Investment Management Certificate

Unit 2 – Investment Practice

Practice and Revision Kit

Syllabus version 12

Contents

ISBN: 9781 4727 1617 0
eISBN: 9781 4727 1625 5

© BPP Learning Media Ltd – December 2014

Printed in United Kingdom by Ricoh
Unit 2, Wells Place, Merstham, RH1 3LG

BPP
LEARNING MEDIA

Investment Management Certificate

Unit 2 – Investment Practice

Question Bank

Note, there are no questions for the preface. This is an introductory chapter and has no learning objectives associated with it.

1. Quantitative Methods

Questions

1. The distribution of firms' turnover in a particular industrial sector is as follows.

£m	%
0-0.5	21
0.6-1.0	19
1.1-2.0	10
2.1-5.0	20
5.1-10	14
10.1-50	12
51+	4

    If there are 20 firms with a turnover of less than £500,000 or greater than £51m, how many firms have a turnover between £1.1m and £5m?

    A 25

    B 32

    C 30

    D 24

2. The proportion of employees in various salary ranges within a major bank are given below. If 150 people earned less than £17,000, how many earned £24,000 and over?

£12,000 – £14,000	0.12
£15,000 – £17,000	0.18
£18,000 – £20,000	0.17
£21,000 – £23,000	0.28
£24,000 and over	0.25

    Important! You should enter the answer only in numbers strictly using this format: 000

    Do not include spaces, letters or symbols (but decimal points and commas should be used if indicated).

3. The height of a bar in a histogram represents

    A The number of items in the band

    B The cumulative number of items to the start of the band

    C The cumulative number of items to the end of the band

    D None of the above

4. **The following sources of data are being utilised.**

  I   Questionnaires

  II   Datastream

  III Published research

  IV   Observation

Which constitute primary data?

A I and IV

B II and III

C I and III

D II and IV

5. **Which description would best categorise fund performance rankings?**

A Continuous data

B Discrete data

C Categorical data

D Ordinal data

6. **Which description would best categorise fund performance statistics?**

A Continuous data

B Discrete data

C Categorical data

D Ordinal data

7. **Which best describes a cumulative relative frequency distribution?**

A A table displaying the number of items in a band

B A table displaying the proportion of items in a band

C A table displaying the number of items less than the upper limit of a band

D A table displaying the proportion of items less than the upper limit of a band

8. **Which of the following categorisations would best describe bond ratings?**

A Continuous data

B Discrete data

C Categorical data

D Ordinal data

9. **Given the following data regarding a fund's asset management, what number of degrees on a pie chart would overseas investments represent?**

UK equities	50%
Japanese equities	10%
UK bonds	15%
US equities	10%
Property	5%
Cash	10%

A 30°

B 36°

C 60°

D 72°

10. **A portfolio is invested in the following areas: US equity £3.72m; UK equity £2.79m; Japanese equity £4.72m; Spanish equity £0.71m; German equity £6.72m.**

Represented on a pie chart, what will be the size of the sector representing the portfolio's exposure to Japanese equity?

A 46°

B 91°

C 40°

D 72°

11. **Which of the following is true of a histogram?**

    I   It displays the frequency of items through the area of the bar

    II   Generally one band is used to represent a range of values per continuous data

    III   The width of the various bands may vary

A I and III

B I, II and III

C II and III

D I and II

12. **What would you plot to see if there was a relationship between two variables?**

A Scatter chart

B Histogram

C Cumulative frequency distribution

D Frequency distribution

13. **If we wish to ensure that each group within a population is represented within a sample which sampling technique should we use?**

A Random sampling

B Quota sampling

C Systematic sampling

D Primary data

14. **If we wish to visualise the relationship between two distributions we should use a**

A Pie chart

B Bar chart

C Histogram

D Scatter graph

15. **Consider the following statements.**

I Non-probability sampling requires no judgement in sample selection

II A random sample is one where each item has an approximately equal chance of selection

III Quota sampling should be representative of the population

Which of the following is correct?

A All are true

B I and II are false, III is true

C I and III are true, II is false

D I is true, II and III are false

16. **Consider the following statements.**

I Pie charts are useful for representing categorical data

II The height of a bar on a histogram reflects the data frequency

III A bar chart cannot be used for continuous data

Which of the following is correct?

A All are true

B I and II are false, III is true

C I and III are true, II is false

D I is true, II and III are false

17. **Which of the following would be most useful to understand the relationship between two variables?**

A Histogram

B Scatter graph

C Bar chart

D Pie chart

18. **A financial analyst uses the following sources of data.**

    I   Original market research

    II   Thomson Reuters and Bloomberg screens

    III   Government publications of financial statistics

    IV   Discussions with company personnel

What constitutes secondary data?

A I and IV

B II and III

C I and II

D III and IV

19. **A research analyst uses the following sources of data.**

    I   Bank of England Quarterly Bulletin

    II   International Monetary Fund's International Financial Statistics

    III   Personally produced charts tracking company share price against the industry

    IV   P/E ratios obtained from company accounts through EXTEL

Which of the above sources constitutes primary data?

A III and IV

B I and II

C III only

D II and IV

20. **You have been asked to explain the differences between a population and a sample.**

    I   A population represents all the members of a specifically defined group

    II   A population represents the majority of members of a specifically defined group

    III   A sample represents a subset of the full population selected

    IV   A sample may not reflect the full population

Which of the above statements are correct?

A I and III are both false; II and IV are both true

B II and IV are both true; I and III are both false

C II and III are both true; I and IV are both false

D I, III and IV are all true whereas II is false

21. **Consider the following statements.**

    I   Continuous data can take any value

    II   Discrete data can take specific values

    III Nominal data is categorised into distinct categories

    IV Ordinal data is categorised into ranked categories

Which of the following is correct?

A I, II, III and IV are all false

B III and IV are false whereas I and II are both true

C I, II, III and IV are all true

D III and IV are true whereas I and II are both false

---

22. **Consider the following statements.**

    I   A bar chart displays the number of items displaying a particular characteristic through the height of the bar

    II   A bar chart shows the number of items displaying a particular characteristic through the area of the bar

    III A bar chart shows the cumulative number of items displaying a particular characteristics

    IV A component bar chart shows the sub-analysis of a particular characteristic

Which of the following is correct?

A I and IV are true whereas II and III are false

B I and II are true whereas III and IV are false

C II and IV are false whereas I and III are true

D II and III are true whereas I and IV are false

---

23. **The rate of change of six corporate bond prices last year was (in %)**

4%, 2%, –1%, 2%, 0%, 5%

The range of the rate of change was

A 2%

B 3%

C 5%

D 6%

---

24. **The monthly rates of return for a security last year were (in %)**

7%, 9%, 5%, –1%, 8%, 0%, –2%, –7%, 7%, 1%, 2%

The modal rate of return was

A 2%

B 3%

C 5%

D 7%

25. An investment manager, with returns of 9%, 7%, 5%, 3% and 8% over five years, wishes to compute an average annual return. Which of the following would be an appropriate measure?

    A   An arithmetic mean

    B   A geometric mean

    C   A harmonic mean

    D   A mode

26. Over a four-year period, an investment fund loses 5%, 6%, 5% and 15% for each of the four years. What is the geometric mean return per annum?

    A   −9.25%

    B   −5.00%

    C   −7.85%

    D   −7.05%

27. The distribution of daily share price changes for a sample of 1,000 UK stocks is as follows.

Interval	Number of Shares
−10% to −0.1%	130
0% to 9.9%	470
10% to 19.9%	270
20% to 29.9%	130

What is the median price change (in % to 1 decimal place)?

Important! You should enter the answer only in numbers strictly using this format: 0.0

Do not include spaces, letters or symbols (but decimal points and commas should be used if indicated).

28. The probability distribution of annual returns from investing in a company is given below.

Return p.a. %	Probability
8	0.2
6	0.3
12	0.3
9	0.2

The mean and standard deviation of the annual rates of return on this investment are

	MEAN	STANDARD DEVIATION
A	8.75%	2.92%
B	8.80%	2.92%
C	8.75%	2.36%
D	8.80%	2.36%

29. The rates of increase of a sample of 200 shares are distributed in intervals as follows.

Interval	I	II	III	IV	V
% Increase	−10 to −0.1	0 to 9.9	10 to 19.9	20 to 29.9	30 to 39.9
No. of shares	28	40	22	48	62

What is the mean rate of change of share prices for the sample (in % to 2 decimal places)?

Important! You should enter the answer only in numbers strictly using this format: 0.00

Do not include spaces, letters or symbols (but decimal points and commas should be used if indicated).

30. A bond had the following quarterly total returns (%) over the last two years

−19%, 8%, 4%, 12%, 6%, −2%, 3%, −7%

What was the geometric mean quarterly return (in % to 2 decimal places)?

Important! You should enter the answer only in numbers strictly using this format: 0.00

Do not include spaces, letters or symbols (but decimal points and commas should be used if indicated).

31. The covariance between two assets is 150. The standard deviation of one asset is 20 and the correlation is 0.5. What is the standard deviation of the other asset?

Important! You should enter the answer only in numbers strictly using this format: 00.0

Do not include spaces, letters or symbols (but decimal points and commas should be used if indicated).

32. The probability distribution of annual returns from investing in Company A is given below.

Return %	Probability
10	0.1
20	0.7
30	0.2

What is the standard deviation of the annual rate of return on this investment (in % to 1 decimal place)?

Important! You should enter the answer only in numbers strictly using this format: 0.0

Do not include spaces, letters or symbols (but decimal points and commas should be used if indicated).

33. The rates of increase of a sample of 200 shares are distributed in intervals as follows.

Interval	I	II	III	IV	V
% Increase	−10 to −0.1	0 to 9.9	10 to 19.9	20 to 29.9	30 to 39.9
No. of shares	28	40	22	48	62

What is the mean rate of change of share prices for the sample (in % to 2 decimal places)?

Important! You should enter the answer only in numbers strictly using this format: 0.00

Do not include spaces, letters or symbols (but decimal points and commas should be used if indicated).

34. A bond had the following quarterly total returns (%) over the last two years

   –19%, 8%, 4%, 12%, 6%, –2%, 3%, –7%

   What was the geometric mean quarterly return (in % to 2 decimal places)?

   Important! You should enter the answer only in numbers strictly using this format: 0.00

   Do not include spaces, letters or symbols (but decimal points and commas should be used if indicated).

35. A sample of 1,000 daily movements in the dollar-sterling exchange rate has the following distribution (in cents).

Interval	Frequency
–4.99 cents to –2.50 cents	30
–2.49 cents to 0.0 cents	270
0.01 cents to 2.50 cents	350
2.51 cents to 4.99 cents	300
5.00 cents to 9.99 cents	50

   What is the median price change (in cents)?

   A 2.50
   B 1.43
   C 1.08
   D 1.37

36. A security has annual rates of return over the last seven years of –9%, 12%, –19%, 22%, 28%, –5%, and 2%. What is the geometric mean return and the median return?

   A 3.8, 4.4
   B 3.8, 2.0
   C 3.2, 2.0
   D 3.2, 4.4

37. A sample of 300 share price changes over a year was as follows

% Change	Number of Shares
−5.0 to −0.1	40
0 to 4.9	27
5 to 9.9	91
10 to 14.9	71
15 to 19.9	71

What is the median price change (in % to 2 decimal places)?

Important! You should enter the answer only in numbers strictly using this format: 0.00

Do not include spaces, letters or symbols (but decimal points and commas should be used if indicated).

38. The rate of return of a share over the last six months has been

12%, 10%, 3%, −5%, 1%, 9%

What was the average monthly return on the share?

A   5.00
B   4.83
C   6.67
D   4.87

39. The distribution of daily share price changes for 1,000 shares is

RANGE	NUMBER
−15 to −5.1	210
−5 to −0.1	330
0 to 4.9	270
5 to 14.9	170
15 to 24.9	20

What is the median price change?

A   3.80
B   −0.60
C   −4.40
D   0.88

40. **The distribution of daily share price changes for 1,000 shares is**

RANGE	NUMBER
−15 to −5.1	210
−5 to −0.1	330
0 to 4.9	270
5 to 14.9	170
15 to 24.9	20

What is the mean price change?

A   7.2

B   0.0

C   3.35

D   −0.15

---

41. **From the following set of data, what is the median (to the nearest one %)?**

−5%, 12%, 3%, 6%, 17%, 1%, 2%

Important! You should enter the answer only in numbers strictly using this format: 0

Do not include spaces, letters or symbols (but decimal points and commas should be used if indicated).

---

42. **Which of the following attempt to establish the central point of a set of data?**

    I   Arithmetic mean

    II   Variance

    III   Standard deviation

    IV   Median

A   I and II

B   II and III

C   I and III

D   I and IV

---

43. **Over the last seven years, the returns on a particular fund have been as follows.**

2%, 7%, 6%, 13%, 11%, −5%, −3%

What is the average return as measured by the arithmetic mean (in % to 1 decimal place)?

Important! You should enter the answer only in numbers strictly using this format: 0.0

Do not include spaces, letters or symbols (but decimal points and commas should be used if indicated).

44. A fund has the following quarterly returns.

QUARTER	RETURN
1	5%
2	7%
3	12%
4	2%

What is the annual return of the fund on both an arithmetic basis, and a geometric basis, of return measurement?

A $r_A = 26\%$ $r_G = 28.3\%$

B $r_A = 6.5\%$ $r_G = 6.4\%$

C $r_A = 26\%$ $r_G = 6.4\%$

D $r_A = 6.5\%$ $r_G = 28.3\%$

45. What is data mining?

A Gathering large amounts of information looking for anything that is relevant

B Sorting through large amounts of information looking for anything that is relevant

C Gathering large amounts relevant information

D Sorting through large amounts of relevant information

46. The method of establishing the parameters 'a' and 'b' when undertaking bivariate regression is referred to as

A The most squared method

B The least squared method

C The sum of the squared errors method

D The sum of the cubed errors method

47. The rate of change of seven corporate bond prices last year was (in %)

4%, 2%, –1%, 2%, 0%, 5%, 3%

What is the inter quartile range of the rate of change (to the nearest one %)?

Important! You should enter the answer only in numbers strictly using this format: 0

Do not include spaces, letters or symbols (but decimal points and commas should be used if indicated).

48. The monthly rates of return for a security last year were (in %)

7%, 9%, 5%, –1%, 8%, 0%, –2%, –7%, 7%, 1%, 2%

What was the median rate of return (to the nearest one %)?

Important! You should enter the answer only in numbers strictly using this format: 0

Do not include spaces, letters or symbols (but decimal points and commas should be used if indicated).

49. **Over a four-year period, an investment fund returns 5%, 10%, 5% and –15% for each of the four years. What is the geometric mean return per annum (in % to 2 decimal places)?**

Important! You should enter the answer only in numbers strictly using this format: 0.00

Do not include spaces, letters or symbols (but decimal points and commas should be used if indicated).

50. **The rates of increase of a sample of 1,000 UK stocks is as follows.**

Interval	Number of Shares
–10% to –0.1%	130
0% to 9.9%	470
10% to 19.9%	270
20% to 29.9%	130

What is the arithmetic mean price change (in % to 1 decimal place)?

Important! You should enter the answer only in numbers strictly using this format: 0.0

Do not include spaces, letters or symbols (but decimal points and commas should be used if indicated).

51. The probability distribution of annual returns from investing in a company is given below.

Return p.a. %	Probability
5	0.1
7	0.3
9	0.4
11	0.2

The mean and standard deviation of the annual rates of return on this investment are

	MEAN	STANDARD DEVIATION
A	8.60%	1.92%
B	8.40%	1.92%
C	8.60%	1.80%
D	8.40%	1.80%

52. The distribution of daily share price changes for a sample of 200 shares are distributed in intervals as follows.

Interval	I	II	III	IV	V
% Increase	−10 to −0.1	0 to 9.9	10 to 19.9	20 to 29.9	30 to 39.9
No. of shares	22	40	62	48	28

The mean rate of change of share prices for the sample is

A 15.5

B 16.0

C 16.5

D 17.0

53. The rates of change of seven corporate bond prices last year were (in %)

+11%, +21%, −7%, −5%, +1%, −35%, +12%

What is your estimate of the median and standard deviation of corporate bond prices based on this sample?

A −0.29%, 14.21%

B +1%, 14.21%

C −0.29%, 18.28%

D +1%, 18.28%

54. **The probability distribution of annual returns from investing in a share is given below.**

Return %	Probability
2	0.1
6	0.6
8	0.3

What is the standard deviation of the annual rate of return on this investment (in % to 2 decimal places)?

Important! You should enter the answer only in numbers strictly using this format: 0.00

Do not include spaces, letters or symbols (but decimal points and commas should be used if indicated).

55. **The rates of increase from a sample of 100 investment funds were distributed as follows.**

Interval	I	II	III	IV
% increase	−10% to −0.1%	0 to 9.9%	10% to 19.9%	20% to 29.9%
Number of salaries	15	17	48	20

The mean rate of change in salaries for the sample is

A   12.3%

B   11.8%

C   12.6%

D   13.4%

56. **Five EC countries have had the following annual rates of GDP growth.**

5.1%, 10.9%, 1.2%, −0.5%, 7.2%

What is the arithmetic mean rate of GDP growth for these countries?

A   4.78%

B   3.20%

C   5.91%

D   4.36%

57. **Which of the following measures must be one of the observed values?**

A   Arithmetic mean

B   Geometric mean

C   Median

D   Mode

58. **What is the major disadvantage of the mode as a measure of central tendency?**

A   It must be one of the observed items

B   It is unaffected by extremes

C   There may be more than one mode

D   It equates to the mean in a symmetrical distribution

59. **A regression exercise has determined the following values.**

$a = 6.3$

$b = 2.7$

$r = 0.6$

What is the estimated value for the dependent variable when the independent variable takes a value of 7?

A   46.8

B   44.7

C   25.2

D   19.5

60. **Consider the following statements.**

I   Interpolation is more risky than extrapolation

II   Strong correlation proves a causal link

III   Least squares regression is only applicable to linear relationships

Which of the following is true?

A   I is true, II and III are false

B   I and II are false, III is true

C   I and III are true, II is false

D   II is true, I and III are false

61. **Consider the following statements.**

I   The dependent variable is driven by the independent variable and is plotted along the x-axis

II   In the regression equation $y = a + bx$, the b coefficient represents the slope of the regression curve

III   Regression coefficients are calculated using the least squares method to determine the line of best fit

Which of the following is true?

A   All are true

B   I and II are true, III is false

C   I and III are true, II is false

D   II and III are true, I is false

62. The following chart is a plot of

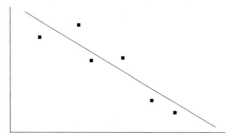

- A Strong positive correlation
- B Weak positive correlation
- C Strong negative correlation
- D Perfect negative correlation

63. In a positively skewed distribution which relationship holds true?

- A Median > Mode > Mean
- B Mean > Mode > Median
- C Mean > Median > Mode
- D Median > Mean > Mode

64. Consider the following statements.

    I   The mean is a measure of dispersion that is heavily affected by extremes

    II   The interquartile range is unaffected by extremes

    III The range is weakly influenced by extremes

Which of the following is true?

- A I and II are false, III is true
- B I and III are false, II is true
- C II and III are false, I is true
- D All are false

65. If an extremely high value item is added to an otherwise perfectly symmetrical distribution then consider the following statements.

    I   The mode would be unaltered

    II   The mode would increase

    III The median stays the same

    IV The median increases

    V   The arithmetic mean stays the same

    VI The arithmetic mean increases

Which of the following is true?

- A I, III and V are all true whereas II, IV and VI are all false
- B II, IV and VI are all true whereas I, III and V are all false
- C I, IV and VI are all true whereas II, III and V are all false
- D III, IV and V are all true whereas I, II and VI are all false

66. **If the plot of two variables X and Y results in a horizontal line, this tells us**

    A   There is a strong positive correlation between the two variables

    B   There is strong negative correlation between the two variables

    C   The two variables are perfectly correlated

    D   There is no correlation between the two variables

67. **Consider the following statements.**

    I   Interpolation of results from regression analysis will provide accurate results

    II   Extrapolation of results from regression analysis is likely to lead to less accurate results than interpolation

    III Regression analysis is only accurate for linear relationships

    IV   Regression analysis will always highlight if a relationship exists between the variables being considered

    Which of the following is true?

    A   I and IV are both true whereas II and III are both false

    B   II and III are both true whereas I and IV are both false

    C   I and II are both false whereas III and IV are true

    D   I and II are both true whereas III and IV are false

68. **With a positively skewed distribution**

    A   The mode will be less than the median, which will be less than the mean

    B   The mean and mode are equal, but greater than the median

    C   The mean and median are equal, but greater than the mode

    D   Mean, mode and median are equal

69. **Dividing the variance by the standard deviation for a sample would give**

    A   Covariance

    B   Correlation coefficient

    C   Beta

    D   Standard deviation

70. **The sample standard deviation is defined as the**

    A   Square of the sample variance

    B   Sample variance divided by the number of observations in the sample

    C   Sample variance divided by the number of the observations in the sample minus one

    D   Square root of the sample variance

71. Calculate the sample variance of the following.

12, 34, 29, 54, 98, 121

A   58

B   38.98

C   1,823.6

D   9,118

---

72. Which would be appropriate as a benchmark for a broadly based portfolio of UK and US shares?

A   S&P 500 and FT All Share

B   S&P 100 and FT 30

C   S&P 100 and FTSE 250

D   S&P 500 and FTSE 100

---

73. To which of the following markets does the Hang Seng Index relate?

A   Osaka

B   Tokyo

C   Hong Kong

D   Singapore

---

74. One disadvantage of the geometric index is that

A   It cannot be weighted

B   It overstates performance

C   It cannot be used as a meaningful benchmark

D   It cannot be calculated for high values

---

75. What is the price-relative geometric index (base was 100) based on the following dates?

ITEM	BASE P_0 £	Q_0	CURRENT P_N £	Q_N
I	5	3	7	4
II	3	3	8	3
III	2	4	9	3

A   256

B   242

C   228

D   214

Answer the next two questions based on the following information.

1960	100	
1961	109	
1990	418	200
1991		220
1992		230

76. **The old index value for 1992 is (to the nearest index point)**

    Important! You should enter the answer only in numbers strictly using this format: 000

    Do not include spaces, letters or symbols (but decimal points and commas should be used if indicated).

    ```
    ┌──────────────┐
    │              │
    │              │
    └──────────────┘
    ```

77. **The new index value for 1961 is**

    A 23.9

    B 26.1

    C 47.8

    D 52.2

78. **One disadvantage of the geometric index is that**

    A It can be weighted

    B It overstates performance

    C It cannot be calculated for high values

    D It cannot always produce a result with negative values

Answer the next *three* questions based on the following information.

ITEM	BASE		CURRENT	
	P_0 £	Q_0	P_N £	Q_N
I	1.00	8	2.50	6
II	1.20	7	2.00	7
III	1.40	6	2.30	6
IV	1.60	5	2.70	7

An index value of 200 was set in the base year for this selection.

79. What is the current unweighted or price-relative arithmetic index (to the nearest index point)?

   Important! You should enter the answer only in numbers strictly using this format: 000

   Do not include spaces, letters or symbols (but decimal points and commas should be used if indicated).

80. What is the current unweighted geometric index (to the nearest index point)?

   Important! You should enter the answer only in numbers strictly using this format: 000

   Do not include spaces, letters or symbols (but decimal points and commas should be used if indicated).

81. What is the weighted arithmetic index?

   A   185
   B   190
   C   369
   D   376

82. A retail price index was originally based on 1970 and has now been rebased on 2006. Express the 1970 value in terms of the 2006 base year, and the 2007 value in terms of the 1970 base year.

	1970 INDEX	2006 INDEX
1970	100	
2005	220	
2006	227	100
2007		110

A 44.05 and 251.2

B 57.12 and 249.7

C 44.05 and 249.7

D 57.12 and 251.2

83. A fund consisting of mainly top continental European shares is best measured against a benchmark of

A Eurotrack 100

B FTSE All Share

C DAX

D S&P 500

84. Which of the following indices is not a value weighted index?

A S&P 500 Index

B FTSE 100 Index

C FTSE All Share Index

D Nikkei 225 Index

85. When constructing a benchmark portfolio for appraising fund manager performance that portfolio

    I   Should be a fair representation of the assets the fund will contain

    II   Should reflect the risk that clients require

    III   Should be constructed for more than one index

A I and II

B II and III

C I, II and III

D I and III

86.   The main index in Japan is

A   SMI

B   Nikkei 225

C   DAX

D   CBS All Share

---

87.   Which of the following indices are said to be value-weighted arithmetic indices?

I   FTSE 100 Index

II   S&P 100 Index

III   Nikkei 225 Index

IV   FTSE All Share Index

A   I, II, III and IV

B   III and IV

C   I and II

D   I, II and IV

---

88.   Which of the following is true of the DAX Index?

A   Weighted and geometric

B   Weighted and arithmetic

C   Unweighted and arithmetic

D   Unweighted and geometric

---

89.   The Nikkei 225 Index is

A   Arithmetic and weighted

B   Arithmetic and unweighted

C   Geometric and weighted

D   Geometric and unweighted

---

90.   The S&P 500 Index relates to which market?

A   Sydney

B   Vancouver

C   New York

D   Frankfurt

---

91.   The Nikkei 225 relates to which market?

A   Tokyo

B   Osaka

C   Singapore

D   Hong Kong

---

92. **Which of the following is likely to be the most attractive investment for a UK private investor seeking long-term capital growth?**

    A Gilts

    B Equity shares

    C Preference shares

    D Eurobonds

93. **The CAC 40 is the index for which market?**

    A France

    B Germany

    C Hong Kong

    D Japan

94. **On how many shares is the Dow Jones Industrial Average based?**

    A 30

    B 33

    C 225

    D 500

95. **Which of the FTSE indices listed below is an unweighted index?**

    A FTSE Ordinary

    B FTSE All Share

    C FTSE 100

    D FTSE 250

96. **Which would be appropriate as a benchmark for a broadly based portfolio of UK and US large and mid-cap shares?**

    A S&P 500 and FT All Share

    B S&P 100 and FT 100

    C S&P 100 and FTSE 250

    D S&P 500 and FTSE 350

97. **There are various ways that market indices can be calculated. The majority of worldwide indices that are used for performance measurement are described as**

    A Value-weighted, arithmetic indices

    B Value-weighted, geometric indices

    C Equally weighted, arithmetic indices

    D Equally weighted, geometric indices

98. **Which of the following indices is not an equally weighted index?**

A   Dow Jones Industrial Average

B   FTSE Ordinary

C   Nikkei 225

D   S&P 500

99. **Which of the following statements concerning equity shares indices are correct?**

I   The Dow Jones Industrial Average is an equally weighted, arithmetic index

II   The Nikkei 225 is an equally weighted, arithmetic index

III   The FT Ordinary Index is an equally weighted, arithmetic index

IV   The S&P 500 Index is a value-weighted, arithmetic index

A   All of the above

B   I, II and III

C   I, II and IV

D   I and II

100. **Which of the following bond indices would be the best to use for benchmarking purposes if you were an American bond investor?**

A   FTSE Gilts All Stocks Index

B   S&P 500 Index

C   Barclays Capital S&P Cantor US Treasury Bond index

D   Barclays Capital DJIA

101. **Which index should holders of US government bonds use?**

A   Barclays US Universal Index

B   Barclays Global Aggregate Index

C   Barclays US Aggregate Index

D   Barclays US Treasury Index

102. **Which of the following is not a use of the FTSE 100 Index?**

I   Benchmark for manager appraisal

II   Indication of small company corporate prospects

III   Indication of growth in the US economy

IV   Pricing of FTSE 100 derivatives

A   I and IV

B   II and III

C   II only

D   I, III and IV

103. **Which of the following is a simple arithmetic aggregate price index?**

    A   Dow Jones Industrial Index

    B   FTSE 100

    C   FT 30 Share Index

    D   CAC 40 Index

104. **An index has the following values in Years 1, 2 and 3: 110, 118, 125. What is the Year 3 value if the index is rebased so that the Year 1 value is 100 (in index points to one decimal place)?**

    Important! You should enter only the answer in numbers (without spaces, letters or symbols) strictly using the following format: 000.0

    Do not include spaces, letters or symbols (but decimal points and commas should be used if indicated).

105. **What is incorrect about a geometric index if used to calculate a stock index?**

    A   If the value of one share in the index drops to zero, the index value becomes zero

    B   Geometric indices are less sensitive to large changes in constituent prices

    C   Geometric indices will always underestimate the performance of the constituents

    D   Geometric indices are the preferred method of index construction

106. **Calculate the current value of an index on a geometric mean basis for three shares, valued at 50p, 25p and 13p in the base year, and 56p, 26p and 17p in the current year. The value of the index in the base year was 100.**

    A   86.9

    B   112.5

    C   115.1

    D   152.3

107. **An asset is purchased for £50. Over the next four quarters, it has quarterly returns of 4%, 5%, 2% and –3%. The value of the asset at the end of the year is**

    A   £51.20

    B   £54.02

    C   £54.12

    D   £56.45

108. What is the value of a bond with an infinite life that pays £100 per annum when the required rate of return is 8% (to the nearest £1)?

Important! You should enter the answer only in numbers strictly using this format: 0,000

Do not include spaces, letters or symbols (but decimal points and commas should be used if indicated).

```
┌─────────────┐
│             │
│             │
└─────────────┘
```

109. You invest £500 at 8% for five years, then withdraw the funds and invest this at 9% for four years. What is the value of the account at the end of nine years (to the nearest £1)?

Important! You should enter the answer only in numbers strictly using this format: 0,000

Do not include spaces, letters or symbols (but decimal points and commas should be used if indicated).

```
┌─────────────┐
│             │
│             │
└─────────────┘
```

110. An investor bought 1,000 shares in Megagrowth plc at 74 pence each and received net dividends of 3 pence per share and 6 pence per share at the end of each of the first two years respectively. He then sold them at the end of the second year for 80 pence each.

The internal rate of return on this investment is

A 9.0%

B 9.3%

C 9.6%

D 9.9%

111. The rate of interest for a repayment mortgage of £150,000 over 25 years is 9%. What is the annual repayment required at the end of each year (to the nearest £1)?

Important! You should enter the answer only in numbers strictly using this format: 00,000

Do not include spaces, letters or symbols (but decimal points and commas should be used if indicated).

```
┌─────────────┐
│             │
│             │
└─────────────┘
```

112. An investment of £15,000 is made at a compound rate of 10% and £1,000 is withdrawn at the end of each year. What is its value after eight years?

A £20,718

B £16,420

C £19,901

D £20,624

113. An investment rises in value from £5,000 to £6,742 over four years. What is its constant annual rate of appreciation (in % to 2 decimal places)?

Important! You should enter the answer only in numbers strictly using this format: 0.00

Do not include spaces, letters or symbols (but decimal points and commas should be used if indicated).

114. What is the present value of £7,000 to be received eight years from now if the annual interest rate is 9% (to the nearest £1)?

Important! You should enter the answer only in numbers strictly using this format: 0,000

Do not include spaces, letters or symbols (but decimal points and commas should be used if indicated).

115. A house purchase requires a repayment loan of £160,000 taken out over 25 years. If the rate of interest is 9%, what is the annual repayment needed at the end of each year (to the nearest £1)?

Important! You should enter the answer only in numbers strictly using this format: 00,000

Do not include spaces, letters or symbols (but decimal points and commas should be used if indicated).

116. A new office computing systems costs £55,000 to buy and depreciates at a constant rate of 20% per annum on the reducing balance basis. What is it worth at the end of four years?

A £22,528
B £32,000
C £11,000
D £23,964

117. Before pressing ahead with a major investment project costing £12m, the managing director of a large engineering firm examines detailed cash flow projections. She believes that the project will yield returns of £3m at the end of each of the first three years, at which point it will still be worth £9m. What is the net present value of this project with a discount rate of 10% (in £m to 2 decimal places)?

      Important! You should enter the answer only in numbers strictly using this format: 0.00

      Do not include spaces, letters or symbols (but decimal points and commas should be used if indicated).

      ```
      ┌─────────────┐
      │             │
      │             │
      └─────────────┘
      ```

118. What does £475 become if it is invested at a compound interest rate of 11% for eight years?

      A   £1,095
      B   £975
      C   £1,125
      D   £995

119. An investor buys 1,000 shares at £3.55 each and receives dividends of 20 pence, 30 pence and 32 pence at the end of the next three years, before selling them at £3.97 each. What is the internal rate of return on this investment?

      A   9.2%
      B   8.1%
      C   11.1%
      D   12.9%

120. How much will an investor have to pay now to receive year-end cash payments of £9,000 beginning six years from now and ending ten years from now, if the interest rate is 10% (to the nearest £1)?

      Important! You should enter the answer only in numbers strictly using this format: 00,000

      Do not include spaces, letters or symbols (but decimal points and commas should be used if indicated).

      ```
      ┌─────────────┐
      │             │
      │             │
      └─────────────┘
      ```

121. The value of an investor's equity portfolio has risen from £18,000 to £20,000 over the last five years. What is the (constant) annual rate of appreciation?

      A   2.1%
      B   2.3%
      C   2.5%
      D   1.7%

122. What is the present value of £540 p.a. forever, if the first payment is in two years' time and the discount rate is 10% (to the nearest £1)?

Important! You should enter the answer only in numbers strictly using this format: 0,000

Do not include spaces, letters or symbols (but decimal points and commas should be used if indicated).

123. An investor buys 750 shares at 103p each and receives a dividend of 5p at the end of the first year, 6p at the end of the second year, and 6.5p at the end of the third year, at which point he sells them for 120p each. What is the internal rate of return on this investment?

A 8.7%

B 9.8%

C 10.3%

D 10.6%

124. A repayment mortgage of £75,000 is taken out over 20 years at a rate of interest of 11.1%. What is the annual repayment required at the end of each year (to the nearest £1)?

Important! You should enter the answer only in numbers strictly using this format: 0,000

Do not include spaces, letters or symbols (but decimal points and commas should be used if indicated).

125. A new piece of machinery costs £125,000 to buy and is worth £15,000 at the end of six years. If it depreciates at a constant rate on the reducing balance basis, what is it worth at the end of the third year (to the nearest £1)?

Important! You should enter the answer only in numbers strictly using this format: 00,000

Do not include spaces, letters or symbols (but decimal points and commas should be used if indicated).

126. What is the present value of £725 to be received seven years from now if the interest rate is 8%?

A £460.11

B £519.92

C £423.03

D £493.42

127. **You have £1,000 to invest for ten years. There are two options (both quoted on a periodic basis rather than annualised)**

      I   2% quarterly compounding

      II   3% semi-annually compounding

  A I is better than II by £402

  B II is better than I by £402

  C I is better than II by £125

  D II is better than I by £125

128. **An annuity is to be purchased now which will return £2,000 p.a. starting in five years and ending ten years from now. If the interest rate is 8%, what will it cost?**

  A £13,420

  B £7,986

  C £6,796

  D £5,434

129. **What is the annual repayment on a £160,000 mortgage over 20 years if interest rates are 7.5%?**

  A £15,695

  B £14,354

  C £14,843

  D £15,161

130. **An investor bought 2,500 shares at a price of 86p each. He received dividends of 4p, 5p and 6p at the end of each of the first three years and sold them at the end of the third year for 95p. What is the internal rate of return on the investment?**

  A 8.5%

  B 9%

  C 9.5%

  D 10%

131. **You invest £7,000 at 7% for four years and 8% thereafter. What is the terminal value at the end of nine years?**

  A £13,482

  B £12,869

  C £13,993

  D £13,493

132. An investment rises from £12,000 to £18,648 over seven years. What is the constant annual rate of appreciation?

   A 6.0%

   B 6.5%

   C 7.0%

   D 7.5%

133. A portfolio of gilts has the following returns each quarter

Quarter 1	(0.5%)
Quarter 2	3.7%
Quarter 3	1.0%
Quarter 4	2.3%

   What is the compounded annualised return from the portfolio?

   A 1.79%

   B 12.5%

   C 7.68%

   D 6.61%

134. How much would an investor be prepared to pay for an investment promising a single payment of £20,000 in ten years' time if the relevant interest rate foregone during the period is 6% (to the nearest £1)?

   Important! You should enter the answer only in numbers strictly using this format: 00,000

   Do not include spaces, letters or symbols (but decimal points and commas should be used if indicated).

135. You have taken out a mortgage of £275,000 over a period of 15 years at a rate of 12½%. What is the annual repayment required at the end of each year?

   A £34,375

   B £41,250

   C £41,460

   D £37,450

136. Your office has installed a new air conditioning system at a cost of £75,000 which is to be written down to £5,000 over 15 years using the reducing balance basis. What is its book value after five years (to the nearest £1)?

Important! You should enter the answer only in numbers strictly using this format: 00,000

Do not include spaces, letters or symbols (but decimal points and commas should be used if indicated).

137. A new fire sprinkler system costs £175,000 and depreciates at a constant rate of 5% on the reducing balance basis. What is it worth at the end of the third year?

A   £148,750

B   £142,696

C   £153,240

D   £150,041

138. An investor buys 500 shares at £4.05 each and receives dividends of 15 pence, 25 pence and 35 pence at the end of the next three years before selling them at £5.15 each. What is the internal rate of return on this investment?

A   10.45%

B   13.87%

C   11.15%

D   12.58%

139. A new plant costs £47,500 and is worth £2,500 at the end of 10 years. If it depreciates at a constant rate on the reducing balance basis, what is it worth at the end of the sixth year?

A   £28,500

B   £20,543

C   £8,118

D   £12,115

140. An investor buys 1,000 shares at 285 pence each and receives dividends of 30 pence and 35 pence before selling them at 305 pence each at the end of the second year. What is the internal rate of return on this investment?

A   11.47%

B   12.74%

C   15.26%

D   14.61%

141. **What would be the annual return from a continuous compounded investment if the annual rate quoted is 34%?**

    A   37.8%

    B   40.5%

    C   34.0%

    D   42.7%

142. **What is the percentage return earned over a three month period for a continuous compounded investment if the annual rate quoted is 27% (in % to 2 decimal places)?**

    Important! You should enter the answer only in numbers strictly using this format: 0.00

    Do not include spaces, letters or symbols (but decimal points and commas should be used if indicated).

    ```
    ┌─────────────┐
    │             │
    │             │
    └─────────────┘
    ```

143. **What is the return earned over a six month period for a continuous compounded investment if the annual rate quoted is 38%?**

    A   20.9%

    B   19.0%

    C   23.1%

    D   46.2%

144. **A repayment mortgage of £212,500 is taken out over 20 years at a rate of 10.5%. What is the annual repayment required at the end of each year (to the nearest £)?**

    Important! You should enter the answer only in numbers strictly using this format: 00,000

    Do not include spaces, letters or symbols (but decimal points and commas should be used if indicated).

    ```
    ┌─────────────┐
    │             │
    │             │
    └─────────────┘
    ```

145. **A repayment mortgage of £127,000 is taken out for a 15 year period at a rate of 8.75%. What is the annual repayment required at the end of each year?**

    A   £14,207

    B   £15,524

    C   £11,113

    D   £12,324

146. Calculate the present value of £500 received at the end of the first quarter of the year when the continuous interest rate is 6.75% (in £ to two decimal places)?

Important! You should enter the answer only in numbers strictly using this format: 000.00

Do not include spaces, letters or symbols (but decimal points and commas should be used if indicated).

147. What is the present value of £1,000 received 45 weeks into the year when the continuous rate is 9.48%?

A £1,094.80

B £1,085.50

C £921.24

D £905.20

148. You have £15,000 to invest over five years and have two options available to you (both interest rates quoted on a periodic, not annual, basis).

    I   2.5% quarterly compound interest

    II   3.5% semi annually compound interest

A I is better than II by £3,420

B II is better than I by £3,420

C I is better than II by £2,250

D II is better than I by £2,250

149. Consider the following statements

    I   Only projects generating positive NPV should be accepted by an investor

    II   Individual firms or investors are able to affect the price of funds

    III NPV assumes that any surplus funds can be reinvested at the same rate of return as the required rate of return

A All are false

B All are true

C II is false whereas I and III are both true

D I is false whereas II and III are both true

150. **£1,000 is invested for two years. What is the difference between 8% compound interest and 8% simple interest on this capital (in £ to two decimal places)?**

Important! You should enter the answer only in numbers strictly using this format: 0.00

Do not include spaces, letters or symbols (but decimal points and commas should be used if indicated).

[   ]

---

151. **An investor has two zero coupon bond holdings. One will mature in five years at £2,000, the other matures in eight years at £2,350. If the investor requires a 6% return what is the difference between the NPVs of these two investments?**

A £2.32

B £16.87

C £20.10

D £28.42

---

152. **Which of the following is not a characteristic of a normal distribution?**

A Symmetrical

B Constant standard deviation

C Autocorrelation

D Increasingly thin tales

---

153. **An investment that averages a return that lies far into one tail of the distribution of expected possible returns may be described as**

A Random

B Unsystematic

C Undiversified

D Statistically significant

---

154. **49% of the UK population are male, 51% are female. What would be the best probability sampling technique to maintain this balance?**

A Random sampling

B Stratified sampling

C Systematic sampling

D Judgement sampling

155. **Which sampling technique may be most useful for investigating a rare or hidden characteristic in a population?**

A Convenience sampling

B Judgement sampling

C Snowball sampling

D Quota sampling

156. **Which of the following statements are true?**

I   Where capital is freely available and investment opportunities only have a single IRR, both NPV and IRR will provide the same conclusion regarding the viability of the investments

II   IRR disregards the scale of any investment opportunities

III A simple investment that, once bought, only provides positive returns cannot have multiple IRRs

A I and II

B I and III

C II and III

D I, II and III

Answers

1. **D**   Turnover < £0.5m =   21%

    Turnover > £51m =   <u>4%</u>

    25% of companies

    25% of total number of companies = 20 companies

    ∴ 100% = 80 companies in total

    30% of companies have turnover in the range of £1.1m to £5m

    ∴ 30% × 80 = **24 companies**

    See Chapter 1 Section 1.4 of your Study Text

2. **125** $\dfrac{150}{0.3} = 500 \times 0.25 = 125$

    See Chapter 1 Section 1.4 of your Study Text

3. **D**   The area of a bar in a histogram represents the number of items in the band

    See Chapter 1 Section 1.6 of your Study Text

4. **A**   Datastream and published data would be examples of secondary data having come from a third-party source

    See Chapter 1 Section 1.1 of your Study Text

5. **D**   By definition, ordinal is ranked data, which is the type required by the question

    See Chapter 1 Section 1.3 of your Study Text

6. **A**   A fund's return can take any value dependent on the accuracy of the figures collected. Data in this form is known as continuous data as opposed to discrete data that can only take a finite range of values

    See Chapter 1 Section 1.3 of your Study Text

7. **D**   A cumulative frequency distribution shows the cumulative number of items that lie below the upper limit of the band, but this question asks about a cumulative relative frequency distribution

    See Chapter 1 Section 1.4 of your Study Text

8. **D**   Credit ratings represent rankings, ie ordinal data

    See Chapter 1 Section 1.3 of your Study Text

9. **D** $360° \times 20\% = 72°$

    See Chapter 1 Section 1.5 of your Study Text

10. **B** $\dfrac{4.72}{18.66} \times 360° = 91°$

    See Chapter 1 Section 1.5 of your Study Text

11. **B** All the points are true

See Chapter 1 Section 1.6 of your Study Text

12. **A** Scatter charts, also known as scatter graphs, are one of the most effective ways of demonstrating the relationship between two variables

See Chapter 1 Section 1.6 of your Study Text

13. **B** Quota sampling is where a sample is selected that is believed to be representative of the population, hence covers all groups in the population. No other sampling technique will necessarily achieve this

See Chapter 1 Section 1.2 of your Study Text

14. **D** A scatter graph shows the relationship between two distributions

See Chapter 1 Section 1.6 of your Study Text

15. **B** I   Non-probability sampling *does* require some judgement
II   Random sampling means each items has an *exactly* equal chance of selection
III   Quota sample is chosen to be representative

See Chapter 1 Section 1.2 of your Study Text

16. **D** I   Pie charts are useful for representing categorical data
II   The *area* of a bar in a histogram reflects the data frequency
III   A bar chart *can* be used for continuous data

See Chapter 1 Section 1.5 and Chapter 1 Section 1.6 of your Study Text

17. **B** A scatter graph shows the relationship between two variables.

See Chapter 1 Section 1.6 of your Study Text

18. **B** Thomson Reuters, Bloomberg and Government publications of financial data are examples of secondary data. Any original market research and discussion with company personnel undertaken by the analyst would be examples of primary data

See Chapter 1 Section 1.1 of your Study Text

19. **C** Personally produced charts constitute primary data as they have been produced by the research analyst. All other sources are examples of secondary data as they have been produced by third parties

See Chapter 1 Section 1.1 of your Study Text

20. **D** A population represents all the members of a specifically defined group whereas a sample represents a subset of the entire population. Whether a sample represents a population depends upon:

- Size of the sample
- Method used for selecting the sample

Thus a small sample is highly unlikely to represent the entire population

See Chapter 1 Section 1.2 of your Study Text

21. **C** All four statements are correct

See Chapter 1 Section 1.3 of your Study Text

22. **A** A bar chart represents the number of items displaying a particular characteristic through the height of the bar whereas a histogram represents the number of items displaying a particular characteristic through the area of a bar. A component bar chart allows further sub analysis of the particular component shown

See Chapter 1 Section 1.5 and Chapter 1 Section 1.6 of your Study Text

23. **D** The range is the difference between the highest and lowest items

5% – (–1%) = 6%

See Chapter 1 Section 2.8 of your Study Text

24. **D** The mode is the most frequently occurring item. 7% occurs most frequently

See Chapter 1 Section 2.4 of your Study Text

25. **B** Since we are given time series data, we use a measure that calculates compound returns, i.e. geometric mean

See Chapter 1 Section 2.5 of your Study Text

26. **C** Geometric mean of $(1 + x) = \sqrt[4]{0.95 \times 0.94 \times 0.95 \times 0.85}$

Corresponding to a loss of $1 - 0.9215 = 0.0785$ or 7.85%

To calculate a 4th root on your Casio calculator, type 4, followed by [shift] then the power button [x■]. The calculator then opens up brackets for you to enter the numbers you want to multiply together. Close the brackets after the final number is entered. A common mistake in these questions is to use the square root button. This will only work if there are two numbers you are taking the geometric mean of

See Chapter 1 Section 2.5 of your Study Text

27. **7.9**

Internal	Number	Cumulative
–10.0% to –0.1%	130	130
0.0% to 9.9%	470	600
10.0% to 19.9%	270	870
20.9% to 29.9%	130	1,000
	1,000	

Median = $\dfrac{n+1}{2} = \dfrac{(1,000+1)}{2} = 500.5^{th}$ item

Median = 500.5th item that falls in the second band that starts after the 130th item and contains 470 items

Median = $0.0\% + \dfrac{500.5 - 130}{470} \times (10\% - 0\%) = 7.9\%$ to one decimal place

See Chapter 1 Section 2.3 of your Study Text

28. D

x	F	fx	$x - \bar{x}$	$(x - \bar{x})^2$	$f(x - \bar{x})^2$
8	0.2	1.6	−0.8	0.64	0.128
6	0.3	1.8	−2.8	7.84	2.352
12	0.3	3.6	3.2	10.24	3.072
9	0.2	1.8	0.2	0.04	0.008
	$\bar{x} =$	8.8		$\sigma^2 =$	5.560
				$\sigma =$	2.358

See Chapter 1 Section 2.2 and Chapter 1 Section 2.8 of your Study Text

29. 18.8

Range	x	f	Fx
−10 to −0.1	−5	28	−140
0 to 9.9	5	40	200
10 to 19.9	15	22	330
20 to 29.9	25	48	1,200
30 to 39.9	35	62	2,170
		200	3,760

$$\bar{x} = \frac{\sum fx}{n} = \frac{3,760}{200} = 18.8$$

See Chapter 1 Section 2.2 of your Study Text

30. 0.17   Geometric mean $= \sqrt[8]{0.81 \times 1.08 \times 1.04 \times 1.12 \times 1.06 \times 0.98 \times 1.03 \times 0.93} - 1$

$$= 1.0017 - 1$$

$$= 0.0017 \text{ or } 0.17\%$$

See Chapter 1 Section 2.5 of your Study Text

31. 15.0   The formula linking correlation and covariance is important to remember, ie

$$cor_{xy} = \frac{Co\,variance(x, y)}{\sigma_x \sigma_y}$$

$$0.5 = \frac{150}{20 \times \sigma_y}$$

$$0.5 \times 20 \times \sigma_y = 150$$

$$\sigma_y = 15.0$$

See Chapter 1 Section 3.2 of your Study Text

32. **5.4**

f	X	fx	$x - \bar{x}$	$(x - \bar{x})^2$	$f(x - \bar{x})^2$
0.1	10	1	−11	121	12.1
0.7	20	14	−1	1	0.7
0.2	30	6	9	81	16.2
		21			29.0

$\bar{x} = 21$

$\sigma = \sqrt{29} = 5.385$

The required format for this question is 0.0% hence you must round to the nearest one decimal place, ie 5.4%

See Chapter 1 Section 2.8 of your Study Text

33. **18.8**

Range	x	f	Fx
−10 to −0.1	−5	28	−140
0 to 9.9	5	40	200
10 to 19.9	15	22	330
20 to 29.9	25	48	1,200
30 to 39.9	35	62	2,170
		200	3,760

$$\bar{x} = \frac{\sum fx}{n} = \frac{3,760}{200} = 18.8$$

34. **0.17** Geometric mean $= \sqrt[8]{0.81 \times 1.08 \times 1.04 \times 1.12 \times 1.06 \times 0.98 \times 1.03 \times 0.93} - 1$

$= 1.0017 - 1$

$= 0.0017$ or 0.17%

35.   **B**

Range	f	Cumulative f
−4.99 to −2.50	30	30
−2.49 to 0.00	270	300
0.01 to 2.50	350	650
2.51 to 4.99	300	950
5.00 to 9.99	50	1,000
	1,000	

Median $= \dfrac{n+1}{2}$ the item $= \dfrac{1,000+1}{2} = 500.5$ the item that falls in the third band that starts after the 300th item and contains 350 items

Median $= 0.0\% + \dfrac{500.5-300}{350} \times (2.5\% - 0.0\%) = 1.43$

See Chapter 1 Section 2.3 of your Study Text

36.   **C**   Geometric mean $= \sqrt[7]{0.91 \times 1.12 \times 0.81 \times 1.22 \times 1.28 \times 0.95 \times 1.02} - 1$

$= 1.032 - 1 = 0.032$ or 3.2%

Median −19, −9, −5, 2, 12, 22, 28

See Chapter 1 Section 2.3 and Chapter 1 Section 2.5 of your Study Text

37.   **9.59**

Range	f	Cumulative f
−5.0 to −0.1	40	40
0.0 to 4.9	27	67
5.0 to 9.9	91	158
10.0 to 14.9	71	229
15.0 to 19.9	71	300

Median item 150.5^{th} item that falls in the third band that starts after the 67th item and contains 91 items

Median $= 5.0 + \dfrac{150.5-67}{91} \times (10 - 5) = 9.59$

See Chapter 1 Section 2.9 of your Study Text

38.   **B** $1 + r = \sqrt[6]{1.12 \times 1.10 \times 1.03 \times 0.95 \times 1.01 \times 1.09} = \sqrt[6]{1.327} = 1.0483$

$r = 0.0483$ or 4.83%

See Chapter 1 Section 2.5 of your Study Text

39. **B** Median term $= \dfrac{n+1}{2} = \dfrac{1{,}001}{2} = 500.5$th item that falls in the second band that starts after the 210th item and contains 330 items

Median $= -5.0 + \dfrac{500.5 - 210}{330} \times (0 - (-5)) = -0.60$

See Chapter 1 Section 2.3 of your Study Text

40. **D**

x	F	fx
−10	210	−2,100
−2.5	330	−825
2.5	270	675
10	170	1,700
20	20	400
	1,000	−150

$\bar{x} = \dfrac{\sum fx}{n} = \dfrac{-150}{1{,}000} = -0.15$

See Chapter 1 Section 2.2 of your Study Text

41. **3** Median $= -5\%, 1\%, 2\%, 3\%, 6\%, 12\%, 17\%$

$= 3\%$ (the middle item)

See Chapter 1 Section 2.3 of your Study Text

42. **D** Variance and standard deviation are measures of dispersion around the central point

See Chapter 1 Section 2.8 of your Study Text

43. **4.4** Arithmetic mean $= \bar{x} = \dfrac{2+7+6+13+11-5-3}{7}$

$= 4.4\%$

See Chapter 1 Section 2.2 of your Study Text

44. **A** r_A $= r1 + r2 + r3 + r4$

$= 5\% + 7\% + 12\% + 2\% = 26\%$

r_G $= (1 + r_1)(1 + r_2)(1 + r_3)(1 + r_4) - 1$

$= (1.05 \times 1.07 \times 1.12 \times 1.02) - 1$

$= 28.3\%$

Please note that you are not being asked to calculate the arithmetic or geometric mean, which is the average return each quarter

See Chapter 1 Section 2.2 and Chapter 1 Section 2.5 of your Study Text

45. **B** Sorting through large amounts of information looking for anything that is relevant

See Chapter 1 Section 3.2 of your Study Text

46. **B** The idea is that in calculating the regression line, we want to identify the line of best fit. The least square method minimises the sum of the vertical distance of each value from the straight line being drawn

See Chapter 1 Section 3.2 of your Study Text

47. **4** The range is the difference between the one quarter and three quarter items in an ordered list

−1%, 0%, 2%, 2%, 3%, 4%, 5%

Given that there are seven items the quartile items will be

$$n_q = \frac{n+1}{4} = \frac{8}{4} = 2$$

From the start and from the end, ie 4% and 0%

Interquartile range = 4% − 0% = 4%

See Chapter 1 Section 2.8 of your Study Text

48. **2** The median is the central item in an ordered list

−7%, −2%, −1%, 0%, 1%, **2%**, 5%, 7%, 7%, 8%, 9%

See Chapter 1 Section 2.3 of your Study Text

49. **0.76** Geometric mean of $(1 + x) = \sqrt[4]{1.05 \times 1.10 \times 1.05 \times 0.85} = 1.00762$
x = 0.00762 or 0.762%

The required format for this answer is 0.00%, hence you must round to the nearest two decimal places, ie 0.76%

To calculate a 4th root on your Casio calculator, type 4, followed by [shift] then the power button [x■]. The calculator then opens up brackets for you to enter the numbers you want to multiply together. Close the brackets after the final number is entered. A common mistake in these questions is to use the square root button. This will only work if there are two numbers you are taking the geometric mean of

See Chapter 1 Section 2.5 of your Study Text

50. **9.0**

Internal	Number (f)	fx	Mid(x)
−10.0% to −0.1%	130	−650	−5.0
0.0% to 9.9%	470	2,350	5.0
10.0% to 19.9%	270	4,050	15.0
20.9% to 29.9%	130	3,250	25.00
	1,000	9,000	

Arithmetic mean = $\frac{9,000}{1,000}$ = 9.0%

See Chapter 1 Section 2.2 of your Study Text

51. **D**

x	f	fx	$x - \overline{x}$	$(x - \overline{x})^2$	$f(x - \overline{x})^2$
5	0.1	0.5	–3.4	11.56	1.156
7	0.3	2.1	–1.4	1.96	0.588
9	0.4	3.6	0.6	0.36	0.144
11	0.2	2.2	2.6	6.76	1.352
	$\overline{x} =$	8.4		$\sigma^2 =$	3.240
				$\sigma =$	1.800

See Chapter 1 Section 2.2 and Chapter 1 Section 2.8 of your Study Text

52. **B**

Range	x	f	fx
–10 to –0.1	–5	22	–110
0 to 9.9	5	40	200
10 to 19.9	15	62	930
20 to 29.9	25	48	1,200
30 to 39.9	35	28	980
		200	3,200

$$\overline{x} = \frac{\sum fx}{n} = \frac{3,200}{200} = 16.0\%$$

See Chapter 1 Section 2.2 of your Study Text

53. **D** Median: –35%, –7%, –5%, *1%*, 11%, 12%, 21%

x	$x - \overline{x}$	$(x - \overline{x})^2$
11	11.29	127.5
21	21.29	453.3
–7	–6.71	45.0
–5	–4.71	22.2
1	1.29	1.7
–35	–34.71	1,204.8
12	12.29	151.0
–2		2,005.5

$$\overline{x} = \frac{\sum x}{n} = \frac{-2}{7} = -0.29$$

Since this is a small sample, we will utilise Bessels correction (n–1), giving

$$\therefore \sigma_{n-1} = \sqrt{\frac{\sum (x - \overline{x})^2}{n-1}} = \sqrt{\frac{2,005.5}{6}} = \sqrt{334.25} = 18.28$$

See Chapter 1 Section 2.3 and Chapter 1 Section 2.8 of your Study Text

54. **1.66**

f	x	fx	$x - \bar{x}$	$(x - \bar{x})^2$	$f(x - \bar{x})^2$
0.1	2	0.2	−4.2	17.64	1.764
0.6	6	3.6	−0.2	0.04	0.024
0.3	8	2.4	1.8	3.24	0.972
		6.2			2.760

$\bar{x} = 6.2$

$\sigma = \sqrt{2.76} = 1.66$

See Chapter 1 Section 2.8 of your Study Text

55. **A**

	m	f	fm
−10% to −0.1%	−5	15	−75
0% to 9.9%	+5	17	85
10% to 19.9%	+15	48	720
20% to 29.9%	+25	20	500
		n = 100	$\sum fm = 1{,}230$

$\bar{x} = \dfrac{\Sigma fm}{n} = \dfrac{1{,}230}{100} = 12.3\%$

See Chapter 1 Section 2.2 of your Study Text

56. **A** Arithmetic mean $= \dfrac{5.1 + 10.9 + 1.2 - 0.5 + 7.2}{5} = 4.78$

See Chapter 1 Section 2.2 of your Study Text

57. **D** The mode is the most frequently occurring value

See Chapter 1 Section 2.4 of your Study Text

58. **C** There may be more than one mode

See Chapter 1 Section 2.4 of your Study Text

59. **C** $y = a + bx = 6.3 + 2.7 \times 7 = 25.2$

See Chapter 1 Section 3.3 of your Study Text

60. **B** I Interpolation is *less* risky than extrapolation

II Strong correlation *does not* prove cause and effect

III Least squares regression is only applicable to linear relationships

See Chapter 1 Section 3 of your Study Text

61. **D**   I   The dependent variable is plotted on the *y-axis*

         II   b is the slope

         III   Regression coefficients are calculated using the least squares method

      See Chapter 1 Section 3 of your Study Text

62. **C**   The relationship is downward sloping, therefore the correlation is negative. The points are not on the line hence it is not perfect.

      See Chapter 1 Section 3.2 of your Study Text

63. **C**   Mean > Median > Mode

      See Chapter 1 Section 2.2 of your Study Text

64. **B**   I   The mean is a measure of *location*

         II   The interquartile range is unaffected by extremes

         III   The range is completely a function of the extremes (Range = Highest – lowest) (not simply weakly affected)

      See Chapter 1 Section 2 of your Study Text

65. **C**   The mode, the most commonly occurring item, is unaltered. The median would be slightly higher as there is now one more item. The arithmetic mean could be significantly higher depending on how extreme the additional item is.

      See Chapter 1 Section 2.6 of your Study Text

66. **D**   The two variables have zero correlation as the value of the y variables is independent from the value of the x variable, it does not change regardless of the value of x.

      See Chapter 1 Section 3.2 of your Study Text

67. **B**   The line of best fit may not be a very accurate line of fit hence the interpolated results will not be accurate. In addition, regression analysis will not highlight any spurious relationships between the two variables being considered as it does not in itself prove causality.

      See Chapter 1 Section 3.2 of your Study Text

68. **A**   The mean is most distorted by extreme values

      See Chapter 1 Section 2.6 of your Study Text

69. **D**   As the variance is standard deviation squared

      See Chapter 1 Section 2.8 of your Study Text

70. **D** $\text{Sample} = \sigma_{n-1} = \sqrt{\dfrac{\sum\left(x-\bar{x}\right)^2}{n-1}} = \sqrt{\text{Sample variance}}$

      The square root of the sample variance

      See Chapter 1 Section 2.8 of your Study Text

71. C $\bar{x} = \dfrac{\sum x}{n} = \dfrac{12 + 34 + 29 + 54 + 98 + 121}{6} = \dfrac{348}{6} = 58$

x	$(x - \bar{x})$	$(x - \bar{x})^2$
12	−46	2,116
34	−24	576
29	−29	841
54	−4	16
98	40	1,600
121	63	3,969
		9,118

∴ Variance = $\sigma_{n-1}^2 = \dfrac{\sum (x - \bar{x})^2}{n - 1} = \dfrac{9,118}{5} = 1,823.6$

The question asks for 'sample' variance. Therefore, use the denominator as n − 1, Bessels correction, rather than dividing by 'n' for a population

See Chapter 1 Section 2.8 of your Study Text

72. A   The respective broad-based equity indices of both the US and the UK equity market would be the most appropriate benchmarks to use

See Chapter 1 Section 4.6 of your Study Text

73. C   The Hang Seng is the Hong Kong equity index

See Chapter 1 Section 4.6 of your Study Text

74. C   A geometric index cannot be used as a meaningful benchmark, since it is virtually impossible for a manager to hold a portfolio that replicates the geometric weighting of the index

See Chapter 1 Section 4.4 of your Study Text

75. A   Price-relative geometric index = $\sqrt[3]{\dfrac{7 \times 8 \times 9}{5 \times 3 \times 2}} \times 100 = 256$

See Chapter 1 Section 4.4 of your Study Text

76. **481**   We need to scale the old index up by the sector that represents the rebasing in 1990

Old index value = $230 \times \dfrac{418}{200} = 481$

See Chapter 1 Section 4.3 of your Study Text

77. D   We need to scale the old index up by the sector that represents the rebasing in 1990

New index value = $109 \times \dfrac{200}{418} = 52.2$

See Chapter 1 Section 4.3 of your Study Text

78. **D** If all values are negative, it may mean taking the root of a negative product, which is not mathematically possible

   See Chapter 1 Section 4.4 of your Study Text

79. **365** Unweighted or price-relative arithmetic index = $\left(\dfrac{2.50 + 2.00 + 2.30 + 2.70}{1.00 + 1.20 + 1.40 + 1.60}\right) \times 200 = 365$

   See Chapter 1 Section 4.4 of your Study Text

80. **369** Unweighted geometric index = $\sqrt[4]{\dfrac{2.50}{1.00} \times \dfrac{2.00}{1.20} \times \dfrac{2.30}{1.40} \times \dfrac{2.70}{1.60}} \times 200 = 369$

   See Chapter 1 Section 4.4 of your Study Text

81. **D**

Item	P_0	Q_0	P_A	Q_n	P_0Q_0	P_nQ_n
I	1.00	8	2.50	6	8.00	15.00
II	1.20	7	2.00	7	8.40	14.00
III	1.40	6	2.30	6	8.40	13.80
IV	1.60	5	2.70	7	8.00	18.90
					32.80	61.70

   Weighted average index = $\dfrac{61.70}{32.80} \times 200 = 376$

   See Chapter 1 Section 4.5 of your Study Text

82. **C** $1970 = \dfrac{100}{227} \times 100 = 44.05$

   $1997 = \dfrac{227}{100} \times 110 = 249.7$

   See Chapter 1 Section 4.3 of your Study Text

83. **A** The others are specific indices of a particular country, i.e. FTSE (UK), DAX (Germany), S&P 500 (USA)

   See Chapter 1 Section 4.6 of your Study Text

84. **D** The Nikkei 225 is unweighted, i.e. not weighted by market capitalisation. Therefore, each of the 225 constituent securities each contribute an equal share towards the index value. This is sometimes referred to as an equally weighted index

   See Chapter 1 Section 4.6 of your Study Text

85. **A** An appropriate benchmark should be relevant and exhibit risk characteristics that reflect the risk that the client requires. This will be due to the fact that there are specific objectives of the fund that are not comparable against a broad published index

   See Chapter 1 Section 4.6 of your Study Text

86. **B** The main index in Japan is the Nikkei 225. This is an arithmetic, unweighted index, where each of the 225 constituent securities each contribute an equal share towards the index value

   See Chapter 1 Section 4.6 of your Study Text

87. **D**   The Nikkei 225 is an unweighted index

See Chapter 1 Section 4.6 of your Study Text

88. **B**   The DAX index is arithmetically calculated and weighted by market capitalisation

See Chapter 1 Section 4.6 of your Study Text

89. **B**   The Nikkei 225 index is arithmetically calculated. However, it is unweighted as each of the 225 shares contribute an equal share

See Chapter 1 Section 4.6 of your Study Text

90. **C**   Standard and Poor's 500

See Chapter 1 Section 4.6 of your Study Text

91. **A**   Osaka and Singapore are where the Nikkei 225 future trades, but the index itself relates to the Tokyo market

See Chapter 1 Section 4.6 of your Study Text

92. **B**   Equity shares are deemed to be the class of asset that will give long-term capital growth

See Chapter 1 Section 4.6 of your Study Text

93. **A**   The CAC is the main French index

See Chapter 1 Section 4.6 of your Study Text

94. **A**   The DJIA is based on 30 American shares

See Chapter 1 Section 4.6 of your Study Text

95. **A**   The FT Ordinary is made up of 30 UK shares representing the breadth of UK industry. Size is not the primary consideration, although all companies are also in the FTSE 100. The other indices are weighted by market capitalisation

See Chapter 1 Section 4.6 of your Study Text

96. **D**   Representing a fair reflection of the UK and US large and mid-cap equity markets

See Chapter 1 Section 4.6 of your Study Text

97. **A**   Weighted by market capitalisation, more specifically using the free float

See Chapter 1 Section 4.6 of your Study Text

98. **D**   The S&P Index is a value-weighted index. The Dow (30), FTSE Ordinary (30) and the Nikkei 225 are all equally weighted indices

See Chapter 1 Section 4.6 of your Study Text

99. **C**   The FT (30) Ordinary index is an equally weighted index, however it is geometrically calculated

See Chapter 1 Section 4.6 of your Study Text

100. **C**   The S&P Cantor US Treasury Bond index is the most suitable given the information provided

   See Chapter 1 Section 4.6 of your Study Text

101. **D**   While all of the indices offered up as possible answers contain US government bonds the US Treasury Index is purely focused on US government bonds and would therefore be the most applicable

   See Chapter 1 Section 4.6 of your Study Text

102. **B**   The FTSE 100 Index is used for many reasons, not least as a benchmark to see if the economy is growing, and for the pricing of its derivative products. However, it focuses on large UK companies only

   See Chapter 1 Section 4.6 of your Study Text

103. **A**   The Dow Jones Industrial Average (DJIA) represents the top 30 American shares. The index is price relative, meaning that each of the constituent items contribute an equal share towards the index value

   See Chapter 1 Section 4.6 of your Study Text

104. **113.6** To rebase the index, scale down so that the old 110 is now equivalent to 100. i.e $125 \times 100/110 = 113.6$

   See Chapter 1 Section 4.3 of your Study Text

105. **D**   Very few indices are calculated using the geometric construction method. The only exception is the FT30.

   See Chapter 1 Section 4.6 of your Study Text

106. **C**   Geometric index $= \sqrt[3]{\dfrac{56 \times 26 \times 17}{50 \times 25 \times 13}} \times 100 = 115.1$

   See Chapter 1 Section 4.4 of your Study Text

107. **B** $£50 \times 1.04 \times 1.05 \times 1.02 \times 0.97 = £54.02$

   See Chapter 1 Section 5.3 and Chapter 1 Section 6.1 of your Study Text

108. **1,250** $£100 \times \dfrac{1}{0.08} = £1,250$

   See Chapter 1 Section 6.1 of your Study Text

109. **1,037** $£500 \times 1.08^5 \times 1.09^4 = £1,037.04$

   The required format for this answer is £0,000, hence you must round to the nearest whole pound, ie £1,037

   See Chapter 1 Section 6.1 of your Study Text

110. **D** You are trying to find the discount rate that gives a NPV of 0. Trial and error gives the following calculation, indicating that 9.9% is the correct answer. Note that we have received assurances that this will not be tested using gap fill style questions

Time	Cash Flow p	DF (9.9%)	PV p
0	(74.00)	1	(74.00)
1	3.00	$\dfrac{1}{1.099^1}$	2.70
2	6.00	$\dfrac{1}{1.099^2}$	5.00
2	80.00	$\dfrac{1}{1.099^2}$	66.30
			0.00

See Chapter 1 Section 7.1 of your Study Text

111. **15,271** Regular payment = $\dfrac{\text{PV of borrowing}}{\text{ADF}}$

$\text{ADF}(1\text{-}25 \text{ @ } 9\%) = \dfrac{1}{0.09}\left(1 - \dfrac{1}{1.09^{25}}\right) = 9.822580$

Annual payment = $\dfrac{£150,000}{9.822580}$ = £15,270.94

The required format for this answer is £00,000, hence you must round to the nearest whole pound, ie £15,271

If you are having problems inputting the numbers into your calculator for the annuity discount factor, try the following keystrokes:

$1 \div 0.09 \times (1 - 1 \div 1.09 \ x^{\blacksquare} \ 25) =$

See Chapter 1 Section 6.2 of your Study Text

112. **A** This can be quite a complicated question. The best method is to calculate the PV of the cash flows, then compound that value for eight years at 10% to give the terminal value

Time	Cash Flow £	DF (10%)	PV £
0	15,000		15,000.00
1-8	(1,000)	$\dfrac{1}{0.1}\left(1 - \dfrac{1}{1.1^8}\right)$	(5,334.93)
			9,665.07

Calculate TV

£9,665.07 × 1.10^8 = £20,717.93, ie £20,718

See Chapter 1 Section 6.2 of your Study Text

113. **7.76** The answer is the value of r that makes £5,000 grow to £6,742 over five years

$$5{,}000 \times (1 + r)^4 = 6{,}742$$

$$1 + r = \sqrt[4]{\frac{6{,}742}{5{,}000}} = 1.0775928$$

r = 0.0776 or 7.76% when rounded to two decimal places as required

See Chapter 1 Section 6.1 of your Study Text

114. **3,513** $PV = £7{,}000 \times \dfrac{1}{1.09^8} = £3{,}513$

See Chapter 1 Section 6.1 of your Study Text

115. **16,289** Regular payment = $\dfrac{\text{PV of borrowing}}{\text{ADF}}$

$$ADF(1\text{-}25 \text{ @ } 9\%) = \frac{1}{0.09}\left(1 - \frac{1}{1.09^{25}}\right) = 9.822580$$

Regular payment = $\dfrac{£160{,}000}{9.822580}$ = £16,289 when rounded to whole pounds as required

See Chapter 1 Section 6.2 of your Study Text

116. **A** This is like compounding, except rather than adding interest, we are taking off 20% every year

£55,000 × (1 − 0.2)⁴ = £22,528

See Chapter 1 Section 5.3 and Chapter 1 Section 6.1 of your Study Text

117. **2.22**

Time	Cash Flow	DF (10%)	PV
0	(12)	1.0000	(12.0000)
1	3	$\frac{1}{1.10}$	2.7272
2	3	$\frac{1}{1.10^2}$	2.4793
3	12	$\frac{1}{1.10^3}$	9.0158
			2.2223

See Chapter 1 Section 6.1 of your Study Text

118. **A** £475 × 1.11⁸ = £1,095

See Chapter 1 Section 5.3 and Chapter 1 Section 6.1 of your Study Text

119. **C** A rate of 11.1% results in a (virtually) zero NPV as follows

Time	Cash Flow p	DF try 11.1%	PV p
0	(355)	1	(355.00)
1	20	$\dfrac{1}{1.111^1}$	18.00
2	30	$\dfrac{1}{1.111^2}$	24.30
3	429	$\dfrac{1}{1.111^3}$	312.83
			0.03

∴ IRR is approximately 11.1%, as this results in a zero NPV

See Chapter 1 Section 7.1 of your Study Text

120. **21,184** The value of investment to the present value of its future cash flows

$$\text{ADF(1-10 @ 10%)} = \frac{1}{0.1}\left(1 - \frac{1}{1.10^{10}}\right) = \quad 6.1445671$$

$$\text{ADF(1-5 @ 10%)} = \frac{1}{0.1}\left(1 - \frac{1}{1.10^{5}}\right) = \quad \underline{(3.7907868)}$$

$$\therefore \text{ADF(6-10)} \qquad\qquad\qquad\qquad \underline{2.3537803}$$

PV = £9,000 × 2.3537803 = £21,184.02

The required format for this answer is £00,000, hence you must round to the nearest whole number of pounds, ie £21,184.

Note, the keystrokes for the ADF, looking at the five year version, are

$1 \div 0.1 \times (1 - 1 \div 1.1\, x^\blacksquare\, 5) =$

See Chapter 1 Section 6.2 of your Study Text

121. **A** The rate of appreciation, r, is the value that is applied to the original £18,000 and compounded over fiver years to grow to £20,000.

£18,000 × (1 + r)^5 = £20,000

$$\text{Rate of appreciation} = \sqrt[5]{\frac{20,000}{18,000}} - 1$$

$$= 1.0213 - 1 = 0.0213 \text{ or } 2.13\%$$

$$= 2.1\% \text{ to one decimal place}$$

See Chapter 1 Section 6.1 of your Study Text

122. **4,909** You can work this out by calculating the PV of the perpetuity, then remove the impact of the cash flow at T1. The resulting perpetuity discount factor (PDF) then only includes Time 2 onwards.

You could also value the perpetuity as normal, then discount the results by one year (i.e. divide by 1.10) to account for your delay.

$$\text{PDF (1 to } \infty) = \frac{1}{r} = \frac{1}{0.1} = \qquad\qquad 10.000000$$

$$\text{Less DF for Time 1} = \frac{1}{1+r} = \frac{1}{1.1} \qquad\qquad \underline{(0.909091)}$$

$$\therefore \text{PDF (2 to } \infty) \qquad\qquad\qquad \underline{9.090909}$$

PV = £540 × 9.090909 = £4,909 to the nearest whole pound

See Chapter 1 Section 6.2 of your Study Text

123. **D** A rate of 10.6% results in a (virtually) zero NPV as follows

Time	Cash Flow p	DF (10.6%)	PV p
0	(103.00)	1	(103.00)
1	5.00	$\frac{1}{1.106^1}$	4.52
2	6.00	$\frac{1}{1.106^2}$	4.91
3	6.50	$\frac{1}{1.106^3}$	4.80
3	120.00	$\frac{1}{1.106^3}$	88.70
			(0.07)

See Chapter 1 Section 7.1 of your Study Text

124. **9,480** $\text{Regular repayment} = \dfrac{\text{PV of borrowing}}{\text{ADF}}$

$$\text{ADF(1-20 @ 11.1\%)} = \frac{1}{0.111}\left(1 - \frac{1}{1.111^{20}}\right) = 7.9115310$$

$\text{Annual payment} = \dfrac{£75,000}{7.9115310} = £9,480$ when rounded to whole pounds as required

Note, the keystrokes for the ADF are

$1 \div 0.111 \times (1 - 1 \div 1.111 \ x^\bullet 20) =$

See Chapter 1 Section 6.2 of your Study Text

125. **43,301** £125,000 $\times$ d^6 = £15,000

Where d = proportion of opening NBV not depreciated at the year-end (1 – Depreciation rate)

Hence, d = $\sqrt[6]{\dfrac{15,000}{125,000}}$ = 0.7023122

Therefore, NBV at end of third year = £125,000 $\times$ 0.7023122^3 = £43,301 to the nearest whole pound

Note that you may find this question easier after studying the accounting section of the syllabus

See Chapter 1 Section 6.1 of your Study Text

126. **C** PV = £725 $\times$ $\dfrac{1}{1.08^7}$ = £423.03

See Chapter 1 Section 6.1 of your Study Text

127. **A**

TV of I = £1,000 $\times$ 1.02^{40} = 2,208.04

TV of II = £1,000 $\times$ 1.03^{20} = $\underline{1,806.11}$

£401.93

See Chapter 1 Section 5.3 and Chapter 1 Section 6.1 of your Study Text

128. **C** ADF(5-10 @ 8%) = ADF(1-10 @ 8%) – ADF(1-4 @ 8%)

ADF(1-10 @ 8%) = $\dfrac{1}{0.08}\left(1-\dfrac{1}{1.08^{10}}\right)$ = 6.71008

ADF(1-4 @ 8%) = $\dfrac{1}{0.08}\left(1-\dfrac{1}{1.08^4}\right)$ = (3.31213)

3.39795

TIME	CASH	DF	PV
5-10	£2,000	3.39795	£6,796

Note, the keystrokes for the 10 year ADF are

1 $\div$ 0.08 $\times$ (1 – 1 $\div$ 1.08 x$^{\bullet}$ 10) =

See Chapter 1 Section 6.2 of your Study Text

129. **A** Regular payment = $\dfrac{\text{PV of borrowing}}{\text{ADF}}$

ADF(1-20 @ 7.5%) = $\dfrac{1}{0.075}\left(1-\dfrac{1}{1.075^{20}}\right)$ = 10.194491

Annual payment = $\dfrac{£160,000}{10.194491}$ = £15,695 when rounded to whole pounds as required

Note, the keystrokes for the ADF are

1 $\div$ 0.075 $\times$ (1 – 1 $\div$ 1.075 x$^{\bullet}$ 20) =

See Chapter 1 Section 6.2 of your Study Text

130. **B** This is another example of using trial and error to find the IRR. We illustrate below the correct answer of 9%, giving an NPV of 0

Time	Cash	DF	PV
0	(86)	1	(86.0)
1	4	$\dfrac{1}{1.09^1}$	3.8
2	5	$\dfrac{1}{1.09^2}$	4.2
3	101 (6+95)	$\dfrac{1}{1.09^3}$	78.0
			0.0

See Chapter 1 Section 7.1 of your Study Text

131. **A**

Time	Cash	CF	TV
0	£7,000	$1.07^4 \times 1.08^5$	£13,482

See Chapter 1 Section 6.1 of your Study Text

132. **B** $£12,000 \times (1 + r)^7 = £18,648$

$(1 + r)^7 = \dfrac{18,648}{12,000} = 1.554$

$1 + r = \sqrt[7]{1.554} = 1.065$

$r = 0.065$ or 6.5%

See Chapter 1 Section 5.3 of your Study Text

133. **D** $r = (1+r_1)(1+r_2)(1+r_3)(1+r_4) - 1$

$= (0.995 \times 1.037 \times 1.01 \times 1.023) - 1$

$= 1.0661 - 1$

$= 0.0661 = 6.61\%$

See Chapter 1 Section 5.3 of your Study Text

134. **11,168** $PV = TV / (1 + r)^n$

$PV = £20,000 / 1.06^{10}$

$PV = £11,168$ to the nearest whole pound

See Chapter 1 Section 6.1 of your Study Text

135. **C**   Annuity discount factor $(1-15 @ 12\frac{1}{2}\%) = \dfrac{1}{0.125}\left(1-\dfrac{1}{1.125^{15}}\right) = 6.632894$

Annual payment $= \dfrac{£275,000}{6.632894} = £41,460$

If you are having problems inputting the numbers into your calculator for the annuity discount factor, try the following keystrokes:

$1 \div 0.125 \times (1 - 1 \div 1.125 \; x^{\blacksquare} \; 15) =$

See Chapter 1 Section 6.2 of your Study Text

136. **30,411** $75,000 \times d^{15}$

where d = proportion of opening NBV not depreciated at the year-end (1 – depreciation rate)

Hence, $d = \sqrt[15]{\dfrac{5,000}{75,000}} = 0.8348221$

Therefore NBV at the end of the 5th year is $75,000 \times 0.8348221^5 = 30,411$ to the nearest whole pound

Note you may find it easier to attempt this question after studying the accounting section of the syllabus

See Chapter 1 Section 6.1 of your Study Text

137. **D**   This is like compounding except rather than adding interest we are deducting 5% each year

$£175,000 \times (1-0.05)^3 = 150,041$

See Chapter 1 Section 5.3 and Chapter 1 Section 6.1 of your Study Text

138. **B**

TIME	CASH FLOW p	DF 13.87%	PV p
0	(405)	1	(405)
1	15	$\dfrac{1}{1.1387}$	13
2	25	$\dfrac{1}{1.1387^2}$	19
3	550	$\dfrac{1}{1.1387^3}$	373
			0

IRR is 13.87% as this results in a zero NPV.

Note that the best approach is trial and error for this sort of question in the exam. You will not be asked to answer this question in a gap-fill format

See Chapter 1 Section 7.1 of your Study Text

BPP LEARNING MEDIA

139. C $47,500 \times d^{10}$

where d = proportion of opening NBV not depreciated at the year-end (1 – depreciation rate)

Hence, $d = \sqrt[10]{\dfrac{2,500}{47,500}} = 0.744946$

Therefore NBV at the end of the 6th year is $47,500 \times 0.744946^6 = 8,118$

Note you may find it easier to attempt this question after studying the accounting section of the syllabus.

See Chapter 1 Section 6.1 of your Study Text

140. D

TIME	CASH FLOW p	DF 14.61%	PV p
0	(285)	1	(285)
1	30	$\dfrac{1}{1.1461}$	26
2	340	$\dfrac{1}{1.461^2}$	259
			0

IRR is 14.61% as this results in a zero NPV.

141. B
$$R = e^{rt} - 1$$
$$= e^{0.34 \times 1} - 1$$
$$= 0.40495 \text{ or } 40.495\% \text{ or } 40.5\%$$

To enter this into your calculator, type SHIFT then the [ln] button (two below the on button) then enter 0.34 to give 1.40495, then subtract 1

See Chapter 1 Section 5.3 of your Study Text

142. 6.98
$$R = e^{rt} - 1$$
$$= e^{0.27 \times 3/12} - 1$$
$$= 0.6983 \text{ or } 6.983\% \text{ or } 6.98\%$$

See Chapter 1 Section 5.3 of your Study Text

143. A
$$R = e^{rt} - 1$$
$$= e^{0.38 \times 6/12} - 1$$
$$= 0.20925 \text{ or } 20.925\% \text{ or } 20.9\%$$

See Chapter 1 Section 5.3 of your Study Text

144. **25,817** Regular payment $= \dfrac{\text{PV of borrowing}}{\text{ADF}}$

$$\text{ADF(1-20 @ 10.5\%)} = \frac{1}{0.105}\left(1 - \frac{1}{1.105^{20}}\right) = 8.230909$$

Annual payment $= \dfrac{£212{,}500}{8.230909} = £25{,}817$ to the nearest whole pound

Note the keystrokes for the ADF calculation are:

$1 \div 0.105 \times (1 - 1 \div 1.105 \; x^{\bullet} \; 20) =$

See Chapter 1 Section 6.2 of your Study Text

145. **B** Regular payment $= \dfrac{\text{PV of borrowing}}{\text{ADF}}$

$$\text{ADF(1-15 @ 8.75\%)} = \frac{1}{0.0875}\left(1 - \frac{1}{1.0875^{15}}\right) = 8.181043$$

Annual payment $= \dfrac{£127{,}000}{8.181043} = £15{,}524$ to the nearest whole pound

Note the keystrokes for the ADF calculation are:

$1 \div 0.0875 \times (1 - 1 \div 1.0875 \; x^{\bullet} \; 15) =$

See Chapter 1 Section 6.2 of your Study Text

146. **491.63** $\text{PV} = 500 \times \dfrac{1}{e^{0.0675 \times 13/52}}$

$= 491.63$

See Chapter 1 Section 6.2 of your Study Text

147. **C** $\text{PV} = 1{,}000 \times \dfrac{1}{e^{0.0948 \times 45/52}}$

$= 921.24$

See Chapter 1 Section 6.2 of your Study Text

148. **A**

TV of I = £15,000 × 1.025$^{(4 \times 5)}$ =	24,579.25
TV of II = £15,000 × 1.035$^{(2 \times 5)}$ =	21,158.98
	3,420.27

See Chapter 1 Section 5.3 and Chapter 1 Section 6.1 of your Study Text

149. **C** NPV model assumes that no single firm is able to affect the price of funds.

See Chapter 1 Section 7.2 of your Study Text

150. **6.40** Simple interest is £1,000 × 8% × 2 = £160.00

Compound interest is $1{,}000 \times 1.08^{2} - 1{,}000 = £166.40$

See Chapter 1 Section 5.2 and Chapter 1 Section 5.3 of your Study Text

151. **C**   Five year bond holding $= \dfrac{£2,000}{1.06^5} =$ 1,494.52

Eight year bond holding $= \dfrac{£2,350}{1.06^8} =$ 1,474.42

Difference   20.10

See Chapter 1 Section 6.1 of your Study Text

152. **C**   Autocorrelation suggests that returns from one period are in some way connected to those of another but is unrelated to normal distributions

See Chapter 1 Section 2.10 of your Study Text

153. **D**   Something is statistically significant if its observed average value is noticeably different from expectations

See Chapter 1 Section 2.11 of your Study Text

154. **B**   Stratified sampling is a technique that can be used when the population can be divided into clear strata or segments that exhibit different characteristics, such as dividing the population into males and females or dividing and equity index into industrial sectors

See Chapter 1 Section 1.2 of your Study Text

155. **C**   Snowball sampling is a technique that is applied when investigating a characteristic that is quite rare or is hidden within the population, characteristics that make it both difficult and costly to locate items with such characteristics

See Chapter 1 Section 1.2 of your Study Text

156. **D**   Where capital is freely available and investment opportunities only have a single IRR, both NPV and IRR will provide the same conclusion regarding the viability of the investments. IRR disregards the scale of any investment opportunities. A simple investment that, once bought, only provides positive returns cannot have multiple IRRs

See Chapter 1 Section 8.2 of your Study Text

2. Micro-economics

Questions

1. **What are the 4 Ps of marketing?**

   A Product, Place, Promotion and Price

   B Profit, Place, Promotion and Price

   C Product, Profit, Place and Promotion

   D Product, Profit, Place and Price

2. **If one firm supplies the entire market through its exclusive patent rights, the resulting market structure is**

   A Natural monopoly

   B Legally protected monopoly

   C Monopolistic competition

   D Perfect competition

3. **The perfectly competitive firm attempting to maximise profits should increase output to the point at which**

   A Average revenue equals average cost

   B Average revenue equals marginal cost

   C The difference between average revenue and average cost is greatest

   D The difference between marginal revenue and marginal cost is greatest

4. **Which of the following would you expect to be the long run attributes of an industry under perfect competition?**

       I   Firms profits maximise

       II   Each firm faces a horizontal demand curve

       III   There is product differentiation

   A I and III

   B II and III

   C I and II

   D None of the above

5. **Which of the following statements about the behaviour of a profit-maximising monopoly is true?**

A It will only produce at the level of output where the price elasticity of demand is greater than one

B It will only produce at the level of output where price is equal to marginal cost

C It will set a price less than marginal cost but greater than average cost

D It will set a price where marginal cost is at a minimum

6. **A demand curve, relating price to output, which is a straight line sloping downwards**

A Has a constant elasticity along its whole length

B Has a falling elasticity as you move down the line

C Has a rising elasticity as you move down the line

D Has an elasticity at each point on the line which has no predictable pattern

7. **Which of the following statements are true?**

    I   If two goods are substitutes, the cross price elasticity of demand is likely to be positive

    II   The total expenditure on a good with elastic demand can be expected to fall when the price rises

    III If two goods are complements, a fall in the price of one reduces the demand for the other

A I, II and III

B II and III

C I and III

D I and II

8. **Which one of the following will not lead to a rightward shift of a supply curve?**

A A reduction in labour charges

B Technological advances

C An increase in supply price

D Increased government subsidies

9. **Monopolies maintain supernormal profits in the long term because**

A They are more efficient than other firms

B Unlike other firms, they benefit from economies of scale

C They can advertise

D There are barriers to the entry of competitors

10. **Which of the following statements about the conditions necessary to achieve optimal outcomes is correct?**

   A Firms wishing to maximise their profits should increase output until marginal revenue exceeds marginal costs

   B Monopolies wishing to maximise sales revenue should produce an output such that the price elasticity of demand is equal to zero

   C Perfectly competitive firms aiming to maximise sales revenue should set price equal to marginal cost

   D Firms wishing to minimise costs should produce such that marginal costs equal average costs

11. **Which of the following does not constitute a barrier to entry into a monopoly market?**

   A Significant economies of scale

   B Constant long-term average costs

   C Heavy advertising costs

   D Large-scale capital requirements

12.

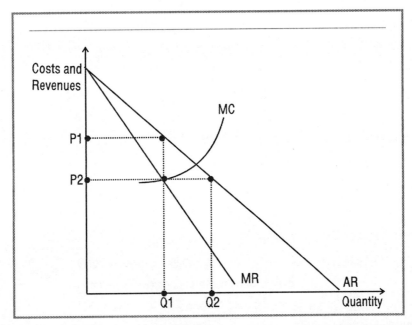

The diagram above shows a profit-maximising monopoly producer of high-definition television sets that was originally producing at Q1 with price P1. Now, as a result of changed conditions (not shown), it sets a price P2.

This change could have occurred because of

   A An increase in consumer incomes

   B A reduction in labour costs

   C An increase in research costs

   D A fall in the price of normal television sets

13. **Which of the following pairs of commodities is likely to have a positive cross-elasticity of demand?**

A   Postage stamps and envelopes

B   Foreign and domestic holidays

C   Airliners and aviation fuel

D   Computers and software

14. **Which of the following might account for diseconomies of scale?**

A   Diversification

B   The Competition Commission

C   Indivisibilities

D   Bureaucracy

15. **An increase in income levels will cause**

A   An increase in demand for normal goods and a decrease in demand for inferior goods

B   A decrease in demand for normal goods and an increase in demand for inferior goods

C   An increase in supply of normal goods and a decrease in supply of inferior goods

D   A decrease in supply of normal goods and an increase in supply of inferior goods

16. **What is the measure that represents the change in aggregate demand for a change in income?**

A   Multiplier

B   Accelerator

C   Marginal propensity to consumer

D   Marginal propensity to save

17. **Consider the following statements.**

I   A change in price causes a movement along a supply curve

II   An increase in the price of complements increases demand

III   As incomes rise demand for inferior goods falls

Which statements are true?

A   All are true

B   I and II

C   I and III

D   II and III

18. If the price of a product is £2.40 then 6,000 units are sold. If the price rises to £2.50 then sales fall by 500 units. What is the elasticity of demand (to two decimal places ignoring the sign)?

Important! You should enter the answer only in numbers strictly using this format: 0.00

Do not include spaces, letters or symbols (but decimal points and commas should be used if indicated).

19. A perfectly elastic demand curve could be

A   A vertical line

B   A 45° downward sloping line

C   A horizontal line

D   A 45° upward sloping line

20. Consider the following statements.

I   Unit elasticity results in a 45° downward sloping straight line

II   Income elasticity of demand is always positive

III   Substitutes do have a positive cross elasticity of demand

Which statements are true?

A   I and III

B   II and III

C   I and II

D   III only

21. Normal profits provide compensation for all but one of the following. Which one?

A   Loss of income proprietors could otherwise have earned

B   Cost in terms of interest lost on capital invested

C   Risks proprietors are undertaking

D   Revenue minus expenditure

22. Which of the following is not one of Porter's five forces?

A   Suppliers' power

B   Buyer power

C   Product life cycle

D   Competitors

23. **Consider the following statements requiring the conditions for perfect competition.**

    I   No barriers to entry

    II   Price discrimination

    III   Homogeneous product

    Which statements are true?

    A   All are true

    B   I and II

    C   I and III

    D   II and III

24. **Demand is the quantity of goods that consumers wish to buy**

    A   Where supply equals demand

    B   Where marginal cost equals marginal revenue

    C   At the average price consumers wish to pay

    D   At each possible price

25. **Which of the following will not lead to an increase in the demand curve?**

    A   Increase in the price of substitutes

    B   Decrease in the price of complements

    C   Rise in income levels

    D   Rise in the price of the goods

26. **Opportunity costs are**

    A   Average variable costs

    B   Marginal costs

    C   The value of the best alternative use

    D   Sunk costs

27. **Which of the following is not an element of SWOT?**

    A   Strengths

    B   Weaknesses

    C   Organisations

    D   Threats

28. **In the short run a firm will produce where marginal costs equal marginal revenue and**

    A   Average variable costs are covered

    B   Average fixed costs are covered

    C   Average total costs are covered

    D   Sunk costs are covered

29. **Marginal cost is, as output rises by one unit**

    A   The increase in average variable cost

    B   The increase in fixed costs

    C   The increase in total costs

    D   The increase in average total costs

30. **Which of the following will not be regarded as complements?**

    A   Bread and butter

    B   Strawberries and cream

    C   Fish and chips

    D   Chalk and cheese

31. **A company that is still gaining the benefit of economies of scale as output levels rise is trading at an output level below its**

    A   Minimum short run average total cost

    B   Minimum short run average variable costs

    C   Minimum long run average total cost

    D   Minimum long run average marginal cost

32. **Consider the following statements.**

    I   The MC curve cuts the average total cost curve before its minimum point

    II   The minimum efficient scale is the minimum point on the short run average total cost curve

    III   Short run costs may rise due to decreasing returns to a factor

    Which statements are true?

    A   I only

    B   II only

    C   III only

    D   None of the statements are true

33. **The supply curve of sofas has shifted to the right. Which of the following could have caused this shift?**

    A   A decrease in the price of sofas

    B   A decrease in the price of futons (a substitute)

    C   A decrease in the cost of horsehair (a raw material)

    D   A decrease in the wage rate in the futon industry

34. **A company increases its output and average costs rise as a result. Which of the following is the best explanation of what is happening in the short run?**

A   The company is experiencing increasing economies of scale

B   Fixed costs are increasing

C   Average variable costs are increasing

D   The company is experiencing diseconomies of scale

35. **When diseconomies of scale exist, which of the following is true?**

A   Marginal cost < Average variable cost

B   Marginal cost > Average variable cost

C   Average fixed costs < Average variable costs

D   Average fixed costs > Average variable costs

36. **In a perfectly competitive market in respect of demand curves faced by individual firms**

A   The elasticity of supply = ∞

B   The elasticity of demand = $-\infty$

C   The elasticity of demand = 0

D   The elasticity of supply = 0

37. **Which one of the following analytical techniques is less likely to be considered when analysing various industrial sectors and companies within those industrial sectors?**

A   Porter's Five Competitive Forces

B   The Four Ps of Marketing

C   An analysis of the strengths, weaknesses, opportunities and threats

D   An analysis of the company's balanced budget

38. **The minimum long run average total cost**

A   Is where profits are maximised

B   Is always less than the minimum short run average total cost curve

C   Is where economies of scale are growing

D   Is the minimum efficient scale

39. **When consumer preference for a good increases, this will cause the equilibrium price to move**

A   To the right along the demand curve

B   To the left along the demand curve

C   To the right along the supply curve

D   To the left along the supply curve

40. **Which of the following statements are true?**

I	Demand becomes less elastic in the long term
II	Supply becomes more elastic in the long term
III	Elasticity of supply is positive

A II only

B II and III

C I and II

D I, II and III

Answers

1. **A**   The 4 Ps help us understand the processes influencing competitive advantage and threats

    See Chapter 2 Section 5.5 of your Study Text

2. **B**   The business is a monopoly due to the legal protection afforded by the patents

    See Chapter 2 Section 4.2 of your Study Text

3. **B**   For the perfectly competitive firm

    Average revenue = Marginal revenue

    and the profit maximisation rule is

    Marginal revenue = Marginal cost

    See Chapter 2 Section 2.1 of your Study Text

4. **C**   There is no production differentiation, firms face a horizontal demand curve but still profit maximise (yielding normal profits)

    See Chapter 2 Section 4.1 of your Study Text

5. **A**   It will produce where MC = MR. Since MC will always be positive, this must be where MR is above the horizontal axis and, therefore, on the elastic portion of the demand curve

    See Chapter 2 Section 2.2 of your Study Text

6. **B**   Elasticity is a relative measure of sensitivity to the price of a good and as such varies along the length of the demand curve from perfectly elastic to perfectly inelastic

    See Chapter 2 Section 1.2 of your Study Text

7. **D**   If two goods are complements, then a fall in the price of one good will lead to an increase in the demand for the other good, as it too becomes more attractive. The strength of the relationship between the two goods is given by the cross-elasticity of demand

    See Chapter 2 Section 1.2 of your Study Text

8. **C**   A rightward shift in the supply curve is an increase in supply. An increase in price would lead to a movement along the supply curve or an increase in quantity supplied

    See Chapter 2 Section 1.1 of your Study Text

9. **D**   Barriers such as legal constraints, minimum efficient scale and integration prevent other firms entering the industry and eroding away the supernormal profit in the long run

    See Chapter 2 Section 4.2 of your Study Text

10. **D**   Beyond the point where marginal cost equals average costs, the marginal cost must be greater than average cost and hence, average costs will be rising

    See Chapter 2 Section 2.1 of your Study Text

11. **B**   The other three are valid barriers to entry, but constant long-term average costs has no impact on the ability of other firms to enter the industry

    See Chapter 2 Section 4.2 of your Study Text

12.   **B**   This will cause a shift in the marginal cost curve to intersect MR at Q_1P_2

The monopolist will always set the production level so that MR = MC, and will fix the cost accordingly. If there was a change in the demand side the optimal price and quantity would move from the prices shown on the graph. The only way for the price to remain on the AR curves is if the only change is a vertical drop in the MC curve, setting a new profit maximising price on the current MR/MC intersection

See Chapter 2 Section 4.2 of your Study Text

13.   **B**   Positive cross-elasticity implies that as the price of a good rises, the quantity demanded of another good rises. This implies that the goods must be substitutes of one another

See Chapter 2 Section 1.3 of your Study Text

14.   **D**   Diseconomies of scale implies increasing long run average costs of production caused by size issues, such as increased bureaucracy, once a firm gets above an optimum level of output

See Chapter 2 Section 3.1 of your Study Text

15.   **A**   The theory of demand and supply states that the demand curve will shift (normally to the right) when a number of factors are considered. Where an individual's income level increases, then this will lead to an increase in the quantity demanded of a normal good. At the same time, when income levels increase, demand for inferior goods will normally fall. Another factor that affect the demand curve are the price of another good, where demand for a normal good increases when the price of a substitute rises or the price of a complement falls

See Chapter 2 Section 1.1 of your Study Text

16.   **A**   The multiplier represents the change in aggregate demand for a change in income

See Chapter 2 Section 1.3 of your Study Text

17.   **C**   An increase in the price of complements reduces demand

See Chapter 2 Section 1.1 of your Study Text

18.   **2.00**   Elasticity of demand = $\dfrac{\left(\dfrac{5{,}500 - 6{,}000}{6{,}000}\right)}{\left(\dfrac{2.50 - 2.40}{2.40}\right)}$ = −2.00 or, ignoring the sign, 2.00

See Chapter 2 Section 1.3 of your Study Text

19.   **C**   Perfect elasticity = horizontal line

See Chapter 2 Section 1.3 of your Study Text

20.   **D**   I   Unit elasticity results in a convex demand curve
        II   Income elasticity is negative for inferior goods
        III   Substitutes have a positive cross elasticity of demand

See Chapter 2 Section 1.3 of your Study Text

21. **D** Revenue minus expenditure gives accounting profits, normal profit is an economic measure

   See Chapter 2 Section 2.1 of your Study Text

22. **C** Product life cycle is not one of Porter's five forces

   See Chapter 2 Section 5.2 of your Study Text

23. **C** There is no price discrimination under perfect competition

   See Chapter 2 Section 4.1 of your Study Text

24. **D** Demand represents the quantity of goods that individuals want to buy given the price

   See Chapter 2 Section 1.1 of your Study Text

25. **D** A change in prices causes a movement along the demand curve

   See Chapter 2 Section 1.1 of your Study Text

26. **C** Opportunity cost is the value of what opportunity is missed by undertaking the chosen alternative (the value of the best alternative use)

   See Chapter 2 Section 2.1 of your Study Text

27. **C** O = opportunities

   See Chapter 2 Section 5.4 of your Study Text

28. **A** A firm must cover average variable costs in the short term. Average total cost must be covered in the long term but not necessarily in the short term

   See Chapter 2 Section 4.1 of your Study Text

29. **C** MC = increase in total cost of producing one extra unit

   See Chapter 2 Section 2.1 of your Study Text

30. **D** Chalk does not go well with cheese

   See Chapter 2 Section 1.1 of your Study Text

31. **C** Economies of scale lead to a reduction of long run average total costs

   See Chapter 2 Section 3.1 of your Study Text

32. **C** Short run costs fall then rise due to increasing then decreasing returns to a factor

   See Chapter 2 Section 2.1 of your Study Text

33. **C** The supply curve has shifted to the right, as a cost has fallen. Therefore, for any given price, producers will be prepared to produce more

   See Chapter 2 Section 1.1 of your Study Text

34. **C** A short-run increase in output will not have any impact on the scale of activities or on fixed costs

   See Chapter 2 Section 2.1 of your Study Text

35.   **B**   Where marginal cost exceeds the AVC it will increase the AVC, hence creating diseconomies of scale

See Chapter 2 Section 3.1 of your Study Text

36.   **B**   Perfect competition, demand for individuals is perfectly elastic, ie PED = $-\infty$

See Chapter 2 Section 1.2 of your Study Text

37.   **D**   The analytical techniques that are likely to be considered when analysing various industrial sectors and companies within those industrial sectors are SWOT (strengths, weaknesses, opportunities and threats) analysis, Porter's Five Competitive Forces, and the Four Ps of Marketing, 'product', 'place', 'promotion', 'price', although you could also consider the seven Ps of marketing, which incorporate 'people', 'process' and 'physical'

See Chapter 2 Section 5 of your Study Text

38.   **D**   The minimum point on the long run average total cost scale is the minimum efficient scale

See Chapter 2 Section 3.1 of your Study Text

39.   **C**   The demand curve itself will shift

See Chapter 2 Section 1.1 of your Study Text

40.   **B**   Elasticity of supply and demand increase in the long term. Elasticity of supply is positive

See Chapter 2 Section 1.3 and Chapter 2 Section 1.4 of your Study Text

3. Macro-economics

Questions

1. **Which of the following would cause structural unemployment to increase?**

   A   Most of the people employed for the Christmas season lose their jobs in January

   B   The labour force expands each summer as school leavers enter the labour market

   C   A domestic steel producing company closes a plant because it cannot produce steel as cheaply as its European competitors

   D   None of the above

2. **Suppose, in a closed economy, that the marginal propensity to save is ¼ and the government reduces its spending by £8m. We would expect**

   A   National income to fall by £32m

   B   National income to rise by £32m

   C   National income to fall by £2m

   D   National income to rise by £2m

3. **If, at some level of aggregate income, aggregate demand is less than output, we would expect**

   A   Aggregate income to rise

   B   Aggregate output to fall

   C   Aggregate demand to rise

   D   No change in aggregate output

4. **A depreciation of the exchange rate may lead to a short-term deterioration in a country's balance of payments because**

   A   Purchasing power parity always holds, thus offsetting any change in the exchange rate

   B   Prices of imports and exports change immediately, but demand for imports and exports take time to change

   C   Domestic goods become less competitive

   D   Demand for imports rise

5. **Which of the following statements is true?**

   A   The Bank of England sets the inflation rate

   B   Falling retail sales would indicate inflationary pressure in the economy

   C   Tourism is not part of the balance of payments

   D   The RPI includes mortgage payments

6. **The marginal propensity to consume is 0.4, the proportional net tax rate is 0.25, and the marginal propensity to import is 0.3. Which of the following statements about the multiplier are true?**

     I   The simple multiplier, ignoring taxes, is 1.67

     II   The simple multiplier, including taxes, is 1.43

     III   The open-economy multiplier, including taxes, is 1.0

A I, II and III

B I only

C I and III

D II and III

7. **Which of the following would be an appropriate action for a monetarist government facing a deflationary gap?**

     I   To repurchase government securities

     II   To increase interest rates to attract foreign investment

     III   To increase the asset reserves that must be held by commercial bank

A I only

B II only

C I and II

D II and III

8. **Which of the following is likely to have a negative cross-elasticity of demand?**

A Aluminium foil and cellophane

B Mars bars and jelly beans

C Big Macs and French fries

D Welsh steel and German steel

9. **The purchasing power parity theory of exchange rate determination holds that**

     I   The exchange rate reflects differences in two countries' price levels

     II   The cost of labour sets the exchange rate

     III   The exchange rate reflects differences in interest rates

     IV   The exchange rate will depreciate if domestic prices fall

Which of the following is correct?

A Only II and III are true

B Only I is true

C Only I and II are true

D Only I and III are true

10. **The demand curve for dollars on the foreign exchange market is downward sloping when plotted against the sterling price of dollars because**

   A   When the dollar depreciates, the price of British exports to the US decreases

   B   A depreciation in the value of the dollar will cause the sterling price of US exports to rise

   C   An appreciation in value of the dollar will cause the sterling price of US exports to fall

   D   When the dollar depreciates, US goods are cheaper in Britain

11.

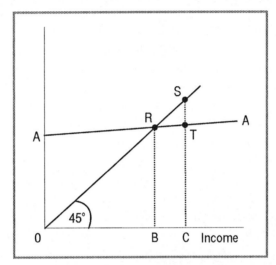

In the diagram above, line AA represents the aggregate demand schedule, given by AD = C ☐ I ☐ G, in a simple closed economy. Suppose the present equilibrium position is OB and OC represents the full employment income level

How much would aggregate demand need to rise to close the deflationary gap?

   A   BC

   B   RS

   C   RT

   D   ST

12. **In an economy, the rate of inflation in a year was 13%, although the money supply rose by only 6%. If the velocity of circulation of money stayed constant, according to the quantity theory of money, what would be the expected percentage changes in the money value of output and the volume of output?**

	MONEY VALUE OF OUTPUT	VOLUME OF OUTPUT
A	6	−7
B	7	6
C	7	−6
D	13	−7

13. **Which of the following is NOT a consequence of inflation being higher than anticipated?**

A   Wealth is redistributed from old to young

B   Business investment plans may be disrupted

C   Wealth is redistributed from debtors to lenders

D   Inflation becomes more uncertain

---

14. **What may cause the demand for sterling to rise in the foreign exchange market?**

A   An increase in UK interest rates

B   An increase in the price of foreign goods sold in the UK

C   The abolition of UK tariffs against foreign goods

D   Increased overseas competition for UK exports

---

15. **Which of the following would you expect to reduce the natural rate of unemployment?**

A   Increased grants for retaining redundant workers

B   Increased unemployment benefit

C   Increased National Insurance contributions

D   Increased numbers entering the labour market

---

16. **Consider the following statements about inflation**

    I   There would be no inflation if unemployment was at its natural level

    II   There would be no inflation if the money supply was held constant

    III   Nobody benefits from inflation

Which of the following is correct?

A   Only I is true

B   Only II is true

C   Only III is true

D   None are true

---

17. **If the marginal propensity to consume out of disposable income is 0.8, the proportional tax rate is 0.25 and the economy-wide marginal propensity to import is 0.2, what is the value of the open-economy multiplier (to 2 decimal places)?**

Important! You should enter the answer only in numbers strictly using this format: 0.00

Do not include spaces, letters or symbols (but decimal points and commas should be used if indicated).

---

18. **Which of the following would reduce the size of the Public Sector Net Cash Requirement?**

    A   Increased corporate taxation

    B   Printing money

    C   Borrowing from abroad

    D   Selling Treasury bills to domestic residents

19. **Which of the following would cause an increase in structural unemployment?**

    A   A total ban on cigarette smoking

    B   Increased numbers of people injured in road accidents

    C   Worldwide recession

    D   An increase in unemployment benefits

20. **In one year, the labour force rose by 1%, labour productivity improved by 3% and the money supply rose by 9%.**

    If all else was fixed, prices rose by

    A   9%

    B   8%

    C   6%

    D   5%

21. **A country is said to be in internal and external balance when**

    A   The PSNCR and the capital account of the balance of payments are both zero

    B   Private savings equal private investment and exports of goods equal imports of goods

    C   Aggregate demand is at full employment and the current account of the balance of payments balances

    D   Inflation is zero and the exchange rate is stable

22. **If fixed investment is very sensitive to changes in interest rates, the most effective method of stimulating the economy would be to**

    A   Increase the money supply

    B   Increase government expenditure

    C   Reduce taxes

    D   Raise pensions

23. **Which of the following may reduce the demand for sterling in the foreign exchange market?**

    A   An increase in UK interest rates

    B   The opening of several plants in the UK that produce import substitutes

    C   A shift of American and Japanese tourists away from the UK

    D   A reduction in American tariffs on imports

24. Central banks have various responsibilities. With regard to the responsibility of setting interest rates independently of the Government, which of the following statements is true?

A   The Bank of England and the European Central bank both have responsibility for setting interest rates independently of the Government, however the US Federal Reserve does not

B   The Bank of England, the European Central Bank, and the US Federal Reserve all have responsibility for setting interest rates independently of the Government

C   The Bank of England and the US Federal Reserve both have responsibility for setting interest rates independently of the Government, however the European Central Bank does not

D   The Bank of England has responsibility for setting interest rates independently of the Government, however both the European Central Bank and the US Federal Reserve do not

25. What is the shape of the long-run Phillips curve?

A   Upward sloping (rising to the right)

B   Downward sloping (falling to the right)

C   Horizontal

D   Vertical

26. The Federal Reserve Bank has responsibility for undertaking which of the following roles?

  I   Sets interest rates and executes monetary policy

  II   Responsible for enforcing banking regulation

  III   Offers a deposit protection scheme

A   I and II

B   II and III

C   I, II and III

D   I and III

27. If the potential money multiplier is 20, what is the cash reserve ratio?

A   5%

B   10%

C   15%

D   20%

28. If the cash reserve ratio is 8% what is the potential money multiplier?

A   8

B   12.5

C   20

D   40

29. **The fractional reserve banking system gives rise to which of the following?**

 A The multiplier effect

 B Automatic stabilisers

 C The consumption function

 D The potential money multiplier

30. **Which of the following is a leading economic indicator?**

 A Unemployment rate

 B Housebuilding activity

 C Outstanding bank loans

 D Labour cost

31. **Which of the following would cause an increase in structural unemployment?**

 A A total ban on cigarette smoking

 B Increased numbers of people injured in road accidents

 C Worldwide recession

 D An increase in unemployment benefits

32. **What is the effect on aggregate demand if the Government raises £1bn from the wealthy (who have a marginal propensity to consume of 0.2), and at the same time increases unemployment benefit by £1bn?**

 A Increases

 B Decreases

 C Stays the same

 D Impossible to tell

33. **Which of the following best describes the balanced budget multiplier?**

 A When government deficits are balanced by sterling borrowing, then there will be no inflationary impact

 B When government spending and revenue are balanced, there will be no impact on national income

 C Even though government spending and revenue are balanced, there will be a positive impact on national income

 D If government spending and revenue are matched, there will be a negative impact on national income

34. **Which of the following policy measures would reduce unemployment and also reduce a current account surplus?**

A   Increase interest rates

B   Reduce the money supply

C   Increase tax

D   Increase government spending

35. **If a country engages in open market operations, to mitigate the effect of a balance of payments trade imbalance on the country's exchange rate, this is known as**

A   Immunisation

B   Neutralisation

C   Sterilisation

D   Equalisation

36. **The consumption function plots**

A   Expenditure against permanent income

B   Expenditure against disposable income

C   Income against permanent expenditure

D   Income against disposable expenditure

37. **The spot euro/sterling exchange rate is quoted in the paper as 0.6885-0.6893. The three-month rate is quoted as 0.20-0.24p dis. This implies that**

A   Euro three-month interest rates are about 0.3% above UK rates

B   UK three-month interest rates are about 0.3% above euro rates

C   UK three-month interest rates are about 1.3% above euro rates

D   UK three-month interest rates are about 5.3% above euro rates

38. **If there was a dramatic increase in the level of UK residents travelling abroad and spending money as tourists, what will be the impact upon the UK balance of payments?**

A   Worsening of visible trade

B   Worsening of invisible trade

C   Worsening of the capital account

D   Improvement in the capital account

39. **Settlement for foreign currency spot deals is usually**

A   One business day

B   Two business days

C   Three business days

D   The day agreed by the participants to the transaction

40. **In the foreign exchange markets in the UK, most currencies are usually quoted against**

A   The US dollar

B   Sterling

C   Gold prices

D   Euro

41. **Which of the following is true of the forward rate between two currencies?**

A   It reflects market expectations of how the spot rate will move

B   It reflects inflation rate differentials between the two currencies

C   It reflects interest rate differentials between the two currencies

D   It is determined by the central banks of the countries concerned

42. **Forward foreign exchange contracts are usually settled**

A   One month after the day of the transaction

B   Three months after the day of the transaction

C   Six months after the day of the transaction

D   At a date agreed by the participants to the transaction

43. **If the US dollar to sterling rate was quoted in London as $1.7770-$1.7850, how may dollars would you receive for £1m?**

A $560,224

B $562,746

C $1,777,000

D $1,785,000

44. **Consider the following statements.**

   I   Currency trades settle T + 3

   II   Exchange rates are usually quoted against the dollar

   III   Currency markets are centralised in London

Which of the following is correct?

A   I only

B   II only

C   III only

D   None of the above

45. The three month interest rates in the UK and Euro zone are 4% and 3% respectively. If the three month forward rate is €1.20:£1 what is the current spot rate (to four decimal places)?

Important! You should enter the answer only in numbers strictly using this format: 0.0000

Do not include spaces, letters or symbols (but decimal points and commas should be used if indicated).

46. An analyst who believes that International Fisher Effect always holds expects one year inflation to be 1.50% in the US and 2.5% in Europe. If European 12 month interest rates are 5% what are US 12 month interest rates (in % to 2 decimal places)?

Important! You should enter the answer only in numbers strictly using this format: 0.00

Do not include spaces, letters or symbols (but decimal points and commas should be used if indicated).

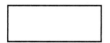

47. The current exchange rate between the dollar and the Japanese yen is ¥91:$1. If interest rates in Japan and the USA are 0.5% and 1.5% respectively what is the six month forward rate?

A 90.548

B 91.905

C 91.454

D 90.103

48. Which of the following is the correct formula for interest rate parity?

A $\text{Spot} = \text{Forward} \times \dfrac{(1+r_v)}{(1+r_f)}$

B $\text{Forward} = \text{Spot} \times \dfrac{(1+r_f)}{(1+r_v)}$

C $\text{Forward} = \text{Spot} \times \dfrac{(1+r_v)}{(1+r_f)}$

D $\text{Spot} = \text{Forward} \times \dfrac{(1+r_f)}{(1+r_v)}$

49. The current exchange rate between sterling and the dollar is $1.46:£1. If UK inflation is 2% p.a. and in the US is 1.5% p.a. what is the expected exchange rate in four years' time (to four decimal places)?

Important! You should enter the answer only in numbers strictly using this format: 0.0000

Do not include spaces, letters or symbols (but decimal points and commas should be used if indicated).

50. A government outspending its revenues through borrowing will obtain its finance first, thereby squeezing up rates of interest for other borrowers. This is known as

A Crowding out

B The accelerator

C The money multiplier

D Open market operations

51. Consider the following statements.

    I   A strengthening currency is good for exporters

    II   Purchasing power parity links to spot and forward rates

    II   Cable is a European terms quote

Which of the following statement is true?

A I only

B II only

C III only

D None of the above

52. The sterling dollar exchange rate is 1.4586 – 1.4674 $ per £1 and the three month forward rate is quoted at 0.27 – 0.28c dis. This implies which of the following about the annualised interest rates?

A US three month rates are 0.19% lower than UK three month rates

B US three month rates are 0.19% higher than UK three month rates

C US three month rates are 0.76% lower than UK three month rates

D US three month rates are 0.76% higher than UK three month rates

53. **Consider the following statements.**

I The spread on forward rates is always greater than on spot rates

II A strengthening foreign currency is good for UK exporters

III Forward rates are a function of interest rate differentials

Which of the following is true?

A I and II are true

B I and III are true

C II and III are true

D All are true

54. **The spot rate with the dollar is 1.52 and is forecast to be 1.57 in six years. If the UK inflation rate is 1.9% pa what is the US inflation rate implied through purchasing power parity.**

A 2.45%

B 2.25%

C 2.05%

D 1.95%

55. **The spot rate with the Euro is €1.26:£1 if three month interest rates for sterling and euro are 4.5% and 3.5% respectively. What is the three month forward rate?**

A 1.2722

B 1.2631

C 1.2569

D 1.2419

56. **The spot rate with the dollar is $1.5275:£1 and the three month forward rate is at a premium at 0.30c. If the three month UK interest rate is 6% what is the three month US rate?**

A 6.0%

B 5.6%

C 5.2%

D 4.8%

57. **If the US dollar spot rate against sterling is 1.5624 and the forward rate is quoted at a premium of 0.5-0.4 to sterling, then the forward quote should be**

A Higher than the spot rate

B Lower than the spot rate

C The same as the spot rate

D Not determinable from such information

58. A investor buys shares at a price of $25 when the sterling dollar exchange rate is $1.5:£1. The shares move to a price of $30 and sterling appreciates by 5% against the dollar. What is the sterling return on the investment?

    A   7.9%

    B   13.9%

    C   26%

    D   12.3%

59. For a currency spot contract, when will the currency be delivered?

    A   The day of the trade

    B   The working day after the day of the trade

    C   Two working days after the day of the trade

    D   Five working days after the day of the trade

60. Which of the following is not part of M0?

        I   Notes and coins in circulation

        II   Banks' operational deposits with the Bank of England

        III   CDs

        IV   Retail deposits with banks and building societies on less than three months' notice

    A   I and II

    B   II, III and IV

    C   III and IV

    D   IV only

61. Which of the following statements is true?

    A   The Taylor rule suggests that a 1% change in inflation (up or down) should be countered by a greater than 1% change in interest rates in the same direction

    B   The Taylor rule suggests that a 1% change in inflation (up or down) should be countered by a less than 1% change in interest rates in the opposite direction

    C   The Taylor rule suggests that a 1% change in inflation (up or down) should be countered by a less than 1% change in interest rates in the same direction

    D   The Taylor rule suggests that a 1% change in inflation (up or down) should be countered by a greater than 1% change in interest rates in the opposite direction

62. The debt deflation or credit cycle theory suggests what?

    A   The credit made available by the financial sector moves with, but lags behing, the economic cycle

    B   The financial sector causes cyclical changes in the economy as a result of their attitude towards credit availability

    C   The non-financial sector causes cyclical changes in the economy due to their changing demand for credit

    D   The credit demanded by the non-financial sector moves with, but lags behing, the economic cycle

63. **What is an optimal currency area?**

A   A geographical region in which a single currency is applied

B   A geographical region where a given currency is considered most appropriate even though it may not be the domestic currency

C   A geographical region in which overall economic efficiency will be maximised through the use of several currencies

D   A geographical region in which overall economic efficiency will be maximised through the use of a single currency

Answers

1. **C** It represents a long-term change in the structure of the labour market due to a decline in a specific industry

   See Chapter 3 Section 3.6 of your Study Text

2. **A** Using the simple multiplier

   $$£8m \times \frac{1}{1-MPC}$$

   $$£8m \times \frac{1}{MPS} \text{ (remember the MPS is } ¼)$$

   £8m × 4 = £32m reduction

   See Chapter 3 Section 2.5 of your Study Text

3. **B** Output will fall as producers adjust to reduced demand for goods

   See Chapter 3 Section 2.5 of your Study Text

4. **B** Prices of imports and exports change immediately, but demand for imports and exports take time to change. Export volumes and values will initially stay the same in sterling terms but I the long term volumes and values will rise as the exchange rate weakens. Import volumes will initially stay the same but values will rise in sterling leading to the short-term deterioration in the balance of payments. In the long-term import volumes (and values) will fall leading to a long-term improvement in exchange rates

   See Chapter 3 Section 4.2 of your Study Text

5. **D** However, RPIX (underlying rate of inflation) and RPIY exclude it

   See Chapter 3 Section 3.7 of your Study Text

6. **A** The simple multiplier is

   $$\frac{1}{1-MPC} = \frac{1}{1-0.4} = 1.67$$

   While the addition of taxes changes this to

   $$\frac{1}{1-\left[MPC(1-\text{tax rate})\right]} = \frac{1}{1-\left[0.40(1-0.25)\right]} = 1.43$$

   The open-economy multiplier is

   $$\frac{1}{1-\left[MPC(1-\text{tax rate})\right]+MPM} = \frac{1}{1-\left[0.40(1-0.25)\right]+0.3} = 1.0$$

   See Chapter 3 Section 2.5 of your Study Text

7. **A** II and III would be contractionary policies which would potentially reduce an inflationary gap in the economy by reducing the money supply

   See Chapter 3 Section 3.8 of your Study Text

8. **C** Negative cross-elasticity implies that as the price of a good rises, then the quantity demanded of another good will fall. This shows that the two goods must be complements of one another

See Chapter 3 Section 3.8 of your Study Text

9. **B** Purchasing power parity holds that differences in price levels or inflation are reflected in exchange rates and that if domestic prices increase relative to the other country, the exchange rate will depreciate

See Chapter 3 Section 4.1 of your Study Text

10. **D** The demand curve for dollars is related to the demand for exports from the US. The lower the price of dollars (exchange rate), the greater the demand for dollars, since the greater the demand for US exports

See Chapter 3 Section 4.1 of your Study Text

11. **D** Aggregate demand could rise due to an expansionary policy such as a reduction in taxation, an increase in government expenditure, an increase in investment or an increase in consumption

See Chapter 3 Section 3.4 of your Study Text

12. **A** MV = PY, but when we consider changes, we use $\Delta M + \Delta V = \Delta P + \Delta Y$

$(6\% + 0\%) = (13\% - ?)$

Volume (Y) must fall by 7% to balance the quantity theory of money

PY = money value

13% − 7% = 6% (also known as the nominal value of output, PY)

See Chapter 3 Section 3.2 of your Study Text

13. **C** The nominal interest rate compensates for the effect of expected inflation so where inflation is in line with expectations there is no wealth transfer between borrower and lender. Where, however, inflation is higher than expected the nominal interest rate will undercompensate for this leading to a redistribution of wealth of wealth from lender to borrower and, consequently from the old to the young. Higher inflation can disrupt investment planning if anticipated real returns fall and higher inflation tends to be more variable and uncertain

See Chapter 3 Section 3.2 of your Study Text

14. **A** Demand for sterling is directly linked to the demand for exports from the UK. Over a shorter term, it is also influenced by the level of UK interest rates attracting flows of overseas cash into the UK

See Chapter 3 Section 4.1 of your Study Text

15. **A** Encouraging firms to retain redundant workers would reduce the numbers registering as unemployed and hence, in the long term help to reduce the natural rate of unemployment

See Chapter 3 Section 3.6 of your Study Text

16. **D** If unemployment was at its natural level, theory states that inflation would be stable and not accelerating

See Chapter 3 Section 3.8 of your Study Text

17. **1.67** $\dfrac{1}{1-\left[MPC\left(1-\text{tax rate}\right)\right]+MPM} = \dfrac{1}{1-\left[0.8\left(1-0.25\right)\right]+0.2} = 1.67$

See Chapter 3 Section 2.5 of your Study Text

18. **A** Increased corporate taxation will increase government revenue and other things being equal reduce the deficit of government expenditure and hence borrowing requirements

See Chapter 3 Section 3.1 of your Study Text

19. **A** Structural unemployment is caused by a long-term decline in a particular industry, in this case potentially a decline in the tobacco industry as a result of regulation

See Chapter 3 Section 3.6 of your Study Text

20. **D** MV = PY, but when we consider changes, we use $\Delta M + \Delta V = \Delta P + \Delta Y$

+9% +0% = ΔP + (+1% +3%)

Prices move by 5%

See Chapter 3 Section 3.2 of your Study Text

21. **C** External balances refers to international trade flows whereas internal balance refers to full employment

See Chapter 3 Section 3.5 and Chapter 3 Section 4.2 of your Study Text

22. **A** An increase in the money supply would reduce interest rates, making private sector investment more attractive to UK firms

See Chapter 3 Section 3.2 of your Study Text

23. **C** Less tourism in the UK would, other things being constant, lead to a decline in the demand for the UK currency, sterling

See Chapter 3 Section 4.1 of your Study Text

24. **B** The Bank of England, the European Central Bank, and the US Federal Reserve all have responsibility for setting interest rates independently of the Government. It is also the case that the Bank of Japan has independence over the setting of interest rates

See Chapter 3 Section 3.9 of your Study Text

25. **D** The long-run Phillips curve is vertical at the natural rate of unemployment.

See Chapter 3 Section 3.8 of your Study Text

26. **A** The Federal Reserve is the central bank of the United States. They have a number of responsibilities, including autonomy in setting interest rates and banking supervision. The Federal Reserve Bank is NOT responsible for deposit protection insurance, as this is operated by the Federal Reserve Insurance Corporation. Along with all the other central banks, being the Bank of England, the Bank of Japan, and the European Central Bank, the Federal Reserve is NOT responsible for managing Government debt

See Chapter 3 Section 3.9 of your Study Text

27. **A**   Potential money multiplier $= \dfrac{1}{\text{Cash reserve ratio}}$

so

Cash reserve ratio $= \dfrac{1}{\text{Potential money multiplier}} = \dfrac{1}{20} = 5\%$

See Chapter 3 Section 3.2 of your Study Text

28. **B**   Potential money multiplier $= \dfrac{1}{\text{Cash reserve ratio}} = \dfrac{1}{0.08} = 12.5$

See Chapter 3 Section 3.2 of your Study Text

29. **D**   Fractional reserve banking gives rise to the potential money multiplier

See Chapter 3 Section 3.2 of your Study Text

30. **B**   Leading indicators include share prices, house building actively, money supply, credit growth and interest rates. Lagging indicators include the unemployment rate, labour costs, business spending, outstanding bank loans.

See Chapter 3 Section 1.1 of your Study Text

31. **A**   Structural unemployment involves changes in unemployment due to changes in demand or production patterns over time. Such changes may require employees to be re-trained or re-located

See Chapter 3 Section 3.6 of your Study Text

32. **A**   The marginal propensity to consume of those on unemployment benefit is likely to be much higher than that of the wealthy. As such, the amount of expenditure (and hence demand) is greater if the money is taken from the wealthy and passed on to those on benefits

See Chapter 3 Section 2.5 of your Study Text

33. **C**   The balanced budget multiplier will generate an increase in overall national income

See Chapter 3 Section 2.5 of your Study Text

34. **D**   The only measure to boost the economy and reduce unemployment is to increase government spending. This may have the impact of increasing the current account deficit through the crowding out effect.

See Chapter 3 Section 3.1 of your Study Text

35. **C**   Sterilisation is the process of offsetting changes in the money supply caused by trade imbalances by using open market operations

See Chapter 3 Section 4.1 of your Study Text

36. **B**   The consumption function plots expenditure against disposable income

See Chapter 3 Section 2.3 of your Study Text

37. C Since sterling is at a discount in the forward market, sterling must have a higher three-month interest rate than the euro. The interest rate parity formula is used to determine the difference in the rates, i.e.

$$\text{Spot} \times (1 + r_v) = \text{Forward} \times (1 + r_f)$$

Using mid-market numbers

Spot = 0.6889

Forward = (0.6889 + 0.0022) = 0.6911

If we now assume the de-annualised three-month euro rate = 1%
(any reasonable number will do here!), then

$$0.6889 \times (1 + r_v) = 0.6911 \times 1.01$$

$$(1 + r_v) = (0.6911 \times 1.01) / 0.6889 = 1.01323$$

The de-annualised sterling rate is therefore 1.323%, hence about 0.323% higher than the euro rate. Annualised, this gives 12/3 × 0.323% = roughly 1.3%

See Chapter 3 Section 4.3 of your Study Text

38. B Tourism is part of the invisible current account

See Chapter 3 Section 4.2 of your Study Text

39. B Spot currency transactions are an exception to the general T + 3 settlement convention, i.e. they settle two business days after the trade, known as T + 2

See Chapter 3 Section 4.3 of your Study Text

40. A This is the convention; the exceptions are £/$ and A$/$. When the dollar is the fixed currency, it is known as an **indirect quote**

See Chapter 3 Section 4.3 of your Study Text

41. C The forward rate is a mathematical projection based on the relevant interest rates in the two countries

See Chapter 3 Section 4.3 of your Study Text

42. D A forward contract is an agreement to exchange two currencies on a future date at a rate agreed today. The benefit is certainty

See Chapter 3 Section 4.3 of your Study Text

43. C £1,000,000 × $1.7770 = $1,777,000

See Chapter 3 Section 4.3 of your Study Text

44. B I   False, currency trades settle T + 2

II   False, currency markets are not centralised

See Chapter 3 Section 4.3 of your Study Text

45. **1.2030** Spot rate $\times (1+r_V) = $ Forward $\times (1+r_F)$

Spot $\times (1 + 0.03 \times 3/12) = 1.20 \times (1 + 0.04 \times 3/12)$

Spot $\times 1.0075 = 1.212$

Spot $= 1.2030$

See Chapter 3 Section 4.3 of your Study Text

46. **3.98** Under the International Fisher Effect

$$\frac{(1+i_V)}{(1+i_F)} = \frac{(1+r_V)}{(1+r_F)}$$

$$\frac{1.015}{1.025} = \frac{(1+r_V)}{1.05}$$

$(1+r_V) = 1.0398$

$r_V = 0.0398$ or 3.98%

See Chapter 3 Section 4.3 of your Study Text

47. **A** Spot $\times (1+r_V) = $ Forward $\times (1+r_F)$

From the quote (¥91:$1) we can see that the fixed currency here is the dollar, hence the six month forward rate can be calculated as

$91 \times (1 + 0.005 \times 6/12) = $ Forward $\times (1 + 0.015 \times 6/12)$

$91.2275 = $ Forward $\times 1.0075$

Forward $= 90.548$

See Chapter 3 Section 4.3 of your Study Text

48. **C** Forward $= $ Spot $\times \dfrac{(1+r_V)}{(1+r_F)}$

See Chapter 3 Section 4.3 of your Study Text

49. **1.4316** For long-term forecasts we can use

Spot rate $\times (1 + i_V) = $ Future rate $\times (1 + i_F)$

Where i_V and i_F are the cumulative effects of four years inflation leased on the quote ($1.46:£1), sterling is the fixed currency giving

$1.46 \times 1.015^4 = $ Future $\times 1.020^4$

$1.5496 = $ Future $\times 1.0824$

Future $= 1.4316$

See Chapter 3 Section 4.3 of your Study Text

50. **A** Where the government carries out deficit finance, the large public sector may 'crowd out' the private sector by absorbing the available resources and potentially forcing up interest rates

See Chapter 3 Section 3.1 of your Study Text

51. **D** I False – a weakening currency is good for exporters as it makes their products cheaper in foreign currency terms

II False – spot and forward rates are linked by interest rate parity

III False – cable is quoted as a number of dollars per pound = American terms quote

See Chapter 3 Section 4.3 of your Study Text

52. **D**

	£1 buys	£1 cost
Spot	1.4586	1.4674
Discount	0.0027	0.0028
Forward rate	1.4613	1.4702

Interest rate parity suggests

Spot rate $(1 + r_V)$ = Forward rate $\times (1 + r_F)$

Using the bid rates this gives

$1.4586 \times (1 + r_V) = 1.4613 \times (1 + r_F)$

If we assume a de-annualised three month rate for sterling at 1% (4% pa) this gives

$1.4586 \times (1 + r_V) = 1.4613 \times 1.01 = 1.4759$

$(1 + r_V) = 1.0119$

$r_V = 0.0119$ or 1.19% for 3 months or 4.76% pa, 0.76% above the UK rate

An alternative approach is to use the fact that the premium or discount, as a percentage is equal to the difference in interest rates. The discount is 0.275 (midpoint) divided by the mid-point of the quote, 1.463. In percentage terms this is 0.19%, which needs to be annualised for the full year

See Chapter 3 Section 4.3 of your Study Text

53. **D** All three statements are true

See Chapter 3 Section 4.3 of your Study Text

54. **A** Spot rate $\times (1 + i_V)$ = Future rate $\times (1 + i_F)$

Where i_V and i_F are the cumulative effects of inflation over the period covered, ie

$1.52 \times (1 + i_\$)6 = 1.57 \times 1.019^6 = 1.7577$

$(1 + i_\$)^6 = 1.1564$

$(1 + i_\$) = 1.0245$

$i_\$ = 0.0245$ or 2.45%

See Chapter 3 Section 4.3 of your Study Text

55. **C** Spot rate $\times (1 + r_V)$ = Forward rate $\times (1 + r_F)$

Based on the quote (€1.26:£1), sterling is the fixed currency, giving

$1.26 \times (1 + 0.035 \times 3/12)$ = Forward $\times (1 + 0.045 \times 3/12)$

1.2710 = Forward $\times 1.01125$

Forward = 1.2569

See Chapter 3 Section 4.3 of your Study Text

56. **C**   Spot rate   1.5275
          Premium   (0.0030)
          Forward rate   1.5245

Spot rate $\times$ (1 + r_V) = Forward rate $\times$ (1 + r_F)

Based on the quote ($1.5275:£1) sterling is the fixed currency, giving

$1.5275 \times (1 + r_V \times 3/12) = 1.5245 \times (1 + 0.06 \times 3/12) = 1.5473675$

$(1 + r_V \times 3/12) = 1.013$

$r_V \times 3/12 = 0.013$ or 1.3%

$r_V = 5.2\%$

See Chapter 3 Section 4.3 of your Study Text

57. **B**   Where the quote is direct, the premium is deducted. It is the dollar trading at a premium to sterling. A good tip is to look at the numbers in the forward adjustment. If they reduce from left to right, subtract them from the spot rate. If they go up, add them

See Chapter 3 Section 4.3 of your Study Text

58. **B** $\dfrac{\$1.5}{0.95}$:£1 $\Rightarrow$ $1.58:£1 is new exchange value. Please note that as sterling appreciates, the dollar depreciates by 5%

$$\left(\frac{\$30}{\$1.58} - \frac{\$25}{\$1.5} \right) / \frac{\$25}{\$1.5} = 0.139 \text{ or } 13.9\%$$

See Chapter 3 Section 4.3 of your Study Text

59. **C**   Otherwise referred to as T + 2

See Chapter 3 Section 4.3 of your Study Text

60. **C**   M0 – the narrowest measure of the money supply

See Chapter 3 Section 3.2 of your Study Text

61. **A**   The Taylor rule suggests that a 1% change in inflation (up or down) should be countered by a greater than 1% change in interest rates in the same direction

See Chapter 3 Section 3.8 of your Study Text

62. **B**   The debt deflation or credit cycle theory suggests that financial sector causes cyclical changes in the economy as a result of their attitude towards credit availability

See Chapter 3 Section 3.13 of your Study Text

63. **D**   An optimal currency area is a geographical region in which overall economic efficiency will be maximised through the use of a single currency

See Chapter 3 Section 5 of your Study Text

4. Accounting

Questions

1. A piece of equipment was purchased for £90,000 four years ago with an estimated useful life of ten years. It has just been sold for £42. Depreciation had been charged at 30% using the reducing balance method

    The accounts for the current year will show

    A   A profit on disposal of £21,567

    B   A profit on disposal of £21,000

    C   A loss of disposal of £21,567

    D   A loss on disposal of £21,000

2. Under the Companies Act, which of the following statements is true?

    A cash flow statement

    A   Must be produced by all overseas companies

    B   Must be produced for each subsidiary and shown in Group Accounts

    C   Need not be produced for companies defined as 'close' companies under the Income and Corporation Taxes Act 1988

    D   Need not be produced for companies defined as 'small' companies under the Companies Act 1989

3. Which of the following payments is not a revenue expense?

    A   Distribution costs

    B   Auditor's fees

    C   Depreciation on machinery

    D   Loan repayment

4. Which of the following is a permitted use of a share premium account reserve?

    A   The payment of dividends

    B   Write-off of expenses incurred in rights issue of shares

    C   Repayment of debenture stock at par

    D   The payment of loan interest

5. In the accounting equation, non-current assets plus working capital equals

    A   Shareholders' funds

    B   Share capital

    C   Shareholders' funds plus long-term loans and provisions

    D   Share capital plus long-term loans and provision

6. **Which of the following would directly affect reserves?**

A A revaluation of non-current assets

B An increase in the deferred tax provision

C A decrease in the provision for bad and doubtful debts

D Revenues

7. **Which of the following accounting concepts gives rise to the inclusion of depreciation in accounting statements?**

A Prudence

B Going concern

C Historical cost

D Accruals

8. **In the accounting equation, reserves equals**

A Share capital

B Shareholders' funds

C Shareholders' funds minus long-term liabilities

D Total assets minus total liabilities, minus share capital

9. **A business has the following assets and liabilities.**

	£
Receivables	72,000
Equipment (written down value)	36,000
Cash	1,890
Inventories	52,500
Motors vehicles (written down value)	44,610
Long-term loan	112,500
Payables	75,000
Buildings (written down value)	75,000

Assuming that the business is a limited company with a paid-up share capital of £45,000 and no other reserves apart from retained profits, what must be the balance of retained profits (to the nearest £1)?

Important! You should enter the answer only in numbers strictly using this format: 00,000

Do not include spaces, letters or symbols (but decimal points and commas should be used if indicated).

10. If a company makes a provision for the first time against the estimated amount of doubtful debts, this will

A Be shown as a note to the accounts only

B Increase reported profits for the year

C Have no effect on profits, but reduce receivables in the balance sheet

D Reduce reported profits for the year

11. A company's authorised share capital is

A The total share capital in the original memorandum of association

B The total amount of share capital the company has currently in issue

C The maximum amount of share capital the company currently has the power to issue

D The amount of share capital the directors intend to issue

12. Which of the following methods of calculating cost will, all other things being equal, produce the lowest value for cost of sales during a period when the purchase (input) price of the item concerned is falling?

A First In First Out

B Last In First Out

C Average cost

D Historic cost

13. A business may make a profit during a period, but have less cash in the bank at the end of the period. This is possible if

A Receivables are taking longer to pay than previously

B The business is not paying its payables

C There has been an issue of shares

D Some non-current assets have been sold during the period

14. In the accounting equation, total assets minus total liabilities equals

A Zero

B Share capital

C Reserves

D Shareholders' funds

15. Post-balance sheet events are

A Adjustments required by the company's auditors

B Events which take place after the company's preliminary results have been announced

C Events which occur between the balance sheet date and the date on which the directors approve the accounts

D Events which take place after the accounts are published

16. Accruals and deferred income would be found in which of the following categories in a company's accounts?

    A Current liabilities

    B Current assets

    C Other income

    D Cash

17. All of the following are categories of non-current assets, except

    A Investments

    B Intangible

    C Tangible

    D Inventories

18. All of the following can be shown as intangible assets on the balance sheet of a printing and publishing company, except

    A Goodwill

    B Computer hardware

    C Publishing rights and titles

    D Licenses

19. Which of the following reserves can be used to make a bonus issue?

    I   Retained earnings

    II   Share premium account reserve

    III Capital redemption reserve

    IV Revaluation reserve

    A I, II, III and IV

    B I, II and III

    C I and II

    D I only

20. Which of the following are legal requirements for a large company's annual accounts?

    I   They must be true and fair

    II   They must comply with the Companies Act 2006

    III They are the responsibility of the directors of the company

    IV They must be audited

    A I, II, III and IV

    B I, II and III

    C I, III and IV

    D II, III and IV

21. **The effect on a company's accounts of borrowing money would be to**

    A Increase assets and increase shareholders' funds

    B Increase assets and decrease liabilities

    C Increase assets and decrease shareholders' funds

    D Increase assets and increase liabilities

22. **Who is responsible for the preparation of a company's annual accounts?**

    A The directors

    B The company secretary

    C The company's auditors

    D The company's registrar

23. **A purchase of a non-current asset on credit will have what effect on a company's accounts?**

    A No effect on net assets; no effect on shareholders' funds

    B Increase net assets; increase shareholders' funds

    C Increase net assets; decrease shareholders' funds

    D Increase net assets; increase liabilities

24. **If a company increases the value of an asset over its initial cost on the balance sheet, the surplus should be shown as part of**

    A Share capital

    B Share premium account

    C Revaluation reserve

    D Income statement

25. **Which of the following would be treated as cash in a company's cash flow statement?**

    I   Cash from a bank overdraft

    II   Bank deposits with one week's notice

    III Foreign currency overdrafts

    IV   Foreign currency bank balances with 24 hours' notice

    A I, II, III and IV

    B II and IV

    C I, II and III

    D I, III and IV

26. **In which of the following categories would prepayments be found in a set of accounts?**

    A Current assets

    B Current liabilities

    C Non-current assets

    D Non current liabilities

27. When reconciling the cash flow statement, the income statement and the balance sheet, you are required to calculate the net cash flow figure for the company. Which of the following would be added to the trading profit figure to arrive at the correct net cash flow figure?

       I   An increase in inventory

      II   A decrease in accounts receivable

     III   An increase in accounts payable

     IV   Depreciation charges on assets

A I and IV

B II, III and IV

C I only

D II and IV

28. Contingent liabilities would be found where within the accounts of a company?

A Balance Sheet

B Cash Flow Statement

C Notes to the Accounts

D Income Statement

29. Given the following information, calculate the net cash flow for the period (to the nearest £1m).

Operating profit	£20m
Stated after charging:	
Depreciation	£4m
Loss on sale of non-current assets	£2m
Other items:	
Increase in receivables	£5m
Increase in inventory	£2m
Increase in payables	£3m

Important! You should enter the answer only in numbers strictly using this format: 00

Do not include spaces, letters or symbols (but decimal points and commas should be used if indicated).

30. Which of the following does not qualify as a revenue expense?

A Interest payments on business loan

B Purchase of a new computer

C Professional fees

D Print and stationery costs

31. **A limited company has the following entries in its financial statements.**

	£
Receivables	55,000
Payables	25,000
Non-current assets (cost)	425,000
Accumulated depreciation at year end	35,000
Annual depreciation charge	7,500
Bad debt provision	15,000
Loan secured against fixed assets	250,000

What is the net book value of non-current assets in the year end financial statements assuming the cost model is applied?

A £390,000

B £382,500

C £140,000

D £447,500

32. **Analysis of company A's accounts highlights the following provisions.**

	£
Bad debt	42,500
Guarantees/warranties provided	50,750
Litigation case outstanding	25,000

What is the liability shown in the balance sheet for company A?

A £118,250

B £42,500

C £75,750

D £93,250

33. **A company may repurchase its own shares in order to**

　　I　　Pay surplus cash back to shareholders

　　II　　Increase share price

　　III　　Reduce the dividend payments to shareholders

　　IV　　Reduce the earnings per share

Which of the following is correct?

A II and III

B I and IV

C III and IV

D I and II

34. A company bought a machine at a cost of £250,000 which is expected to last 5 years with no residual value. At the end of year 5, the machine was sold for £2,500. What was the annual depreciation charge using the straight line method (to the nearest £1)?

Important! You should enter the answer only in numbers strictly using this format: 00,000

Do not include spaces, letters or symbols (but decimal points and commas should be used if indicated).

35. A company bought an asset for £50,000 with a residual value of £5,000. The asset is to be depreciated over 5 years using the reducing balance method.

The annual depreciation rate would be

A 36.9%

B 70.6%

C 18.0%

D 52.4%

36. A company bought its inventory as follows.

Date		£
1/1	10 units @ £20	200
1/3	10 units @ £25	250
1/6	20 units @ £20	400

On 1/7 it sold 15 units for £550. Assuming the company uses a FIFO basis for inventory valuation, how much profit would be reported by the company?

A £50

B £175

C £225

D £150

37. Which of the following is not a recognised reason for qualifying an audit report?

A Limitation in scope

B Material disagreement

C Ethical disagreement

D Fundamental disagreement

38. Which one of the following non-current assets is not normally required to be depreciated?

A Buildings

B Machinery

C Freehold land

D Leasehold property

39. A business has the following assets and liabilities.

Receivables	£38,000
Shop premises (net book value)	£60,000
Payables	£40,000
Cash at bank	£ 1,260
Secured five-year loan	£65,000
Plant and machinery (net book value)	£14,000
Inventory	£25,000
Short-term investments	£19,740

Is the business solvent?

A In both the short and the long term

B In neither the short nor the long term

C In the long term only

D In the short term only

40. A company has operating profits of £300,000 and interest payable of £25,000. Its shareholders' funds are £1,000,000 and long-term loans are £100,000. What is its return on capital employed, where capital employed is defined as non current assets plus working capital (in % to 1 decimal place)?

Important! You should enter the answer only in numbers strictly using this format: 00.0

Do not include spaces, letters or symbols (but decimal points and commas should be used if indicated).

41. A company has inventory of £3m, receivables of £5m, cash balances of £1m, short-term payables of £6m and long-term payables of £1m. What is its acid test (quick) ratio (to two decimal places)?

Important! You should enter the answer only in numbers strictly using this format: 0.00

Do not include spaces, letters or symbols (but decimal points and commas should be used if indicated).

42. If a company has net assets of £100, non-current assets of £100, current assets of £200, inventory of £40 and long-term liabilities of £40, what is the quick ratio?

A 1.00×

B 1.25×

C 0.80×

D 0.50×

43. Using the figures provided by the previous question, what is the current ratio?

A   1.00×

B   1.25×

C   0.80×

D   0.67×

44. Working capital is said to be

A   Total assets – Total liabilities

B   Net current assets

C   Total assets – Current liabilities

D   Current assets – Total liabilities

45. According to International Accounting rules, if Co X has an investment in Co Y and exerts no significant influence, how is Co Y accounted for in Co X's accounts?

A   Minority investment

B   Subsidiary

C   Associate

D   Investment

46. In general, we would expect a manufacturing company with large work in progress inventory when compared to a retail company to have

A   Lower current ratio

B   Higher current ratio

C   Lower capital requirements

D   Higher quick ratio

47. A company has operating profits £450,000 and interest payable of £37,500. Its shareholders' funds are £1,500,000 and long term loans are £175,500. What is its return on capital employed, where capital employed is defined as non current assets plus working capital?

A   26.9%

B   30.0%

C   29.1%

D   32.5%

48. **A company has the following income statement**

	£'000
Revenue	37,500
Cost of sales	8,650
Gross profit	28,850
Distribution costs	2,900
Administration cost	1,960
Operating profit	23,990
Interest receivable	3,750
Interest payable	4,050
Profit on ordinary activities before taxation	23,690
Tax on profit on ordinary activities	4,750
Profit on ordinary activities after tax	18,940

The company's balance sheet is as follows

	£'000	£'000
Fixed assets		250,000
Current assets:		
Inventory	25,000	
Debtors	10,000	
Cash	5,000	
		40,000
Long term liabilities		
Bank loan		10,000
Current liabilities		
Creditors	7,500	
Tax due in 9 months	3,400	
		10,900
		269,100
Share capital		200,000
Retained earnings		69,100
		269,100

What is the company's return on capital employed?

A   9.94%

B   7.04%

C   8.80%

D   8.60%

49. **A firm is looking to increase its interest cover ratio. This could be achieved by**

A   Increasing the cash balance

B   Increasing non-current assets

C   Decreasing reserves

D   Decreasing non-current liabilities

50. **Which of the following is the best definition of the quick (acid test) ratio?**

A Cash and deposits divided by short-term borrowings

B Receivables, cash and deposits divided by payables

C Cash and deposits divided by payables and short-term borrowings

D Receivables, cash and deposits divided by payables and short-term borrowings

51. **If a company buys 75% of another company, which of the following would be included in the consolidated balance sheet?**

A 75% of the net assets and a minority interest

B 100% of the net assets and a minority interest

C 75% of the net assets and no minority interest

D 100% of the net assets and no minority interest

52. **A company with a low gearing ratio will**

A Have a high level of debt finance

B Have a high level of equity finance

C Have a low ratio of current assets to current liabilities

D Have a low return on capital employed

53. **A firm has shareholders' funds of £3,600,000, long term liabilities of £1,000,000 and current liabilities of £300,000. Calculate the capital employed.**

A £3,600,000

B £3,900,000

C £4,600,000

D £4,900,000

54. **Calculate the gearing ratio for a company which has total assets of £100m, and shareholders equity of £70m (to two decimal places).**

Important! You should enter the answer only in numbers strictly using this format: 0.00

Do not include spaces, letters or symbols (but decimal points and commas should be used if indicated).

55. **If a company has cumulative redeemable preference shares in issue, in addition to ordinary shares, which of the following statements is true?**

A If the preference dividend is not paid this year, the ordinary shareholders cannot receive a dividend until all arrears of the preference dividend have been paid

B If the preference dividend is not paid this year, then the ordinary shareholders may still receive a dividend next year, provided next year's preference dividend is paid

C No more ordinary shares may be issued until the preference shares have been redeemed

D Until the ordinary shareholders have received a dividend, no preference dividend can be paid

56. **An investor receives a dividend of £3.75. The tax credit attached to the dividend cheque is for how much (in £ to two decimal places)?**

Important! You should enter the answer only in numbers strictly using this format: 0.00

Do not include spaces, letters or symbols (but decimal points and commas should be used if indicated).

57. **Which of the following may not be a type of preference share?**

A A-share

B Participating share

C Redeemable

D Convertible

58. **Consider the following statements**

I Ordinary shareholders share in voting and dividends

II MTFs should lower transaction costs

III SDRT is payable on all equity purchases

Which statements are true?

A I and II

B I and III

C II and III

D I only

59. **Consider the following statements. Which is true?**

A A preference share must always pay its dividend

B Preference shares never have voting rights

C Preference shares share in the residual assets of the business when it is wound up

D Preference share dividends are classed as franked investment income

60. **Why would an investor invest in convertible preference shares?**

A   Investor requires income now, but also wants the opportunity to make capital gains in the future

B   Income now, and no risk of making capital losses in the future

C   Possibility of capital gain now and the certainty of income later

D   Certainty of capital gains now and the possibility of income later

Answers

1. **C** The profit or loss on disposal is the difference between the asset's NBV at the point of disposal and the proceeds. NBV is established by applying 30% reducing balance depreciation for four years

	£
Cost	90,000
1st year Deprn. 30%	(27,000)
	63,000
2nd year Deprn. 30%	(18,900)
	44,100
3rd year Deprn. 30%	(13,230)
	30,870
4^{the} year Deprn. 30%	(9,261)
Net book value	21,609
Proceeds	(42)
Loss	£21,567

See Chapter 4 Section 2.5 of your Study Text

2. **D** This is an exemption for small companies. Small companies are defined as companies meeting two of the following three tests: less than 50 employees; turnover of less than £5.6m and assets of less than £2.8m. This definition can change over time

See Chapter 4 Section 1 of your Study Text

3. **D** A loan repayment would be shown as a reduction in assets and a reduction in liabilities on the company balance sheet; it would have no impact on the income statement for the year. Note that 'revenue expense' is a slightly confusing term, but it should be taken to mean an expense that shows in the income statement

See Chapter 4 Section 2.2 of your Study Text

4. **B** The share premium account reserve is a non-distributable reserve and as a result cannot be used to pay a dividend to shareholders. It is not based on past or present profits of the company

See Chapter 4 Section 2.14 of your Study Text

5. **C**

Non-current assets	×
Plus working capital	×
Total assets	×
Long-term loans	×
Liabilities + shareholders' funds	×

Assets = Liabilities + shareholders' funds

See Chapter 4 Section 2 of your Study Text

6. **A** Revaluation would have a direct impact on reserves. The other items would eventually affect reserves through the impact on retained profits

   See Chapter 4 Section 2.14 of your Study Text

7. **D** The accruals/matching concept states that costs should be allocated to the periods where revenues are generated. Depreciation involves allocating the costs of a fixed asset over its useful economic life

   See Chapter 4 Section 2.5 of your Study Text

8. **D**

Total assets	×
	×
Share capital	×
Reserves	×
Total liabilities	×
	×

   See Chapter 4 Section 2 of your Study Text

9. **49,500**

	£
Assets	
Receivables	72,000
Equipment	36,000
Cash	1,890
Inventory	52,500
Vehicles	44,610
Buildings	75,000
	282,000
Liabilities	
Loan	(112,500)
Payables	(75,000)
Net assets	94,500
Share capital	45,000
Retained profits (balancing figure)	49,500
Shareholders' funds	94,500

   See Chapter 4 Section 2 and Chapter 4 Section 2.2 of your Study Text

10. **D** The increase in the provision will represent the full amount of the charge for the year. Effectively we are recognising the cost by putting the provision in the account

    See Chapter 4 Section 2.8 of your Study Text

11. **C** Authorised share capital is the share capital that the company is allowed to issue. Since some of it may have been retained for future issue (warrants and convertibles), it may not all be shown on the balance sheet

See Chapter 4 Section 2.14 of your Study Text

12. **B** This is logical since we are assuming that the most recent items sold are the most recently purchased. If the purchase price in reducing , and we are using LIFO accurately, this will result in the lowest value for cost of sales

Therefore, requires the highest closing stock to give the lowest cost of sales.

With prices falling, LIFO will give the highest value

See Chapter 4 Section 2.8 of your Study Text

13. **A** All the others would have the effect of raising cash

See Chapter 4 Section 2.8 of your Study Text

14. **D** Total assets minus total liabilities equals net assets

See Chapter 4 Section 2 of your Study Text

15. **C** Post-balance sheet events (FRS 21/IAS 10) can either be classified as adjusting or non-adjusting, depending on whether the events are based on an existing condition at the balance sheet date or a new event since the statement date

See Chapter 4 Section 2.15 of your Study Text

16. **A** As a result of the accruals/matching concept, accruals are liabilities owed for services used during the chargeable accounting period, but not yet paid for, e.g. gas bill which is paid in arrears

See Chapter 4 Section 2.11 of your Study Text

17. **D** Inventory would be a current asset, in that it has been acquired by the company for conversion into cash. It is the least liquid of current assets

See Chapter 4 Section 2.8 of your Study Text

18. **B** This would be a tangible non-current asset. Both tangibles and intangibles will be depreciated or amortised

See Chapter 4 Section 2.5 of your Study Text

19. **A** All reserves within shareholders' funds can be used for a bonus or capitalisation issue

See Chapter 4 Section 2.14 of your Study Text

20. **A** All four of these are statutory requirements under the Companies Act 2006 for all large UK companies, unless they are dormant during the accounting period. Small companies (as defined in the Act) are exempt from the need to have the accounts audited

See Chapter 4 Section 1 and Chapter 4 Section 1.1 of your Study Text

21. **D** Borrowing money would increase cash (current assets) and increase liabilities. As a result, it would have no impact on the net assets of the company

See Chapter 4 Section 2 and Chapter 4 Section 2.10 of your Study Text

22.　**A**　Under the Companies Act 2006, the directors have responsibility for the preparation of the accounts, which must be audited prior to their release to shareholders

See Chapter 4 Section 1 of your Study Text

23.　**A**　Both assets and liabilities will increase by the same amount and as a result, net assets will remain unchanged

See Chapter 4 Section 2 of your Study Text

24.　**C**　The value of non current assets will increase as will therefore net assets. The revaluation reserve will be increased by the same amount, increasing shareholders' funds. As a result, the accounting equation will still hold

See Chapter 4 Section 2.5 of your Study Text

25.　**D**　Cash, overdrafts and deposits payable without notice and without penalty or within 24 hours where agreed

See Chapter 4 Section 5.1 of your Study Text

26.　**A**　Prepayments will occur if a company has paid for a service, but not yet had the benefit during the accounting period. The service owed to the company is shown at the year-end as a current asset

See Chapter 4 Section 2.8 of your Study Text

27.　**B**　When reconciling the cash flow figure from the profit figure, you have to consider what is good or bad from a cash flow perspective. If inventory is increasing, it suggests that the company is spending cash on increasing this current asset, and so this is bad from a cash flow point of view. However, if accounts receivable are decreasing, then the company is receiving cash from those debtors – good. If accounts payable are increasing, then the company is not paying those creditors as quickly as they maybe should – good. If depreciation is being charged on assets, this is also good from a cash flow perspective, as the company is not actually spending any money on depreciation, as it is an accounting entry only

See Chapter 4 Section 5.1 of your Study Text

28.　**C**　Contingent liabilities should NOT be recognised in the accounts, however, there should be a brief description of the contingent liability, and for each class of contingent liability the nature of the contingency, and an estimate of its financial effect. This would therefore be included in the notes of the accounts

See Chapter 4 Section 2.12 of your Study Text

29. **22**   Operating profit   £20m   (to obtain the cash flow)

   Stated after charging
       Depreciation   +£4m   (added back to operating profits)
       Loss on sale of   +£2m   (added back to operating profits)
       non current assets
   Other items
       Increase in receivables   −£5m   (a cash outflow)
       Increase in inventories   −£2m   (a cash outflow)
       Increase in payables   +£3m   (a cash inflow)
   Net cash inflow   £22m

   See Chapter 4 Section 5.1 of your Study Text

30. **B**   Computer equipment is regarded as capital expenditure whilst the other expenditure listed is regarded as revenue expenditure

   See Chapter 4 Section 2.3 of your Study Text

31. **A**   Assuming the cost model is applied, the net book value of non-current assets is the original cost less accumulated depreciation to date.

Cost of non-current assets	425,000
Less accumulated depreciation at year end	35,000
Net book value	390,000

   See Chapter 4 Section 2.5 of your Study Text

32. **B**   Guarantees/warranties provided by the company and an outstanding litigation case are both examples of contingent liabilities and not shown in the accounts whilst the bad debt provisions represents an amount likely to be written off by the company and hence is included in the accounts

   See Chapter 4 Section 2.12 of your Study Text

33. **D**   Companies can repurchase their own shares in order to pay surplus cash back to shareholders as an alternative to dividends and to increase the share price and earnings per share

   See Chapter 4 Section 2.14 of your Study Text

34. **50,000**   Asset should be depreciated over its useful life

   Cost of machine: £250,000 with no residual value

   Useful life of machine: 5 years

   Thus depreciation charge = $\dfrac{250,000}{5}$ = £50,000

   Note the sale proceeds of the asset of £2,500 at the end of its useful life are not relevant in determining the depreciation charge

   See Chapter 4 Section 2.5 of your Study Text

35.   **A**   Depreciation rate $= 1 - \sqrt[n]{\dfrac{\text{Residual value}}{\text{Cost}}}$

$= 1 - \sqrt[5]{\dfrac{5,000}{50,000}} = 36.9\%$

See Chapter 4 Section 2.5 of your Study Text

36.   **C**

		£
15 units sold for 550		550
Cost of units sold:		
10 @ 20	200	
5 @ 25	125	
		325
		225

See Chapter 4 Section 2.8 of your Study Text

37.   **C**   There is no such thing as an ethical disagreement. There are either limitations in scope (may be referred to as 'uncertainty') or disagreements. Both can be fundamental or material

See Chapter 4 Section 1.2 of your Study Text

38.   **C**   Land is not required to be depreciated

See Chapter 4 Section 2.5 of your Study Text

39.   **A**   Balance Sheet

	£	£
Non current assets		
Premises		60,000
Plant and machinery		14,000
		74,000
Current assets		
Inventory	25,000	
Investments	19,740	
Cash	1,260	
Receivables	38,000	
	84,000	
Payables	(40,000)	
Net current assets		44,000
Loan		(65,000)
Net assets		53,000

Both net current assets (£44,000) and net assets (£53,000) are positive implying that the business is solvent in the short and long term

See Chapter 4 Section 7.3 of your Study Text

40. **27.3** $\text{ROCE} = \dfrac{£300,000}{£1,100,000} = 0.273 \text{ or } 27.3\%$

There are a few ways of establishing capital employed, all leading to the same number. Given the information presented, we can't use their definition. We have to use shareholders' funds plus long term liabilities

See Chapter 4 Section 7.2 of your Study Text

41. **1.00** $\dfrac{\text{Current assets (excluding inventory)}}{\text{Current liabilites}} = (\text{Receivables} + \text{Cash}) \div \text{Short-term Payables}$

$$= \frac{(£5m + £1m)}{£6m} = 1\times$$

See Chapter 4 Section 7.3 of your Study Text

42. **A**

	£
Non current assets	100
Current assets	200
Current liabilities (missing figure)	(160)
	140
Long-term liabilities	(40)
Net assets	100

$$\text{Quick ratio} = \frac{\text{Current assets (excluding inventory)}}{\text{Current liabilities}} = \frac{200 - 40}{160} = 1\times$$

See Chapter 4 Section 7.3 of your Study Text

43. **B** $\text{Current ratio} = \dfrac{\text{Current assets}}{\text{Current liabilities}} = \dfrac{£200}{£160} = 1.25\times$

See Chapter 4 Section 7.3 of your Study Text

44. **B** Working capital is defined as net current assets, ie current assets – current liabilities

See Chapter 4 Section 7.3 of your Study Text

45. **D** If there was significant influence it would be an associate; if there was control it would be a subsidiary

See Chapter 4 Section 6.1 of your Study Text

46. **B** High stock levels result in high current assets and therefore a higher current ratio (current assets: current liabilities)

See Chapter 4 Section 7.3 of your Study Text

47. **A** $\dfrac{450,000}{1,675,500} = 0.269 \text{ or } 26.9\%$

See Chapter 4 Section 7.2 of your Study Text

48.   **A** $ROCE = \dfrac{\text{Profit before interest payable and tax}}{\text{Capital employed}}$

$\dfrac{23,990 + 3,750}{269,100 + 10,000} = \dfrac{27,740}{279,100}$

$= 0.994 \text{ or } 9.94\%$

See Chapter 4 Section 7.2 of your Study Text

49.   **D**   The interest cover ratio is EBIT/interest expense. This ratio can be increased by either increasing EBIT or decreasing interest expense. If the company reduces their non-current liabilities, then there would be less interest to pay, and hence a lower interest rate

See Chapter 4 Section 7.3 of your Study Text

50.   **D**   This is the best description, as the acid test ratio is the current assets excluding inventory divided by the current liabilities

See Chapter 4 Section 7.3 of your Study Text

51.   **B**   Where one company controls another, the balance sheet will record the group's share of the net assets of the subsidiary company. This is carried out by recording 100% of the subsidiary assets and then making a deduction to reflect minority interests

See Chapter 4 Section 6.1 of your Study Text

52.   **B**   Gearing is the ratio of debt to equity. A low gearing is indicative of a high level of equity or a low level of debt

See Chapter 4 Section 7.3 of your Study Text

53.   **C**   Capital employed is shareholder funds plus long-term liabilities. It does not include current liabilities

See Chapter 4 Section 7.2 of your Study Text

54.   **0.43**   The most common form of the gearing ratio is the debt to equity ratio (debt / equity). Debt + equity is equal to total assets, therefore by rearranging the equation, Debt equals total assets (100) less equity (70), so debt equals £30m. The gearing ratio is, therefore, £30m / £70m = 0.42857 or 0.43 to two decimal places

See Chapter 4 Section 7.3 of your Study Text

55.   **A**   Preference shareholders have preference on capital repayment on liquidation and on receipt of dividends. This is generally cumulative in that preference dividend arrears must be paid before any ordinary dividends

See Chapter 4 Section 2.14 of your Study Text

56.   **0.42** $\dfrac{£3.75}{0.9} \times 0.1 = £0.4166$

The required format for this question is £0.00, hence this must be rounded to £0.42

See Chapter 4 Section 2.14 of your Study Text

57. **A** A-shares are a class of ordinary shares

See Chapter 4 Section 2.14 of your Study Text

58. **A** I Ordinary shareholders *do* share votes and dividends
II MTFs *are* expected to reduce trading costs
III Stamp duty is payable on certificated purchases and SDRT is payable on electronic dematerialised transfers of shares

See Chapter 4 Section 2.14 and Chapter 9 Section 5.2 of your Study Text

59. **D** Preference share dividends are classed as franked investment income

See Chapter 4 Section 2.14 of your Study Text

60. **A** With convertible preference shares, a fixed preference dividend is paid now, but the investor has the opportunity to convert those preference shares into ordinary equity shares in the future. Preference shares do not experience an increase in value as the company grows, so would be unlikely to deliver capital gain, whereas capital gains would be a possibility with ordinary equity shares. Even with preference shares there is a risk of making a capital loss, if the company goes into liquidation

See Chapter 4 Section 2.14 of your Study Text

5. Equities

Questions

1. A stock is priced 190p cum dividend. It will trade ex-dividend of 5p during the next week. A corporate financier works out over the weekend the theoretical ex-rights price if there is to be a 2 for 5 rights issue at 140p, with the new shares ranking pari passu except for the dividend. The theoretical ex-rights price would be

    A   175.7p
    B   172.1p
    C   170.0p
    D   167.0p

2. A share has just paid its annual dividend of 20p. Next year's dividend is expected to be 22p and, thereafter, the dividend is expected to grow at 10% per annum. The required rate of return is 17%. What should the price of the shares be (in £ to two decimal places)?

    Important! You should enter the answer only in numbers strictly using this format: 0.00

    Do not include spaces, letters or symbols (but decimal points and commas should be used if indicated).

3. Earnings per share is usually defined as

    A   Net profit before tax divided by the number of authorised ordinary shares
    B   Net profit after tax, preference dividends and minority interests, divided by the number of issued ordinary shares
    C   Net profit after dividends and tax divided by the number of issued ordinary shares
    D   Net profit after dividends divided by the number of authorised ordinary shares

4. A company requires fresh capital. Which of the following would not raise extra capital for the company?

    A   A 1 for 3 rights issue
    B   A placing of convertible preference shares
    C   A 1 for 3 scrip issue
    D   A placing of unsecured loan stock

5. A company has dividend cover of 1.25, a net dividend of 12p and a P/E ratio of 20. What is the net dividend yield (in % to 2 decimal places)?

Important! You should enter the answer only in numbers strictly using this format: 0.00

Do not include spaces, letters or symbols (but decimal points and commas should be used if indicated).

```
┌─────────────┐
│             │
│             │
└─────────────┘
```

6. Which is true of a scrip issue?

    A   The shares are issued for at least nominal value
    B   It is an issue to shareholders pro rata their shareholdings
    C   Cash is raised by the issuer
    D   It is a flotation

7. If a company does a 1 for 4 rights issue, at a price of £0.90, and the cum rights price is £1.00 per share, what will be the value of a nil-paid right?

    A   £0.02
    B   £0.08
    C   £0.90
    D   £0.98

8. Which of the following is the best description of a rights issue?

    A   A company buying back shares from its shareholders pro rata to their existing shareholding in the company
    B   A free issue of shares to shareholders pro rata to their existing shareholding in the company
    C   An issue of shares to shareholders for cash pro rata to their existing shareholding in the company
    D   A public offer with preferential treatment for existing shareholders

9. A pre-emptive share issue is one where

    A   Existing shareholders receive new shares pro rata to their existing shareholding in the company by means of a capitalisation of reserves
    B   Existing shareholders are given preferential treatment in a public offer for sale of shares in the company
    C   Existing shareholders have agreed by ordinary resolution in general meeting that they wish new shares to be issued to new shareholders
    D   Existing shareholders receive the right to subscribe for shares pro rata to their existing shareholding in the company

10. **Which of the following relationships is true?**

    A Price-to-earnings ratio multiplied by earnings per share equals price per share

    B Price-to-earnings ratio divided by earnings per share equals price per share

    C Price per share multiplied by price-to-earnings ratio equals earnings per share

    D Price per share multiplied by earnings per share equals price-to-earnings ratio

11. **Which of the following best describes an offer for subscription?**

    A The company issuing shares sells the shares directly to the investors

    B The company issuing shares sells the shares to an issuing house, which sells the shares to investors

    C The existing shareholders in the company sell shares directly to new investors

    D The existing shareholders in the company sell shares to an issuing house, which sells the shares to investors

12. **All of the following are the same except for**

    A Scrip issues

    B Capitalisation issues

    C Open issues

    D Bonus issues

13. **Which of the following share issues would not normally be underwritten?**

    A Placing

    B Deep discounted rights issue

    C Open offer

    D Offer for subscription

14. **Last year, a firm earned 20p per share and these earnings are expected to grow at 12% per annum. There is a constant dividend payout ratio of 30%, and the current share price, immediately following the payment of a dividend, is 110p. What is the implied gross total return required by investors?**

    A 18.10%

    B 12.92%

    C 14.31%

    D 9.80%

15. In the 'Brewers and Distillers' section of the London Share Price service, the following information on four companies on a given day was recently presented.

STOCK	PRICE	NET DIVIDEND YIELD	P/E
Allied-Lyons	631	4.0	15.0
Bass	548	4.3	11.9
Boddington	179	4.5	12.9
Eldridge Pope	105	3.3	24.1

Consider the following statements.

I   It is possible that the P/E ratio for Eldridge Pope is about twice that of the P/E ratio of Bass because the former's earnings are expected to grow faster than those of Bass

II   Investors are willing to pay over 24 times the current year's earnings for Eldridge Pope

III   The yield is the latest published dividend less 10% tax per share divided by the current share price

IV   Net dividend per share is a complete measure of holding period return

Which of the following is correct?

A   I is true; the rest are false

B   II and IV are false; the rest are true

C   IV is false; the rest are true

D   II and III are false; the rest are true

16. The share price of XYZ plc is currently 30p per share. Last year's earnings per share was 6p, and the company has a constant dividend payout ratio of 10%. If future earnings growth per share is expected to continue at 20% per annum, what annual return do investors require to hold this share (in % to 1 decimal place)?

Important! You should enter the answer only in numbers strictly using this format: 00.0

Do not include spaces, letters or symbols (but decimal points and commas should be used if indicated).

17. Who issues ADRs?

A   US corporations

B   Non-US corporations

C   US government

D   Non-US government

18. If a company does a 1 for 5 bonus issue, the cum bonus price is £3.60 per share. What will be the theoretical price after the issue (in £ to two decimal places)?

Important! You should enter the answer only in numbers strictly using this format: 0.00

Do not include spaces, letters or symbols (but decimal points and commas should be used if indicated).

```

```

19. Which of the following is the best definition for an ADR?

   A Shares issued by US banks for US investors

   B Shares in non-US companies which can be traded on US share exchanges

   C Shares in US companies for investment by non-US residents

   D Shares issued by UK banks for UK investors

20. Which of the following is a reason a company might give for paying a scrip dividend?

   A To reduce losses

   B Desire to conserve cash

   C To reduce cash balance

   D Lack of profits

21. How may the dividend growth rate 'g' be estimated?

   A Return on equity × Payout ratio

   B Return on equity × Retained earnings ratio

   C Return on debt × Payout ratio

   D Return on debt × Retained earnings ratio

22. Which of the following is not an option in respect of a rights issue?

   A Sell rights fully paid

   B Allow rights to lapse

   C Exercise rights, buy and hold the shares

   D Exercise the rights, buy then sell the shares

23. Which of the following could not be a valid long term dividend policy?

   A Achieve 5% annual dividend growth

   B Achieve a dividend cover of 2×

   C Distribute 120% of annual profits

   D Achieve dividend growth in excess of inflation

24. **Which would not be a likely implication for a share buy-back?**

A   Increase EPS

B   Increase ROCE

C   Increase financial gearing

D   Increase current ratio

25. **Consider the following statements.**

I   Dividends must be paid from the current year's profits

II   Directors set a dividend policy as they believe stockholders prefer a stable/steady/predictable dividend

III   An asset based valuation is particularly useful for a service business

Which statements are true?

A   I and III are true, II is false

B   I and II are true, III is false

C   I is true, II and III are false

D   II is true, I and III are false

26. **A share is currently trading at £2.40. What will be the theoretical ex-rights price if it undertakes a 1 for 6 rights issue at a price of £1.00?**

A   2.15

B   2.20

C   2.25

D   2.30

27. **The dividend currently payable by a company is 36p. The dividend paid 4 years ago was 30p. What is the annual growth rate (in % to 2 decimal places)?**

Important! You should enter the answer only in numbers strictly using this format: 0.00

Do not include spaces, letters or symbols (but decimal points and commas should be used if indicated).

28. **A share was bought for £2.40. One year later it paid a 20p dividend and was then worth £2.50. Calculate the holding period return.**

A   4.00%

B   4.17%

C   8.33%

D   12.50%

29. **A company undertakes a 3 for 1 stock split. What does this mean?**

    A   One new share is issued for every three held, taking the number of shares up to four

    B   After the issue there will be three new shares in place of every one old share that existed

    C   Three new shares will be issued for every one existing share, taking the number of shares up to four

    D   After the issue there will be one new share in place of every three hold shares that existed

30. **Consider the following statements**

    I   A primary market cannot also be a secondary market

    II   An offer for sale is a secondary market deal

    III   A placing is a marketing operation

    Which of the following statement is correct?

    A   I is true, II and III are false

    B   I and III are true, II is false

    C   III is true, I and II are false

    D   II and III are true, I is false

31. **What will be the growth rate in dividends if 60% of profits are distributed as a dividend, the profit margin is 12% and the rate of return on reinvested income is 15%?**

    A   9.0%

    B   7.2%

    C   6.0%

    D   4.8%

32. **Which is true of a rights issue?**

    A   Shares are usually issued at the current market price

    B   No new finance is raised

    C   Shareholders must take up their rights

    D   It is a primary market issue

33. **The historical dividend pattern of a share is as follows.**

YEAR	DIVIDEND
1	50.0
2	52.5
3	55.1
4	57.9
5	60.8

    Using the first and last dividends, assess the dividend growth rate.

    A   4.0%

    B   5.0%

    C   6.0%

    D   7.0%

34. A share was bought one year ago for £5.76, it is now worth £5.84 having just paid a 30p dividend. What are the holding period and the dividend yield respectively?

   A   3.4%, 5.1%

   B   3.4%, 5.2%

   C   6.6%, 5.1%

   D   6.6%, 5.2%

35. A share is priced at £5.20 and about to pay a dividend of 20p. It is growing at 5% pa. What return do shareholders require (in % to 1 decimal place)?

   Important! You should enter the answer only in numbers strictly using this format: 0.0

   Do not include spaces, letters or symbols (but decimal points and commas should be used if indicated).

   ┌─────────────┐
   │   │
   │   │
   └─────────────┘

36. A company undertakes a 4 for 1 share split. The share price before the split was £6.00. What is the price after?

   A   £2.00

   B   £1.50

   C   £1.20

   D   £1.00

37. A business has assets that cost £100,000, have a replacement value of £120,000, a realisable value of £80,000 and a residual value of £50,000. What is the minimum price a seller should accept for the business?

   A   £50,000

   B   £80,000

   C   £100,000

   D   £120,000

38. Consider the following statements.

   I   Shares may be repurchased as an alternative to paying a dividend

   II   Share repurchases will reduce gearing

   III   Share repurchases will increase EPS

   Which of the above are true?

   A   I and II

   B   I and III

   C   II and III

   D   I, II and III

39. **What is the most likely action of a shareholder in a rights issue where the subscription price is above the market price?**

    A Sell the nil paid right

    B Let the right expire

    C Buy share at beneath the TERP

    D Exercise right and buy at below the subscription price

40. **If a company goes through a 1 for 4 bonus issue, what will the price of the company's shares be following the bonus issue, if the share price was £1.20 before the bonus issue?**

    A £1.20

    B £1.00

    C £0.96

    D £0.24

41. **Which of the following is not a feature of an ADR?**

    A Freely transferable

    B Able to receive dividends

    C Able to take ownership of underlying shares

    D Depositary receipts are not tradable on an exchange

42. **A company has earnings of £1m and 5 million shares in issue. Its dividend per share is 12p. What is its dividend cover?**

    A 0.133×

    B 0.167×

    C 1.67×

    D 1.33×

43. **Given a dividend of 10p, a share price (ex-dividend) of 255p and a growth rate of 5%, calculate the required return of shareholders?**

    A 4.9%

    B 8.9%

    C 9.1%

    D 10.5%

44. **Which of the following is not a method of marketing a new issue of shares?**

    A Offer for sale

    B Placing

    C Offer for subscription

    D Sponsored listing

45. **Which of the following issue methods raises cash for the company?**

        I   Placing

        II   Bonus issue

        III   Rights issue

        IV   Capitalisation issue

A   I, III and IV

B   I, II and IV

C   III and IV

D   I and III

46. **An investor has 10,000 shares in Rolls plc at 76p. If a 1 for 25 scrip issue occurs, what will be the effect on the share price?**

A   It will rise

B   It will be unchanged

C   It will fall

D   It may either fall or rise

47. **A company's shares are trading at 180p. If its latest earnings were 9p per share, which of the following is the P/E ratio?**

A   0.05×

B   5×

C   20×

D   2×

48. **In a tender, you bid 260p, the lowest bid was 230p, the highest bid 290p and the acceptance level was 245p. What price will you pay?**

A   230p

B   260p

C   245p

D   290p

49. **In a 1 for 3 rights issue at £1.50, the value of the rights nil paid is 25p. What was the cum rights price?**

A   £1.75

B   £2.33

C   £1.83

D   £2.00

50.   A share is priced at 300p. The dividend that has just been paid is 20p. Investors want a 12% return. Assuming the share is correctly priced per the Gordon Growth Model, what is the percentage expected growth rate (in % to 1 decimal place)?

Important! You should enter the answer only in numbers strictly using this format: 0.0

Do not include spaces, letters or symbols (but decimal points and commas should be used if indicated).

51.   If a company does a 5 for 4 bonus issue and the cum bonus price of the shares is £8.00, what will the share price be after the bonus issue (in £ to two decimal places)?

Important! You should enter the answer only in numbers strictly using this format: 0.00

Do not include spaces, letters or symbols (but decimal points and commas should be used if indicated).

52.   A company has dividend cover of 1.25×, a net dividend of 12p and a P/E ratio of 20. What is the net dividend yield?

   A   5%

   B   4%

   C   5.3%

   D   6.25%

53.   If the dividend per share is 10.5p, dividend cover is 1.5x and net dividend yield 7%, what is the P/E ratio?

   A   11.9×

   B   9.5×

   C   13.2×

   D   8.4×

54.   A share has a P/E ratio of 10, EPS of 30p and dividend cover of 2.4×. What is the net dividend yield (in % to 2 decimal places)?

Important! You should enter the answer only in numbers strictly using this format: 0.00

Do not include spaces, letters or symbols (but decimal points and commas should be used if indicated).

55. **If a company has a high P/E ratio, it is likely that it will have**

   A   A high dividend yield and low earnings yield

   B   A high dividend yield and a high earnings yield

   C   A low dividend yield and a low earnings yield

   D   A low dividend yield and a high earnings yield

56. **What is the price of a share if the P/E ratio is 16 and the earnings per share is 21p?**

   A   336p

   B   373p

   C   380p

   D   382p

57. **A company pays a dividend of 15p. The dividend yield for this company is 7% and its dividend cover is 4. Calculate the associated price/earnings ratio.**

   A   4.2

   B   1.05

   C   0.28

   D   3.57

58. **A company has dividend cover of 2.5, a net dividend of 15p and a P/E ratio of 20. What is the net dividend yield (in % to 1 decimal place)?**

   Important! You should enter the answer only in numbers strictly using this format: 0.0

   Do not include spaces, letters or symbols (but decimal points and commas should be used if indicated).

   ☐

59. **A company has a current share price of 330p and an EPS figure of 14.32p. What is the P/E ratio?**

   A   15.72

   B   14.32

   C   23.05

   D   4.34

60. A company pays a dividend of 25p. The dividend yield is 10% and its dividend cover is 5. Calculate the associated price/earnings ratio (to one decimal place).

Important! You should enter the answer only in numbers strictly using this format: 0.0

Do not include spaces, letters or symbols (but decimal points and commas should be used if indicated).

_____

61. What is the price of a share if the P/E ratio is 35 and the earnings per share is 28p (in £ to two decimal places)?

Important! You should enter the answer only in numbers strictly using this format: 0.00

Do not include spaces, letters or symbols (but decimal points and commas should be used if indicated).

_____

62. Calculation of earnings per share defines earnings as

A Consolidated profits before minority interest and preference dividends

B Consolidated profits after minority interest but before tax

C Consolidated profit after interest, tax, minority interest and preference dividends

D Consolidated profit before interest, tax, minority interest and preference dividends

63. The price-earnings (P/E) ratio is given by

A Current share price divided by latest total earnings

B Current share price divided by average total earnings over the past month

C Current share price divided by average earnings per share over the last three years

D Current share price divided by earnings per share declared for the last financial year

64. All of the following are means of effecting an offer for sale, except

A Fixed price offer

B Bookbuilding

C Tender offer

D Rights

65. **Which of the following would be included in a company's basic earnings per share calculation?**

        I   Ordinary shares ranking for dividend

        II   Preference shares

        III Warrants

        IV Convertibles

A I, II, III and IV

B I, II and III

C I and II

D I only

---

66. **What impact does a scrip issue have on return on capital employed?**

A No impact

B Increase

C Decrease

D Not possible to tell

Answers

1. **B**   Ex-div price 190p – 5p = 185p

	NUMBER	PRICE £	VALUE £
Before	5	1.85	9.25
Rights issue	2	1.40	2.80
After	7		12.05

Theoretical price after = $\dfrac{12.05}{7}$ = £1.721

See Chapter 5 Section 2.3 of your Study Text

2. **3.14**   This is an example of a growing perpetuity. The dividend in one year's time is 22p and it then grows at 10%

$$E_{xd} = \frac{d_1}{r_e - g} = \frac{20 \times 1.10}{0.17 - 0.10} = \frac{22p}{0.07} = 314p \text{ (ex-dividend) or £3.14}$$

See Chapter 5 Section 3.3 of your Study Text

3. **B**   Note that earnings per share is calculated using the number of shares issued and not the total authorised share capital of the company concerned

See Chapter 5 Section 3.5 of your Study Text

4. **C**   Scrip, bonus or free issues do not raise cash, but are undertaken to bring the share price down into a more marketable range

See Chapter 5 Section 2.4 of your Study Text

5. **4.00**   Net div 12p

EPS = Dividend cover × Net dividend per share (dps)

= 1.25 × 12p

= 15p

Share price = EPS × P/E ratio

= 15p × 20

= 300p

Net dividend yield = $\dfrac{dps}{Price} = \dfrac{12p}{300} = 0.04$ or 4%

The required format for this question is 0.00%, hence this must be noted as 4.00%

See Chapter 5 Section 3.2 of your Study Text

6. **B**   A scrip issue (bonus or capitalisation issue) is an issue of free shares pro rata to an existing holding in order to dilute the share price into a more marketable range

See Chapter 5 Section 2.3 of your Study Text

7. B

	NUMBER	PRICE £	VALUE £
Before	4	1.00	4.00
Rights issue	1	0.90	0.90
After	5		4.90

Theoretical price after $= \dfrac{4.90}{5} = £0.98$

Value of the nil paid rights = 8p (98p – 90p)

See Chapter 5 Section 2.3 of your Study Text

8. C A rights issue is an issue of shares pro rata to existing holdings, usually at a discount to current market prices, to raise cash for the issuing company. The need for a rights issue is due to the existence of pre-emption rights

See Chapter 5 Section 2.3 of your Study Text

9. D This is a requirement of the UKLA Listing Requirement and means that a rights issue must take place as opposed to a new issue of shares to non-shareholders of the company

See Chapter 5 Section 2.3 of your Study Text

10. A $P/E = \dfrac{\text{Market price}}{\text{EPS}}$

Therefore

$P/E \times EPS = \text{Market price}$

See Chapter 5 Section 3.6 of your Study Text

11. A This would be without the involvement of an issuing house, and is a method generally only used by investment banks or investment trusts who would have the experience in-house to administer all aspects of the issue

See Chapter 5 Section 2.2 of your Study Text

12. C All of the others are the same. Scrip, capitalisation and bonus issues relate to an issue of free shares pro rata to an existing shareholding in order to dilute the share price. An open offer/issue is a rights issue in non-renounceable form. In other words, shareholders cannot sell their rights to a third party

See Chapter 5 Section 2.4 of your Study Text

13. B The deeper the discount, the more likely investors are to subscribe and as a result, underwriting would not be necessary

See Chapter 5 Section 2.2 of your Study Text

14.   **A**   This is a difficult question requiring you to put the values of D, g and P into the dividend valuation model to work out what the required return is. But you have to use the EPS and payout ratio to work out the dividends first

EPS = 20p
∴ Dividend = D_0 = 30% × 20p = 6p

Using Gordon's growth model

MV ex-dividend = $\dfrac{D_0(1+g)}{r-g}$

110p = $\dfrac{6(1.12)}{r-0.12}$

Therefore, r = 0.181 or 18.1%

See Chapter 5 Section 3.3 of your Study Text

15.   **A**   I   True

II   False, the P/E is based on the most recent historic earnings

III   False, published dividend is the net figure, no tax need be deducted

IV   False, it ignores any capital gain

See Chapter 5 Section 3.2 and Chapter 5 Section 3.6 of your Study Text

16.   **22.4** d_0 = EPS × 10% = 6p × 10% = 0.6p

g = 20%

$r_e = \dfrac{d_0(1+g)}{E_{ex\text{-}div}} + g = \dfrac{0.6\times1.2}{30p} + 0.2 = 0.224$ or 22.4%

See Chapter 5 Section 3.3 of your Study Text

17.   **B**   American Depository Receipts (ADRs) are issued by UK companies to enhance the attractiveness of their shares to US investors, and hence as a way of raising finance from them

See Chapter 5 Section 1.3 of your Study Text

18.   **3.00**

	NUMBER	PRICE £	VALUE £
Before	5	3.60	18.00
Bonus issue	1	0.00	0.00
After	6		18.00

Theoretical price after = $\dfrac{18.00}{6}$ = £3.00

See Chapter 5 Section 2.3 of your Study Text

19.   **B**   American Depository Receipts (ADRs) are the conventional form of trading a UK share in the US. ADRs help facilitate the trading of non-US company shares within the US, where international trading on the NYSE is largely made up of such ADRs. These ADRs are denominated in US dollars, pay a US dollar dividend and settle T + 3

See Chapter 5 Section 1.3 of your Study Text

20.   **B**   A scrip dividend is one paid in shares. This may be done to conserve cash

See Chapter 5 Section 2.4 of your Study Text

21.   **B**   A company grows by making profits and reinvesting them within the company. Or, in a formula, $g = r \times b$

Where r = Return on equity and
b = Proportion of profits retained

See Chapter 5 Section 3.3 of your Study Text

22.   **A**   The shares can be sold nil paid, not fully paid

See Chapter 5 Section 2.3 of your Study Text

23.   **C**   Long-term it is not sustainable to distribute 120% of profit each year

See Chapter 5 Section 3.2 of your Study Text

24.   **D**   Since cash is paid out the current ratio would be reduced

See Chapter 5 Section 2.6 and Chapter 4 Section 1 of your Study Text

25.   **D**   I   Dividends *do not* have to be paid from current year's profits

II   Directors *do* set dividend policy to satisfy shareholders

III   Asset based valuation is most appropriate for capital intensive businesses, not service businesses

See Chapter 5 Section 3.2 and Chapter 5 Section 3.4 of your Study Text

26.   **B**

	NUMBER	PRICE £	VALUE £
Before	6	2.40	14.40
Rights issue	1	1.00	1.00
After	7		15.40

Theoretical price after $= \dfrac{15.40}{7} = £2.20$

See Chapter 5 Section 2.3 of your Study Text

27.   **4.66**   Dividends now = Dividends n years ago $\times (1 + g)^n$

$36 = 30 \times (1 + g)^4$

$(1 + g) = \sqrt[4]{\dfrac{36}{30}} = \sqrt[4]{1.20} = 1.20 = 1.0466$

$g = 0.0466$ or 4.66%

See Chapter 5 Section 3.3 of your Study Text

28.   **D**   Holding period return $= \dfrac{(d_1 + V_1) - V_0}{V_0} = \dfrac{(20 + 250) - 240}{240} = 0.125$ or 12.5%

See Chapter 5 Section 3.7 of your Study Text

29. **B** A 3 for 1 stock split results in 3 new shares replacing every 1 old share that existed

See Chapter 5 Section 2.5 of your Study Text

30. **C**
I   A primary market (eg LSE) *can* also be a secondary market
II   An offer for sale is a *primary* market issue
III   A placing *is* a marketing operation

See Chapter 5 Section 2.2 of your Study Text

31. **C** $g = rb$ where r = rate of return on reinvested income (15%) and b = proportion of profits retrained (0.4 since 0.6 is paid out)

$g = 15\% \times 0.4 = 6.0\%$

See Chapter 5 Section 3.3 of your Study Text

32. **D** A rights issue is a new issue (primary market) undertaken at a discount to the current price to raise new finance. Shareholders do not have to take up their rights

See Chapter 5 Section 2.3 of your Study Text

33. **B** Dividend now = Dividend n years ago $\times (1 + g)^n$

Dividend now = 60.8

Dividend n years ago = 50

n = 4 (in year 5, year 1 was four years ago)

$60.8 = 50 \times (1 + g)^4$

$1 + g = \sqrt[4]{\dfrac{60.8}{50.0}} = 1.050$

$g = 0.050$ or 5.0%

See Chapter 5 Section 3.3 of your Study Text

34. **C** Holding period return = $\dfrac{(d_1 + V_1) - V_0}{V_0} = \dfrac{(30 + 584) - 576}{576} = 0.066$ or 6.6%

Dividend yield = $\dfrac{d}{E_{XD}} = \dfrac{30}{584} = 0.051$ or 5.1%

Note: dividend yield is based on the current share price

See Chapter 5 Section 3.2 and Chapter 5 Section 3.7 of your Study Text

35. **9.2** About to pay a dividend implies that it is currently cum-div

$E_{ex.div} = E_{cum.div} - d_0 = 5.20 - 0.20 = 5.00$

$d_1 = d_0 \times (1 + g) = 20 \times 1.05 = 21$

$r_e = \dfrac{d_1}{E_{ex.div}} + g = \dfrac{21}{500} + 0.05 = 0.092$ or 9.2%

See Chapter 5 Section 3.3 of your Study Text

36. **B** In a share split no value is lost and so one £6.00 share will be replaced by four £1.50 shares
(4 × £1.50 = £6.00)

See Chapter 5 Section 2.5 of your Study Text

37. **B** Minimum price to the seller = realisable value = £80,000

See Chapter 5 Section 3.4 of your Study Text

38. **B**   I   Shares may be repurchased as an alternative to paying a dividend
    II   Share repurchases *increase* gearing
    III   Share repurchases *will* increase EPS

See Chapter 5 Section 2.6 of your Study Text

39. **B** It would not be possible to sell the nil paid right, as it would be worth nothing (the value in the nil paid right comes from the excess of the current share price over the subscription price), and there is no value from the shareholder's point of view in buying a share for more than its current price. So the best course of action is to let the right expire

See Chapter 5 Section 2.3 of your Study Text

40. **C** Following the bonus issue, each shareholder will be given (for free) an extra 1 share for each 4 shares previously held. So where an investor held 4 shares before the bonus issue, after the bonus issue that investor would hold 5 shares. No extra funds have been raised, so the share price following the bonus issue will be £0.96 (£1.20 × 4/5), or

	NUMBER	PRICE £	VALUE £
Before	4	1.20	4.80
Rights issue	1	0.00	0.00
After	5		4.80

Theoretical price after = $\dfrac{4.80}{5}$ = £0.96

See Chapter 5 Section 2.3 of your Study Text

41. **D** Depositary receipts are tradable on an exchange

See Chapter 5 Section 1.3 of your Study Text

42. **C** $\dfrac{£1,000,000}{5,000,000 \times 12p}$ = 1.67×

See Chapter 5 Section 3.2 of your Study Text

43. **C** Rearranging Gordon's Growth Model

10p × 1.05 = 10.5p (Value of dividend at Time 1)

(10.5/255) + 0.05 = 0.091 or 9.1%

Note. You can assume the dividend you are being provided with is the dividend at Time 0

See Chapter 5 Section 3.3 of your Study Text

44.   **D**   The four permitted issue methods are an offer for subscription, an offer for sale, a placing and an introduction

See Chapter 5 Section 2.2 of your Study Text

45.   **D**   The placing and a rights issue will raise cash for the company. The bonus issue and capitalisation issue are where shares are distributed freely, with no money being raised

See Chapter 5 Section 2.2 of your Study Text

46.   **C**   The share price will fall as a result of the scrip issue, also known as a bonus issue

	NUMBER	PRICE £	VALUE £
Before	10,000	0.76	7,600
Scrip issue (1:25)	400	0.00	0
After	10,400		7,600

Theoretical price after $= \dfrac{7,600}{10,400} = £0.731$

The share value falls from 76p to 73.1p

See Chapter 5 Section 2.5 of your Study Text

47.   **C** $P/E = \dfrac{\text{MV of shares}}{\text{EPS}} = \dfrac{180p}{9p} = 20$

See Chapter 5 Section 3.6 of your Study Text

48.   **C**   In a tender offer, all accepted bids receive shares at a common price, known as the common strike price. Therefore, if a bid is higher than the common strike price, the applicant of the shares will only pay the common strike price

See Chapter 5 Section 2.2 of your Study Text

49.   **C**   £1.50 + £0.25 = £1.75   = Theoretical ex-rights price

4 × £1.75 = £7.00   = Value of new holding (after rights issue)

£7.00 − £1.50 = £5.50   = Total value of original holding

550p/3 = 183p   = Cum rights price

See Chapter 5 Section 2.3 of your Study Text

50. **5.0** The share price is given by the formula:

$$E_{xd} = \frac{d_1}{r_e - g} = \frac{d_0 \times (1+g)}{r_e - g}$$

$$300 = \frac{20 \times (1+g)}{0.12 - g}$$

To work out g we need to rearrange this equation

$300 \times (0.12 - g) = 20 \times (1 + g)$

$36 - 300g = 20 + 20g$

$16 = 320g$

$g = 0.050$ or 5.0%

See Chapter 5 Section 3.3 of your Study Text

51. **3.56**

	NUMBER	PRICE £	VALUE £
Before	4	8.00	32.00
Bonus issue	5	0.00	0.00
After	9		32.00

Theoretical price after = $\dfrac{£32.00}{9}$ = £3.56

See Chapter 5 Section 2.3 of your Study Text

52. **B** Net div 12p

Dividend cover 1.25×, therefore

EPS = 12p × 1.25× = 15p

P/E = 20   EPS = 15p

Market price = P/E × EPS

= 20 × 15p = 300p

Net dividend yield = $\dfrac{12p}{300p}$ × 100 = 0.04 or 4%

See Chapter 5 Section 3.2 of your Study Text

53.　**B**　$\dfrac{EPS}{DPS}$ = Dividend cover

Hence

EPS = Dividend cover × DPS = 1.5× × 10.5p = 15.75p

$\dfrac{Dividend}{Price}$ = Net dividend yield

Hence

$\dfrac{Dividend}{Net\ dividend\ yield}$ = Price

$\dfrac{10.5p}{0.07}$ = 150p = price

$\dfrac{P}{E} = \dfrac{Price}{EPS} = \dfrac{150p}{15.75p} = 9.5×$

See Chapter 5 Section 3.6 of your Study Text

54.　**4.17**　EPS = 30p, P/E = 10

Therefore

Price　= P/E × EPS

　　　　= 10 × 30p = £3

EPS = 30p

Dividend cover = 2.4× = $\dfrac{EPS}{DPS}$

Therefore

Net dividend　= $\dfrac{EPS}{Dividend\ cover}$

　　　　= $\dfrac{30p}{2.4×}$ = 12.5p

$\dfrac{12.5p}{£3}$ × 100 = 0.0417 or 4.17%

See Chapter 5 Section 3.5 of your Study Text

55.　**C**　A high P/E ratio indicates that the share price is high relative to current company performance. If profits are low relative to the share price, the dividend and earnings yields will also be low

See Chapter 5 Section 3.6 of your Study Text

56.　**A**　Price per share/Earnings per share = 16

Therefore

Price per share = Earnings per share × 16 = 21p × 16 = 336p

See Chapter 5 Section 3.6 of your Study Text

57.   **D**   The trick to answering this question is to compare what you want with what you have per the question

We are asked for the P/E ratio, ie $\dfrac{\text{Share price}}{\text{Earnings per share}}$

We are given

   Dividend cover $= {}^{EPS}\!/_{DPS} = 4$ and

   Dividend yield $= {}^{DPS}\!/_{PPS} = 0.07$

Therefore,

Earnings per share (EPS)   = Dividend cover × Dividend per share

$\qquad\qquad\qquad = 4 \times 15p\ \ = 60p$

Price per share $= \dfrac{\text{Dividend per share}}{\text{Dividend yield}}$

$\qquad\qquad\qquad = \dfrac{15p}{0.07}$

$\qquad\qquad\qquad = 214.29p$

Price/earnings ratio $= \dfrac{\text{Share price}}{\text{Earnings per share}}$

$\qquad\qquad\qquad = \dfrac{214.29p}{60p}$

$\qquad\qquad\qquad = 3.57\times$

See Chapter 5 Section 3.6 of your Study Text

58.   **2.0**   Net dividend 15p

Dividend cover 2.5×

EPS = 15p × 2.5× = 37.5p

P/E = 20   EPS = 37.5p

Market price   = P/E × EPS

$\qquad\qquad = 20 \times 37.5 = 750$

Net dividend yield $\dfrac{15}{750} \times 100 = 0.02$ or 2%

See Chapter 5 Section 3.2 of your Study Text

59.   **C**   Price/Earnings $= \dfrac{330}{14.32}$

$\qquad\qquad = 23.05$

See Chapter 5 Section 3.6 of your Study Text

60. **2.0** P/E ratio $= \dfrac{\text{Share price}}{\text{Earnings per share}}$

Dividend cover $= \dfrac{\text{EPS}}{\text{DPS}} = 5$

Dividend yield $= \dfrac{\text{DPS}}{\text{PPS}} = 1.0$

Therefore

EPS = Dividend cover × Dividend per share

= 5 × 25 = 125

Price per share $= \dfrac{\text{Dividend per share}}{\text{Dividend yield}}$

$= \dfrac{25}{0.10} = 250.0\text{p}$

P/E $= \dfrac{250}{125} = 2.0\times$

See Chapter 5 Section 3.6 of your Study Text

61. **9.80** $\dfrac{\text{Price / share}}{\text{Earnings per share}} = 35$

Price/share = EPS × 35

= 28 × 35

= 980p

See Chapter 5 Section 3.6 of your Study Text

62. **C**

See Chapter 5 Section 3.5 of your Study Text

63. **D** P/E $= \dfrac{\text{Current market price per share}}{\text{Earnings per share}}$

See Chapter 5 Section 3.6 of your Study Text

64. **D** Rights issues are offers to the existing shareholders

See Chapter 5 Section 2.3 of your Study Text

65. **D** Earnings per share is earnings attributable to ordinary shareholders only

See Chapter 5 Section 3.5 of your Study Text

66. **A** A scrip issue has no impact on the operating profit of the company. Nor is it raising finance and so has no impact on the capital employed in the business. Therefore it will have no overall impact

See Chapter 5 Section 2.4 of your Study Text

6. Fixed Income

Questions

1. **Which of the following is true of issues of T-bills?**

   A   They are competitively auctioned on a bid price basis

   B   They are issued on a yield basis

   C   The bills are released directly into the secondary market via taps

   D   They are issued by fixed price offer for subscription

2. **All of the following are true of UK Treasury bills, except**

   A   They usually have a 91-day life

   B   They pay interest only on redemption

   C   They have a minimum denomination of £25,000

   D   They are denominated in sterling

3. **Which of the following is true of a repo?**

   I   The user of a repo may be adversely affected if gilt prices rise before the repurchase occurs

   II   A repo can only be conducted by money market institutions

   III   An open repo has no predetermined date for the repurchase element

   IV   The Bank of England conducts its interest rate policy through its repo operations

   A   I, II and III

   B   I, III and IV

   C   III and IV

   D   I, II, III and IV

4. **What is the credit risk on a Certificate of Deposit?**

   A   Reinvestment risk

   B   Legal risk

   C   Issuer defaulting

   D   Interest rate risk

5. **What is the discount rate on a treasury bill priced at £98.62 with 58 days to maturity (in % to 2 decimal places)?**

   Important! You should enter the answer only in numbers strictly using this format: 0.00

   Do not include spaces, letters or symbols (but decimal points and commas should be used if indicated).

6. Consider the following statements.

    I   The FSCS covers the first £85,000 of each deposit

    II CP is normally unsecured

    III CDs may have a term above one year

    Which statements are true?

    A   All are true

    B   I and II

    C   I and III

    D   II and III

7. **Which of the following is not a role of the Bank of England and DMO in the money markets?**

    A   Lender of last resort

    B   Set LIBOR

    C   Issue Treasury Bills

    D   Operate any quantitative easing programme

8. **A security which preserves the value of its purchasing power over time, despite increases in the general price level, is known as**

    A   A risk-free asset

    B   An indentured security

    C   An inflation hedge

    D   A negative correlation inflation stock

9. Consider the following statements.

    I   The minimum deposit for a CD is usually £25,000

    II Treasury bills trade on a discount basis

    III CP is normally unsecured

    Which statements are true?

    A   I and III

    B   I and II

    C   II and III

    D   III only

10. **Consider the following statements.**

   I   Cash deposits below £85,000 have a negligible risk

   II The DMO is part of the Bank of England

   III The MPC determines the base rate

   Which statements are true?

   A   I and II

   B   I and III

   C   II and III

   D   I, II and III

11. **Which of the following do not trade at a discount?**

   A   Treasury bills

   B   CP

   C   CD

   D   Bill of exchange

12. **Consider the following statements.**

   I   An eligible bill is one accepted by a bank

   II CP typically has a maturity of up to five years

   III The discount rate on a treasury bill always exceeds the yield

   Which statements are true?

   A   None are true

   B   I and III

   C   II and I

   D   II and III

13. **What is the interest if we repo bonds with a value of £110,000 at a repo rate of 4% for 89 days (to the nearest £1)?**

   Important! You should enter the answer only in numbers strictly using this format: 0,000

   Do not include spaces, letters or symbols (but decimal points and commas should be used if indicated).

14. **What is Standard and Poor's highest credit rating for CP?**

   A   A+1+

   B   A–1+

   C   A+1

   D   A–1

15. **Place the following securities in order by maturity (shortest to longest).**

CP, CDs, Treasury bills

A Treasury bills < CDs < CP

B CP < Treasury bills < CDs

C Treasury bills < CP < CDs

D CP < CDs < Treasury bills

16. **Consider the following statements.**

    I   CDs trade on a yield basis

    II   FRNs pay a coupon linked to money market rates

    III   The minimum block size for Treasury bills is £20,000

Which statements are true?

A I, II and IIIj

B I and II

C I and III

D II and III

17. **What is the yield on Commercial Paper priced at 95.42 with 267 days to maturity?**

A 19.25%

B 18.37%

C 6.56%

D 6.26%

18. **Consider the following statements.**

    I   FRNs pay a guaranteed income

    II   A repo is a form of unsecured loan

    III   An eligible debt security is a bill of exchange

Which statements are true?

A I only

B II only

C III only

D All are false

19. **Which of the following is the most likely reason for investing in Commercial Paper?**

A Capital gain

B Income gain

C Low risk arising from security

D Long-term investment horizon

20. **Which of the following is the most usual form of FRN?**

    A Long-term notes with a variable rate of interest

    B Long-term notes with a fixed rate of interest

    C Short-term notes with a variable rate of interest

    D Short-term notes with a fixed rate of interest

21. **As interest rates fall, which of the following statements is true of a FRN?**

    A The price will rise and the yield will fall

    B The price will fall and the yield will rise

    C The price will remain constant and the yield will fall

    D The price will remain constant and the yield will rise

22. **3% Treasury 2019 currently has a gross redemption yield of 5.5%. 10.25% Exchequer 2016 has a gross redemption yield of 6.4%. Which of the following investors would you expect to prefer the low coupon stock?**

    A UK pension fund

    B Widow on state benefits

    C Company director who earns £50,000 p.a.

    D A high-income unit trust

23. **When is Treasury 6¾% 2016-2019 repayable?**

    A 2016

    B At a time selected by the Debt Management Office between 2016-2019

    C 2019

    D At a time selected by the investor between 2016-2019

24. **It is 31 December. You own £1m nominal of Treasury 10% 2017, repayable on 31 December 2017. Which of the following are true?**

    I   The clean price of the gilt is the same as the dirty price

    II   Each half-year, you will receive income of £100,000 net of tax

    III   You can always sell the gilt holding for £1m

    A I and III

    B I, II and III

    C None of the above

    D I only

25. If the coupon rate on a bond increases, the duration of the bond will

A   Increase

B   Decrease

C   Remain unchanged

D   Change in an unpredictable fashion

26. In the 1970s, high inflation reduced institutional demand for

A   Index-linked gilts

B   Non-indexed linked gilts

C   Equities

D   Property

27. What is the market value of a fixed rate irredeemable bond?

A   Coupon rate divided by yield

B   Yield divided by coupon rate

C   Coupon rate multiplied by yield

D   Nominal value divided by yield

28. Who are usually trustees for an issue of corporate bonds?

A   A specialist trustee company

B   An appointee of the debt holders

C   The issuing company

D   The official receiver

29. Which of the following relationships would be true for a gilt trading above par?

A   Flat yield > GRY < NRY

B   Flat yield < GRY > NRY

C   Flat yield < GRY < NRY

D   Flat yield > GRY > NRY

30. Which of the following are true of GEMMs?

   I   They have access to the IDB system

   II   They are obliged to make a firm two-way price in all gilts

   III   They are outside the Financial Services and Markets Act requirements for authorisation

A   I only

B   I and II

C   I and III

D   I, II and III

31. **Which of the following bonds will have the greatest duration?**

   A   0% 2015

   B   12% 2018

   C   14% 2020

   D   2% 2029

32. **Which is the normal style of coupon payment for gilts?**

   A   Annually, gross

   B   Annually, net of basic rate tax

   C   Semi-annually, net of basic rate tax

   D   Semi-annually, gross

33. **All of the following are true of Eurobonds, except**

   A   They are usually registered securities

   B   They are issued outside of the country in whose currency they are denominated

   C   They are held in safe custody by Clearstream or Euroclear

   D   Interest on them is paid without any tax being deducted

34. **Which of the following yield calculations for a gilt would be most useful for a higher rate taxpayer?**

   A   Flat yield

   B   Gross redemption yield

   C   Net redemption yield

   D   Grossed-up net redemption yield

35. **What does the symbol ● mean beside a gilt price?**

   A   It is a tap stock

   B   It is a FOTRA stock

   C   It is being traded in 'when issued' form

   D   It is subject to a reverse auction

36. **Which of the following regulates the Eurobond market?**

   A   ICMA

   B   AIBD

   C   Euroclear

   D   Clearstream

37. **Which of the following are true of Eurobonds?**

    I   They are registered securities

    II   No stamp duty is payable on their transfer

    III   Settlement is interoffice

    IV   Settlement is usually for three business days

A I, II, III and IV

B II, III and IV

C I, III and IV

D II and IV

38. **Gilts which are classified as longs have what minimum period to run to redemption?**

A More than 10 years

B More than 15 years

C More than 20 years

D More than 25 years

39. **If interest rates increase, which of the following statements would be true for gilts?**

A Prices would rise and yields would fall

B Prices would rise and yields would rise

C Prices would fall and yields would rise

D Prices would fall and yields would fall

40. **In order to establish the income return on a gilt investment, which of the following yield calculations is most useful?**

A Flat yield

B Gross redemption yield

C Net redemption yield

D Grossed-up net redemption yield

41. **What is the Japanese gross redemption yield of a bond investment which cost £98.00 per £100 of par value, where the bond pays a coupon of 5% and there were five years to maturity of the bond when it was purchased?**

A 5.0%

B 5.5%

C 6.4%

D 7.0%

42. **Which of the following is the most suitable investment for an investor with a marginal tax rate of 40% who believes that interest rates will fall?**

   A   FRNs

   B   Low-coupon, long-dated gilts

   C   High-coupon, short-dated gilts

   D   Equities

43. **Which of the following are true of GEMMs?**

   I   They must quote prices on request to brokers

   II   They apply to the Stock Exchange to act as GEMMs

   III   Their activities will be regulated by the FSA

   A   II and III

   B   I and III

   C   I and II

   D   I only

44. **A bond is priced at £113.75 and has a modified duration of 3.45. If yields rise by ½%, what will the new price of the bond be (in £ to two decimal places)?**

   Important! You should enter the answer only in numbers strictly using this format: 000.00

   Do not include spaces, letters or symbols (but decimal points and commas should be used if indicated).

45. **Gilts which are classified as shorts by the Debt Management Office have what maximum period to run to maturity?**

   A   One year

   B   Five years

   C   Seven years

   D   Ten years

46. **A long and short-dated gilt both have a market price of £90. If interest rates increase, which of the following statements is true?**

   A   The short gilt price will increase more than the long gilt price

   B   The long gilt price will increase more than the short gilt price

   C   The short gilt price will fall more than the long gilt price

   D   The long gilt price will fall more than the short gilt price

47. **If a gilt has a maturity of 2015-2018 and a coupon of 6%, and current interest rates are 4%, which of the following statements are true?**

A   The DMO would immediately buy the gilt in the market place to reissue at cheaper rates

B   The DMO will aim to redeem the gilt at the earliest opportunity

C   The DMO will aim to redeem the gilt at the latest possible opportunity

D   The DMO will be indifferent as to any of the above courses of action

---

48. **Consider the following statements.**

    I   A callable bond may be sold to the issuer at any time

    II   Senior unsecured debt has a lower risk than subordinated debt

    III   A serial note is where a proportion of bonds in issue are redeemed each year

Which of the above are true?

A   I is true, II and III are false

B   II is true, I and III are false

C   III is true, I and II are false

D   All are false

---

49. **A 6% 'long' government bond pays interest half-yearly. Two months after payment of interest, the dirty price is £62.50. What is the interest yield (in % to 2 decimal places)?**

Important! You should enter the answer only in numbers strictly using this format: 0.00

Do not include spaces, letters or symbols (but decimal points and commas should be used if indicated).

---

50. **Calculate the redemption yield of a bond bought for £91.99 with four full years to maturity and paying a 7% annual coupon.**

A   8.9%

B   9.3%

C   9.5%

D   9.8%

---

51. **The 'worst case' interest rate scenario for a bond portfolio refers to**

A   The percentage change in the average coupon of the bonds, given the worst possible fall in interest rates over a specified period

B   The worst possible decline in the capital values of the bonds held in the portfolio, given the largest possible expected fall in interest rates over a specified period

C   The worst possible decline in the capital values of the bonds held in the portfolio, given the largest possible expected rise in interest rates over a specified period

D   The worst possible decline in the duration of the bond portfolio held, given the largest possible expected rise in interest rates over a specified period

52. A 6% 'long' Treasury security pays twice-yearly interest and the price, including accrued interest two months prior to a payment, is £60. What is the gross flat yield?

    A 6.00%
    B 10.34%
    C 9.21%
    D 10.00%

53. A bond has three years before being redeemed at par at maturity and pays a 9% coupon at the end of each of the three years. The one, two and three-year spot rates are 11%, 10% and 7% respectively. Calculate the price of this bond (in £ to two decimal places).

    Important! You should enter the answer only in numbers strictly using this format: 000.00

    Do not include spaces, letters or symbols (but decimal points and commas should be used if indicated).

54. If a 5% 'long' government bond pays interest twice a year and the price (including accrued interest) one month after an interest payment is £48.50, what is the gross interest yield (in % to 2 decimal places)?

    Important! You should enter the answer only in numbers strictly using this format: 00.00

    Do not include spaces, letters or symbols. (but decimal points and commas should be used if indicated).

55. If a eurosterling bond has three years to redemption, pays a 9% annual coupon, with interest rates at 10%, and is priced at £97.51, what is the duration of the eurosterling bond?

    A 2.76 years
    B 2.78 years
    C 2.82 years
    D 2.65 years

56. A £100 bond is priced at £101.73 with an 11% coupon payable at the end of each of the three years, and redeemable at par. What is its yield to maturity?

    A 10.95%
    B 10.75%
    C 10.30%
    D 10.15%

57. When the investor's required rate of return equals the coupon rate of a fixed income security, then

A The par value of the security is greater than its redemption value

B The par value of the security equals its present value

C The par value of the security will be greater than its present value

D The redemption value of the security will be greater than the par value of the security

58. A bond with a life of two years will pay an 8% coupon at the end of each of the two years. The bond will be redeemed at par. If the one-year spot rate is 10% and the two-year spot rate is 9%, what is the price of this bond (in £ to two decimal places)?

Important! You should enter the answer only in numbers strictly using this format: 00.00

Do not include spaces, letters or symbols (but decimal points and commas should be used if indicated).

59. A bond where a proportion of the capital is redeemed each year along with the interest payment is referred to as a

A Bullet

B Sinker

C Purchase fund bond

D Serial note

60. Which one of the following statements about index-linked gilts best describes the government bond?

A The interest payment, otherwise known as the coupon payment, is linked to the retail price index, either three or eight months prior to the date in question

B The redemption value, otherwise known as the maturity payment, is linked to the retail price index, either three or eight months prior to the date in question

C Neither the interest payment, otherwise known as the coupon payment, nor the redemption value, otherwise known as the maturity payment, are linked to the retail price index, either three or eight months prior to the date in question

D Both the interest payment, otherwise known as the coupon payment, and the redemption value, otherwise known as the maturity payment, are linked to the retail price index, either three or eight months prior to the date in question

61. How are UK government bonds, otherwise known as gilts, quoted on the London Stock Exchange?

A 16ths of a pound sterling

B 32nds of a pound sterling

C 64ths of a pound sterling

D 100ths of a pound sterling

62. **What is the correct order for repayment in the event of a liquidation of a company?**

   A   Deferred shares, ordinary shares, cumulative preference shares

   B   Ordinary shares, deferred shares, cumulative preference shares

   C   Cumulative preference shares, ordinary shares, deferred shares

   D   Ordinary shares, cumulative preference shares, deferred shares

63. **What is the highest junk bond credit rating?**

   A   BBB+

   B   BBB–

   C   BB+

   D   BB–

64. **In relation to any price prediction based on modified duration, convexity means**

   A   The actual price always falls below what has been predicted

   B   The actual price exceeds the predicted price if rates fall but falls below if rates rise

   C   The actual price exceeds the predicted price if rates raise but falls below if rates fall

   D   The actual price always exceeds the predicted price

65. **Consider the following statements.**

   I   A convertible may be converted at the issuer's option

   II   A putable bond may be sold back at the holder's option

   III   A callable bond may be redeemed at the issuer's option

   Which are true?

   A   All are true

   B   I and II are true

   C   I and III are true

   D   II and III are true

66. **A bond has a modified duration of 8.67 and is priced at £93.47. If rates rise by 0.4% what will the price become (in £ to two decimal places)?**

   Important! You should enter the answer only in numbers strictly using this format: 00.00

   Do not include spaces, letters or symbols (but decimal points and commas should be used if indicated).

67. A bond pays a 4% coupon and will be redeemed in 17 years. What is its price if it is yielding 5%?

A 84.55

B 86.94

C 88.73

D 89.42

68. Irredeemable debentures issued by a company

A Can never be redeemed

B Can be redeemed at the request of the company

C Can be redeemed at the request of the investor

D Can be redeemed if a majority of the debenture holders vote for redemption

69. Which of the following ratios would a credit analyst have least interest in?

A Current ratio

B Interest cover

C Debt to equity

D Price to earnings

70. Consider the following statements

    I   Labour intensive industries are considered a better credit risk

    II   Greater competition increases credit risk

    III   Volatile raw material costs increase credit risk

Which statements are true?

A I and II

B I and III

C II and III

D III only

71. What is the best definition of convexity?

A Convexity is the error in duration

B Convexity is the price movement for a 1% yield change

C Convexity is a measure of the relative volatility of a bond

D Convexity is the difference between actual prices and modified duration predictions

72. **Rank the following in order of priority on liquidation.**

    I   Preferential creditors

    II   Amounts subscribed for warrants in the company's shares

    III Debt secured by floating charges

    IV   Ordinary shares

    A   I, II, III, IV

    B   II, I, III, IV

    C   II, I, IV, III

    D   I, III, IV, II

73. **Which of the following best describes an index-linked gilt?**

    A   A bond where coupon payments are linked to the rate of inflation

    B   A bond where coupon payments are related to the rate of interest

    C   A bond where the price is linked to the rate of inflation

    D   A bond where the coupon and redemption value are linked to the rate of inflation

74. **The gross redemption yield is**

    A   The annual rate of return to redemption for an investor who pays tax

    B   The annual rate of return to redemption for an investor who pays no tax

    C   The annual rate of return to redemption for an investor who pays no tax on coupons, but pays tax on capital gains

    D   The annual rate of return to redemption for an investor who pays no tax on capital gains, but pays tax on coupons

75. **Which of the following bonds would rise to the greatest extent for a given fall in interest rates?**

    A   Low-coupon, short-dated

    B   Low-coupon, long-dated

    C   High-coupon, short-dated

    D   High-coupon, long-dated

76. **A three year bond has the following features.**

    Par value £80,000,000

    Coupon £7,200,000

    Yield 9%

    What price will the bond trade at?

    A   £72,000,000

    B   £80,000,000

    C   £88,000,000

    D   We cannot derive the price from this information

77. A company has in issue cumulative preference shares, ordinary shares and deferred shares and convertible bonds. Which one will rank last In the event of liquidation?

   A Cumulative preference shares

   B Ordinary shares

   C Deferred shares

   D Convertible bonds

78. A bond is rated as BBB– . It is downgraded by 1 notch by S&P. What will the new credit rating be?

   A BBB

   B BB

   C BB+

   D BBB–

79. A one year bond is trading on a yield of 4%. The one year forward rate in one years' time is 5%. What will the yield be on a two year bond?

   A 4%

   B 4.5%

   C 5%

   D 5.5%

80. An inverted yield curve reflects the expectation that

   A Short-term interest rates will rise

   B Long-term interest rates will fall

   C Short-term interest rates will fall

   D Long-term interest rates will rise

81. One-year zero-coupon bonds have a yield of 7% and two-year zero-coupon bonds have a yield of 8%. What is the two-year spot rate?

   A 7.5%

   B 8%

   C 9%

   D 15%

82. Which of the following best describes a droplock FRN?

   A Where there is a limit to the maximum interest paid

   B Where there is a limit to the minimum interest paid

   C Where the bond is allowed to be converted into a conventional bond to maturity if interest rates fall to a particular level

   D Where the bond is allowed to be converted into a conventional bond to maturity if interest rates rise to a particular level

Answers

1. **B** UK government bonds, otherwise known as gilts, may be issued via the other methods

   See Chapter 6 Section 1.1 of your Study Text

2. **B** They pay no interest and are therefore issued at a discount

   See Chapter 6 Section 1.1 of your Study Text

3. **C** The user of a repo may be adversely affected if gilt prices fall, since additional security may be required. They will not, however, be adversely affected if gilt prices rise

   See Chapter 6 Section 1.3 of your Study Text

4. **C** A Certificate of Deposit (CD) can only be issued by those institutions with a UK banking licence, being highly rated banks and other financial organisations, and therefore carry a limited credit risk. However, the credit risk that does exist, albeit limited, is with the issuing bank

   See Chapter 6 Section 1.3 of your Study Text

5. **8.68** Discount rate = $\dfrac{100.00 - 98.62}{100.00} \times \dfrac{365}{58} = 0.0868$ or 8.68%

   See Chapter 6 Section 1.1 of your Study Text

6. **D** I   The FSCS covers the first £85,000 per person per separately authorised firm
   II   CP is normally unsecured
   III CDs may have a term up to five years

   See Chapter 6 Section 1 of your Study Text

7. **B** LIBOR is set by commercial banks, not the Bank of England or DMO. The Bank sets the base rate that influences LIBOR through its weekly Treasury Bill auction programme

   See Chapter 6 Section 1.2 of your Study Text

8. **C** Inflation is a measure of the purchasing power

   See Chapter 6 Section 2.5 of your Study Text

9. **C** I   Minimum deposit for a CD is normally £100,000
   II   Treasury bills trade on a discount basis
   III CP is normally unsecured

   See Chapter 6 Section 1 of your Study Text

10. **B** I   Due to the FSCS this is true
    II   The DMO is a department of the Treasury
    III The MPC does determine the base rate

    See Chapter 6 Section 1.2 of your Study Text

11. **C** CDs provide a return by paying interest. Treasury bills, CP and Bills of Exchange do not pay interest but give a return by trading at a discount

    See Chapter 6 Section 1 of your Study Text

12. **A**   I   False – It is one accepted by an eligible bank

           II   False – CP marketing is typically ≤ 12 months

           III   False – The yield exceeds the discount rate as it uses the (lower value) price on the denominator rather than the higher maturity value

           See Chapter 6 Section 1 of your Study Text

13. **1,073**   Interest $= 100{,}000 \times 0.04 \times \dfrac{89}{365} = £1{,}072.88$

           The required format for this question is £0,000, hence you must round to the nearest whole pound, ie £1,073.

           See Chapter 6 Section 1.3 of your Study Text

14. **B**   The highest is A–1+

           See Chapter 6 Section 1.3 of your Study Text

15. **C**   Treasury bills (91 days) < CP (12 months) < CDs (up to 5 years)

           See Chapter 6 Section 1 of your Study Text

16. **B**   I   True – CDs trade on a yield basis

           II   True – FRN coupons are linked to money market rates

           III   False – Minimum block size = £25,000

           See Chapter 6 Section 1 of your Study Text

17. **C**   Yield $= \dfrac{100.00 - 95.42}{95.42} \times \dfrac{365}{267} = 0.0656$ or 6.56%

           See Chapter 6 Section 1.1 of your Study Text

18. **D**   I   False – The coupon on an FRN varies

           II   False – A repo is effectively a secured debt

           III   False – An EDS is a dematerialised instrument that can be settled through CREST

           See Chapter 6 Section 1 and Chapter 6 Section 1.2 of your Study Text

19. **A**   Commercial Paper is a short-term instrument, issued by a company with no security attached to it and with no interest. To create a rate of return, commercial paper is issued at a discount to its par value, and hence an investor will experience an increase in value, from the discount purchase price up to the par value, when held to maturity. The investor will therefore experience a capital gain

           See Chapter 6 Section 1.3 of your Study Text

20. **A**   Floating rate notes that pay a variable coupon and as a result trade near par. They are generally long term despite trading as money market instruments

           See Chapter 6 Section 2.6 of your Study Text

21. **C**   The coupon is adjusted regularly to interest rates and consequently, the price remains constant

           See Chapter 6 Section 2.6 of your Study Text

22. **C** Low coupon means less income tax and the capital gain on the gilt is tax free

See Chapter 6 Section 4.1 of your Study Text

23. **B** The bond is repayable at a time selected by the Debt Management Office between 2016-2019 though it must be redeemed by the DMO by 2019

See Chapter 6 Section 2.1 of your Study Text

24. **C** Gilts pay ½ the coupon on a semi-annual basis. The payments will be made on 30 June/31 December in this case. The settlement date for the bargain would be one business day later. Thus, accrued interest would be charged for two days

See Chapter 6 Section 2.1 and Chapter 6 Section 2.3 of your Study Text

25. **B** Low-coupon bonds are more sensitive to interest rates than higher coupon bonds and therefore have higher durations

See Chapter 6 Section 2.3 of your Study Text

26. **B** The others are real assets that are protected from inflation, which is important to investors with long-term investment horizons

See Chapter 6 Section 2.5 of your Study Text

27. **A** Apply the perpetuity discount factor to the equal cash flow to give the present value, i.e. the price

See Chapter 6 Section 2.3 of your Study Text

28. **A** Normally a specialist company

See Chapter 6 Section 2.6 of your Study Text

29. **D** Trading above par means that there will be a loss to redemption. As a result, the loss will reduce the total return. NRY is just the redemption yield, net of relevant tax

See Chapter 6 Section 4.1 of your Study Text

30. **B** GEMMs are conducting investment business and therefore are required to be covered by the Financial Services and Markets Act

See Chapter 6 Section 2.2 of your Study Text

31. **D** Low-coupon long-dated stock are the most sensitive to interest rate changes

See Chapter 6 Section 2.3 of your Study Text

32. **D** Gilts pay a semi-annual gross coupon except 2½% consolidated, which pays a quarterly coupon

See Chapter 6 Section 2.2 of your Study Text

33. **A** Most Eurobonds are bearer. There are global bonds which are registered in key markets

See Chapter 6 Section 2.6 of your Study Text

34. **C** Net of the appropriate tax rate. Assuming that the investor is concerned with after-tax total returns, then the net redemption yield is the most appropriate, since it takes into account after-tax cash flows from coupons

See Chapter 6 Section 4.1 of your Study Text

35. **A** When the DMO retains some nominal value of a new gilt issue for issue in to the secondary market at a later date, it is referred to as tap stock

See Chapter 6 Section 2.2 of your Study Text

36. **A** International Capital Market Association (ICMA) is the key regulator in the Eurobond market (formerly known as ISMA)

See Chapter 6 Section 2.6 of your Study Text

37. **D** Eurobonds are bearer documents and as a result, no stamp duty is payable on purchase. Eurobonds settle through Euroclear and Clearstream

See Chapter 6 Section 2.6 of your Study Text

38. **B** Note that the default classification is the version used by the Debt Management Office. Note though that for long-dated gilts, the London Stock Exchange and Financial Times have identical classification

See Chapter 6 Section 2.2 of your Study Text

39. **C** Gilt prices have an inverse relationship to changes in interest rates/yields. The sensitivity of a particular bond to yield changes is measured by duration

See Chapter 6 Section 3.1 of your Study Text

40. **A** The flat yield (also known as current, interest, income or running yield) only assesses the income return and ignores the capital gain or loss on redemption. It is most appropriate for irredeemable bonds

See Chapter 6 Section 4.1 of your Study Text

41. **B** Annualised capital gain = (100 – 98)/5 = £0.40

Gross redemption yield = (£5 [coupon] + £0.40)/£98 = 5.5%

See Chapter 6 Section 4.1 of your Study Text

42. **B** With falling interest rates bond prices will be rising. Low-coupon, long-dated gilts will be most sensitive to this and rise the furthest giving the holder a substantial (tax-free) gain

See Chapter 6 Section 2.2 of your Study Text

43. **B** They apply to the DMO to act as GEMMs and are regulated by the FSA

See Chapter 6 Section 2.2 of your Study Text

44. **111.79** $-3.45 \times 0.005 \times £113.75 = -£1.96$

£113.75 – £1.96 = £111.79

See Chapter 6 Section 2.2 of your Study Text

45. **C** The DMO classifies short-dated gilts as having up to seven years until maturity. This is the default classification, but note that the LSE/FT would classify shorts as having up to five years until maturity

See Chapter 6 Section 2.2 of your Study Text

46. **D** Longer dated stock is more volatile and would have the highest duration

See Chapter 6 Section 2.2 of your Study Text

47. **B** The DMO will redeem at the earliest opportunity if it is possible to replace with a lower coupon issue, ie a lower cost borrowing

See Chapter 6 Section 2.1 of your Study Text

48. **B** I   False – A callable bond may be called by the issuer, not sold to the issuer (that is a putable bond)

   II   True – Senior unsecured has lower risk than subordinated

   III   False – A serial note is where a proportion of the capital is repaid each year, a sinking fund is where a proportion of the bonds in issue are redeemed each year

See Chapter 6 Section 2.6 of your Study Text

49. **9.76** Interest yield $= \dfrac{\text{Coupon}}{\text{Clean price}} = \dfrac{£6}{£62.50 - \left(£6 \times \dfrac{2}{12}\right)} = 0.0976$ or 9.76%

See Chapter 6 Section 4.1 of your Study Text

50. **C** By trial and error

Time	Cash Flow £	DF (9.5%)	PV £
0	(91.99)	1	(91.99)
1	7.00	$\dfrac{1}{1.095}$	6.39
2	7.00	$\dfrac{1}{1.095^2}$	5.84
3	7.00	$\dfrac{1}{1.095^3}$	5.33
4	107.00	$\dfrac{1}{1.095^4}$	74.43
			–

Yield = 9.5%

See Chapter 6 Section 2.3 and Chapter 6 Section 4.1 of your Study Text

51. **C** Bond prices are inversely related to interest rates

See Chapter 6 Section 2.2 of your Study Text

52. **B**

Dirty price	£60.00
Accrued interest $\left(£6 \times \dfrac{4}{12}\right)$	(2.00)
Clean price	£58.00

Gross flat yield $= \dfrac{£6}{£58} = 0.1034$ or 10.34%

See Chapter 6 Section 2.3 and Chapter 6 Section 4.1 of your Study Text

53. **104.52**

T	Cash Flow £	DF	PV £
1	9	$\dfrac{1}{1.11}$	8.108
2	9	$\dfrac{1}{1.10^2}$	7.434
3	109	$\dfrac{1}{1.07^3}$	88.976
			104.522

See Chapter 6 Section 4.3 of your Study Text

54. **10.40**

	£
Dirty price	48.50
Accrued interest £5 × $\frac{1}{12}$	(0.42)
Clean price	48.08

Gross interest yield $= \dfrac{£5}{£48.08} = 0.1040$ or 10.40%

See Chapter 6 Section 2.3 and Chapter 6 Section 4.1 of your Study Text

55. **A**

Time	Cash Flow £	DF(10%)	PV £	tPV £
1	9.00	$\dfrac{1}{1.10}$	8.18	8.18
2	9.00	$\dfrac{1}{1.10^2}$	7.44	14.88
3	109.00	$\dfrac{1}{1.10^3}$	81.89	245.67
			97.51	268.73

Duration $= \dfrac{£268.73}{£97.51} = 2.76$ years

See Chapter 6 Section 2.3 of your Study Text

56. **C** By trial and error

Time	Cash Flow £	DF (10.3%)	PV £
0	(101.73)	1	(101.73)
1	11.00	$\dfrac{1}{1.103}$	9.97
2	11.00	$\dfrac{1}{1.103^2}$	9.04
3	111.00	$\dfrac{1}{1.103^3}$	82.72
			–

See Chapter 6 Section 2.3 and Chapter 6 Section 4.1 of your Study Text

57. **B** If the investor's required rate of return, i.e. the effective discount factor, is the same as the coupon, then when applying normal discounting rules, the present value of the discounted cash flows would be equal to par

See Chapter 6 Section 3.1 of your Study Text

58. **98.17**

Time	Cash Flow £	DF	PV £
1	8	$\dfrac{1}{1.10}$	7.27
2	108	$\dfrac{1}{1.09^2}$	90.90
			98.17

See Chapter 6 Section 4.3 of your Study Text

59. **D** Similar to a repayment mortgage and enables the issuing company to spread cash flow obligations over the life of a bond instead of just on the maturity date

See Chapter 6 Section 2.6 of your Study Text

60. **D** With regards to index-linked gilts (ILGs), both the interest payment, otherwise known as the coupon payment, and the redemption value, otherwise known as the maturity payment, are linked to the retail price index (RPI) either three or eight months prior to the date in question. ILGs are described as 'real' returning assets, as they offer protection against inflationary pressure, which is why both the coupon and the redemption proceeds are scaled up by the inflationary uplift, as measured by the RPI

See Chapter 6 Section 2.5 of your Study Text

61. **D** UK government bonds, otherwise known as gilts, quoted on the London Stock Exchange, are quoted in decimal. That is, 100ths of a pound sterling, otherwise referred to as a quotation in pence

See Chapter 6 Section 2.2 of your Study Text

62. **C** The correct order for repayment in the event of a company going into liquidation is preference shares, ordinary shares and then deferred shares. However, it is possibly to have warrants issued to subscribe to new shares in the company, and if this is the case, then these warrants would rank last, after deferred shares, in the liquidation priority. It is also worth noting that most preference shares are deemed to be cumulative in terms of their dividend entitlements. However, there are some preference shares that are described as being non-cumulative

    See Chapter 6 Section 2.6 of your Study Text

63. **C** BB+ is the highest junk bond rating, BBB– is the lowest investment bond rating

    See Chapter 6 Section 2.6 of your Study Text

64. **D** Convexity ensures the actual price always exceeds the modified duration prediction

    See Chapter 6 Section 2.4 of your Study Text

65. **D** A convertible may be converted at the *holder's* option

    See Chapter 6 Section 2.6 of your Study Text

66. **90.23** With a modified duration of 8.67, a 1% change in yields will give rise to an 8.67% change in prices, ie £8.10 (93.47 × 8.67%). If rates rise 0.4% then prices will fall by £3.24 (8.10 × 0.4) to £90.23 (93.47 – 3.24)

    See Chapter 6 Section 2.3 of your Study Text

67. **C**

TIME	CASH FLOW (£)	DF (5%)	PV (£)
1-17	4	$\dfrac{1}{0.05}(1-\dfrac{1}{1.05^{17}})$	45.10
17	100	$\dfrac{1}{1.05^{17}}$	43.63
			88.73

    See Chapter 6 Section 2.3 of your Study Text

68. **A** A bond that is irredeemable is a bond that has no maturity or redemption date, i.e. it can never be redeemed, and so is valued as a perpetuity

    See Chapter 6 Section 2.6 of your Study Text

69. **D** The price to earnings ratio gives little insight into the ability of a company to service its debt

    See Chapter 6 Section 2.6 of your Study Text

70. **C** Labour intensive industries are considered a poorer credit risk

    See Chapter 6 Section 2.6 of your Study Text

71. **D** Convexity is the difference between actual prices and modified duration predictions

    See Chapter 6 Section 2.4 of your Study Text

72. **D** Normally, ordinary shareholders rank last. However, the warrant will effectively be worthless and thus could be looked at as ranking last if it must be ranked at all

See Chapter 6 Section 2.6 of your Study Text

73. **D** ILGs are linked to the rate of inflation using the Retail Price Index (RPI)

See Chapter 6 Section 2.5 of your Study Text

74. **B** The gross redemption yield is assuming no tax is paid

See Chapter 6 Section 4.1 of your Study Text

75. **B** As duration is the greatest, it reacts to the greatest extent

See Chapter 6 Section 2.3 of your Study Text

76. **B** There is no need to do a calculation here as the coupon is the same as the required return (yield of 9%) so the bond will trade at par.

See Chapter 6 Section 3.1 of your Study Text

77. **C** The order will be the bonds, preference shares, ordinary shares, deferred shares

See Chapter 6 Section 2.6 of your Study Text

78. **C** BB is below BBB.

See Chapter 6 Section 2.6 of your Study Text

79. **B** $(1+r)^2 = 1.04 \times 1.05$

$1+r = 1.045$

See Chapter 6 Section 4.3 of your Study Text

80. **C** An inverted yield curve is where the short-term rates are high, but the market anticipates that this can't last for long, therefore the short-term interest rates are expected to fall

See Chapter 6 Section 4.2 of your Study Text

81. **B** The zero-coupon rate is the spot rate

See Chapter 6 Section 4.3 of your Study Text

82. **C** With a droplock, once the interest hits a specified minimum, the bond locks into that rate for its remaining life

See Chapter 6 Section 2.6 of your Study Text

7. Derivatives

Questions

1. You own a portfolio of gilts and are concerned that interest rates may rise in the near future. Which of the following strategies could you employ to protect the value of your portfolio?

    I   Sell a gilt put option

    II   Buy a stock with high volatility and sell a lower volatility stock

    III   Sell a long gilt future

    IV   Buy a gilt call option

    A   I and IV

    B   I and II

    C   III only

    D   II and III

2. If a call option with an exercise price of £3 is purchased for £1, the maximum loss is

    A   £1

    B   £2

    C   £3

    D   Unlimited

3. You own 50 contracts of the December FTSE 100 Index future. Under which of the following circumstances would you expect to have to increase your margin commitment?

    I   The FTSE 100 Index falls 50 points in a day

    II   You buy 10 more contracts

    III   You sell 20 of the December contracts and buy 20 March

    A   I and III

    B   None of the above

    C   II and III

    D   I and II

4. If the underlying share is at £1.30, what is the intrinsic value of a £1.50 call which was bought for a premium of 20p when the underlying share was trading at £1.65?

    A   15p

    B   20p

    C   35p

    D   Nil

5. **An equity put option contract will specify which of the following?**

    I   The amount of shares to be sold

    II   The exercise price for the shares

    III The expiry date

    IV The particular share on which the contract is based

    A I and II

    B I, II and III

    C I, III and IV

    D I, II, III and IV

6. **If you are depositing cash in August and are worried that rates will fall, which of the following would be an appropriate hedging transaction?**

    A Sell June short sterling

    B Sell September short sterling

    C Buy June short sterling

    D Buy September short sterling

7. **What would be the appropriate hedge ratio when hedging £2,000,000 of equities with the FTSE 100 Index future with a price of 6081?**

    A 65 contracts

    B 329 contracts

    C 32 contracts

    D 33 contracts

8. **If a warrant is priced at £1.70 and has the right to subscribe for £2.00 for a share with a market price of £3.00.**

    A The warrant has time value of 70p

    B The warrant has time value of £1.00

    C The warrant has time value of 30p

    D The warrant has no time value

9. **If a warrant is priced at £2.00 and has the right to subscribe £5.00 for a share with a market price of £3.00. What is the time value of the warrant (in £ to two decimal places)?**

    Important! You should enter the answer only in numbers strictly using this format: 0.00

    Do not include spaces, letters or symbols (but decimal points and commas should be used if indicated).

10. **Five FTSE 100 Index futures are sold at 5850 and bought back at 5870. The tick is 0.5 and the tick value £5. What is the profit/loss?**

   A   £500 profit

   B   £1,000 profit

   C   £1,000 loss

   D   £500 loss

11. **Which of the following statements is true?**

   A   A futures contract does not involve obligations to buy or sell an asset

   B   A future is standardised

   C   A future requires delivery of an asset

   D   A long future is the equivalent of a long put/short call at the same exercise price

12. **A call option is in-the-money if**

   A   It has a positive time value

   B   The position is in profit

   C   The exercise price is below the asset price

   D   The exercise price is above the asset price

13. **What does 'LCH' in the acronym LCH.Clearnet stand for?**

   A   Local Capital Holder

   B   Limited Cash Handler

   C   London Clearing House

   D   Long Convergence Hedger

14. **If a warrant on its expiry date has the right to subscribe for a share at a price of £3.00 and the share price is £5.00**

   A   The warrant has a time value of £5.00

   B   The warrant has a time value of £3.00

   C   The warrant has a time value of £2.00

   D   The warrant has no time value

15. **Which of the following indices is used as the basis for a NYSE Liffe stock index future?**

   A   FT Ordinary Share Index

   B   FT All-Share Index

   C   FTSE 100 Index

   D   FTSE 350 Index

16.   When a warrant is out-of-the-money

A   Its exercise price equals the underlying share price

B   Its exercise price is less than the underlying share price

C   Its exercise price is more than the underlying share price

D   It is just about to expire worthless

17.   All of the following are true of interest rate swaps, except

A   They are commonly based upon LIBOR and a fixed rate

B   They are used commonly by companies and individuals

C   They can be based upon two different currencies

D   They are usually exceedingly liquid instruments in their simplest forms

18.   An investor wishes to find out where covered warrants are traded in the UK. When asked by the investor which market he should go to, your response would be that covered warrants

A   Do not trade in the UK, and that the investor would have to go to the NYSE to trade covered warrants

B   Trade over-the-counter, as they are OTC products

C   Trade on the London Stock Exchange

D   Trade on NYSE Liffe, the main derivatives exchange in London

19.   Which of the following best describes the measure of sensitivity of the change in the option price known as 'theta'?

A   The sensitivity of change in the option price with respect to a change in the underlying asset price is known as theta

B   The sensitivity of change in the option price with respect to a change in the volatility of the underlying asset is known as theta

C   The sensitivity of the change in the option price with respect to a change to the passing of interest rates is known as theta

D   The sensitivity of the change in the option price with respect to a change to the passing of time is known as theta

20.   What rights does a warrant give to the holder?

I   The right to buy a new share

II   The potential obligation to buy a new share

III   The right to sell a new share

A   I and II

B   II and III

C   II only

D   I only

21. A convertible was issued several years ago at £103 per £100 of nominal value with the right to subscribe for 30 shares. The existing share price is £3 and the market price of the convertible is £95. What is the conversion premium (in % to 1 decimal place)?

    Important! You should enter the answer only in numbers strictly using this format: 0.0

    Do not include spaces, letters or symbols (but decimal points and commas should be used if indicated).

22. Consider the following statements.

    I   Forwards are standardised OTC products

    II   American options may be exercised before expiry

    III Currency swaps usually involve an exchange of principal

    Which statements are true?

    A I and II

    B I and III

    C II and III

    D All of them

23. **What is the notional coupon on the long gilt future?**

    A 4%

    B 5%

    C 6%

    D 7%

24. An investor went short 62 FTSE 100 contracts when the index stood at 5200. If he closed out when the index level was 4900 what profit was made?

    A +372,000

    B +186,000

    C −186,000

    D −372,000

25. **Consider the following statements.**

    I   It will take more futures to hedge a portfolio with a beta of 0.8 than it will to hedge an accurate tracker of the same value

    II   A CDS is a securitised investment vehicle into which risky assets can be transferred

    III   No sterling swaps require an exchange of principal

    Which are false?

    A   I and II

    B   I and III

    C   II and III

    D   All are false

26. **An investor who has a short straddle position expects**

    A   Prices to increase

    B   Prices to decrease

    C   Price volatility to increase

    D   Price volatility to decrease

27. **What is the percentage hedge efficiency if when the share price rises 10% from its original price of 120, the futures price rises 9% from its original price of 124 (to the nearest one %)?**

    Important! You should enter the answer only in numbers strictly using this format: 00

    Do not include spaces, letters or symbols (but decimal points and commas should be used if indicated).

    ```
    ┌─────────────┐
    │             │
    │             │
    └─────────────┘
    ```

28. **An investor wishes to hedge a £30m deposit against a fall in rates. What action should he take with the Short Sterling future?**

    A   Long 60 contracts

    B   Long 30 contracts

    C   Short 30 contracts

    D   Short 60 contracts

29. **A day trader sells 5,000 FTSE 100 index futures short at the start of the day when the index starts at 5400. He buys 3,000 back midday when the index has moved to 5100 and buys the remaining 2000 back at the end of the day when the index is 5200. What is his profit or loss?**

    A   +£15m

    B   +£13m

    C   +£10m

    D   –£15m

30. **What would be the impact on an options price of an increase in interest rates?**

	CALL PREMIUM	PUT PREMIUM
A	Up	Up
B	Up	Down
C	Down	Up
D	Down	Down

31. **An investor has entered into an interest rate swap under which they pay 5% fixed and receive LIBOR. If LIBOR is 5.25% what is paid/received?**

A   5% paid, 5.25% received

B   5.25% paid, 5% received

C   0.25% paid, nothing received

D   0.25% received, noting paid

32. **Consider the following statements.**

I   Initial margin is a returnable deposit based on the worst probable one day price movement

II   Initial margin is only payable by futures buyers

III   Variation margin must be paid in cash

Which statements are true?

A   I and II

B   I and III

C   II and III

D   I, II and III

33. **Which of the following is not a characteristic of futures?**

A   Standardisation of quantities

B   Standardisation of delivery dates

C   Standardisation of asset

D   Standardisation of strike prices

34. **A convertible was bought at a price of £102 but is now worth £102.50. It gives the right to convert into 40 shares that are currently priced at £2.40, though they were priced at £2.30 when the convertible was bought. What is the current conversion premium?**

A   6.25%

B   6.77%

C   10.87%

D   11.41%

35. **Consider the following statements.**

    I   The unit of trade for the short sterling future is £500,000

    II The tick size on the FTSE 100 future is 0.5

    III The long gilt future coupon is cash settled

    Which are true?

    A   I and II

    B   I and III

    C   II and III

    D   I, II and III

36. **Consider the following statements.**

    I   A call option with a strike price below the current share price is in-the-money

    II A put option with a strike price above the current share price is out-of-the-money

    III Time value can never exceed the total premium

    Which statements are true?

    A   I and II

    B   I and III

    C   II and III

    D   I, II and III

37. **What is a tranche of a CDO?**

    A   A class of securities a CDO invests in

    B   A method of issuing securities

    C   A class of securities a CDO issues

    D   A method of investing in securities

38. **A synthetic CDO is an investment vehicle that**

    A   Invests in a portfolio of risky securities

    B   Invests in high quality debt and boosts its income by selling CDSs

    C   Avoids risk by buying CDSs

    D   Only invests in high quality debt to offer a very safe return

39. **A protective put position entails an investor being**

    A   Long in the put, short in the stock

    B   Long in the put, long in the stock

    C   Short in the put, short in the stock

    D   Short in the put, long in the stock

40. **Naked put writing occurs when the writer**

A Does not hold sufficient amounts of the stock to deliver the stock if required

B Does not have sufficient cash in his/her brokerage account to purchase the stock if required

C Does not specify the exercise price

D Writes a put which can be exercised at any time before expiration

---

41. **An 'in-the-money' call option is one where**

A The exercise price is higher than the current stock price

B The exercise price is lower than the current stock price

C The stock has outperformed the option premium

D The stock has underperformed the option premium

---

42. **The variation margin paid in respect of a futures position is based on**

A The price movement that day

B The price movement in the contract to date

C The price movement of the previous day

D The greatest expected price movement on a given day

---

43. **Which is the most risky transaction to undertake in the equity index option markets if the stock market is expected to increase substantially after the transaction is completed?**

A Write an uncovered call option

B Write an uncovered put option

C Buy a call option

D Buy a put option

---

44. **A warrant has a subscription price of £5. The shares are trading at £6.50. The warrant gives the right to subscribe for 4 shares. What is the intrinsic value of the warrant (in £ to two decimal places)?**

Important! You should enter the answer only in numbers strictly using this format: 0.00

Do not include spaces, letters or symbols (but decimal points and commas should be used if indicated).

---

45. **Which of the following is correct regarding interest rate and currency swaps?**

A They always involve the exchange of one fixed and one floating flow

B They are always used by participants based in different countries

C They are exchange traded contracts

D They are based on the notion of comparative advantage

---

46.   **Which of the following are true of warrants?**

I   An increase in the underlying share price will cause the warrant price to increase

II   An increase in the underlying share price will cause the warrant price to decrease

III   An increase in the exercise price of the warrant will cause its price to increase

IV   An increase in the exercise price of the warrant will cause its price to decrease

A   I and III

B   I and IV

C   II and III

D   II and IV

Answers

1. **C**   Buying a put not selling a put would be effective. A long gilt future is a ten-year gilt future

    See Chapter 7 Section 1.1 of your Study Text

2. **A**   When buying any option (either a call or a put option), the maximum amount that the holder can lose is the premium paid. This is still considered risky since it would equate to a 100% loss

    See Chapter 7 Section 1.2 of your Study Text

3. **D**   Initial margin is a refundable good faith deposit based on the worst probable one day's loss. It is calculated as a net figure by Ice Clear Europe. Since III involves an element of netting-off, it would not require additional margin

    See Chapter 7 Section 1.1 of your Study Text

4. **D**   Since the call option is out-of-the-money (it has no profit if exercised now), it will have no intrinsic value. All of the premium is time value

    See Chapter 7 Section 1.4 of your Study Text

5. **D**   A put option gives the holder the right to sell a standard quantity of a specified asset on a fixed future date at a price agreed today

    See Chapter 7 Section 1.2 of your Study Text

6. **D**   September is the best hedge, as it relates to future interest rates for three months from September

    See Chapter 7 Section 1.1 of your Study Text

7. **D** $\dfrac{£2,000,000}{6081 \times £10}$ = 33 to nearest whole contract

    See Chapter 7 Section 1.1 of your Study Text

8. **A**   Warrant price – Intrinsic value = Time value

    £1.70 – (£3 – £2) = 70p

    See Chapter 7 Section 3.2 of your Study Text

9. **2.00**   The warrant has no immediate appeal, zero intrinsic value, but does have the chance of making future profits (time value) so its entire value of £2.00 is time value

    See Chapter 7 Section 3.2 of your Study Text

10. **C**   40 ticks × £5 × 5 contracts = £1,000

    The future was bought for more than it was sold, so a loss will occur

    See Chapter 7 Section 1.1 of your Study Text

11. **B**   A future involves an obligation to buy or sell an asset. These obligations are either for physical delivery or cash settlement. A long put/short call position would create a synthetic short future position

    See Chapter 7 Section 1.1 of your Study Text

12. **C** If you have the right to buy at below the market price. The option would have intrinsic value

See Chapter 7 Section 1.4 of your Study Text

13. **C** ICE Clear Europe and LCH.Clearnet are responsible for administering and guaranteeing the performance of the majority of exchange-traded derivatives contracts in the UK

See Chapter 7 Section 1.1 of your Study Text

14. **D** Since the warrant is on its expiry date, it has no potential to make any further profit in the future and as a result would have no time value, the price paid for the chance of further profits

See Chapter 7 Section 3.2 of your Study Text

15. **C** The FTSE 100 Index future is available for trading on NYSE Liffe and is cash settled at £10 per point. It has four potential delivery months, being March, June, September and December

See Chapter 7 Section 1.1 of your Study Text

16. **C** Thus, it has no intrinsic value, only time value if before expiry

See Chapter 7 Section 1.2 and Chapter 7 Section 3.4 of your Study Text

17. **B** There is no role for an individual in the swaps market as the principals involved are generally large

See Chapter 7 Section 2.3 of your Study Text

18. **C** Covered warrants trade on the London Stock Exchange (LSE) in the UK, and settlement is carried out through CREST. Typically, covered warrants are issued by investment banks rather than by the company themselves, who issue ordinary warrants. The two types of covered warrant are call warrants (the right to buy) and put warrants (the right to sell)

See Chapter 7 Section 3.2 of your Study Text

19. **D** Theta is described as the sensitivity in the option price with respect to the passing of Time. Delta is with respect to a change in the underlying asset price, Vega is with respect to a change in the Volatility of the underlying asset, and Rho is with respect to a change in interest Rates

See Chapter 7 Section 1.4 of you Study Text

20. **D** Warrants offer investors the right to buy a new share at set date(s) in the future

See Chapter 7 Section 2.3 of your Study Text

21. **5.7** $\frac{£95}{30}$ = £3.17 per share, therefore at a premium of 17p over the price of £3

$\frac{17p}{£3}$ = 0.05667 or 5.7%

See Chapter 7 Section 3.1 of your Study Text

22. **C** Forwards are not standardised

See Chapter 7 Section 1.2 and Chapter 7 Section 2.3 of your Study Text

23. **A** The long gilt future has a 4% notional coupon

See Chapter 7 Section 1.1 of your Study Text

24. **B** Profit = Ticks quote movement × Tick value × No. contracts

= 600 × £5 × 62 = £186,000

See Chapter 7 Section 1.1 of your Study Text

25. **A** I A portfolio with a beta of 0.8 will only need 80% of the contracts required to hedge an accurate tracker of the same value

II A CDS is a form of credit insurance. The definition given is a CDO

III True – only currency swaps that are not wholly sterling do require an exchange of principal

See Chapter 7 Section 2.3 of your Study Text

26. **D** A price volatility decrease is the motivation for a short straddle

See Chapter 7 Section 1.2 of your Study Text

27. **93** Hedge efficiency = $\dfrac{\text{Absolute gain on future}}{\text{Absolute gain on cash market}} = \dfrac{124 \times 9\%}{120 \times 10\%} = 0.93$ or 93%

See Chapter 7 Section 1.1 of your Study Text

28. **A** Depositors go long to hedge. One contract hedges £500,000 principal, hence 60 are needed to hedge £30m

See Chapter 7 Section 1.1 of your Study Text

29. **B**

	pts	
Sell	5400	5400
Buy	5100	5200
Gain	300	200
	= 600 ticks	= 400 ticks

Profit =	ticks × tick value × no. contracts	
	600 × £5 × 3,000 =	9,000,000
	400 × £5 × 2,000 =	4,000,000
		13,000,000

See Chapter 7 Section 1.1 of your Study Text

30. **B** An increase in interest rates increases the value of a call but reduces the value of a put

See Chapter 7 Section 1.4 of your Study Text

31. **D** Interest rate swap flows are netted hence 0.25% (5.25% – 5.00%) will be received

See Chapter 7 Section 2.3 of your Study Text

32. **B** II False – initial margin is paid by both buyer and seller

See Chapter 7 Section 1.1 of your Study Text

33. **D**   Futures do not have strike prices

See Chapter 7 Section 1.1 of your Study Text

34. **B**   The current premium must be based on current prices

$$\text{Premium} = \frac{(102.50 / 40) - 2.40}{2.40} = 0.0677 \text{ or } 6.77\%$$

See Chapter 7 Section 3.1 of your Study Text

35. **A**   The gilt future is physically settled through the delivery of £100,000 nominal of gilts

See Chapter 7 Section 1.1 of your Study Text

36. **B**   II   A put option is out of the money when the share price is above the strike price

See Chapter 7 Section 1.4 of your Study Text

37. **C**   CDOs issue various tranches of securities

See Chapter 7 Section 4.1 of your Study Text

38. **B**   Synthetic CDOs invest in high quality debt and boost income by selling CDSs, increasing return at an increased risk

See Chapter 7 Section 4.1 of your Study Text

39. **B**   The put increases in value if the share price falls, thus protecting the portfolio value in total

See Chapter 7 Section 1.2 of your Study Text

40. **B**   The writer of a put is required to buy the stock if the holder exercises

See Chapter 7 Section 1.2 of your Study Text

41. **B**   A call option is the right to buy an asset and, if this is in-the-money, then the option has intrinsic value, i.e. the strike price is lower than the value of the underlying asset

See Chapter 7 Section 1.4 of your Study Text

42. **C**   The variation margin is a daily marking-to-market procedure, ensuring that losses on derivative positions are paid on the exchange

See Chapter 7 Section 1.1 of your Study Text

43. **A**   The short call is a bearish trade with an unlimited maximum loss if it is uncovered

See Chapter 7 Section 1.2 and Chapter 7 Section 1.2 of your Study Text

44. **6.00**   The intrinsic value is the difference between the subscription price of £5.00 and the current share price of £6.50, multiplied by the number of shares the warrant covers.

See Chapter 7 Section 1.4 of your Study Text

45. **D**   The first swaps were created as a result of the theory of comparative advantage, whereby one party could borrow in one country and swap with a counterparty in another country. The same applied with fixed and floating rates. Now that swaps are done through a dealer this is less clear, but still true

See Chapter 7 Section 2.3 and Chapter 7 Section 2.3 of your Study Text

46. **B**   A warrant is effectively a long-term call option

       See Chapter 7 Section 3.2 of your Study Text

8. Alternative Investments

Questions

1. **Which of the following is not a common feature of collectables?**

   A They can be difficult to value

   B They generate high income

   C They are expensive to store

   D Dealing costs are high

2. **Which of the following is not a class of commodity?**

   A Hards

   B Energy

   C Softs

   D Biotechnology

3. **All of the following could be considered to be significant influences on commodity prices, except**

   A Weather

   B Tariffs

   C Interest rates

   D Substitution

4. **Consider the following statements.**

   I   Commodities have volatile values

   II Collectible holding costs are low

   III Commodities provide a good hedge against natural disasters

   Which statements are true?

   A I and II

   B I and III

   C II and III

   D I, II and III

5. **Which of the following is not a characteristic expected of collectibles investment?**

   A No income

   B Long term real return

   C Low volatility

   D Diversification through low correlation

6. **Coffee may be classified as**

A Collectibles

B Hards

C Softs

D Energy

7. **Which of the following are among the advantages of investing in alternatives?**

    I   Low transaction costs

    II   Low correlations with other asset classes

    III   High liquidity

A I only

B II only

C I and II

D I and III

8. **Consider the following statements.**

    I   ETC is an indirect route to investing in collectibles

    II   Collectibles have low marketability

    III   Commodities do not deteriorate over time

Which statements are true?

A I and II

B II only

C II and III

D I and III

9. **Which of the following characteristics distinguishes commodities from collectibles?**

A Income generation

B Volatility

C Marketability

D Holding costs

10. **Which of the following is not a possible reason for holding hards in a portfolio?**

A Hedge against inflation

B Hedge against natural disasters

C Portfolio diversification

D Income generation

11. **Which of the following is not a requirement in order for a company to qualify as a REIT?**

    A UK resident closed-ended company

    B Pay out at least 90% of its net taxable profits to investors

    C Obtain a listing on the LSE main market

    D No one investor owning more than 10% of the share of the REIT

12. **What are property bonds?**

    I   A form of indirect investment into property

    II   A scheme sold mostly through insurance companies

    III A scheme where yields move inversely to property prices

    A I only

    B II and III

    C I, II and III

    D III only

13. **Which of the following is not a characteristic of property?**

    A Homogenous

    B Higher transaction costs

    C Indivisible compared to other investments

    D Illiquid

14. **A property is bought for £425,000. Legal fees are £2,000 and estate agent's fees are 2%. What is the total price paid assuming the appropriate rate of Stamp Duty Land Tax is 3%?**

    A £448,250

    B £439,750

    C £435,500

    D £427,000

15. **Which of the following is not a typical characteristic of commercial property?**

    A Medium to long term leases

    B Tenant repairing

    C Mainly income returns

    D Annual rent reviews

16. **Consider the following statements**

  I   The main class of property investors is private individuals

  II   Residential property investors primarily seek capital returns

  III   The supply of property is elastic

Which of the above are true?

A   I is true, II and III are false

B   II is false, I and III are true

C   III is true, I and II are false

D   I and III are false, II is true

17. **Consider the following costs**

  I   Estate agent's fees

  II   Legal fees

  III   Stamp duty land tax

Which are paid by a buyer?

A   I and II

B   I and III

C   II and III

D   All the above

18. **Which of the following is not a usual valuation method?**

A   Comparative

B   Profits

C   Differentiated

D   Investment

19. **Which of the following is not a method of direct property investment?**

A   Freehold

B   REIT

C   Life interest

D   Leasehold

20. **Which is not true of a REIT?**

A   UK resident open ended fund

B   Must pay out at least 90% of profits

C   Requires a listing

D   Must receive at least 75% of profits from property letting business

21. A property is sold for £600,000. Stamp duty land tax is 4%, estate agent's fees are 2%, legal fees are £3,000. What is the net received (to the nearest £1)?

    Important! You should enter the answer only in numbers strictly using this format: 000,000

    Do not include spaces, letters or symbols (but decimal points and commas should be used if indicated).

    ┌─────────────┐
    │   │
    │   │
    └─────────────┘

22. Which of the following is not a method of indirect property investment?

    A   Limited liability partnership

    B   Property OEIC

    C   ETC

    D   Derivatives

23. Which of the following is not a common characteristic of property investment?

    A   Government intervention

    B   High management costs

    C   Homogeneity

    D   Inelastic supply

24. Consider the following three statements.

    I   Property bonds are issued by life assurance companies

    II   REITs are closed-ended funds

    III   Limited liability partnership suffer SDLT

    Which are true?

    A   All are true

    B   I and II are true

    C   I and III are true

    D   II and III are true

25. Consider the following statements.

    I   Freehold is the highest form of direct property ownership

    II   Commercial property leases are typically medium to long term

    III   REITs can list on AIM

    Which are true?

    A   All are true

    B   I and II are true

    C   I and III are true

    D   II and III are true

26. **Which of the following is most likely to be classified as an indirect property investment?**

A   Buying a house

B   Investing in an office

C   Investing in a REIT

D   Buying a flat with the intention of renting it out

27. **Which of the following are characteristics of the property market?**

I   A decentralised market

II   Loose government regulation

III   Management cost considerations

A   I only

B   I and III

C   II and III

D   I, II and III

28. **Which of the following are possible explanations for the supply of property being relatively inelastic?**

I   Supply can be readily increased

II   Planning constraints

III   Geographical immobility

A   III only

B   I and II

C   II and III

D   I, II and III

29. **Which of the following is not true of property?**

A   It is homogenous

B   It is indivisible

C   Transaction costs may be high

D   There is no centralised market

30. **The main exchanges for energy derivatives are**

A   NYME and NYSE Liffe

B   Liffe and ICE

C   CME and NYSE Liffe

D   NYME and ICE

31. **The primary exchange for agricultural derivatives is**

A   NYSE Liffe

B   NYME

C   CME

D   LME

32. **Which of the following are genuine property derivatives?**

    I   IPD Index swaps

    II   FTSE UK Commercial Property Index

    III   Property income certificates

A   I and II

B   I and III

C   II and III

D   I, II and III

33. **Which of the following is not a valid commodity index?**

A   Dow Jones-AIG

B   FTSE World Commodity Index

C   Goldman Sachs Commodities Index

D   Rogers International Commodity Index

34. **Which of the following statements are true? Commodity futures are negatively correlated to**

    I   Equities

    II   Bonds

    III   Inflation

A   I and II

B   I and III

C   II and III

D   All are true

35. **Which of the following is not an index of credit risk?**

A   CDX

B   CDX.EM

C   iTraxx

D   IPD

Answers

1. **B** They tend not to generate income

   See Chapter 8 Section 1.4 of your Study Text

2. **D** Biotechnology is not a category

   See Chapter 8 Section 1.1 of your Study Text

3. **C** Although interest rates may have an effect on individual producers, it is the least likely of these factors to have a significant influence on commodity prices

   See Chapter 8 Section 1.3 of your Study Text

4. **B** Collectibles have high holding costs

   See Chapter 8 Section 1.4 of your Study Text

5. **C** Collectibles have high volatility

   See Chapter 8 Section 1.4 of your Study Text

6. **C** Coffee = foodstuffs, ie softs

   See Chapter 8 Section 1.1 of your Study Text

7. **B** The downside of alternatives include high transaction costs and illiquidity, but they can offer diversification benefits.

   See Chapter 8 Section 1.4 of your Study Text

8. **B** I   ECT is an indirect form of commodity investment
        III Softs may deteriorate over time

   See Chapter 8 Section 1.1 and Chapter 8 Section 1.4 of your Study Text

9. **C** Collectibles have low marketability/liquidity, the liquidity of commodities is high

   See Chapter 8 Section 1.1 and Chapter 8 Section 1.4 of your Study Text

10. **D** Commodities do not generate income

    See Chapter 8 Section 1.1 of your Study Text

11. **C** The company must obtain a listing, though this does not have to be on the main market, it may be on AIM or any recognised overseas market

    See Chapter 8 Section 2.7 of your Study Text

12. **C** All of these apply. The yield on a property can be calculated by taking the rental income and dividing it by the property's value. As property values increase it may take some time before rental values increase, creating in the short term a drop in yields

    See Chapter 8 Section 2.1 of your Study Text

13. **A** Property comes in all different shapes and sizes making them heterogeneous rather than homogenous. All the others are characteristics of property

    See Chapter 8 Section 2.2 of your Study Text

14. **B**

	£
Purchase price	425,000
Add Legal fees	2,000
SDLT (425,000 × 3%)	12,750
	439,750

Estate agent's fees are paid by the seller

See Chapter 8 Section 2.5 of your Study Text

15. **D** Commercial leases normally have rent reviews every 5 years

See Chapter 8 Section 2.4 of your Study Text

16. **D** I The main class of property investors is pension and life companies
II Residential property investors primarily seek capital returns
III Supply is inelastic

See Chapter 8 Section 2.2 of your Study Text

17. **C** Estate agent's fees are payable by sellers

See Chapter 8 Section 2.5 of your Study Text

18. **C** Differentiated is not a usual valuation method

See Chapter 8 Section 2.5 of your Study Text

19. **B** REITs are indirect investment vehicles

See Chapter 8 Section 2.7 of your Study Text

20. **A** REITs are UK resident *closed-ended* funds

See Chapter 8 Section 2.7 of your Study Text

21. **585,000**

	£
Sale proceeds	600,000
Less Estate agent's fees (600,000 × 2%)	(12,000)
Legal fees	(3,000)
Net proceeds received	585,000

Note stamp duty land tax is only payable by the buyer

See Chapter 8 Section 2.5 of your Study Text

22. **C** ETC = exchange traded commodity, not a property investment

See Chapter 8 Section 2.7 of your Study Text

23. **C** Property is heterogeneous not homogeneous

See Chapter 8 Section 2.8 of your Study Text

24. **A** All are true

See Chapter 8 Section 2.7 of your Study Text

25. **A** Freehold refers to ownership of property into perpetuity and is the highest form of direct holding. Commercial property leases typically have a minimum term of 5 years and are often much longer. Originally REITs could not be listed on AIM but, since 6 April 2012 they have been permitted to do so, and they may also be listed on a recognised overseas exchange

See Chapter 8 Section 2.7 of your Study Text

26. **C** Investing in an REIT (Real Estate Investment Trust) is an investment in a fund. The fund will then subsequently purchase property, but it will not be directly held by the investor in the REIT

See Chapter 8 Section 2.7 of your Study Text

27. **B** The property market is heavily regulated, with various legislation in place such as the 1977 Rent Act and the Housing Acts in force. Other state regulations, such as planning permission and controls also add to the regulatory burden. Property is also geographically immobile, reflecting a decentralised market place

See Chapter 8 Section 2.8 of your Study Text

28. **C** The supply of property cannot be readily increased, due to planning constraints and the availability of land to build on, as land is said to be a finite resource. It is also true that property is said to be geographically immobile. Therefore, it is fair to say that the supply of property is relatively inelastic. This is also why property prices tend to be dominated by the economic forces of demand, rather than supply

See Chapter 8 Section 2.8 of your Study Text

29. **A** Property investments tend to be unique or heterogeneous in terms of location, design, condition or size. The general property market is highly decentralised, and costs may be high through repairs and maintenance

See Chapter 8 Section 2.8 of your Study Text

30. **D** The main exchanges for energy derivatives are NYME and ICE Futures Europe

See Chapter 8 Section 1.1 of you Study Text

31. **C** The Chicago Mercantile Exchange (CME)

See Chapter 8 Section 1.1 of you Study Text

32. **B** IPD index swaps and property income certificates

See Chapter 8 Section 2.3 of you Study Text

33. **B** The other three are valid commodities indices

See Chapter 8 Section 1.2 of you Study Text

34. **A** Commodities (and commodity futures) are positively correlated to inflation

See Chapter 8 Section 1.1 of your Study Text

35. **D** IPD = Investment property data bank, a provider of property indices

See Chapter 8 Section 2.3 of your Study Text

9. Portfolio Management

Questions

1. As a portfolio becomes increasingly well diversified, which of the following will be driven towards zero?

    A   Total risk

    B   Systematic risk

    C   Non-systematic risk

    D   Market risk

2. An investor can choose between four portfolios with the following expected return and standard deviations.

	EXPECTED RETURN	STANDARD DEVIATION OF RETURN
A	8%	20%
B	6%	21%
C	8%	21%
D	7%	22%

    Which portfolio should the investor choose?

    A   Portfolio A

    B   Portfolio B

    C   Portfolio C

    D   Portfolio D

3. If a security has a total risk of 30% and a systematic risk of 20% (both in standard deviation terms), what is the security's non-systematic risk, expressed in standard deviation terms to the nearest percentage point?

    A   3.0%

    B   10.0%

    C   22.4%

    D   50.0%

4. **Consider the following statements**

   I   The Jensen measure of portfolio performance is the same for a well-diversified portfolio representing all of an investor's wealth and a portfolio representing only part of an investor's wealth

   II   A beta of zero suggests that a portfolio return is perfectly correlated with the market return

   III   The Sharpe and Treynor measures of portfolio performance are identical in a bull market

Which of the above are correct?

A I, II and III

B I only

C I and III

D None of the above

---

5. Securities A and B have expected returns of 12% and 16%, respectively. If 25% of a portfolio is invested in security A with the rest invested in B, what is the expected percentage portfolio return (to the nearest one %)?

Important! You should enter the answer only in numbers strictly using this format: 00

Do not include spaces, letters or symbols (but decimal points and commas should be used if indicated).

```
┌──────────────┐
│              │
│              │
└──────────────┘
```

---

6. **Positive correlation implies that returns on two securities**

A Move in the same direction to the same extent

B Move in the same direction to a smaller extent

C On average, move in the same direction to the same extent

D On average, move in the same direction

---

7. **Uncorrelated securities**

A Move together on average

B Move in opposite directions on average

C Show no relationship

D Show an exact relationship

---

8. **Which of the following is true of idiosyncratic risk?**

A It is related to market forces and can be diversified away

B It is related to market forces and cannot be diversified away

C It is specific to an investment and can be diversified away

D It is specific to an investment and cannot be diversified away

---

9. **If the market crashes over the next six months what would we expect to happen to the share's correlation with the market?**

    A Remain stable

    B Move towards 0

    C Move towards +1

    D Move towards –1

10. **The total risk of an investment is 25%. Its unsystematic risk is 15%. What is the percentage market risk (to the nearest one %)?**

    Important! You should enter the answer only in numbers strictly using this format: 00

    Do not include spaces, letters or symbols (but decimal points and commas should be used if indicated).

11. **The total risk of an investment is 20%. Its specific risk is 16%. What is its idiosyncratic risk?**

    A 20%

    B 16%

    C 12%

    D 4%

12. **Four securities offer the following risks and returns.**

	RETURN %	RISK %
I	16	6
II	17	5
III	18	7
IV	19	8

    Which should be considered by a risk-averse investor?

    A II only

    B I, II and IV

    C I and III

    D II, III and IV

13. The market risk on an investment is 10%; the risk of the market portfolio is 12%; the risk-free return is 8% and the market risk premium is 5%. What is the expected return on the investment (in % to 1 decimal place)?

Important! You should enter the answer only in numbers strictly using this format: 00.0

Do not include spaces, letters or symbols (but decimal points and commas should be used if indicated).

14. An investment tends to move against the market but is less volatile. Which of the following betas is consistent with this?

A 1.2

B 0.4

C −0.6

D −1.8

15. An investment has a beta of 1.2. Market risk is 12%, risk premium is 8% and the risk-free rate is 7%. What is the expected return (in % to 1 decimal place)?

Important! You should enter the answer only in numbers strictly using this format: 00.0

Do not include spaces, letters or symbols (but decimal points and commas should be used if indicated).

16. An investment is expected to return 14% when the market is returning 16%. Its beta is 0.8. What is the risk-free rate (in % to 1 decimal place)?

Important! You should enter the answer only in numbers strictly using this format: 0.0

Do not include spaces, letters or symbols (but decimal points and commas should be used if indicated).

17. An investment on average moves with the market, but is more volatile. Its beta is

A Positive and greater than one

B Positive, but less than one

C Negative and greater than one

D Negative, but less than one

18. **Which of the following portfolios would be selected by a risk-averse investor?**

	RETURN %	RISK %
A	18	6
B	17	7
C	16	6
D	18	7

19. **A portfolio is fairly valued under the Capital Asset Pricing Model. The risk-free return is 6%; the market return 18%; the portfolio systematic risk 15% and the market risk is 20%. What return may be expected from the portfolio?**

    A 12%

    B 15%

    C 18%

    D 20%

20. **The beta of a security is 1.2 and the market risk is 18%. What is the covariance of the returns between the security and the market?**

    A 18.0

    B 21.6

    C 324.0

    D 388.8

21. **An investor must choose between the following portfolios. Which would be considered as possibilities?**

	RETURN	RISK
I	17	15
II	15	17
III	19	19
IV	18	18

    A II only

    B I, II and IV

    C I only

    D I, III and IV

22. **If an investment on average moves against the market but is more volatile, then its beta is**

    A Positive and greater than one

    B Positive but less than one

    C Negative and greater than one

    D Negative but less than one

23. **Which of the following investments would a rational investor choose?**

SECURITY	RETURN	STANDARD DEVIATION
A	6%	10%
B	7%	10%
C	8%	8%
D	9%	8%

A   Security A

B   Security B

C   Security C

D   Security D

24. **Which of the following cannot be reduced through diversification?**

   I   Systematic risk

   II   Undiversifiable risk

   III   Specific risk

   IV   Market risk

A   I, II and III

B   I, II and IV

C   II, III and IV

D   II and IV

25. **Which of the following is a measure of the relationship between securities within a portfolio?**

A   Variance

B   Standard deviation

C   Arithmetic mean

D   Covariance

26. **Which of the following would be the beta of the market portfolio?**

A   Beta = 0

B   Beta > 1

C   Beta < 1

D   Beta = 1

27. **If a portfolio has a beta of greater than 1, which of the following could be the portfolio return, where the market return is 8%?**

    I   6%

    II   8%

    III 9%

    IV 12%

A I only

B I and II

C III and IV

D II only

28. **Which of the following can increase the overall risk of a portfolio?**

    I   Selecting riskier stocks

    II   Using borrowed funds to increase the leverage of the portfolio

    III Using futures or options

    IV Selecting stocks that are negatively correlated to each other

A I and II

B I, II and III

C I, III and IV

D III and IV

29. **When a stock has a beta of less than one, this indicates that**

A It will on average give a return below the yield on the market

B It will on average give a return in excess of that of a stock with a beta of greater than one

C It will have a high level of systematic risk

D It will have a high level of unsystematic risk

30. **Beta could be correctly described as**

    I   The correlation coefficient of the security and the market

    II   The proportion of a given fund that would have to be invested in the market portfolio to create a given risk/return profile

    III An index of a security's systematic risk relative to that of the market

A I, II and III

B III only

C II and III

D I and III

31. Which of the following risks will normally remain within a randomly selected portfolio of securities?

    I   Market risk

    II   Specific risk

    III   Systematic risk

    IV   Diversifiable risk

A I and II

B II and IV

C I and III

D III and IV

32. With regard to the following portfolios, which is said to have the highest beta according to the Capital Asset Pricing Model assuming the same risk free rate of return?

PORTFOLIO	MARKET RETURN	PORTFOLIO RETURN EXPECTED
A	7%	7%
B	7%	10%
C	7%	6%
D	7%	14%

A Portfolio A

B Portfolio B

C Portfolio C

D Portfolio D

33. If the beta of a portfolio is 0.8, the risk-free rate is 4% and the market risk premium is 6%, what is the expected return from the portfolio?

A 8.8%

B 5.6%

C 8.0%

D 1.6%

34. An investment is sensitive to two factors, A and B. The risk premia for each factor is 2% and 1% respectively. The investment has unit sensitivity to factor B and a sensitivity of 0.8 to factor A. If the risk-free rate is 4% what is the expected return (in % to 1 decimal place)?

Important! You should enter the answer only in numbers strictly using this format: 0.0

Do not include spaces, letters or symbols (but decimal points and commas should be used if indicated).

35. A stock has a beta of 0.8 and the risk-free return is 9%. If the market return is 15%, what would be the expected return on the stock (in % to 1 decimal place)?

   Important! You should enter the answer only in numbers strictly using this format: 00.0

   Do not include spaces, letters or symbols (but decimal points and commas should be used if indicated).

   ┌─────────────┐
   │   │
   │   │
   └─────────────┘

36. Which of the portfolios with the following betas, made up of five equally weighted shares, will most closely track the market?

Portfolio A	+1.0, +0.7, −0.1, +0.6, +1.2
Portfolio B	+1.2, +0.8, +0.3, +0.7, +0.9
Portfolio C	+1.7, +0.2, −0.2, +1.3, −0.3
Portfolio D	+1.0, +1.1, +1.2, −0.1, +0.4

   A Portfolio A

   B Portfolio B

   C Portfolio C

   D Portfolio D

37. If a portfolio has no specific or systematic risk, what rate of return will be obtained?

   A Risk-free rate

   B Market return

   C Market risk premium

   D Nil

38. A rational investor will

   A Expect to receive a higher return on an investment that has a lower risk

   B Expect to receive a lower return on an investment that has a lower risk

   C Expect to receive a higher return on an investment that has a higher risk

   D Expect to receive a lower return on an investment that has a higher risk

39. All of the following cannot be reduced through diversification, except for

   A Systematic risk

   B Undiversifiable risk

   C Specific risk

   D Market risk

40. If the beta of a portfolio is 1.2, the risk-free rate is 5% and the expected return of the market is 9%, what is the risk premium (in % to 1 decimal place)?

Important! You should enter the answer only in numbers strictly using this format: 0.0

Do not include spaces, letters or symbols (but decimal points and commas should be used if indicated).

41. If the portfolio has a beta of 0.75, the market premium is 6%, and the expected market return is 11%, what is the expected return from the portfolio?

A 9.75%

B 9.5%

C 5.75%

D 5%

42. A drawdown of 20% implies what?

A 20% has been withdrawn from an investment

B 20% income has been received from an investment

C The value of an investment has fallen by 20% from its peak

D The total return on the investment is 20%

43. The best way to diversify is to

A Pick shares from across the whole market

B Pick shares from one market sector

C Choose shares that are uncorrelated

D Choose shares that are correlated

44. The expected return on an investment is 7.46% when the risk-free rate is 4.5%. The investment is sensitive to two factors F_1 and F_2 that have risk premia of 1.6% and 1.5% respectively. If the sensitivity to F_2 is 0.8 what is the sensitivity to F_1?

A 0.9

B 1.0

C 1.1

D 1.2

45. **The value by which an investment may fall over a given period of time to a given level of probability is**

A   Drawdown

B   VAR

C   Semi-deviation

D   Tracking error

46. **Consider the following statements**

    I   APT is a single factor model

    II   APT does not specify the factors

    III   The assessment of APT betas is simple and reliable

Which of the statements are true?

A   None of the statements

B   I only

C   II only

D   III only

47. **The effectiveness of any diversification primarily depends on**

A   Standard deviation

B   Autocorrelation

C   Statistical significance

D   Correlation

48. **Drawdown is 8%. What does this signify?**

A   The value has fallen by 8% since investing

B   8% of the initial investment has been withdrawn

C   The investment is yielding 8%

D   The investment is 8% below its peak value

49. **Suppose a pension fund's trustees have set a beta for a fund containing UK shares of 0.85. If the risk-free rate of return is 8% and the return on the FT All Share Index for the last year was 15%, the return on a benchmark portfolio suggested by the CAPM is**

A   5.95%

B   9.25%

C   13.95%

D   20.75%

50. The Capital Asset Pricing Model asserts that portfolio returns are best explained by

A Economic factors

B Specific risk

C Systematic risk

D Diversification

---

51. Within the context of the Capital Asset Pricing Model (CAPM), assume

Expected return on the market = 15%

Risk-free rate = 8%

Actual rate of return on XYZ security = 17%

Beta of XYZ security = 1.25

Which one of the following is correct?

A XYZ is overpriced

B XYZ is fairly priced

C XYZ's alpha is –0.25%

D XYZ's alpha is 0.25%

---

52. An investment has a beta of 1 and an expected return of 11%. An investment with a beta of 1.2 has an expected return of 12.2%. What is the risk free rate (in % to 1 decimal place)?

Important! You should enter the answer only in numbers strictly using this format: 0.0

Do not include spaces, letters or symbols (but decimal points and commas should be used if indicated).

---

53. The covariance of the returns of two securities can be calculated as

A The correlation of the securities divided by the product of their variances

B The correlation of the securities divided by the product of their standard deviations

C The correlation of the securities multiplied by the product of their variances

D The correlation of the securities multiplied by the product of their standard deviations

---

54. A fund has a one week VAR of £1m at a 95% level, what does this mean?

A There is a 95% chance that the fund will be worth £1m at the end of a week

B There is a 95% chance that the fund will lose £1m or more over a week

C The fund is expected to lose £1m or more one week in every 20

D The fund is expected to lose less than £1m one week in every 20

55. **The liabilities of pension funds are predominantly**

    A   Long-term real liabilities

    B   Long-term fixed liabilities

    C   Short-term real liabilities

    D   Short-term fixed liabilities

56. **Which of the following gilts would a higher rate taxpayer find most suitable to invest in if he expected interest rates to fall?**

    A   High coupon shorts

    B   Low coupon shorts

    C   High coupon longs

    D   Low coupon longs

57. **Which of the following is the best description of the long term correlation between bonds and commodities?**

    A   No correlation

    B   Strong positive correlation

    C   Strong negative correlation

    D   Weak positive correlation

58. **Which of the following best describes a yield curve ride?**

    A   A switch out of a short-dated stock into a longer dated issue to exploit a perceived change in the yield curve

    B   A switch out of one bond and into another in order to exploit a difference in the historic pattern of prices between the two bonds

    C   A switch out of the cash market and into the derivatives market in order to enhance the utilisation of assets

    D   A switch out of one bond and into another in order to exploit differences in tax treatment

59. **Which of the following can also be referred to as market timing?**

    A   Tactical asset allocation

    B   Security selection

    C   Strategic asset allocation

    D   Full replication

60. **Which of the following is not one of the main objectives of measuring the performance of a portfolio?**

    A   To monitor the progress of investments

    B   To determine relative performance

    C   To identify fund managers with good historical performance records

    D   To identify the most efficient use of resources available to the fund manager

61. An investor in an indexed equity fund is exposed to which of the following?

       I   Specific risk

      II   Systematic risk

     III   Tracking error

A III only

B I and III

C I and II

D II and III

62. All of the following are main methods adopted by a passive fund manager when constructing an index fund, except

A Full replication

B Sector selection

C Optimisation

D Stratified sampling

63. A fund manager wishes to actively manage his portfolio. He is likely to engage in which of the following?

       I   Tracking

      II   Market timing

     III   Stock selection

A I, II, III

B I only

C II only

D II and III

64. Which of the following assets is said to be relatively illiquid?

A Fixed interest bonds

B Equity securities

C Cash

D Property

65. Which of the following is the best description of passive fund management?

A The trustee does not appraise the performance of the fund manager

B The trustee does not have any involvement with the investment decisions

C The fund manager tries to pick stocks that will outperform the market

D The fund manager attempts to achieve the return on a benchmark of the appropriate risk

66. **The two major approaches to investment management are described as**

    A   Capital growth and income

    B   Equities and debt instruments

    C   Active and passive

    D   Domestic and international securities

67. **Market timing is another description of which of the following?**

    A   Strategic asset allocation

    B   Tactical asset allocation

    C   Security selection

    D   Equity style management

68. **Which of the following is not a fundamental analysis technique?**

    A   Share price charts and patterns

    B   Discounted cash flow valuations

    C   Analysis of economic profit

    D   Analysis of business performance and strategic environment

69. **Which one of the following statements is true?**

    A   UK pension funds hold a higher proportion of their assets in equities than do German and French pension funds

    B   UK pension funds hold the same proportion of their assets in equities as do German and French pension funds

    C   UK pension funds hold a smaller proportion of their assets in equities than do German and French pension funds

    D   UK pension funds hold a higher proportion of their assets in bonds than do German and French pension funds

70. **The required rate of return on a final salary scheme will be dependent on which of the following factors?**

    I   Mortality rates

    II   Investments returns

    III   Length of service

    A   I and II

    B   II and III

    C   I and III

    D   I, II and III

71. **Which of the following are valid approaches to indexation?**

    I   Full replication

    II   Stratified sampling

    III   Factor matching

    A I and II

    B I and III

    C II and III

    D I, II and III

72. **Which of the following is least likely to be trading at its fair value?**

    A Emerging market short bond

    B CDO based on mortgage backed securities

    C 3 month FTSE futures

    D Near dated soya bean futures

73. **Which of the following is not normally associated with passive fund management techniques?**

    A Optimisation

    B Stratified sampling

    C Full replication

    D Security selection

74. **The four stages of the investment management process are best described as which of the following?**

    A Investment Objectives, Investment Policy, Profit Maximisation, Risk Analysis

    B Investment Objectives, Annual Review, Asset Allocation, Measurement and Evaluation

    C Investment Objectives, Investment Policy, Asset Allocation, Measurement and Evaluation

    D Investment Objectives, Annual Review, Profit Maximisation, Risk Analysis

75. **General insurance business relates to which of the following types of insurance policy?**

    A Endowment policies

    B Term assurance policies

    C Whole of life insurance policies

    D Buildings Insurance policies

76. **Which of the following is not an SRI approach?**

    A Tactical asset allocation

    B Positive screening

    C Negative screening

    D Engagement

77. **In order to achieve a high return/high risk profile, you would invest in**

    A   A US equity fund

    B   A US fixed income fund

    C   A Japanese fixed income fund

    D   A South American equity fund

78. **Consider the following statements.**

    I   Diversification between asset classes is more effective than diversification within asset classes

    II   Higher liquidity results in fairer asset prices

    III   Asset class correlations are very stable

    Which statements are true?

    A   I and II

    B   III only

    C   I and III

    D   II and III

79. **Immunisation risk is minimised in a**

    A   Bullet portfolio

    B   Barbell portfolio

    C   Portfolio of bonds with an even spread of durations

    D   Dedicated portfolio

80. **Strategic asset allocation is**

    A   Selecting individual securities for a portfolio

    B   Allocating the portfolio across various asset classes and currencies

    C   Short-term variations in selected stocks

    D   Making strategic changes to the asset classes invested in

81. **What is the aim of LDI?**

    A   To maximize the risk-adjusted returns for a fund

    B   To ensure fund returns exceed what is required to fund liabilities

    C   To match fund assets and liabilities

    D   To minimise the risks to a liability matching fund

82. **The permitted range of any tactical asset allocation limits is liable to be wider if**

    A   Asset prices are higher

    B   Transaction costs are higher

    C   Liquidity is higher

    D   Risks are higher

83. **Negative screening is**

A A passive bond management technique

B An approach to LDI

C An approach to SRI

D A bottom up approach

84. **In time of market distress, what tends to happen to the correlation between different assets?**

A Moves to +1

B Moves to 0

C Moves to −1

D Tends to reduce

85. **Which is one of the main risks of an LDI strategy?**

A Fund beta

B Immunisation risk

C Fund standard deviation

D Fraud

86. **Consider the following statements**

I In extreme market conditions correlation coefficients move towards zero

II ETFs are continuously priced open-ended investments

III More liquid assets will trade closer to fair values

Which statements are true?

A I and II

B I and III

C II and III

D All are true

87. **The following zero coupon bonds are available.**

BOND	MATURITY	PRICE
Y	1 year	£95
Z	2 years	£90

If an investor has a one year investment horizon what is the extra return available from a yield curve ride assuming no move in the yield curve?

A 0.1%

B 0.2%

C 0.3%

D 0.4%

88. **The practice of 'cash matching' in bond portfolio management involves which of the following?**

    I   Reinvestment risk

    II   Interest rate risk

    III   Dedicated portfolios

    A   I only

    B   III only

    C   II and III

    D   I and II

89. **Which of the following would generally have the shortest investment horizon?**

    A   A unit trust

    B   A pension fund

    C   An investment trust company

    D   A general insurance company

90. **A one-year bond yields 7%. The implied yield of a one-year bond in the second year is 5%. What is the implied two-year yield?**

    A   6%

    B   12.35%

    C   5%

    D   7%

91. **Which of the following are key issues facing a tracker fund manager?**

    I   Market timing

    II   Method of index replication

    III   Frequency of portfolio rebalancing

    A   I only

    B   II only

    C   III only

    D   II and III

92. **In comparing a UK private pension against EU private pensions, which of the following is true?**

    A   The UK pension will generally have a lower equity exposure

    B   The UK pension will generally have a lower overseas equity exposure

    C   The UK pension will generally have a lower fixed income exposure

    D   The UK pension will generally have a similar asset mix

93. Riding the yield curve is

A Selling a low duration bond and buying a high duration bond to benefit from a fall in interest rates

B Matching bond durations to liability timescales

C Responding to a change in the tax treatment of a bond

D Buying a bond with a duration greater than the liability timescale to benefit from higher yields

94. The assets required by a mature pension fund are

A Long term, high risk

B Short term, high risk

C Long term, low risk

D Short term, low risk

95. Market timing is best described as

A Altering the allocation of assets

B Altering the specific investments held

C Altering the beta of the portfolio in anticipation of a market movement

D Using futures as a short hedge on the portfolio

96. If a market is weak form efficient

A All analysts can make superior profits

B Technical analysts can make superior profits, fundamental analysts cannot

C Fundamental analysts can make superior profits, technical analysts cannot

D No analysts can make superior profits

97. Which of the following is not a heuristic bias?

A Representativeness

B Loss aversion

C Familiarity

D Availability bias

98. Which of the following is not a form of EMH?

A Weak

B Medium

C Semi-strong

D Strong

99. **Which of the following is true of a semi-strong market?**

   A Technical analysts will be able to discover new information allowing them to predict price movements

   B All public and private information is reflected in the current share price

   C Fundamental analysts will be able to discover new information from company accounts and announcements that will allow them to benefit

   D The current price reflects all publically available information

100. **An analyst focuses too much on recently observed asset price behaviour when trying to forecast future returns. What bias is he exhibiting?**

   A Overconfidence

   B Conservatism

   C Memory bias

   D Regret avoidance

101. **Which of the following is true of a weakly efficient market?**

   A Technical analysts, fundamental analysts and insider dealers can all profit from the information they hold

   B Only fundamental analysts and insider dealers can all profit from the information they hold

   C Only insider dealers can all profit from the information they hold

   D It is not possible to make gains in such a market

102. **A pension fund with an increasing average age will**

   A Invest more in property

   B Invest more in equities

   C Invest more in fixed interest securities

   D Invest in riskier assets to increase returns

103. **A broker-dealer principal does which of the following?**

   I   Buys and sells shares on their own behalf

   II   Buys and sells shares on behalf of clients

   III Provides a facility for anonymous dealing between market makers

   IV   Quotes prices on SEAQ

   A I and II

   B III and IV

   C III only

   D I, II and III

104. **Consider the following statements.**

    I   MTF arises from MiFD, the euro-wide directive, and stands for multilingual trading facility

    II MIFID only allows shares to be traded on an exchange

    III MTFs will not affect trading costs

    Which statements are true?

    A   None of them

    B   I only

    C   II only

    D   III only

105. **Which of the following is the correct order of increasing maturity?**

    A   Bills, bonds, notes

    B   Bills, notes, bonds

    C   Notes, bills, bonds

    D   Notes, bonds, bills

106. **When dealing in UK debenture stock, when would you normally expect to settle the bargain?**

    A   Three business days hence

    B   Two days hence

    C   The next day

    D   On account day

107. **Settlement for gilts occurs after how many days?**

    A   One business day

    B   Two business days

    C   Three business days

    D   Five business days

108. **Which of the following costs are incurred by an institutional investor who trades directly with the dealer dealing bonds?**

    I   Bid-offer spread

    II Commission

    III Stamp duty reserve tax

    A   I, II and III

    B   I and II

    C   II and III

    D   I only

109. **Which of the following correctly describes a GEMM?**

    A   A gilt-edged money maker

    B   A gilt-edged money market

    C   A German market maker

    D   A gilt-edged market maker

110. **Which of the following best describes immunisation?**

    A   Matching the portfolio's assets and liabilities

    B   Tracking an index

    C   Holding short-dated assets for long-dated liabilities

    D   Obtaining the client's consent for the risk profile of the fund

111. **Which of the following describes how UK bonds are traded?**

    A   They are traded through a market making system

    B   They are traded through an order-book system

    C   They may be traded either through market makers or an order-book system

    D   They trade on a centralised market

112. **If an investor buys £40,000,000 of gilts, what is the commission likely to be?**

    A   0%

    B   0.5%

    C   1.0%

    D   1.5%

113. **An investor buys 7,500 certified AIM shares for £1.36. Calculate the total price paid assuming his broker charges 0.4% commission.**

    A   10,240.80

    B   10,292.80

    C   10,296.80

    D   10,241.80

114. **Which of the following is NOT and IMA investment fund classification?**

    A   Unclassified

    B   Income

    C   Classified

    D   Specialist

Answers

1.   **C**   Diversification can only eliminate unsystematic risk. This can also be referred to as specific or non-systematic risk

See Chapter 9 Section 1.2 of your Study Text

2.   **A**   Highest return, lowest risk

See Chapter 9 Section 1.1 of your Study Text

3.   **C**
$$\sigma_i^2 = \sigma_s^2 + \sigma_u^2$$
$$30^2 = 20^2 + \sigma_u^2$$
$$\sigma_u^2 = 500$$
$$\sigma_u = 22.4\%$$

See Chapter 9 Section 1.2 of your Study Text

4.   **D**   A beta of zero represents a portfolio with no correlation to the market and therefore, no market risk (a risk-free asset)

See Chapter 9 Section 3.1 of your Study Text

5.   **15** $r = (0.25 \times 12\%) + (0.75 \times 16\%) = 15\%$

See Chapter 9 Section 3.1 of your Study Text

6.   **D**   Note that perfect positive correlation implies that they move in the same direction to the same extent

See Chapter 9 Section 1.2 of your Study Text

7.   **C**   Securities that are not correlated to one another show no relationship between their returns. Combining uncorrelated securities within a portfolio gives risk reduction (diversification)

See Chapter 9 Section 1.2 of your Study Text

8.   **C**   Idiosyncratic risk is also known as specific risk or unsystematic risk and can be reduced through diversification. Systematic or market risk cannot be reduced through diversification

See Chapter 9 Section 1.2 of your Study Text

9.   **C**   In stock market crashes share correlations tend to move towards +1 as all shares fall together

See Chapter 9 Section 1.2 of your Study Text

10.   **20**
$$\sigma_i^2 = \sigma_s^2 + \sigma_u^2$$
$$25^2 = \sigma_s^2 + 15^2$$
$$\sigma_s^2 = 400$$
$$\sigma_s = 20\%$$

See Chapter 9 Section 1.2 of your Study Text

11.   **B**   Idiosyncratic risk = Specific risk

See Chapter 9 Section 1.2 of your Study Text

12. **D** I is a dominated security, in that it has a lower return for higher risk than II. We believe that Security III and IV should be considered, as they do offer additional return for additional risk

See Chapter 9 Section 1.1 of your Study Text

13. **12.2** $\beta = \dfrac{\sigma_s}{\sigma_m} = \dfrac{10}{12} = 0.8333$

$r = r_f + \beta(r_m - r_f) = 8\% + (0.83 \times 5\%) = 12.2\%$

If you are concerned about rounding having an impact on your answers, make sure you keep the original answer as calculated by your calculator. Rounding 0.83 in the first calculation will give an answer of 12.15%. But if you use the whole number as calculated you will get 12.16666667, which we round to 12.2%. In this case both are correctly rounded to 12.2% as the question asks for one decimal place, but it is something to be aware of in these gap-fill questions

See Chapter 9 Section 3.1 of your Study Text

14. **C** Moving against the market implies a negative beta, being less volatile implies a value less than one

See Chapter 9 Section 3.1 of your Study Text

15. **16.6** $r = r_f + \beta(r_m - r_f) = 7\% + (1.2 \times 8\%) = 16.6\%$

See Chapter 9 Section 3.1 of your Study Text

16. **6.0** $r = r_f + \beta(r_m - r_f)$

$14\% = r_f + 0.8(16\% - r_f)$

$14\% = r_f + 12.8\% - 0.8r_f$

$0.2\, r_f = 1.2\%$

$r_f = 6\%$

See Chapter 9 Section 3.1 of your Study Text

17. **A** An investment that moves in the direction of the market will have a positive beta and if more sensitive, its beta will be greater than one

See Chapter 9 Section 3.1 of your Study Text

18. **A** The others are all dominated portfolios either with higher risk and lower return, or higher risk and the same return

See Chapter 9 Section 1.1 of your Study Text

19. **B** $r = r_f + \beta(r_m - r_f) = 6\% + \dfrac{15}{20}(18\% - 6\%) = 15\%$

See Chapter 9 Section 3.1 of your Study Text

20.   **D** $\beta = \dfrac{\text{Covariance(i,m)}}{\text{Variance of market}}$

Covariance(i,m) = $\beta \times$ Variance of market = $\beta\sigma_m^2$ = 1.2×18^2 = 388.8

See Chapter 9 Section 3.1 of your Study Text

21.   **D**   Higher return realised for higher risk

See Chapter 9 Section 1.1 of your Study Text

22.   **C**   The sign indicates with (positive) or against (negative) the market

The value indicates more (>1) or less (<1) volatile

See Chapter 9 Section 3.1 of your Study Text

23.   **D**   As it has the highest return for the lowest level of risk

See Chapter 9 Section 1.1 of your Study Text

24.   **B**   Only specific risk can be reduced through diversification

See Chapter 9 Section 1.2 of your Study Text

25.   **D**   Covariance looks at how securities interact with the portfolio that they are part of

See Chapter 9 Section 3.1 of your Study Text

26.   **D**   The beta of the market is always 1

See Chapter 9 Section 3.1 of your Study Text

27.   **C**   The portfolio would return more than the market return of 8% if it has a beta of greater than 1

See Chapter 9 Section 3.1 of your Study Text

28.   **B**   The selection of stocks that are negatively correlated to each other would reduce the level of overall risk in the portfolio

See Chapter 9 Section 1.2 and Chapter 9 Section 1.4 of your Study Text

29.   **A**   If beta is less than 1, the security will return less than the market, which has a beta of 1, assuming that the market is returning a positive return

See Chapter 9 Section 3.1 of your Study Text

30.   **C**   Mainly from assumptions from the Capital Asset Pricing Model (CAPM)

See Chapter 9 Section 3.1 of your Study Text

31.   **C**   Market/Systematic risk cannot be diversified away

See Chapter 9 Section 1.2 of your Study Text

32. **D** CAPM suggests that the portfolio with the highest beta will have the highest expected return

See Chapter 9 Section 3.1 of your Study Text

33. **A** $E(R) = r_f + \beta\,(r_m - r_f)$

$= 4\% + (0.8 \times 6\%)$

$= 8.8\%$

See Chapter 9 Section 3.1 of your Study Text

34. **6.6** $r = r_f + b_1 F_1 + b_2 F_2 = 4 + 0.8 \times 2 + 1 \times 1 = 6.6\%$

See Chapter 9 Section 3.1 of your Study Text

35. **13.8** $E(R) = r_f + \beta\,(r_m - r_f)$

$= 9\% + 0.8\,(15\% - 9\%) = 13.8\%$

See Chapter 9 Section 3.1 of your Study Text

36. **B** The beta of a portfolio is simply a weighted average of what is in the portfolio. As the shares are equally weighted, we just add up the betas and divide by 5 to take the average

A $\dfrac{1 + 0.7 - 0.1 + 0.6 + 1.2}{5} = 0.68$

B $\dfrac{1.2 + 0.8 + 0.3 + 0.7 + 0.9}{5} = 0.78$

C $\dfrac{1.7 + 0.2 - 0.2 + 1.3 - 0.3}{5} = 0.54$

D $\dfrac{1 + 1.1 + 1.2 - 0.1 + 0.4}{5} = 0.72$

B has the beta closest to 1, so it will most closely track the market (beta = 1)

See Chapter 9 Section 3.1 of your Study Text

37. **A** If there is not risk, we can only expect to earn the risk-free rate of return (R_f)

See Chapter 9 Section 3.1 of your Study Text

38. **C** As the higher return is compensation for taking higher risk on board. A rational investor will wish for this. However, a risk averse investor will focus on a lower risk investment

See Chapter 9 Section 1.1 of your Study Text

39. **C** Specific risk, also referred to as diversifiable risk

See Chapter 9 Section 1.2 of your Study Text

40. **4.0** Risk Premium $= r_m - r_f = 9\% - 5\% = 4\%$

The required format for this question is 0.0%, hence this must be noted as 4.0%

See Chapter 9 Section 3.1 of your Study Text

41. **B** $E(R)$ $= r_f + \beta\,(r_m - r_f)$

$= 5\% + (0.75 \times 6\%)$

$= 9.5\%$

See Chapter 9 Section 3.1 of your Study Text

42. **C** The value of an investment has fallen by 20% from its peak.

See Chapter 9 Section 1.1 of your Study Text

43. **C** Shares that are uncorrelated mean that if one goes up in value, the other does not, hence diversifying the portfolio and reducing risk without necessarily reducing returns. Negatively correlated shares would also be a good way to achieve this

See Chapter 9 Section 1.2 of your Study Text

44. **C** Under APT we have

$r = r_f + b_1 F_1 + b_2 f_2$

$7.46 = 4.5 + b_1 \times 1.6 + 0.8 \times 1.5$

$1.76 = b_1 \times 1.6$

$b_1 = 1.1$

See Chapter 9 Section 3.1 of your Study Text

45. **B** VAR is defined as the value by which an investment may fall over a given period of time to a given level of probability

See Chapter 9 Section 1.1 of your Study Text

46. **C** APT is a multi-factor model in which the factors are not specified. One of its limitations is the difficulty in establishing relevant betas and their stability

See Chapter 9 Section 3.1 of your Study Text

47. **D** Diversification depends on investment correlation

See Chapter 9 Section 1.2 of your Study Text

48. **D** Drawdown is the amount by which an investment has fallen from its peak value

See Chapter 9 Section 1.1 of your Study Text

49. **C** $r = r_f + \beta(r_m - r_f)$

$r = 8\% + 0.85(15\% - 8\%) = 13.95\%$

See Chapter 9 Section 3.1 of your Study Text

50. **C** The model relates expected return to the relative systematic risk of the portfolio to the risk of the market portfolio (Beta)

See Chapter 9 Section 3.1 of your Study Text

51. **D** Required return = 8% + 1.25(15% − 8%) = 16.75%

Actual return = 17%

Alpha is 17% − 16.75% = +0.25%

See Chapter 9 Section 3.1 and Chapter 9 Section 6.2 of your Study Text

52. **5.0** This question requires you to set up two equations and solve to find out what the risk free rate is. If MRP is the market risk premium ($r_m − r_f$), then

1. $r_f + 1 \times$ MRP = 11

2. $r_f + 1.2 \times$ MRP = 12.2

Multiply equation 1 by 1.2 to make the MRP terms equal

3. $1.2\ r_f + 1.2 \times$ MRP = 13.2

Now take equation 2 from equation 3

$0.2\ r_f = 1$

$r_f = 5.0$

See Chapter 9 Section 3.1 of your Study Text

53. **D** By definition

$$\text{Correlation}_{xy}\ \frac{\text{Co var iance}(x,y)}{\sigma_x \sigma_y}$$

Hence

$\text{Covariance}(x,y) = \text{Correlation}_{xy} \times \sigma_x \times \sigma_y$

See Chapter 9 Section 1.2 of your Study Text

54. **D** A one week VAR of £1m at 95% may be interpreted in one of four ways

- There is a 95% chance of losing less than £1m in any one week
- The fund is expected to lose less than £1m for 19 weeks in every 20
- There is a 5% chance the fund will lose £1m or more in any one week
- The fund is expected to lose £1m or more for one week in every 20

See Chapter 9 Section 1.1 of your Study Text

55. **A** Assuming we are dealing with a young pension fund, then it has a long-term investment horizon where the liabilities it needs to meet in the future are linked to inflation (real)

See Chapter 9 Section 6.1 of your Study Text

56. **D** This will be the most volatile bond, as it has the highest duration and thus gives the greatest capital gain

See Chapter 9 Section 7.2 of your Study Text

57. **C** Commodities tend to be negatively correlated with bonds, with that correlation increasing with investment horizon, so for long term bonds, the correlation will be strongly negative.

See Chapter 9 Section 2.1 of your Study Text

58. **B** A switch out of a short-dated stock into a longer dated issue to exploit a perceived change in the yield curve

See Chapter 9 Section 7.6 of your Study Text

59. **A** Tactical asset allocation determines when the manager will go into, and come out of, the market

See Chapter 9 Section 6.1 of your Study Text

60. **D** One of the other main objectives of performance measurement is to use the analysis of past performance to allocate current and future funds

See Chapter 9 Section 6.1 of your Study Text

61. **D** The assumption is that the specific risk has been diversified away, because the investor has a fund of various equities

See Chapter 9 Section 6.2 of your Study Text

62. **B** Sector selection is an active management technique

See Chapter 9 Section 6.2 of your Study Text

63. **D** Tracking is a passive management technique

See Chapter 9 Section 6.1 and Chapter 9 Section 6.2 of your Study Text

64. **D** Property is deemed to be relatively illiquid. Equities and fixed interest bonds are exchange-traded, therefore liquid, and cash is the most liquid asset

See Chapter 9 Section 6.1 of your Study Text

65. **D** Passive management, sometimes referred to as indexing, suggests that passive fund managers seek to replicate the returns on an index, or pre-defined benchmark, i.e. they are attempting to achieve the return on such an index

See Chapter 9 Section 6.2 of your Study Text

66. **C** Active and passive fund management

See Chapter 9 Section 6.2 of your Study Text

67. **B** Market timing involves the short-term variation of the asset allocation of the fund in order to take advantage of market changes and potential market fluctuations

See Chapter 9 Section 6.1 of your Study Text

68. **A** Technical analysis includes share price charts and market volume indicators

See Chapter 9 Section 6.1 of your Study Text

69. **A** UK based pension schemes tend to hold a higher proportion of their assets in equities compared to German and French pension funds, as they tend to hold a higher proportion of their assets in bonds. The main reason why UK pension funds have a higher proportion in equities is that they are aiming to achieve 'real' returns over a long-term time horizon, where equity investment also offer a degree of inflation protection

See Chapter 9 Section 6.1 of your Study Text

70. **D** A final salary scheme, also known as a defined benefits scheme, is one type of Occupational Pension Scheme (OPS). The employer has the responsibility of ensuring that the pension scheme is sufficiently funded to ensure that all future liabilities are met, i.e. the assets of the scheme will meet the liabilities as they arise, as the employees retire. All these are factors that will affect the funding of the final salary scheme, as the employer must consider length of service of each employee, as this is used to determine the pension, the mortality rates are also important as this will assist in ensuring that these future liabilities can be meet for the required period. Investment returns are also important, as if they fall below the required rate of return in any one year then the future required returns must rise to compensate

    See Chapter 9 Section 6.1 of your Study Text

71. **D** All are valid

    See Chapter 9 Section 6.2 of your Study Text

72. **B** The least liquid assets are likely to be furthest from the fair value and this will include OTC derivatives and securities on illiquid markets. The emerging market short bond can be valued using DCF techniques, whereas the CDO will be opaque and hard to value

    See Chapter 9 Section 2.1 of your Study Text

73. **D** Security selection is associated with active fund management

    See Chapter 9 Section 6.2 of your Study Text

74. **C** The four objectives follow on from each other in a continual fashion

    See Chapter 9 Section 6.1 of your Study Text

75. **D** General insurance business relates to insurance policies such as building insurance policies, contents insurance policies, and car insurance policies, such as fully comprehensive and fire and theft insurance policies. Life assurance business relates to policies such as endowments, whole of life policies and term assurance policies

    See Chapter 9 Section 6.1 of your Study Text

76. **A** Tactical asset allocation is not an SRI approach

    See Chapter 9 Section 6.3 of your Study Text

77. **D** Equities are more risky than fixed income, and South American equities are more risky than US equities

    See Chapter 9 Section 6.1 of your Study Text

78. **A** I   True – Diversification between asset classes is most effective

    II True – Correlated coefficients vary and variations can be significant in extreme circumstances

    See Chapter 9 Section 2.1 of your Study Text

79. **A** A bullet portfolio minimises immunisation risk

    See Chapter 9 Section 7.3 of your Study Text

80. **B** Strategic asset allocation = allocating the fund to various asset classes/currencies

    See Chapter 9 Section 6.1 of your Study Text

81. **C** LDI seeks to match fund assets and liabilities

   See Chapter 9 Section 7.8 of your Study Text

82. **C** Higher liquidity makes tactical asset allocation easier

   See Chapter 9 Section 6.1 of your Study Text

83. **C** Negative screening is an SRI approach where certain activities are screened out

   See Chapter 9 Section 6.3 of your Study Text

84. **A** In extreme market movements, correlations tend towards +1 (i.e. all assets might go down at the same time)

   See Chapter 9 Section 2.1 of your Study Text

85. **B** LDI aims to match funds assets and liabilities and its main risks are credit risk and immunisation risk

   See Chapter 9 Section 7.8 of your Study Text

86. **C** I   False – in extreme market conditions correlation coefficients move higher in value, ie towards + 1 and –1

   See Chapter 9 Section 6.1 of your Study Text

87. **C** Return from investing in a one year bond = $\dfrac{100-95}{95}$ = 0.0526 or 5.26%

   Return from holding the two year bond for one year = $\dfrac{95-90}{90}$ = 0.0556 or 5.56%

   Extra return from yield curve ride = 0.30% (5.56% – 5.26%)

   See Chapter 9 Section 7.6 of your Study Text

88. **B** Cash matching is also known as 'perfect immunisation'. This means that the investor is not exposed to reinvestment risk or interest rate fluctuations, as the future liability has been matched exactly in both timing and amount. This is undertaken by buying a bond where the redemption of that bond meets the date of the liability, and the proceeds upon maturity meet the size of the liability

   See Chapter 9 Section 7.1 of your Study Text

89. **D** A general insurance company such as home or car insurance

   See Chapter 9 Section 6.1 of your Study Text

90. **A** If the yield for the first year is 7% and for the second year is 5%, then the two-year yield must be a weighted average of 5% and 7%. The best answer is therefore 6%

   See Chapter 9 Section 7.6 of your Study Text

91. **D** Market timing is associated with an active fund manager. A tracker fund manager would be described as passive, and therefore not concerned with market timing. However, the method in index replication is important, as is the frequency of portfolio rebalancing, to ensure that the index being tracked is reflected in the relevant fund

   See Chapter 9 Section 6.1 of your Study Text

92. **C** UK pensions tend to have a higher percentage of equities in their fund than fixed income securities, such as gilts, whereas European pension funds tend to have a higher exposure to fixed income securities

   See Chapter 9 Section 6.1 of your Study Text

93. **D** A yield curve ride is one of the active fund management techniques, where the aim is to invest in a bond, where the duration of that bond is greater than the date of the liability. The intention is then to sell what is left of the bond (i.e. the remaining life of the bond) upon meeting the date of the liability. The overall aim is to enhance returns, over those that could have been achieved by simply buying a bond where the duration is the same as the liability

   See Chapter 9 Section 7.6 of your Study Text

94. **D** A mature pension fund is said to be where the average age of the investors within the pension fund is older than other funds, i.e. they are close to retirement. If this is the case, the fund manager will wish to invest in lower risk investments that have shorter maturities, as these are deemed to be safer. Examples may include moving investments into money market instruments or short-dated gilts

   See Chapter 9 Section 6.1 of your Study Text

95. **C** Market timing is a form of active fund management where the fund manager will attempt to alter the profile of the portfolio, in anticipation of potential movements in the market. This can be achieved by altering the beta of an equity-based portfolio, or altering the duration of a bond portfolio

   See Chapter 9 Section 6.1 of your Study Text

96. **C** Weak form efficiency implies that any information that can be established from charts of post price movements is already factored into the price. Charting therefore reveals no new information whereas fundamental analysis does

   See Chapter 9 Section 4.1 of your Study Text

97. **B** Loss aversion is an example of mental frames

   See Chapter 9 Section 4.2 of your Study Text

98. **B** Weak, semi-strong and strong are the three forms of EMH

   See Chapter 9 Section 4.1 of your Study Text

99. **D** In a semi-strong form market all information contained in past price movements and all information published by the company and available to the public is reflected in the current price. As a result technical analysts who track price movements and fundamental analysts who analyse company accounts and announcements are deriving no new information, hence cannot beat the market. In contrast, insider dealers are aware of unpublished information that is not known to the market, hence can benefit.

   See Chapter 9 Section 4.1 of your Study Text

100. **C** The answer here is memory bias, which is defined as giving too much weight to recent experience when forecasting.

   See Chapter 9 Section 4.2 of your Study Text

101. **B** In a weak form market all information contained in past price movements is reflected in the current price. As a result technical analysts who track price movements are deriving no new information, hence cannot beat the market. In contrast, fundamental analysts and insider dealers discover new information that is not known to the market, hence can benefit.

See Chapter 9 Section 4.1 of your Study Text

102. **C** In order to reduce risk as the investment horizon shortens, ie the average age of the pension fund investors is increasing, which means that the time until retirement is shortening

See Chapter 9 Section 6.1 of your Study Text

103. **A** III is an inter-dealer broker and IV is a market maker

See Chapter 9 Section 5.2 of your Study Text

104. **A** I   MTF = multilateral trading facility
         II   MiFID permits off-exchange trading
         III MTFs *are* expected to reduce costs

See Chapter 9 Section 5.2 of your Study Text

105. **B** It is possible to refer to medium-term debt as Treasury notes as is the convention in the US

See Chapter 9 Section 5.3 of your Study Text

106. **A** The only exceptions to the general $T + 3$ convention are UK gilts and US government bonds $(T + 1)$

See Chapter 9 Section 5.3 of your Study Text

107. **A** International settlement is $T + 3$. Two exceptions in the fixed interest market are UK gilts and US government bonds

See Chapter 9 Section 5.3 of your Study Text

108. **D** An institutional investor who trades directly with the dealer will only suffer the bid-offer spread. An investor who uses a broker will suffer commission. Bond trades do not attract stamp duty reserve tax

See Chapter 9 Section 5.3 of your Study Text

109. **D** A GEMM is a gilt-edged market maker. The GEMMs are all FSA firms, who have been allowed by the Debt Management Office (DMO) to become GEMMs in the gilt market. The DMO, as regulator of the gilt market, ensures that the GEMMs fulfil their obligations as GEMMs, such as participating in gilt auctions

See Chapter 9 Section 5.3 of your Study Text

110. **A** Immunisation is where a portfolio will provide an asset return over a specific time horizon, irrespective of interest rate changes. Therefore, the aim is to select a portfolio where the duration of the portfolio is the same as that of the liability it is intended to meet

See Chapter 9 Section 7.7 of your Study Text

111. **A** UK bonds only trade on a market making system with no centralised market

See Chapter 9 Section 5.3 of your Study Text

112. **A**   Purchases in excess of £1m tend to attract no commission.

See Chapter 9 Section 5.3 of your Study Text

113. **D**

	£
Purchase cost (7,500 × £1.36)	10,200.00
Add: commission (10,200 × 0.4%)	40.80
PTM levy	1.00
	10,241.80

AIM shares are exempt stamp duty and SDRT

See Chapter 9 Section 5.2 of your Study Text

114. **C**   IMA classifications are: Capital protection, Income – subdivided into fixed income, equity, mixed asset, Growth – subdivided into equity, mixed asset, Specialist, Unclassified.

See Chapter 9 Section 6.4 of your Study Text

10. Investment Products

Questions

1. **Which of the following best describes an investment trust?**

   A A type of savings plan

   B A type of life assurance

   C A trust in which clients invest

   D A company in which clients invest

2. **Which of the following best describes a unit trust?**

   A A savings plan referred to as a unit trust, which relies on stock market growth and dividends to achieve capital gains for investors

   B A means of life assurance referred to as a unit trust, which involves investing in the stock market with certain tax advantages if the unit investments are held for a specified period of time

   C A listed company referred to as a unit trust, which relies on stock market growth and dividends to achieve capital gains

   D A fund referred to as a unit trust, which relies on stock market growth and dividends to achieve capital gains for investors

3. **Which of the following best describes a wrap account?**

   A An investment platform that enables investors to hold funds from many different portfolios in a single account

   B A fund that offers tax advantages

   C A fund where the tactical and strategic asset allocation functions are outsourced

   D A fund that operates under SRI principles

4. **Which of the following is not an advantage of indirect investment?**

   A Control over the assets held in the fund

   B Broad diversification even at small investment levels

   C No tax payable when assets are traded within the fund, only when the fund is traded

   D Professionally managed fund

5. **Which of the following statements about investment trusts and unit trusts is true?**

   A A unit trust is a registered trust, whereas an investment trust is a public limited company

   B A unit trust is a public limited company, whereas an investment trust is a registered trust

   C A unit trust cannot invest in overseas property, whereas an investment trust can

   D An investment trust cannot invest in overseas land, whereas a unit trust can

6. A European investment fund manager of a UCITS scheme wishes to purchase non-approved Eastern European securities for inclusion in the fund. What is the maximum amount of these shares that could be included in the fund (to the nearest one %)?

    Important! You should enter the answer only in numbers strictly using this format: 00

    Do not include spaces, letters or symbols (but decimal points and commas should be used if indicated).

7. Under COLL rules, what restriction is there on permanent borrowings for a UCITS retail fund?

    A   Maximum of 10% of the value of the fund

    B   Maximum of 25% of the value of the fund

    C   Maximum of 5% of the value of the fund

    D   No permanent borrowings permitted

8. A higher rate taxpayer receives a dividend from a holding of shares in a European Smaller Companies investment trust. How much additional tax must he pay?

    A   10% of the net dividend

    B   22.5% of the gross dividend

    C   20% of the gross dividend

    D   32.5% of the net dividend

9. Which one of the following statements about unit trusts is incorrect?

    A   A unit trust must be authorised if it is to be advertised and promoted to private customers

    B   All unit trusts must be authorised

    C   An authorised unit trust is an open-ended investments

    D   Authorised unit trusts are regulated by the FCA

10. In respect of an Open Ended Investment Company, the chief responsibility of the Depository is

    A   To safeguard the assets of the OEIC

    B   To manage the day-to-day transactions

    C   To prepare reports for investors, twice a year

    D   To manage the investments of the OEIC

11. The manager of a unit trust that operates on a historical pricing basis must, on the request of the investor, move to a forward pricing basis if the value of the trust is believed to have moved by at least what (to the nearest one %)?

    Important! You should enter the answer only in numbers strictly using this format: 0

    Do not include spaces, letters or symbols (but decimal points and commas should be used if indicated).

    _____

12. What circumstances can lead to a unit trust manager holding a 'box'?

    A   A move from dual pricing of units to single pricing

    B   A switch from historic pricing to forward pricing

    C   A year-end valuation of the fund

    D   Re-purchase of units from unit holders

13. An authorised unit trust that is not a tracker fund is generally not permitted to invest more than X of the total fund in any one security or to acquire more than Y of the shares in any one company that is not itself a collective investment scheme. Which one of the following shows the correct values of X and Y?

    A   X: 5%   Y: 10%

    B   X: 10%   Y: 10%

    C   X: 20%   Y: 5%

    D   X: 10%   Y: 5%

14. Investment trust companies are

    A   Always closed-ended

    B   Always open-ended

    C   Open-ended if they are approved schemes

    D   Closed-ended except for reinvestment of dividends

15. Which of the following is NOT a type of structured product?

    A   Structured capital protected products

    B   Structured capital and income product

    C   Structured capital at risk products

    D   Structured deposits

16. To say that an investment trust is trading at a discount means that

A A special offer is being made to reduce management charges below the normal level

B The net asset value per share exceeds the share price

C The share price exceeds the net asset value per share

D The bid/offer spread has fallen below 1% of the share price

17. Under COLL Sourcebook rules, a non-UCITS retail scheme is permitted to borrow

A On a temporary basis only, up to 25% of fund value

B On a permanent basis, up to 10% of fund value

C Up to 100% of fund value

D On a temporary basis only, up to 10% of fund value

18. Which of the following is true of split capital trusts?

A Trusts where capital is divided equally between different classes of share

B Trusts where capital shares are paid for in two or more instalments

C Trusts where income is paid on capital shares during the fixed life of the trust

D Trusts where capital shares are paid any surplus assets on the winding up of the trust

19. Which of the following best describes the significance of UCITS?

A A classification of funds enabling cross-border marketing within the European Union

B A classification of funds determining its tax status for the purpose of international tax treaties

C A term used for funds not authorised by the Financial Conduct Authority

D A fund management group based in Luxembourg

20. What determines the price of shares in an investment trust?

A Voluntary industry guidelines

B The value of the underlying assets per share

C A FCA formula

D Supply and demand for the shares in the investment trust

21. A dilution levy is most likely to be applied in respect of an Open Ended Investment Company when

A Shares are bought and sold by a single holder on the same day

B There are exceptionally large funds outflows

C The OEIC is being launched

D There is an increase in the tax liability of the fund

22.   **Which one of the following statements is incorrect?**

A   An Individual Savings Account can hold investments in OEICs

B   OEIC equity fund distributions are paid with a 10% tax credit

C   OEICs are dual-priced, with a spread between the buying and selling prices of shares

D   Many unit trusts are dual-priced, with a spread between the buying and selling prices of units

23.   **The ICVC regulations cover**

A   Open Ended Investment Companies

B   Unit Trusts

C   Investment Trusts

D   Individual Savings Accounts

24.   **Sam receives an interest payment from a gilt unit trust amounting to £240 after deduction of income tax. Sam is a higher rate taxpayer. What additional tax liability does Sam have (in £ to two decimal places)?**

Important! You should enter the answer only in numbers strictly using this format: 00.00

Do not include spaces, letters or symbols (but decimal points and commas should be used if indicated).

25.   **Jo has an annual salary of £23,000 and pays tax at the basic rate of 20%. She received a distribution of £600 during the year from an Equity Unit Trust which is not held in an ISA. The distribution does not include an equalisation payment. What is the tax position?**

A   There is further tax of £72.00 to pay

B   A tax repayment of £66.67 is due

C   There is no further tax to pay

D   There is further tax of £80.00 to pay

26.   **Which of the following is not a possible advantage to the investor of an investment in an Open Ended Investment Company (OEIC)?**

A   OEIC shares have a single price, with no bid/offer spread

B   OEIC shares may be held in an ISA

C   An investment in an OEIC can provide diversification

D   It is possible to buy OEIC shares in the market when their valuation stands at a discount to the aggregate market value of its shares

27. What is true of the pricing of an OEIC in comparison with Unit Trusts?

A   Have a narrower bid/offer spread

B   Price can be altered

C   Mostly single-priced but can be dual-priced

D   Charges are lower

28. Which of the following does an investor in a unit trust not benefit from?

A   Ability to select individual equities

B   Benefit from increase in value of a portfolio of equities, government and corporate bonds

C   An independent trustee

D   Fund management

29. Which of the following could a UCITS fund not invest in?

A   Warrants

B   Money market instruments

C   Futures and options

D   Single property

30. Which of the following is NOT an ARC Private Client Index?

A   ACR Equity Risk PCI

B   ACR Steady Income PCI

C   ACR Steady Growth PCI

D   ACR Cautious PCI

31. Which of the following is true of a hedge fund?

A   Priced according to NAV

B   Generally located overseas

C   Benefit from low initial investment amount

D   Benefit from low management charges

32. Why would an investor choose a short/long hedge fund?

A   To have a market neutral exposure

B   To benefit from low management charge

C   To benefit from low initial investment

D   To increase investment returns in a rising market

33. **A fund that tries to maximise returns using warrants, derivatives and equities and is not risk averse is known as**

    A Capital fund

    B Derivatives fund

    C Hedge fund

    D Managed fund

34. **Which is true of unit trusts, ICVCs and investment trusts respectively?**

    A Open-ended, open-ended, open-ended

    B Open-ended, open-ended, closed-ended

    C Open-ended, closed-ended, closed-ended

    D Closed-ended, closed-ended, open-ended

35. **Which of the following investment vehicles is subject to the Companies Act?**

    A UK authorised unit trust

    B US mutual fund

    C UK investment trust company

    D UK unregulated collective investment scheme

36. **An investor pays £22,000 for a single premium unit-linked bond with a life of 10 years. Which of the following patterns of withdrawal will give rise to a chargeable event during the first three years of the bond?**

    A Year 1: £550 Year 2: £1,100 Year 3: £1,100

    B Year 1: £2,100 Year 2: £Nil Year 3: £Nil

    C Year 1: £Nil Year 2: £2,100 Year 3: £1,100

    D Year 1: £Nil Year 2: £Nil Year 3: £2,750

37. **Which of the following investment vehicles is subject to the Companies Act?**

    A UK authorised unit trust

    B US mutual fund

    C UK investment trust company

    D UK unregulated collective investment scheme

Answers

1. **D** The legal form of an investment trust is a public company

   See Chapter 10 Section 1.2 of your Study Text

2. **D** A legal trust structure, where investors buy units in the fund that distributes income and achieves capital gains

   See Chapter 10 Section 1.2 of your Study Text

3. **A** A fund that offers tax advantages may be referred to as a tax wrapper. However, a wrap account allows funds from many providers to be held in a single account

   See Chapter 10 Section 1.2 of your Study Text

4. **A** Investors do not control exactly what assets are held

   See Chapter 10 Section 1.1 of your Study Text

5. **A** Unit trusts are legal trusts, whereas investment trusts are plc's listed on the LSE. Both unit trusts and investment trusts can invest in overseas equity

   See Chapter 10 Section 1.2 of your Study Text

6. **10** Since is a UCITS fund, non-approved securities are restricted to 10%. This means that at least 90% of the fund's value must be invested in transferable securities that are approved securities, being securities traded on a listed exchange in the EU, or traded on an eligible market

   See Chapter 10 Section 1.2 of your Study Text

7. **D** Unlikely to be an investment trust, a UCITS retail scheme may not borrow on a permanent basis

   See Chapter 10 Section 1.2 of your Study Text

8. **B** Investment trust dividends are treated in exactly the same way as normal equity dividends. The higher rate taxpayer's liability is, therefore, 32.5% of the gross dividend, to which a 10% tax credit applies. The sector in which the trust is classified is not relevant

   See Chapter 10 Section 1.2 of your Study Text

9. **B** Unauthorised unit trusts exist but cannot be promoted to the public

   See Chapter 10 Section 1.2 of your Study Text

10. **A** The Depository is an independent authorised person

    See Chapter 10 Section 1.2 of your Study Text

11. **2** Most trusts now operate on a forward pricing basis

    See Chapter 10 Section 1.2 of your Study Text

12. **D** The units held in the 'box' enables the manager to match buyers and sellers of units

    See Chapter 10 Section 1.2 of your Study Text

13.   **B**   10% and 10% respectively are the answers. Under COLL rules, tracker funds have higher limits

See Chapter 10 Section 1.2 of your Study Text

14.   **A**   Investment trusts are closed-ended because they have fixed share capital

See Chapter 10 Section 1.2 of your Study Text

15.   **B**   The three main types of structured products are: Structured capital protected products, Structured capital at risk products, Structured deposits

See Chapter 10 Section 1.2 of your Study Text

16.   **B**   The share price is lower than the net asset value per share

See Chapter 10 Section 1.2 of your Study Text

17.   **B**   10% permanent borrowings are permitted for non-UCITS retail funds

See Chapter 10 Section 1.2 of your Study Text

18.   **D**   Capital shares receive the remainder of the investment trust's funds once the other classes of shares have been paid on winding-up. This makes them generally the most risky type of share to hold in the investment trust

See Chapter 10 Section 1.2 of your Study Text

19.   **A**   The UCITS classification was created to facilitate cross-border marketing of collective funds

See Chapter 10 Section 1.2 of your Study Text

20.   **D**   Shares in an investment trust are traded on the stock market and the price reflects supply and demand

See Chapter 10 Section 1.2 of your Study Text

21.   **B**   A dilution levy may be applied when there are exceptionally large outflows of funds

See Chapter 10 Section 1.2 of your Study Text

22.   **C**   Open Ended Investment Companies are mostly single-priced

See Chapter 10 Section 1.2 of your Study Text

23.   **A**   ICVC stands for 'Investment Company with Variable Capital'

See Chapter 10 Section 1.2 of your Study Text

24.   **60.00**   20% tax is deducted at source, and a higher rate taxpayer is subject to a further 20% charge. The interest grossed up is £300 so that the total tax liability at 40% is £120 of which £60 was deducted at source and £60 is payable

See Chapter 10 Section 1.2 of your Study Text

25.   **C**   Equity unit trusts are taxed as equities. There is a tax credit of 10%. There is no further tax liability for a basic rate tax payer, and no tax can be reclaimed

See Chapter 10 Section 1.2 of your Study Text

26. **D** The market price of OEIC shares will reflect the Net Asset Value

See Chapter 10 Section 1.2 of your Study Text

27. **C** Until October 2006 OEICs could only be single-price but since that time can be dual-priced

See Chapter 10 Section 1.2 of your Study Text

28. **A** The whole point of investing in a unit trust is that you purchase units representing a large number of investments of shares, bonds etc. You effectively are buying a tiny piece of each of those investments but the selection of investments is left to the unit trust manager

See Chapter 10 Section 1.1 of your Study Text

29. **D** Although a UCITS fund could invest in property, for example via shares in a property company, it cannot invest in single properties

See Chapter 10 Section 1.2 of your Study Text

30. **B** Arc Private Client Indices are available for four risk classes: ACR Cautious PCI, ACR Balances PCI, ACR Steady Growth PCI, ACR Equity Risk PCI

See Chapter 10 Section 1.2 of your Study Text

31. **B** Hedge funds are generally located offshore

See Chapter 10 Section 2.1 of your Study Text

32. **A** If the hedge fund is made up of both short and long positions that will roughly equate to a market neutral position

See Chapter 10 Section 2.1 of your Study Text

33. **C** This fits the description of what a hedge fund tries to do

See Chapter 10 Section 2.1 of your Study Text

34. **B** Investment trusts are closed-ended because they have fixed share capital. Unit trusts and ICVCs are open-ended

See Chapter 10 Section 1.1 of your Study Text

35. **C** Investment trusts are companies whose trading objectives are to profit from investing in securities. As companies, they are governed by company law which, in the UK, is the Companies Act

See Chapter 10 Section 1.2 of your Study Text

36. **B** The limit on withdrawals is 5% on a cumulative basis. A withdrawal of more than £1,100 in the first year exceeds this limit

See Chapter 10 Section 1.2 of your Study Text

37. **C** Investment trusts are companies whose trading objectives are to profit from investing in securities. As companies, they are governed by company law which, in the UK, is the Companies Act

See Chapter 10 Section 1.2 of your Study Text

11. Performance Measurement

Questions

1. If small capitalisation stocks outperform all other stocks, the difference between returns on the FT All Share Index and the returns on the FTSE 100 Index will be

    A   Zero
    B   Negative
    C   Positive
    D   Indeterminate

2. What is the average annual time-weighted return of a £60m investment based on the following portfolio year-end values (in % to 1 decimal place)?

    Year 1   £70m   Following the receipt into the fund of £5m
    Year 2   £75m   Following the receipt into the fund of £2m
    Year 3   £88m   No receipt this year

    Important! You should enter the answer only in numbers strictly using this format: 0.0

    Do not include spaces, letters or symbols (but decimal points and commas should be used if indicated).

3. £20m is invested in a fund that pays an annual dividend. The year-end dividend and fund value prior to the payment are

	YEAR 1	YEAR 2	YEAR 3
Year-End Value	£23m	£25m	£26m
Dividend	£2m	£3m	£3m

    What is the average annual time-weighted return?

    A   −2.6%
    B   9.1%
    C   17.4%
    D   19.3%

4.   A portfolio returns 10%, has a beta of 2 and a variance of returns of 16. If the risk-free return is 6% and market return is 7.5%, what is the Treynor measure of the above portfolio (in % to 1 decimal place)?

Important! You should enter the answer only in numbers strictly using this format: 0.0

Do not include spaces, letters or symbols (but decimal points and commas should be used if indicated).

5.   What is the Jensen measure of the above portfolio?

A   1.0

B   2.0

C   2.5

D   5.0

6.   The Jensen measure of portfolio performance is otherwise known as

A   Risk

B   Beta

C   Expected return

D   Abnormal return

7.   Which of the following portfolios shows the greatest performance, given a risk-free rate of 6% and a market portfolio duration of five years?

	RETURN %	DURATION (YEARS)
A	8	5
B	9	7
C	10	10
D	11	15

8. A fund manager has invested 80% of his portfolio in the UK and 20% in the US. The fund has a value of £80m at the start of the year and £87m by the year-end. Comparison benchmark indices for each part of the portfolio had the following values.

	UK	US
Start of year	5,500	800
End of year	6,000	860

Based on the above portfolio details, but given that the fund managers asset allocation differs from that suggested by the client of 75% UK, 25% US, what gain or loss has the fund manager generated through the activities of stock selection and asset allocation?

	STOCK SELECTION GAIN	ASSET ALLOCATION GAIN
A	0.2%	0.8%
B	0.8%	0.2%
C	−0.2%	0.8%
D	−0.8%	0.2%

Answer the next *three* questions based on the following information.

A fund returns 22%, has a beta of 0.9 and a risk (expressed as a standard deviation) of 16%. The risk-free return is 8%, the market return is 20% and the market risk is 15%. The client's stated preference is for a portfolio that has a beta of 0.8 on average

9. What is the Sharpe measure of fund performance (to three decimal places)?

    Important! You should enter the answer only in numbers strictly using this format: 0.000

    Do not include spaces, letters or symbols (but decimal points and commas should be used if indicated).

10. What is the Treynor measure of fund performance?

    A 0.875
    B 3.206
    C 15.556
    D 17.500

11. What is the Jensen measure of fund performance (in % to 2 decimal places)?

    Important! You should enter the answer only in numbers strictly using this format: 0.00

    Do not include spaces, letters or symbols (but decimal points and commas should be used if indicated).

12. A US investor buys one million yen at 105 to the dollar to hold for six months in a euroyen account yielding 4½% p.a. If the yen are sold at the end of the period for 99 to the dollar, what is the dollar holding period return?

    A 7.6%

    B 7.9%

    C 8.4%

    D 8.9%

13. A firm has just paid a dividend (net of tax) of 5p per share. An analyst believes that the firm's dividends will grow at 8% per annum forever. If the current share price is 79p, what is the expected annual net holding period return?

    A 9.10%

    B 13.92%

    C 11.21%

    D 14.83%

14. An international investor uses £100,000 to purchase dollars on the spot market at $1.7546 and places them on a six-month eurodollar deposit at an annual rate of 11%. If at the same time, she sells the proceeds forward at $1.7410, what is the holding period return (in % to 2 decimal places)?

    Important! You should enter the answer only in numbers strictly using this format: 0.00

    Do not include spaces, letters or symbols (but decimal points and commas should be used if indicated).

    _____

15. Supergrowth plc has just paid an annual dividend of 4p per share and the current share price is £1.36 per share. If analysts foresee continuing dividend growth of 8% p.a., what is the expected net holding period return from holding this share for one year?

    A 8.00%

    B 11.18%

    C 9.42%

    D 10.11%

16. A German investor buys 1,000 shares in a US bank for $147 each, holds them for two years and receives dividends of $10 and $15 per share at the end of each year. The first dividend is invested in a one-year dollar term deposit paying 8%. The investor sells the shares at $130 each at the end of the second year. When the investor bought the shares the euro-dollar exchange rate was €1.60 to the dollar, and when the shares were sold the rate was €1.52 per dollar. What is the holding period euro return?

   A   0.69%

   B   2.13%

   C   3.92%

   D   4.93%

17. A US investor buys £50,000 to hold for three months in eurosterling account yielding 13% p.a. If the sterling is bought at $2.0135 per £ and sold at $1.8400, what is the dollar holding period return?

   A   6.50%

   B   −19.10%

   C   33.08%

   D   −5.65%

18. An analyst believes that a firm's dividends will grow at 10% p.a. indefinitely. If the current share price is £1.95, and last year's dividend, which has just been paid, was 10p per share, what is the expected annual net holding period return (in % to 2 decimal places)?

   Important! You should enter the answer only in numbers strictly using this format: 00.00

   Do not include spaces, letters or symbols. (but decimal points and commas should be used if indicated).

19. The value of a portfolio at the end of Year 1 is £106m, from a value at the beginning of the year of £26m. What is the return over the period in question?

   A   75.5%

   B   162.3%

   C   250.4%

   D   307.7%

20. A fund has a return over the last year of 17.5%. If the fund had a beta of 0.7 and a standard deviation of 11%, with the risk-free rate being 5%, what is the reward to variability as measured by the Sharpe measure?

   A   17.86

   B   9.55

   C   3.63

   D   1.14

21. A stock picker will try and do which of the following?

   A   Select stocks with a positive alpha

   B   Select stocks with a negative alpha

   C   Select stocks with a beta greater than one

   D   Select stocks with a beta less than one

Based on the following information, answer the next three questions.

Portfolio	Return on Portfolio R_μ	Standard Deviation σ	Sharpe Measure
A	8%	0.5	4
B	9.5%	1.7	Q22
C	Q23	0.6	5.2
D	11.3%	Q24	6.6

22. What is the Sharpe measure for Portfolio B (to 2 decimal places)?

   Important! You should enter the answer only in numbers strictly using this format: 0.00

   Do not include spaces, letters or symbols (but decimal points and commas should be used if indicated).

23. What is the return on Portfolio C?

   A   −2.88%

   B   13.12%

   C   9.12%

   D   0.91%

24. **What is the standard deviation measure for Portfolio D (in % to 2 decimal places)?**

Important! You should enter the answer only in numbers strictly using this format: 0.00

Do not include spaces, letters or symbols (but decimal points and commas should be used if indicated).

25. **A fund has a return over the last year of 12%. If the fund had a standard deviation of 2%, and a beta of 1.5, what is the reward to variability as measured by the Sharpe measure, if the risk-free rate was 4%?**

A 4

B 19

C 5.33

D 15

26. **The Sharpe measure identifies a manager's ability to**

A Diversify a portfolio efficiently and select winners

B Diversify a portfolio efficiently

C Diversify away systematic risk in a portfolio

D Select winners

27. **A fund has the following values and cash flows.**

	YEAR 1	END OF YEAR 2	YEAR 3
Value	100	95	140
Cash flow at year-end		30	

What is the time-weighted rate of return from the fund over the two years (in % to 1 decimal place)?

Important! You should enter the answer only in numbers strictly using this format: 0.0

Do not include spaces, letters or symbols (but decimal points and commas should be used if indicated).

28. **For a fund with both investments and withdrawals, which is the best measure of performance?**

A Jensen

B Paasche index

C Money-weighted return

D Simple interest

Based on the following information, answer the next *two* questions.

Portfolio	Return on Portfolio R_p	Beta β	Risk-Free Rate of Return R_f	Jensen's Alpha α
A	Q29	0.8	5.5%	3.1
B	11.6%	Q30	5.5%	6.1
C	14%	1.2	5.5%	7.08

29. **What is the return on Portfolio A (in % to 2 decimal places)?**

    Important! You should enter the answer only in numbers strictly using this format: 0.00

    Do not include spaces, letters or symbols (but decimal points and commas should be used if indicated).

    ☐

30. **What is the β of Portfolio B?**

    A 6.1

    B 0

    C 0.1

    D 0.42

31. **If a UK fund invests in UK and US mid-sized companies, a combination of which of the following two indices would be the most appropriate?**

    A FTSE 100 and Dow Jones

    B S&P 500 and FTSE All Share

    C FTSE 250 and S&P Mid-Cap 500

    D FTSE 100 and S&P 500

32. **Which of the following is not normally a form of comparable analysis with regard to relative investment performance measures?**

    A Comparison to a relevant stock or bond index

    B Comparison to another fund manager's performance

    C Comparison to a similar fund

    D Comparison to a custom benchmark

33. A fund's performance over the past year has been measured using the Treynor measure at 0.02. If the fund had a beta of 1.3 and a standard deviation of 12%, and the risk-free rate was 6%, what is the return from the fund (in % to 1 decimal place)?

    Important! You should enter the answer only in numbers strictly using this format: 0.0

    Do not include spaces, letters or symbols (but decimal points and commas should be used if indicated).

34. A fund has a return of 22% over the last 12 months, with a beta of 1.7 and a standard deviation of 23%. The risk-free rate is 6%. What is the excess return, if any, as measured by Jensen's Alpha, if the market return is 9% (in % to 1 decimal place)?

    Important! You should enter the answer only in numbers strictly using this format: 00.0

    Do not include spaces, letters or symbols (but decimal points and commas should be used if indicated).

35. Which of the following is not a popular measure of risk?

    A Sharpe measure

    B Jensen measure

    C Lintner measure

    D Treynor measure

Answer the next *two* questions based on the following information.

Portfolio A has a return of 18%, with a portfolio β of 1.4 and a Treynor measure of 7.1

Portfolio B has a return of 7.2% and a portfolio β of 1

Portfolio C has a β measure of 0.6 and a Treynor measure of 9.33

36. What is the Treynor measure for Portfolio B?

    A 0.86

    B −0.86

    C −0.0086

    D 0.0086

37. **What is the return of Portfolio C?**

A 0.13%

B 13.66%

C –2.46%

D –0.02%

38. **If the risk-free rate of return is 4%, what is the Treynor measure for the following portfolio (in % to 2 decimal places)?**

	PROPORTION OF FUND (%)	RETURN (%)	BETA
Stock A	30	12	1.3
Stock B	40	8	1
Stock C	30	9	1.2

Important! You should enter the answer only in numbers strictly using this format: 0.00

Do not include spaces, letters or symbols (but decimal points and commas should be used if indicated).

39. **Which of the following best describes performance attribution?**

A Performance attribution measures how a portfolio's return compares to the overall market return

B Performance attribution is the way in which fund managers can be either active or passive in their approach to fund management

C Performance attribution attempts to explain why the portfolio has had a certain return during the period in question

D Performance attribution evaluates the level of expected risk and related return from a portfolio

40. **Performance attribution can assist in identifying which of the following about a portfolio manager and the investment firm?**

A Risks and rewards

B Passive and active management

C Strengths and weaknesses

D Skill or luck

41. Which of the following statements concerning performance attribution is true?

    I   Performance attribution can assist in identifying good asset allocation

    II   Performance attribution can assist in identifying the effects of market timing on the overall return in the portfolio

    III Performance attribution can assist in identifying which securities are over or undervalued before selecting them

    IV Performance attribution can assist in identifying which fund managers are the better performing fund managers

A I, II and III

B I, III and IV

C II and IV

D I, II and IV

42. A life assurance fund has a value of £60m at the start of the year that has risen to £80m by the end of the year. If £10m was invested mid year when the fund value after this investment was £74m, what is the time weighted return for the year?

A 14.29%

B 15.31%

C 15.87%

D 16.67%

43. A fund manager runs an international equity portfolio that had a value of £200m at the start of the year and that is benchmarked against the FTSE 350 and S&P500 indices. At the end of the year the fund value is £215m and over the same periods the FTSE 350 and S&P500 have risen by 8% and 6% respectively. If the US:UK asset allocation is 20%:80% which of the following is true?

A The manager has outperformed by 1.1%

B The manager has outperformed by 0.5%

C The manager has underperformed by 0.1%

D The manager has underperformed by 0.8%

44. An undiversified investor is looking to determine which appraisal method would be most appropriate for him to use. Which measure would you recommend?

A Sharpe measure

B Treynor measure

C Jensen measure

D Information ratio

45. **Fund A has returned 12% and Fund B has returned 11% when the risk free rate is 6%. The standard deviations of A and B are 16% and 14% respectively and their betas are 0.9 and 0.7. Which of the following is true?**

   A   Fund A has outperformed Fund B on both bases

   B   Fund A has underperformed Fund B on both bases

   C   Fund A has outperformed on a Sharpe measure basis and underperformed on a Treynor measure basis

   D   Fund A has outperformed on a Treynor measure basis and underperformed on a Sharpe measure basis

46. **An investment is bought for £2.56. One year later it pays a dividend of 14p and is then valued at £2.74. What are the income and gain components of the total return?**

	INCOME	GAIN
A	5.1%	6.6%
B	5.5%	6.6%
C	5.1%	7.0%
D	5.5%	7.0%

47. **A fund manager is given the objective of outperforming the return on an equity portfolio of various UK stocks, which are being used as a benchmark. The beta of the portfolio is estimated at 1.3. During the year the risk-free rate of return is 4.2%, and the return on the market portfolio is 8.7%. If the fund manager achieved an actual rate of return of 11.6%, which of the following statements would be true?**

   A   The fund manager has underperformed the benchmark by 1.55%

   B   The fund manager has outperformed the benchmark by 3.91%

   C   The fund manager has underperformed the benchmark by 3.91%

   D   The fund manager has outperformed the benchmark by 1.55%

48. **The essential idea behind portfolio performance evaluation is to judge the performance**

   A   On an absolute basis

   B   On a relative basis

   C   Disregarding risk considerations

   D   Disregarding exchange rate considerations

49. **A fund manager starts the year with a fund value of £500m. The fund is composed of UK equities (80%) and US equities (20%). At the end of the year, the fund value has risen to £527m during which time the FTSE All Share Index showed a return of 10% and the S&P Index showed a return of 7%. Which of the following may be concluded?**

   A   The fund manager is good at stock selection

   B   The fund manager has outperformed the benchmark

   C   The fund manager has underperformed the benchmark

   D   The fund manager is good at market timing

50. A fund manager achieves a return of 8% one year with a standard deviation of 5%. If the risk-free rate of return over the period was 4%, what is the Sharpe measure of performance?

A 1.0

B 0.4

C 0.8

D 0.6

51. A portfolio returns 15%, has a beta of 1.6 and variance of 49. The risk-free rate is 8% and market return is 12%.

What is the Treynor measure of the above?

A 4.38

B 1.00

C 0.60

D 0.14

52. A portfolio returns 15%, has a beta of 1.6 and variance of 49. The risk-free rate is 8% and market return is 12%.

What is the Sharpe measure of fund performance?

A 4.38

B 1.00

C 0.60

D 0.14

53. A benchmark is constructed of 70% FTSE 100 and 30% DJIA. The FTSE rises from 4600 to 5014 and the overall benchmark rises by 12%. The DJIA starts 9800. What does it end at (in index points to 1 decimal place)?

Important! You should enter the answer only in numbers strictly using this format: 00000

Do not include spaces, letters or symbols (but decimal points and commas should be used if indicated).

54. An investment is worth 125 at the end of a two year period. 40 was invested at the end of the first year and the average annual money weighted return over the period was 12%. What was the original investment (in £ to two decimal places)?

Important! You should enter the answer only in numbers strictly using this format: 00.00

Do not include spaces, letters or symbols (but decimal points and commas should be used if indicated).

55. **Which of the following is the closest to money weighted return on a fund which has £100m invested at the beginning of the year, a further £25m invested six months into the year, and is worth £142m at the end of the year**

   A   6.5%

   B   10.5%

   C   14.5%

   D   18.5%

Answers

1. **D** The All Share index is composed of the FTSE 100, the FTSE 250 and the small cap stocks. If the FTSE 250 performed extremely badly, the FTSE 100 return could exceed the All Share index return

   See Chapter 11 Section 1 of your Study Text

2. **9.9**
   $$r_1 = \frac{(70-5)-60}{60} \times 100\% = 8.3\%$$

   $$r_2 = \frac{(75-2)-70}{70} \times 100\% = 4.3\%$$

   $$r_3 = \frac{88-75}{75} \times 100\% = 17.3\%$$

   $(1+r)^3 = 1.083 \times 1.043 \times 1.173 = 1.325$

   $1+r = \sqrt[3]{1.325} = 1.099$

   $r = 0.099$ or 9.9%

   See Chapter 11 Section 2.2 of your Study Text

3. **C**
   $$r_1 = \frac{23-20}{20} \times 100\% = 15.0\%$$

   $$r_2 = \frac{25-(23-2)}{(23-2)} \times 100\% = 19.0\%$$

   $$r_3 = \frac{26-(25-3)}{(25-3)} \times 100\% = 18.2\% \; r$$

   $(1+r)^3 = 1.150 \times 1.190 \times 1.182 = 1.618$

   $1+r = \sqrt[3]{1.618} = 1.174$

   $r = 0.174$ or 17.4%

   See Chapter 11 Section 2.2 of your Study Text

4. **2.0** Treynor Measure $= \dfrac{r_p - r_f}{\beta} = \dfrac{10\% - 6\%}{2} = 2.0\%$

   See Chapter 11 Section 4.1 of your Study Text

5. **A** $r = r_f + \beta(r_m - r_f) = 6\% + 2(7.5\% - 6\%) = 9\%$

   Jensen measure $= r_p - r = 10.0\% - 9.0\% = 1.0\%$

   See Chapter 11 Section 4.1 of your Study Text

6. **D** The Jensen measure states the return over and above that predicted by the Capital Asset Pricing Model. It is also known as the abnormal return or alpha

   See Chapter 11 Section 4.1 of your Study Text

7.   **B**   Excess return to relative duration for each portfolio is

$$A = \frac{8\% - 6\%}{1.0} = 2.000\%$$

$$B = \frac{9\% - 6\%}{1.4} = 2.143\%$$

$$C = \frac{10\% - 6\%}{2.0} = 2.000\%$$

$$D = \frac{11\% - 6\%}{3.0} = 1.667\%$$

See Chapter 11 Section 4.1 of your Study Text

8.   **C**   Actual portfolio performance = $\frac{87 - 80}{80}$ = 8.75%

Timing portfolio performance = $\left[0.80 \times \left(\frac{6000 - 5500}{5500} \right) + 0.20 \times \left(\frac{860 - 800}{800} \right) \right]$ = 8.77%

Original benchmark performance = $\left[0.75 \times \left(\frac{6000 - 5500}{5500} \right) + 0.25 \times \left(\frac{860 - 800}{800} \right) \right]$ = 8.69%

Giving

Actual Portfolio Performance	+8.75%	} −0.02% Stock Selection Gain
Timing Portfolio Performance	+8.77%	
Original Benchmark Performance	+8.69%	} +0.08% Asset Allocation Gain

See Chapter 11 Section 4.4 of your Study Text

9.   **0.875**   Sharpe Measure = $\frac{r_p - r_f}{\sigma_p} = \frac{22\% - 8\%}{16\%}$ = 0.875

See Chapter 11 Section 4.1 of your Study Text

10.   **C**   Treynor Measure = $\frac{r_p - r_f}{\beta_p} = \frac{22\% - 8\%}{0.9}$ = 15.556%

See Chapter 11 Section 4.1 of your Study Text

11.   **3.20** $r = r_f + \beta(r_m - r_f) = 8\% + 0.9(20\% - 8\%) = 18.8\%$

Jensen measure = $r_p - r = 22.0\% - 18.8\% = 3.20\%$

See Chapter 11 Section 4.1 of your Study Text

12.   **C**   Value of $1 end = $\dfrac{\$1 \times 105 \times \left(1 + \frac{4.5\%}{2} \right)}{99}$ = \$1.084 a gain of 8.4%

See Chapter 11 Section 1 of your Study Text

13. **D** Holding period return $= \dfrac{V_e - V_s}{V_s}$

Current cum div price = 79p + 5p = 84p

Cum div price in one year = 84p × 1.08 = 90.72p (growth 8% p.a.)

Holding period return $\dfrac{90.72p - 79p}{79p}$ = 0.148 or 14.8%

See Chapter 11 Section 1 of your Study Text

14. **6.32**

Spot dollar value (£100,000 × $1.7546) = $175,460

Interest for six months at 11% p.a. = <u>9,650</u>

($175,460 × 0.11 × 6/12)

<u>$185,110</u>

Sterling proceeds $\dfrac{\$185,110}{1.7410}$ = £106,324

Holding period return $= \dfrac{£106,324 - £100,000}{£100,000}$ = 6.32%

See Chapter 11 Section 1 of your Study Text

15. **B**

Next year's dividend (4p × 1.08)   4.32

Next year's share price (136p × 1.08)   <u>146.88</u>

<u>151.20p</u>

Holding period return $= \dfrac{151.2p - 136.0p}{136.0p}$ × 100% = 11.18%

See Chapter 11 Section 1 of your Study Text

16. **A**

	$
Value at end:	
Shares	130.00
1st div $10 × 1.08	10.80
2nd div	<u>15.00</u>
	<u>$155.80</u> × 1.52 = €236.816

Cost at start $147 × 1.60 = €235.2

Holding period return $= \dfrac{236.816 - 235.200}{235.200}$ = 0.0069 or 0.69%

See Chapter 11 Section 1 of your Study Text

17. **D** Cost = £50,000 × $2.0135 = $100,675

Final sterling value = $£50,000 \times \left(1 + \dfrac{0.13}{4}\right) = £51,625$

Final value in dollars = £51,625 × $1.84 = $94,990

Holding period return = $\dfrac{\$94,990 - \$100,675}{\$100,675} = -0.0565$ or –5.65%

See Chapter 11 Section 1 of your Study Text

18. **15.64** Holding period return = $\dfrac{[(195p + 10p) \times 1.1] - 195p}{195p} = 15.64\%$

See Chapter 11 Section 1 of your Study Text

19. **D** $r = \dfrac{V_1 - V_0}{V_0}$

$= \dfrac{£106m - £26m}{£26m} = \dfrac{£80m}{£26m} = 3.077$ or 307.7%

See Chapter 11 Section 1 of your Study Text

20. **D** Sharpe measure = $\dfrac{r_p - r_f}{\sigma_p}$

$= \dfrac{17.5\% - 5\%}{11\%}$

$= 1.14$

See Chapter 11 Section 4.1 of your Study Text

21. **A** A positive alpha means that the shares are offering an excess return for their level of market risk

See Chapter 11 Section 4.1 of your Study Text

22. **2.06** From information on Portfolio A

Sharpe $= \dfrac{r_p - r_f}{\sigma}$

$\therefore r_f = r_p - (\text{Sharpe} \times \sigma)$

$= 8\% - (4 \times 0.5)$

$= 8\% - 2$

$= \underline{6\%}$

Therefore, for Portfolio B

Sharpe $= \dfrac{r_p - r_f}{\sigma}$

$= \dfrac{9.5\% - 6\%}{1.7\%}$

$= 2.06$

See Chapter 11 Section 4.1 of your Study Text

23.　**C**　From information on Portfolio A

Sharpe $= \dfrac{r_p - r_f}{\sigma}$

∴ r_f　$= 8\% - (4 \times 0.5)$

　　$= 6\%$

Therefore, for Portfolio C

Sharpe $= \dfrac{r_p - r_f}{\sigma}$

∴ r_p　$= (\text{Sharpe} \times \sigma) + rf$

　　$= (5.2 \times 0.6) + 6\%$

　　$= 3.12 + 6\%$

　　$= 9.12\%$

See Chapter 11 Section 4.1 of your Study Text

24.　**0.80**　From information on Portfolio A

Sharpe $= \dfrac{r_p - r_f}{\sigma}$

∴ Rf　$= 8\% - (4 \times 0.5)$

　　$= 6\%$

Therefore, for Portfolio D

Sharpe $= \dfrac{r_p - r_f}{\sigma}$

∴ σ　$= \dfrac{r_p - r_f}{\text{Sharpe}}$

　　$= \dfrac{11.3\% - 6\%}{6.6}$

　　$= 0.80\%$

See Chapter 11 Section 4.1 of your Study Text

25.　**A**　Sharpe $= \dfrac{r_p - r_f}{\sigma_p}$

　　$= \dfrac{12\% - 4\%}{2\%}$

　　$= 4$

See Chapter 11 Section 4.1 of your Study Text

26.　**A**　The Sharpe ratio is based upon total portfolio return (less the risk-free rate) and the portfolio total risk, ie after the benefits of diversification

See Chapter 11 Section 4.1 of your Study Text

27. **6.4** $r_1 = \dfrac{95-100}{100} \times 100 = -5\%$

$r_2 = \dfrac{140-125}{125} \times 100 = 12\%$

Total return $= (1 + r_1)(1 + r_2) - 1$

$= (0.95 \times 1.12) - 1 = 6.4\%$ over 2 years

See Chapter 11 Section 2.2 of your Study Text

28. **C**   The MWRR is the most appropriate measure to deal with both cash inflows and cash outflows

See Chapter 11 Section 2.1 of your Study Text

29. **9.55**   From information on Portfolio C

Jensen's Alpha $(\alpha) = r_p - \left[r_f + \beta (r_m - r_f) \right]$

$\therefore r_p - \alpha = r_f + \beta (r_m - r_f)$

$\therefore \dfrac{r_p - \alpha - r_f}{\beta} = r_m - r_f$

$\therefore r_m = \dfrac{r_p - \alpha - r_f}{\beta} + r_f$

$= \dfrac{14\% - 7.08 - 5.5\%}{1.2} + 5.5\%$

$\therefore r_m = \mathbf{6.683\%}$

Therefore, for Portfolio A

Jensen's Alpha $(\alpha) = r_p - \left[r_f + \beta (r_m - r_f) \right]$

$\therefore r_p = \alpha + r_f + \left[\beta (r_m - r_f) \right]$

$= 3.1\% + 5.5\% + [0.8 (6.683\% - 5.5\%)]$

$= \mathbf{9.55\%}$

See Chapter 11 Section 4.1 of your Study Text

30. **B**   From information on Portfolio C

Jensen's Alpha $(\alpha) = r_p - \left[r_f + \beta\left(r_m - r_f\right)\right]$

$\therefore r_p - \alpha = r_f + \beta(r_m - r_f)$

$\therefore \dfrac{r_p - \alpha - r_f}{\beta} = r_m - r_f$

$\therefore r_m = \dfrac{r_p - \alpha - r_f}{\beta} + r_f$

$= \dfrac{14\% - 7.08 - 5.5\%}{1.2} + 5.5\%$

$\therefore r_m = \mathbf{6.683\%}$

Therefore, for Portfolio B

Jensen's Alpha $(\alpha) = r_p - \left[r_f + \beta\left(r_m - r_f\right)\right]$

$\therefore r_p - \alpha = r_f + \beta\left(r_m - r_f\right)$

$\therefore \dfrac{r_p - \alpha - r_f}{\left(r_m - r_f\right)} = \beta$

$= \dfrac{11.6\% - 6.1\% - 5.5\%}{\left(6.683\% - 5.5\%\right)} = \mathbf{0}$

See Chapter 11 Section 4.1 of your Study Text

31. **C**   This would be the most appropriate combination of indices where the fund invests in both the UK and US mid-sized companies

See Chapter 11 Section 3.1 of your Study Text

32. **B**   The performance of a fund can be compared against that of another fund manager, where the investment objectives are similar. However, the three main forms of comparable analysis are to relevant indices, customised benchmarks or similar funds

See Chapter 11 Section 3.1 of your Study Text

33. **8.6**   Treynor $= \dfrac{r_p - r_f}{\beta_p}$

$\therefore 2\% = \dfrac{r_p - 6\%}{1.3}$

$\therefore 2.6\% = rp - 6\%$

$\therefore r_p = 8.6\%$

See Chapter 11 Section 4.1 of your Study Text

34. **10.9**   Jensen's Alpha (α) $= r_p - [r_f + \beta_p(r_m - r_f)]$

$= 22\% - [6\% + 1.7 \times (9\% - 6\%)]$

$= 0.109 \text{ or } 10.9\%$

See Chapter 11 Section 4.1 of your Study Text

35. **C** Sharpe, Treynor and Jensen's Alpha are all associated with risk-adjusted performance

See Chapter 11 Section 4.1 of your Study Text

36. **B** Portfolio A:

$$\text{Treynor} = \frac{r_p - r_f}{\beta}$$

$$\therefore r_f = r_p - (\text{Treynor} \times \beta)$$

$$= 18\% - (7.1 \times 1.4)$$

$$= 18\% - 9.94$$

$$= 8.06\%$$

Therefore, for Portfolio B

$$\text{Treynor} = \frac{r_p - r_f}{\beta}$$

$$= \frac{7.2\% - 8.06\%}{1}$$

$$= -0.86\%$$

See Chapter 11 Section 4.1 of your Study Text

37. **B** Portfolio A

$$\text{Treynor} = \frac{r_p - r_f}{\beta}$$

$$\therefore r_f = r_p - (\text{Treynor} \times \beta)$$

$$= 18\% - (7.1 \times 1.4)$$

$$= 18\% - 9.94$$

$$= 8.06\%$$

Therefore, for Portfolio C

$$\text{Treynor} = \frac{r_p - r_f}{\beta}$$

$$\therefore r_p = (\text{Treynor} \times \beta) + r_f$$

$$= (9.33 \times 0.6) + 8.06\%$$

$$= 5.598 + 8.06\%$$

$$= 13.66\%$$

See Chapter 11 Section 4.1 of your Study Text

38. **4.78**   This question requires you to identify the weighted return (9.5%) and the weighted Beta measure of the portfolio (1.15). The Treynor measure identifies the return of the portfolio (R_p) over the return on the risk-free asset (R_f) being 9.5% – 4% and divides it by the Beta (1.15).

Weighted return = (12% × 0.30) + (8% × 0.40) + (9% × 0.30) = 9.5%

Weighted beta = (1.3 × 0.30) + (1 × 0.40) + (1.2 × 0.30) = 1.15

$$\text{Treynor} = \frac{r_p - r_f}{\beta} = \frac{9.5\% - 4.0\%}{1.15} = 4.78\%$$

See Chapter 11 Section 4.1 of your Study Text

39. **C**   Performance attribution assesses where the return has been achieved, such as good stock selection or asset allocation

See Chapter 11 Section 4.4 of your Study Text

40. **C**   Performance attribution can assist in identifying the fund managers' strengths and weaknesses with respect to their asset allocation, stock selection choices

See Chapter 11 Section 4.4 of your Study Text

41. **D**   The main areas of performance attribution are asset allocation/sector choice and security selection and assessing how successful the fund manager is

See Chapter 11 Section 4.4 of your Study Text

42. **B**

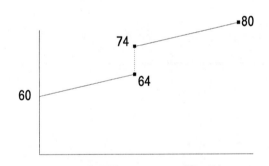

$$r_1 = \frac{64 - 60}{60} \qquad r_2 = \frac{80 - 74}{74}$$

$$= 0.0667 \qquad\qquad = 0.081$$

$$\text{or } 6.67\% \qquad\qquad \text{or } 8.01\%$$

$$(1 + r_{yr}) = (1 + r_1)(1 + r_2)$$

$$= 1.0667 \times 1.0810 = 1.1531$$

$$r_{yr} = 0.1531 \text{ or } 15.31\%$$

See Chapter 11 Section 2.2 of your Study Text

43. **C**   Actual return $\left(\dfrac{215 - 200}{200}\right)$ 7.5%

           } 0.1% Underperformance

Benchmark return (0.8 × 8% + 0.2 × 6%) =   7.6%

See Chapter 11 Section 3.2 of your Study Text

44. **A**   The Sharpe measure is appropriate for undiversified investors

     See Chapter 11 Section 4.1 of your Study Text

45. **C**

Measure	Fund A	Fund B
Sharpe	$\dfrac{12-6}{16} = 0.375$	$\dfrac{11-6}{14} = 0.357$
Treynor	$\dfrac{12-6}{0.9} = 6.67\%$	$\dfrac{11-6}{0.7} = 7.14\%$

     Fund A has outperformed on a Sharpe measure basis but underperformed on a Treynor measure basis

     See Chapter 11 Section 4.1 of your Study Text

46. **D**   Income return $= \dfrac{D_1}{V_0} = \dfrac{14}{256} = 0.055$ or 5.5%

     Gain return $= \dfrac{V_1 - V_0}{V_0} = \dfrac{274 - 256}{256} = 0.070$ or 7.0%

     See Chapter 11 Section 1 of your Study Text

47. **D**   Under CAPM the expected return is $r = r_f + \beta\,(r_m - r_f)$

     $\therefore r \quad = 4.2\% + [1.3(8.7\% - 4.2\%)]$

           $= 4.2\% + 5.85\%$

           $= 10.05\%$

     The actual return was 11.6% therefore the manager has outperformed by 1.55%

     See Chapter 11 Section 4.1 of your Study Text

48. **B**   Performance evaluation is used essentially to judge the performance of one fund relative to another, rather than on an absolute basis

     See Chapter 11 Section 3.1 of your Study Text

49. **C**   The benchmark fund would be worth

     (£500m × 0.8 × 1.10) + (£500m × 0.2 × 1.07) = £547m

     See Chapter 11 Section 3.2 of your Study Text

50. **C**   Sharpe $= \dfrac{r_p - r_f}{\sigma} = \dfrac{8\% - 4\%}{5\%} = 0.8$

     See Chapter 11 Section 4.1 of your Study Text

51. **A**   Treynor measure $= \dfrac{r_p - r_f}{\beta} = \dfrac{15\% - 8\%}{1.6} = 4.38\%$

     See Chapter 11 Section 4.1 of your Study Text

52. **B**   Sharpe measure $= \dfrac{r_p - r_f}{\sigma} = \dfrac{15\% - 8\%}{7\%} = 1.0$

     See Chapter 11 Section 4.1 of your Study Text

53. **11662** This is quite a tricky one.

The FTSE has risen by 9%

$12\% = 0.7 \times 9\% + 0.3 \times DJIA\%$

$12\% = 6.3\% + 0.3 \times DJIA\%$

$5.7\% = 0.3 \times DJAI\%$

$DJIA\% = 5.7\%/0.3 = 19\%$

Therefore, the closing DJIA value, is 11662 (9800×1.19)

See Chapter 11 Section 3.1 of your Study Text

54. **63.90** We can solve this by discounting at 12%, but taking the year 1 cash flow as negative to take account of the fact that the investor would have to pay in that amount to the investment.

$-40/(1.12) + 125/(1.12)^2 = 63.90$

See Chapter 11 Section 2.1 of your Study Text

55. **C** The money weighted return is an IRR calculation, so the answer is the discount rate which gives a NPV of closest to zero.

Cash flows: time 0: −£100m

Time 0.5: −£25m (cash flow occurs after 6 months

Time 1: £142m

NPV calculation = −£100m − £25/1.1450.5 + £142m/1.1451 = 0.65 (closest to zero from available options

See Chapter 11 Section 2.1 of your Study Text

Practice
Examinations

Contents

	Page Number	
	Questions	Answers
Practice Examination One	283	305
Practice Examination Two	319	341
Practice Examination Three	355	377
Practice Examination Four	389	413
Practice Examination Five	425	447

Important note

The Unit 2 (Investment Practice) examination consists of 105 questions to be answered in 2 hours and 20 minutes. Please note that there will be a small number of additional questions which will not be marked as these are new questions included for valuation purposes. You examination is, therefore, based on 105 marked questions, though you cannot see from the exam which are marked and which are not.

The majority of the questions are of the four-part multiple choice variety although the exam will contain a number of gap-fill questions for numerical areas. With a gap-fill question no possible answers are offered, rather the result of your calculator must be entered into the space provided.

We have produced five practice exams each with 105 questions (the number that are marked in the examination) that should be completed in 2 hours and 20 minutes.

PRACTICE EXAMINATION ONE

(105 questions in 2 hours and 20 minutes)

Questions

1. Which of the following will be LEAST RELEVANT impact on a corporate bond's credit spread?

   A Maturity

   B Coupon

   C Economic circumstances

   D Credit rating

2. Given a dividend of 60p per share, a growth rate of 7% and a required return of 12%, what is the share price (in £ to two decimal places)?

   Important! You should enter the answer only in numbers strictly using this format: 00.00

   Do not include spaces, letters or symbols (but decimal points and commas should be used if indicated).

3. A bond is priced at 100.36 – 100.40. If 10,000 nominal is sold through a broker who charges 0.3% commission what will be the net proceeds?

   A 10,006

   B 10,010

   C 10,066

   D 10,070

4. Which of the following are true for preference shares?

       I   They have no voting rights

       II   Their dividend is normally fixed

       III   Their dividend may be passed by the company

   A I, II and III

   B I and II

   C I and III

   D II and III

5. **Where payments are made into a pension scheme to buy investments and the benefits are solely determined by the returns achieved on these investments, then the scheme is**

    A   An occupational scheme

    B   A defined benefit scheme

    C   A retirement annuity scheme

    D   A defined contribution scheme

6. **Which of the following is generally true for a general insurance company compared to a life assurance company?**

    A   It will have assets with shorter maturities

    B   It will invest more in equities

    C   Its investments will be more illiquid

    D   Its liabilities will be longer dated

7. **The yield curve is the plot of**

    A   Spot rates against time

    B   Forward rates against time

    C   Redemption yields against time

    D   Flat yields against time

8. **12,000 shares are sold at a price of 82p. If the broker charges 0.3% commission, what is the net receipt (in £ to two decimal places)?**

    Important! You should enter the answer only in numbers strictly using this format: 0,000.00

    Do not include spaces, letters or symbols (but decimal points and commas should be used if indicated).

9. **Which of the following is true of UK government index-linked securities?**

    A   The trading price and the coupon are fixed by a formula relating to the RPI

    B   Only the coupon is fixed by a formula relating to the RPI

    C   The redemption price and the coupon are fixed by a formula relating to the RPI

    D   Only the trading price is fixed by a formula relating to the RPI

10. **A bond has a current price of £98.15 and a GRY of 8.73%. Its Macaulay duration is 3.2 years. What is the impact on price of a 25 basis point rise in yields?**

    A   +0.722

    B   +0.785

    C   −0.785

    D   −0.722

11. £150 is deposited in an account quoting an annual flat rate of 10% compounding monthly. What is the value of the deposit at the end of one year (to the nearest £1)?

    Important! You should enter the answer only in numbers strictly using this format: 000.00

    Do not include spaces, letters or symbols (but decimal points and commas should be used if indicated).

12. A company, which has just paid its annual dividend, has a payout ratio of 50%, an expected dividend growth rate of 2% p.a. compound and a rate of return on equity of 12% p.a. What is the company's historic P/E ratio (to 1 decimal place)?

    Important! You should enter the answer only in numbers strictly using this format: 0.0

    Do not include spaces, letters or symbols (but decimal points and commas should be used if indicated).

13. Which of the following companies would find net assets per share the most useful measure?

    A   A technology company
    B   A high growth training company
    C   A property company
    D   A manufacturing company

14. £200 is deposited in an account quoting an annual nominal rate of 7.5% compounding quarterly. What is the value of the deposit after two years (to the nearest £1)?

    Important! You should enter the answer only in numbers strictly using this format: 000.00

    Do not include spaces, letters or symbols (but decimal points and commas should be used if indicated).

15. A firm has a constant dividend payout ratio of 30%, and last year the company earned 10 pence per share. Earnings are expected to grow at 11% per annum, and investors require a gross total return of 15% p.a. on these shares. What should be the current price of a share in pence, assuming the dividend has just been paid (in £ to two decimal places)?

    Important! You should enter the answer only in numbers strictly using this format: 00.00

    Do not include spaces, letters or symbols. (but decimal points and commas should be used if indicated).

16. **Which of the following is the usual definition of total holding period return?**

   A   Change in share price plus income (including reinvested income) over the period

   B   Change in share price over the period

   C   Change in share price plus income (including reinvested income) over the period divided by the opening share price

   D   Change in share price plus income (including reinvested income) over the period divided by the closing share price

17. **When a stock has a beta of less than one, this indicates that**

   A   It will on average give a return below the yield on the market

   B   It will on average give a return in excess of that of a stock with a beta of greater than one

   C   It will have a high level of systematic risk

   D   It will have a high level of unsystematic risk

18. **In which of the following circumstances could the Jensen measure be used to evaluate portfolio performance?**

   A   When the portfolio is poorly diversified

   B   Only when there is unsystematic risk in the portfolio

   C   Only when there is systematic risk in the portfolio

   D   When the beta of the portfolio can be pre-specified

19. **A 20-year repayment mortgage has annual payments of £2,000. If interest rates are 8% what was the original sum borrowed closest to?**

   A   £20,000

   B   £19,000

   C   £8,500

   D   £400

20. **A manager has a three-month investment horizon. Three-month bills are priced at £98.50 and six-month bills are priced at £96.30. What annualised yield will the manager obtain from riding the yield curve by buying six-month bills and selling them in three months' time, assuming the yield curve remains unchanged?**

   A   9.12%

   B   9.87%

   C   8.72%

   D   7.34%

21. **£5,000 is deposited in a building society account quoting a flat annual rate of 5% compounding quarterly. What is the value of the deposit at the end of five years?**

    A £6,250.00

    B £5,062.50

    C £6,025.19

    D £6,410.19

22. **What percentage shareholding in an undertaking would normally be held before Consolidated Accounts are produced?**

    A 10% or more

    B 20% or more

    C 30% or more

    D 50% or more

23. **Which of the following is equal to non-current assets less long-term liabilities?**

    A Shareholders' funds + Current assets – Current liabilities

    B Profit and loss reserve + Share capital

    C Shareholders' funds – Current assets + Current liabilities

    D Current assets + Net assets – Share capital

24. **An investment had a value of £125 at the beginning of the year. After six months, the investment stood at £135. Then a further £10 was invested. If the investment was worth £150 at the end of the year, what is the percentage time weighted rate of return over the year (in % to 1 decimal place)?**

    Important! You should enter the answer only in numbers strictly using this format: 00.0

    Do not include spaces, letters or symbols (but decimal points and commas should be used if indicated).

25. **Which of the following is an expense in the income statement?**

    A Depreciation

    B Company formation expenses

    C Legal expenses incurred on the purchase of buildings

    D Cost of fixtures and fittings

26. The rate of interest for a repayment mortgage of £150,000 over 25 years is 6.5%. What is the annual repayment required at the end of each year (to the nearest £1)?

   Important! You should enter the answer only in numbers strictly using this format: 00,000

   Do not include spaces, letters or symbols (but decimal points and commas should be used if indicated).

   ```
   ┌──────────────┐
   │              │
   │              │
   └──────────────┘
   ```

27. A company has inventory of £5m, receivables of £4m, cash balances of £2m, current liabilities of £7m and non-current liabilities of £2m. What is its current ratio (to two decimal places)?

   Important! You should enter the answer only in numbers strictly using this format: 0.00

   Do not include spaces, letters or symbols (but decimal points and commas should be used if indicated).

   ```
   ┌──────────────┐
   │              │
   │              │
   └──────────────┘
   ```

28. A new office computing system costs £115,000 and depreciates at a constant rate of 10% per annum on a reducing balance basis. What is it worth at the end of five years?

   A £57,500
   B £67,906
   C £65,900
   D £56,432

29. If a company has shareholders' funds of £10m, non-current assets of £2m and long-term loans of £5m, what is the total value of its capital employed, defined as total assets less current liabilities (to the nearest £1m)?

   Important! You should enter the answer only in numbers strictly using this format: 00

   Do not include spaces, letters or symbols (but decimal points and commas should be used if indicated).

   ```
   ┌──────────────┐
   │              │
   │              │
   └──────────────┘
   ```

30. If a company's net earnings yield is 10% and it has a dividend cover of 2×, what is the company's net dividend yield?

   A 22.00%
   B 20.00%
   C 6.25%
   D 5.00%

31. A benchmark is established using 20% FTSE 100 and 80% S&P 500. The FTSE started off at 5600 when the S&P was at 1500. The combined benchmark ended the period showing 9% growth and the FTSE ended at 6000. What was the ending S&P Index value (to the nearest index point)?

    Important! You should enter the answer only in numbers strictly using this format: 0000

    Do not include spaces, letters or symbols (but decimal points and commas should be used if indicated).

    ```
    ┌─────────────┐
    │             │
    │             │
    └─────────────┘
    ```

32. From the following set of data, what is the range (to the nearest one %)?

    7%, 2%, 12%, –3%, 6%, 6%, 1%

    Important! You should enter the answer only in numbers strictly using this format: 00

    Do not include spaces, letters or symbols (but decimal points and commas should be used if indicated).

    ```
    ┌─────────────┐
    │             │
    │             │
    └─────────────┘
    ```

33. Which of the following are true?

    I   The long-run average cost curve passes through the lowest points of each short-run average cost curve

    II   Minimum efficient scale is the point at which long-run average costs cease to fall

    III The long-run average cost curve rises beyond a particular level of output because of diseconomies of scale

    A   I and II
    B   II and III
    C   I and III
    D   I, II and III

34. Which of the following statements about the short-run marginal cost curve is false?

    A   Marginal cost equals average cost when average cost is at a minimum
    B   Marginal cost depends in part upon fixed costs
    C   When average cost is falling, marginal cost will be below average cost
    D   Marginal cost will be rising under conditions of diminishing returns

35. If an investor is using the Jensen measure, which of the following would be most appropriate as a comparison?

    A   A passive benchmark portfolio with a given standard deviation the same as that of the portfolio
    B   An active benchmark portfolio with a given standard deviation the same as that of the portfolio
    C   A passive benchmark portfolio with a given beta the same as that of the portfolio
    D   An active benchmark portfolio with a given beta the same as that of the portfolio

36. **If an increase in the level of the nominal money supply results in no change in the level of money income, then which of the following is true?**

    A Interest rates must have increased

    B The velocity of money must have fallen

    C Taxes must have risen

    D The price level must have risen

37. **Which of the following pairs of goods would be most likely to have a cross-elasticity of demand of –0.9?**

    A Apples and pears

    B Mustard and bananas

    C Strawberries and cream

    D Books and newspapers

38. **The Phillips curve shifts from PC1 to PC2 in the figure below.**

    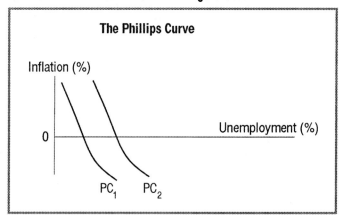

    Which of the following reasons is most likely to cause such a movement in the Phillips curve?

    A The expectation of a future rise in the inflation rate

    B The expectation of a future rise in the unemployment rate

    C A change in the natural rate of unemployment

    D A shift in labour supply

39. **What is the arithmetic mean and geometric mean respectively of the following?**

    104, 109, 103, 102, 103

	ARITHMETIC	GEOMETRIC
A	104.20	104.17
B	104.17	104.20
C	103.00	104.17
D	104.17	103.00

40. **Rank the following investments in order of risk, with the riskiest first.**

    I   Traded options

    II   Equity shares in quoted companies

    III   Convertible debt in quoted companies

    IV   Gilts

A I, II, III, IV

B I, III, II, IV

C II, I, III, IV

D III, II, I, IV

41. **A bond had the following quarterly total returns (%) over the last two years.**

–12%, 7%, 4%, 9%, 8%, –3%, 5%, –6%

What was the geometric mean quarterly return?

A 1.24%

B 1.95%

C 3.02%

D 2.86%

42. **When the equilibrium income level increases due to an increase in disposable income, this is due to**

A The accelerator principle

B The multiplier principle

C The permanent income theory

D Inflation augmented expectations

43. **Which of the following are advantages for the geometric mean over the arithmetic mean?**

    I   It is less distorted by extreme values

    II   It is intuitively better for a series which is growing over time

    III   It can be calculated for negative values

A I, II and III

B I and II

C II and III

D I only

44. **Which of the following would be the most appropriate way to assess the risk and return attitude of a client?**

A Ask what the highest return they wish to receive is

B Ask how much they need to receive in excess of inflation

C Ask them to pick from portfolios on their efficient frontier

D Ask them what the highest risk they will accept is

45. **A Eurodollar account yields 5% per annum. A US investor places £100,000 on deposit for three months at an exchange rate of $1.43 to the £ and sells the proceeds forward for that period at $1.40 per £. What is the dollar holding period return?**

    A   3.42%

    B   1.98%

    C   0.72%

    D   1.25%

46. **Four bonds are available with durations of 6 years, 10 years, 13 years and 15 years. What will be the duration of a portfolio with weightings 20:20:30:30 respectively?**

    A   44 years

    B   11.6 years

    C   11.0 years

    D   10.4 years

47. **If you had expectations of high inflation you would**

    A   Increase fixed income exposure and reduce equity exposure

    B   Increase fixed income exposure and reduce property exposure

    C   Increase equity exposure and reduce fixed income exposure

    D   Increase fixed income exposure and reduce commodity exposure

48. **A firm in perfect competition**

    A   Follows the market price

    B   Has a downward sloping demand curve

    C   Has an upward sloping demand curve

    D   Is a price maker

49. **In a positively skewed distribution**

    A   The mode is greater than median and the median is greater than the mean

    B   The mode is less than the median and the median is less than the mean

    C   The mode, median and mean are the same

    D   The relationship between the mode, median and mean cannot be determined

The following information relates to questions 50 to 55

An exporter has contracted to sell an item to a US client in three months' time for $1.8m. The current spot rate is 1.5040 - 1.5061 and the three month premium is 0.32 – 0.30c. UK interest rates are 5% pa. The product is manufactured in the UK using local labour, though the raw materials are imported from the US. At the current exchange rate the labour cost, raw materials cost and profit each equate to one third of the revenue figure. The company has a policy of hedging their exchange rate exposure on both exports and imports through the use of forward exchange contracts and hedging changes in the sterling prices of commodities used in the manufacturing process.

50. **If the exporter hedges the sale with a forward exchange contract how much sterling will he receive (to the nearest £1)?**

   Important! You should enter the answer only in numbers strictly using this format: 0,000,000

   Do not include spaces, letters or symbols (but decimal points and commas should be used if indicated).

51. **Using the 1.5040 spot rate as a starting point, determine the current US interest rate (in % to 2 decimal places)**

   Important! You should enter the answer only in numbers strictly using this format: 0.00

   Do not include spaces, letters or symbols (but decimal points and commas should be used if indicated).

52. **What is the net impact on the balance of trade from manufacturing and selling the asset?**

   A   No impact

   B   Increases a surplus/reduces a deficit

   C   Increases a deficit/reduces a surplus

   D   Increases either a surplus or deficit

53. **How would the forward exchange contract used to hedge the export be reflected in the accounts of the exporter?**

   A   A financial asset recognised at amortised cost

   B   A financial liability recognised at amortised cost

   C   A financial asset or liability recognised at amortised cost

   D   A financial asset or liability recognised at fair value

54. **If the company did not hedge its currency exposure and the dollar appreciated by 20% what would be the sterling operating profit margin on the item (in % to 1 decimal place)?**

   Important! You should enter the answer only in numbers strictly using this format: 00.0

   Do not include spaces, letters or symbols (but decimal points and commas should be used if indicated).

55.   Which of the following may be used by the manufacturer to hedge future commodity purchases?

A   Long put

B   Long future

C   Short call

D   Short future

---

56.   The level of natural unemployment arises

A   When the economy is in equilibrium

B   When the economy is not in equilibrium

C   Due to people moving jobs

D   Due to structural changes in the economy

---

57.   What is the weighted arithmetic index based on the following (Base 200)?

	BASE		CURRENT	
	P_O	Q_O	P_N	Q_N
I	3	1	7	3
II	4	3	6	3
III	6	4	7	2

A   140

B   189

C   272

D   379

---

58.   A share has a beta of nil, the risk-free rate is 3% and the market premium for risk is 6%. What is the required return on the share (in % to 1 decimal place)?

Important! You should enter the answer only in numbers strictly using this format: 0.0

Do not include spaces, letters or symbols (but decimal points and commas should be used if indicated).

---

59.   When government expenditure increases interest rates and reduces private sector investment, this is referred to as

A   Crowding out

B   Crowding in

C   The accelerator effect

D   The multiplier effect

60. **If a company changes its depreciation method so as to reduce the depreciation charge each year, the impact of this is to**

    A   Increase profits

    B   Reduce profits

    C   Increase cash flow

    D   Reduce cash flow

61. **A company has a share price of 90p and does a scrip issue so that one new share is issued for every two shares. What will the share price be after the scrip issue?**

    A   60p

    B   90p

    C   45p

    D   30p

62. **What is the duration in years of a portfolio consisting of three equally weighted bonds with durations of 3, 4 and 6 years (in years to 1 decimal place)?**

    Important! You should enter the answer only in numbers strictly using this format: 0.0

    Do not include spaces, letters or symbols (but decimal points and commas should be used if indicated).

    ```
    ┌─────────────┐
    │             │
    │             │
    └─────────────┘
    ```

63. **For a zero-coupon bond, which of the following is true of its modified duration?**

    A   It will equal the bond's maturity

    B   It will equal the bond's duration

    C   It will be less than the bond's duration

    D   It may be greater than the bond's duration

64. **What is the real yield on a bond held for the last year?**

    A   Nominal yield less expected inflation

    B   Nominal yield plus expected inflation

    C   Actual inflation for the last year

    D   Nominal yield less actual inflation for the last year

65. **The covariance of the returns of A and B is 0.004 and the standard deviations of their returns are 6% and 9% respectively. What is the correlation coefficient for their returns?**

    A   0.86

    B   0.74

    C   0.55

    D   0.00

66. A company paid a dividend last year of 20p. Dividends are expected to grow at 7% and shareholders' required returns are 17%. What is the share price (in £ to two decimal places)?

    Important! You should enter the answer only in numbers strictly using this format: 0.00

    Do not include spaces, letters or symbols (but decimal points and commas should be used if indicated).

    ┌──────────┐
    │   │
    │   │
    └──────────┘

67. A margined bank account would be used for settlement of which of the following?

    I   UK share transactions

    II   Overseas share transactions

    III Futures and options transactions

    A III only

    B I, II, III and IV

    C II and III

    D I and III

68. According to the expectations hypothesis, which of the following is true for the forward rate?

    A It will always be less than the current spot rate

    B It represents the consensus market opinion as to the expected spot rate

    C It is unrelated to the expected spot rate

    D It is equal to the current spot rate

69. Which of the following equals working capital less shareholders' funds?

    A Non-current assets less long-term debt

    B Non-current assets plus long-term debt

    C Long-term debt less non-current assets

    D Share capital plus long-term debt

70. What impact does a rights issue have on return on capital employed?

    A No impact

    B Increase

    C Decrease

    D Not possible to tell

71. **If prices are rising, which of the following methods of inventory valuation would give the highest profit?**

    A LIFO

    B FIFO

    C Weighted average

    D All would give the same profit

72. **Which of the following should prepare a cash flow statement under the requirements laid out by the Companies Act?**

    A All companies, public and private

    B Only public companies

    C All companies except those defined as small under the Companies Act

    D Only companies with 100% owned subsidiaries

73. **The marginal propensity to save is 0.2. Calculate the marginal propensity to consume and the multiplier?**

    A MPC = 0.2   Multiplier = 5

    B MPC = 0.2   Multiplier = 0.2

    C MPC = 0.8   Multiplier = 0.8

    D MPC = 0.8   Multiplier = 5

74. **The Sharpe measure identifies a manager's ability to**

    A Diversify a portfolio efficiently and select winners

    B Diversify a portfolio efficiently

    C Diversify away systematic risk in a portfolio

    D Select winners

75. **Which of the following is true for a corporate debenture?**

    A It may be bearer stock

    B Any charge must be registered with the registrar of companies

    C It will be unsecured

    D It cannot be convertible into equity

76. Which of the following accounts would need to be audited?

    I   Limited liability company

    II   Partnership

    III   Dormant limited liability company

    IV   Sole trader

A   I, II, III and IV

B   I and III

C   I, II and III

D   I only

77. Which of the following futures are traded on NYSE Liffe?

    I   US$

    II   Short-term US interest rates

    III   Short-term £ interest rates

    IV   Long-term £ interest rates

A   I, II and III

B   III only

C   II, III and IV

D   I, II, III and IV

78. A straddle consists of

A   A long call and long put with different expiries

B   A long call and long put with different strikes

C   A long call and long put with different strikes/expiries

D   A long call and long put with the same strikes/expiries

79. Which of the following is true?

    I   Stock indices generally include capital gain only

    II   Bond indices generally include reinvested income and capital gain

    III   Stock indices and bond indices both generally include reinvested income

A   I and II

B   II and III

C   III only

D   I and III

80. Which of the following is true of an interest rate swap and/or a currency swap?

A   There is always an exchange of principal for both types of swap

B   There is always the exchange of the difference between a floating rate payment against a fixed rate payment with an interest rate swap

C   There is never an exchange of principal with a currency swap

D   There is always a comparative advantage from entering into the swap

The following information relates to questions 81 to 86

A company has developed a product on which it has a worldwide patent. In the entire world there are only five manufacturers who build the product under licence. The following is an extract from the company's accounts.

	£M
BALANCE SHEET	
Non-current assets	200
Current assets	100
	300
Current liabilities	80
Non-current liabilities (4 year 7% annual coupon bond)	60
Shareholder's funds	
– Ordinary share capital and reserves	130
– Preference shares	30
	300
INCOME STATEMENT	£M
Turnover	120
Operating profit	16

The non-current asset was originally bought two years ago, it has six years life remaining and is being depreciated using the cost model on a straight line basis down to a residual value of £20m. The company has invested its cash surplus in a Treasury bill that is currently priced at 98.82 and has 86 days to maturity. The current risk-free rate is 5% and the yield on bonds with a similar term and similar credit rating to that of the company is 6%.

81. **What is the return on capital employed for the company (in % to 2 decimal places)?**

    Important! You should enter the answer only in numbers strictly using this format: 0.00

    Do not include spaces, letters or symbols (but decimal points and commas should be used if indicated).

82. **What industrial structure do the manufacturers have?**

    A   Monopoly

    B   Oligopoly

    C   Monopolistic competition

    D   Perfect competition

83. **What is the price of the company's bonds closest to?**

    A   101.56

    B   102.80

    C   103.47

    D   109.01

84. **Which of the following is not a common characteristic of a preference share?**

    A Cumulative

    B Participating

    C Voting

    D Convertible

85. **What was the original cost of the non-current asset (to the nearest £1m)?**

    Important! You should enter the answer only in numbers strictly using this format: 000

    Do not include spaces, letters or symbols (but decimal points and commas should be used if indicated).

86. **What is the compound annual return the company is getting on the Treasury bill investment (in % to 2 decimal places)?**

    Important! You should enter the answer only in numbers strictly using this format: 0.00

    Do not include spaces, letters or symbols (but decimal points and commas should be used if indicated).

87. **A stock picker will try and**

    A Select stocks with a positive alpha

    B Select stocks with a negative alpha

    C Select stocks with a beta greater than one

    D Select stocks with a beta less than one

88. **When using the indirect method to calculate cash flow from operations, what should be added back to profit before tax?**

    A Depreciation

    B Increase in inventory

    C Decrease in payables

    D Increase in receivables

89. **Which of the following is not a typical hedge fund strategy?**

    A Long/short

    B Market-neutral

    C Global macro

    D Index tracking

90. A portfolio generates a total annual return of 8%. The portfolio is split equally between two gilts: a 6% treasury and a 5% Treasury. The price per £100 N.V. per each gilt at the start of the year is as follows:

Bond 1:   6% Treasury   £100

Bond 2:   5% Treasury   £95

At the end of the year the 6% Treasury has a price of £103. Calculate the end price of Bond 2?

A   £95

B   £97

C   £99

D   £101

91. Which of the following is least important to an investor concerned with controlling risk:

A   Other assets held

B   Length of investment

C   Mix of income versus capital growth

D   Level of collateral

92. Which of the following is not a problem with the rate of unemployment?

A   Inclusion of unemployed not looking for work

B   Inclusion of unemployed working in the black economy

C   Exclusion of unemployed who turn down job offers

D   Exclusion of unemployed who have accepted job offers but not yet started the job yet

93. How is a put option which has a strike price of 56p described if the current market price of the 60p

A   In the money

B   At the money

C   Out of the money

D   Has intrinsic value

94. Which of the following is the best description of the value of exports less imports?

A   Public Sector Net Cash Requirement

B   Balance of Payments

C   Current Account

D   Capital Account

95. **Which of the following is the best justification for entering into a long futures position?**

   A Belief that the underlying asset price will rise

   B Belief that the underlying asset price will fall

   C Belief that the underlying asset price will remain the same

   D Belief that the underlying asset price will be volatile but ultimately down

96. **Which of the following statements are true with regards to defined benefit pension schemes?**

   I   The sponsoring company contributes a fixed amount to the scheme per year, relative the each employees current salary

   II   The employee receives a pension based on their salary at the firm when they retire or leave the firm

   III The risk for ensuring there is sufficient funds within the pension scheme lies with the sponsoring company

   A II only

   B I and II

   C I and III

   D II and III

97. **Which of the following should not be considered when identifying a client's objectives and constraints?**

   A Investment horizon

   B Stock selection

   C Requirements for cash

   D Risk tolerance

98. **Which of the following is a requirement of the Companies Act 2006?**

   A A Chairman's Statement

   B A statement of fundamental concepts

   C A balance sheet

   D A summary of the firm's business plans

99. **Which of the following is a problem with the government borrowing to finance government spending?**

   A Increase in taxes

   B Reduction in demand for cash balances from companies

   C Increase in private investment

   D Increase in the exchange rate

100. **Which of the following is/are advantages of investing through collective investment vehicles?**

      I   Any capital gains made are exempt from capital gains tax

      II   Economies of scale through larger assets under management

      III   Easier to access benefits of diversification

  A I only

  B I and II

  C II and III

  D I, II and III

101. **Which of the following is least likely to have an effect on consumer spending?**

  A Exchange rates

  B Consumer confidence

  C Inflation expectations

  D Marginal propensity to save

102. **What is a disadvantage of holding CFDs?**

  A Inability to enter into a margin trade

  B No capital gain

  C No voting rights

  D Inability to short sell

103. **Which of the following institutions would be classed as having real liabilities?**

  A Life insurance

  B Pension

  C Non-life insurance

  D Endowments

104. **Identify the best description of a conventional warrant**

  A An obligation to buy a new share in the company

  B An obligation to buy an existing share in the company

  C A right to buy a new share in the company

  D A right to buy an existing share in the company

105. **An investor currently holds an equities portfolio. Which of the following equity index options strategies would provide the best hedge against downside risk?**

  A Buy a call option

  B Buy a put option

  C Sell a call option

  D Sell a put option

Answers

1. **B** A bond's coupon will have little impact on a corporate bond's credit spread

   See Chapter 6 Section 2.6 of your Study Text

2. **12.84** Using Gordon's Growth Model:

   60p × 1.07 = 64.2p (value of the dividend at Time 1)

   64.2/(0.12 – 0.07) = 1,284p = £12.84

   See Chapter 5 Section 3.3 of your Study Text

3. **A**

Gross proceeds =	10,000 × 100.36	10,036
Commission =	10,036 × 0.3%	(30)
Net proceeds		10,006

   See Chapter 9 Section 5.3 of your Study Text

4. **A** The dividend may not be paid, but would normally be paid cumulatively in arrears thereafter

   See Chapter 4 Section 2.14 of your Study Text

5. **D** A defined contribution scheme, also known as a money purchase scheme, invests money now in order to achieve a general increase in the value of contributions made

   See Chapter 9 Section 6.1 of your Study Text

6. **A** General insurance covers house, holiday and car insurance, where the maturities of liabilities are much shorter. A life assurance company generally has a longer time horizon

   See Chapter 9 Section 6.1 of your Study Text

7. **C** The yield curve is a graphical representation of the structure of interest rates, plotting the yield offered by bonds against maturity, i.e. the gross redemption yield against time

   See Chapter 6 Section 4.2 of your Study Text

8. **9,810.48**

Sale proceeds	9,840.00
Less commission (9,840 × 0.3%)	(29.52)
PTM levy (Nil as < £10,000)	(0.00)
	9,810.48

   See Chapter 9 Section 5.2 of your Study Text

9. **C** Both coupon and redemption value are protected

   See Chapter 6 Section 2.5 of your Study Text

10. **D** To establish the change in price we need to first convert Macaulay's Duration to modified duration

$$\text{Modified duration} = \frac{\text{Duration}}{1 + \text{GRY}} = \frac{3.2}{1.0873} = 2.943$$

$$\Delta P = \Delta Y \times \text{Price} \times -\text{MD}$$

$$\therefore \Delta P = 0.0025 \times £98.15 \times -2.943 = -£0.722$$

ie the price will fall by 72.2p

See Chapter 6 Section 2.3 of your Study Text

11. **165.71** Rate per month $\frac{10\%}{12} = 0.83333\%$

Value of deposit at end of one year would be:

$150 \times (1 + 0.0083333)^{12} = 165.71$

See Chapter 1 Section 5.3 of your Study Text

12. **5.1** You can use the ratios for this, or just take any number as the dividend and work out what the earnings and price would be. As long as the numbers are correct in proportion to each other, the trial answer for the P/E will be correct. We have assumed a dividend just paid of 10p

Using Gordon's Growth Model, Share price $= \dfrac{10p \times 1.02}{0.12 - 0.02} = 102p$

Assuming our dividend of 10p, then the EPS must be 20p, as the payout ratio is 50%

EPS 20p therefore P/E = 102/20 = 5.1

See Chapter 5 Section 3.6 of your Study Text

13. **C** Since all assets are valued appropriately on the balance sheet

See Chapter 5 Section 3.4 of your Study Text

14. **232.04** Rate per quarter $\frac{7.5\%}{4} = 1.875\%$

Value of deposit at end of two years would be

$200(1 + 0.01875)^8 = £232.04$

See Chapter 1 Section 5.3 of your Study Text

15. **83.25** $\text{Exd} = \dfrac{d_1}{r_e - g} = \dfrac{d_0(1+g)}{r_e - g} = \dfrac{(10p \times 0.3) \times 1.11}{0.15 - 0.11} = 83.25p$

Please note that $d_0 = 3p$, as the EPS = 10p, and the dividend payout ratio is 30%

See Chapter 5 Section 3.3 of your Study Text

16. **C** The holding period return is simply the gain during the period (money received less cost) divided by the initial cost, ie

$$r = \frac{D_1 + V_1 - V_0}{V_0}$$

See Chapter 11 Section 1 of your Study Text

BPP LEARNING MEDIA

17. **A**   The market has a beta of 1. Companies with a beta of less than 1 are often described as 'defensive stocks'

See Chapter 9 Section 3.1 of your Study Text

18. **D**   A peculiarly worded exam question. This is the most acceptable answer of those available

See Chapter 11 Section 4.1 of your Study Text

19. **A**   Using the annuity formula, the present value is

£2,000 × 9.81815 = £19,636.29

The required format for this question is £00,000 hence you must round to the nearest whole pound, ie £19,636

See Chapter 1 Section 6.2 of your Study Text

20. **A** $\dfrac{£98.50 - £96.30}{£96.30} = 2.28\%$

2.28% × 4 = 9.12%

We assume that the exam question is looking for an annualised return, using the money market convention of quoting a flat yield

See Chapter 9 Section 7.6 of your Study Text

21. **D**   Rate per quarter $\dfrac{5\%}{4} = 1.25\%$

Value of deposit after five years would be

$5,000 \times (1 + 0.0125)^{20} = £6,410.19$

See Chapter 1 Section 5.3 of your Study Text

22. **D**   A holding in a subsidiary company is where another company owns ≥ 50%

See Chapter 4 Section 6.1 of your Study Text

23. **C**   A rearrangement of the accounting equation, where

Non-current assets + Current assets – Current liabilities – Long-term liabilities = Shareholders' funds

See Chapter 4 Section 2 of your Study Text

24. **11.7**   We are asked to calculate the TWR. This involves calculating the holding period returns between cash flows and compounding them together

Return over first six months

(£135 – £125) / £125 = 0.08 or 8%

Return over second six months

(£150 – £145) / £145 = 0.0345 or 3.45%

*Note at the end of the first six months a further £10 is invested bringing up the value of the investment to £145. This then represents the base amount at the start of the second six months

TWR = (1.08 × 1.0345) –1 = 0.117 or 11.7%

See Chapter 11 Section 2.2 of your Study Text

25. **A** The others are either capitalised or deducted straight from equity

    See Chapter 4 Section 2.3 of your Study Text

26. **12,297**

    Annuity discount factor $(1 - 25 @ 6.5\%) = \dfrac{1}{0.065}\left(1 - \dfrac{1}{1.065^{25}}\right) = 12.1978767$

    Annual payment $= \dfrac{£150,000}{12.1978767} = £12,297$ to the nearest whole number of pounds

    If you are having problems inputting the numbers into your calculator for the annuity discount factor, try the following keystrokes:

    $1 \div 0.065 \times (1 - 1 \div 1.065 \text{ x}^{\blacksquare} 25) =$

    See Chapter 1 Section 6.2 of your Study Text

27. **1.57** $\dfrac{£5m + £4m + £2m}{£7m} = 1.57$

    See Chapter 4 Section 7.3 of your Study Text

28. **B** This is like compounding except rather than adding interest we are deducting 10% each year.

    $£115,000 \times (1 - 0.1)^5 = 67,906$

    See Chapter 1 Section 5.3 and Chapter 1 Section 6.1 of your Study Text

29. **15** £10m + £5m = £15m

    See Chapter 4 Section 2 of your Study Text

30. **D** $\dfrac{\text{Earnings yield}}{\text{Dividend yield}} = \text{Dividend cover}$

    $\therefore$ Earnings yield/Dividend cover $= \dfrac{\text{Earnings yield}}{\text{Dividend yield}} = \text{Dividend yield}$

    $\therefore \dfrac{10\%}{2\times} = 5\%$

    Note: both earnings yield and dividend yield are net figures

    See Chapter 5 Section 3.2 of your Study Text

31. **1642** Return on the FTSE portion

    $(6000 - 5600) / 5600 = 0.0714$ or 7.14% = Return on the FTSE 100

    But this only made up 20% of our portfolio – 7.14% × 20% = **1.43% contribution**

    The S&P portion within the portfolio must therefore have returned 9% – 1.43% = 7.57%.

    However, we only obtained 80% of the return on the S&P 500, so the index must have gone up by more than 7.57%

    S&P Index return × 0.8 = 7.57%

    S&P Index return = 9.46%

    Therefore the S&P index must have finished the period at a level of 1500 × 1.0946 = 1642

    See Chapter 11 Section 4.4 of your Study Text

32. **15**   The range is the difference between the highest and lowest items

   12% – (–3%) = 15% range

   See Chapter 1 Section 2.9 of your Study Text

33. **D**   The long run is simply viewed as a combination of all the short-run possibilities, and so the long-run cost curve does pass through the lowest points of each short-run cost curve. The MES is deemed to be where the LRATC becomes horizontal. Thereafter, the LRATC begins to increase, reflecting diseconomies of scale

   See Chapter 2 Section 3.1 of your Study Text

34. **B**   Marginal cost only considers the variable element of cost

   See Chapter 2 Section 2.1 of your Study Text

35. **C**   The comparison to such a portfolio will provide the Jensen measure or excess return

   See Chapter 11 Section 4.1 of your Study Text

36. **B**   MV = PY, thus if M increases, V must fall in order for the equation to remain in balance

   See Chapter 3 Section 3.2 of your Study Text

37. **C**   As they are complements

   See Chapter 2 Section 1.1 of your Study Text

38. **C**   A shift in the Phillips curve is likely to be caused by a change in the natural rate of unemployment, sometimes referred to as NAIRU (the Non-Accelerating Inflation Rate of Unemployment)

   See Chapter 3 Section 3.8 of your Study Text

39. **A**   Arithmetic mean: $\dfrac{104 + 109 + 103 + 102 + 103}{5} = 104.20$

   Geometric mean: $\sqrt[5]{104 \times 109 \times 103 \times 102 \times 103} = 104.17$

   See Chapter 1 Section 2.2 and Chapter 1 Section 2.5 of your Study Text

40. **A**   Gilts are less risky than company debt as backed by the government

   See Chapter 9 Section 6.1 of your Study Text

41. **A**   Geometric mean $= \sqrt[8]{0.88 \times 1.07 \times 1.04 \times 1.09 \times 1.08 \times 0.97 \times 1.05 \times 0.94} - 1$

   $= 1.0124 - 1$

   $= 0.0124$ or 1.24%

   See Chapter 1 Section 2.5 of your Study Text

42. **B**   The multiplier looks at ways in which an increase in the level of demand is transmitted through the economy. Keynes viewed consumption as being based upon the level of income, which as it increases, the beneficiaries also increase their spending

   See Chapter 3 Section 2.5 of your Study Text

43. **B**   Both the geometric and arithmetic means can be calculated for negative values

   See Chapter 1 Section 2.2 and Chapter 1 Section 2.5 of your Study Text

44. **C** The efficient frontier is simply a diagram, plotting the expected return against risk for the various investment possibilities. The client would then select the best combination of risk and return, i.e. a point on the efficient frontier

See Chapter 9 Section 1.1 of your Study Text

45. **D** Dollar holding period return = $\dfrac{5\%}{4}$ = 1.25%. Most of the information in the question is irrelevant

See Chapter 11 Section 1 of your Study Text

46. **B** Portfolio duration is the weighted average of the bond durations

Portfolio duration = $0.2 \times 6 + 0.2 \times 10 + 0.3 \times 13 + 0.3 \times 15 = 11.6$ years

See Chapter 9 Section 7.7 of your Study Text

47. **C** As cash flows are fixed with fixed income instruments, they become worth less in terms of high inflation

See Chapter 3 Section 3.8 of your Study Text

48. **A** Perfectly competitive firms are price takers

See Chapter 2 Section 4.1 of your Study Text

49. **B** Of the three measures, the mean is the most distorted by extreme values

See Chapter 1 Section 2.6 of your Study Text

50. **1,197,525**

	£ buys		£ costs
Spot	1.5040	-	1.5061
Premium	(0.0032)	-	(0.0030)
Forward rate	1.5008	-	1.5031

Sterling receipt $= \dfrac{1,800,000}{1.5031} = £1,197,525$

See Chapter 3 Section 4.3 of your Study Text

51. **4.14** Using interest rate parity we have

Spot $\times (1 + r_V)$ = Forward $\times (1 + r_F)$

The current sterling interest rate is 5% pa or 1.25% per quarter, hence

$1.5040 \times (1 + r_V) = 1.5008 \times 1.0125$

$(1 + r_V) = 1.010346$

$r_V = 0.010346$ or 1.0346% per quarter, a quoted rate of 4.14% pa

See Chapter 3 Section 4.3 of your Study Text

52. **B** Since the asset is being sold at a profit the export value of the completed unit exceeds the import value of the raw materials. This will either increases a balance of trade surplus or reduce a a balance of trade deficit

See Chapter 3 Section 4.2 of your Study Text

53. **D** Whether the forward exchange contract is an asset or liability depends on how exchange rates vary prior to the payment date. If the dollar depreciates, the sterling value of the dollar receivables asset will fall and the forward contract will offer a compensating gain being recognised as an asset. Alternatively, if the dollar appreciates, the sterling value of the dollar receivables asset will rise and the forward contract will produce a compensating loss, thereby being recognised as a liability. This asset or liability must be reflected at fair value

See Chapter 4 Section 3 of your Study Text

54. **38.9** This can most conveniently be established by considering the impact on the sterling value of revenue and cost at present and following a 10% appreciation of the dollar based on £3 of spot rate revenue. At the spot rate we know that the labour cost, raw materials cost and profit each all one third of the revenue figure. We can then factor in the dollar appreciation as follows

	SPOT RATE VALUE	20% APPRECIATION VALUE
	£	£
Sales revenue ($ denominated)	3.0	3.6
Raw materials ($ denominated)	(1.0)	(1.2)
Labour (£ denominated)	(1.0)	(1.0)
Operating profit	1.0	1.4

Margin = $\dfrac{1.4}{3.6}$ = 0.389 or 38.9%

See Chapter 4 Section 7.2 of your Study Text

55. **B** The manufacturer wishes to buy an asset at a future date at a price agreed today – the definition of a long future

See Chapter 7 Section 1.1 of your Study Text

56. **A** The natural rate of unemployment is the rate of unemployment when the labour market is in equilibrium

See Chapter 3 Section 3.6 of your Study Text

57. **C**

Item	P_0	Q_0	P_N	Q_N	P_0Q_0	P_NQ_N
I	3	1	7	3	3	21
II	4	3	6	3	12	18
III	6	4	7	2	24	14
					39	53

Weighted arithmetic index = $\dfrac{53}{39}$ × 200 = 272

See Chapter 1 Section 4.5 of your Study Text

58. **3.0** $r_e = r_f + \beta(r_m - r_f)$

r_e = 3% + (0 × 6%) = 3.0%

See Chapter 9 Section 3.1 of your Study Text

59. **A** Crowding out is where the government does indulge in deficit finance. However, the large public sector will 'crowd out' the private sector by potentially forcing interest rates to rise

See Chapter 3 Section 3.1 of your Study Text

60. **A** Depreciation is merely an accounting entry and has no impact on cash flows

   See Chapter 4 Section 2.5 of your Study Text

61. **A** $\dfrac{2 \times 90p}{3} = 60p$

   See Chapter 5 Section 2.4 of your Study Text

62. **4.3** $\dfrac{3+4+6}{3} = 4.3$ years

   See Chapter 6 Section 2.3 and Chapter 9 Section 7.7 of your Study Text

63. **C** Modified duration = $\dfrac{\text{Duration}}{1+\text{Yield}}$

   The duration (in years) for a zero coupon bond will be equal to the time left to maturity. The MD will always be less than this

   See Chapter 6 Section 2.3 of your Study Text

64. **D** The nominal return (r) from a bond is the real return (R) plus an allowance to reflect inflation (i)

   $(1 + r) = (1 + R)(1 + i)$

   See Chapter 6 Section 4.1 and Chapter 3 Section 3.8 of your Study Text

65. **B** $Cor_{xy} = \dfrac{Co\,variance\,(x,\,y)}{\sigma_x \sigma_y}$

   $\sigma_x = 6\%$ or 0.06

   $\sigma_y = 9\%$ or 0.09

   $Cor_{xy} = \dfrac{0.004}{0.06 \times 0.09}$

   See Chapter 1 Section 3.2 of your Study Text

66. **2.14** Price = $\dfrac{20p \times 1.07}{0.17 - 0.07}$ = 214p or £2.14

   See Chapter 5 Section 3.3 of your Study Text

67. **A** Margins are due on derivatives only

   See Chapter 7 Section 1.1 of your Study Text

68. **B** The expected spot rate in the future is given by the purchasing power parity (PPP) theorem, ie the forward rate represents what the exchange rate (spot) will be in the future

   See Chapter 3 Section 4.3 of your Study Text

69. **C** Non-current assets   x
         plus: Working capital   x
         Less Long-term debt   (x)
         Net assets   x

     Net assets = Shareholders' funds

     ∴ Working capital – Shareholders' funds = Debt – Non-current assets

     See Chapter 4 Section 2 of your Study Text

70. **C** Rights issues result in raising new equity finance. In the short term, operating profit is unlikely to be significantly affected, but capital employed (Shareholder's funds + Long-term liabilities) will increase. This will lead to a reduction in the return on capital employed. Note the examiner does not stipulate whether he is discussing the short or long term. We have made the assumption that he is interested in the immediate short-term effect

     See Chapter 5 Section 2.3 of your Study Text

71. **B** Since FIFO includes most recent purchases in closing inventory

     See Chapter 4 Section 2.8 of your Study Text

72. **C** All companies must prepare a cash flow statement, unless defined as a small company, that is, turnover of less than or equal to £6,500,000 and total assets less than or equal to £3,260,000, and less than or equal to 50 employees

     See Chapter 4 Section 1 of your Study Text

73. **D** In a closed economy: MPC + MPS = 1. Therefore MPC = 0.8. The multiplier is 1/(1– MPC)

     See Chapter 2 Section 1.3 of your Study Text

74. **A** Since it is based on total portfolio return (less the risk-free rate) and the portfolio's total risk (i.e. after the benefits of diversification)

     See Chapter 11 Section 4.1 of your Study Text

75. **B** Corporate debentures are secured registered stock

     See Chapter 6 Section 2.6 of your Study Text

76. **D** There is no need for dormant companies to be audited

     See Chapter 4 Section 1.2 of your Study Text

77. **B** There are no currency contracts on NYSE Liffe. The short-term (3m) sterling interest rate future is cash settled

     See Chapter 7 Section 1.1 of your Study Text

78. **D** Straddles are constructed with one call option and one put option, where the two options have the same strike price and the same expiry date. This would be an example of a long straddle

     See Chapter 7 Section 1.2 of your Study Text

79. **A** Stock indices only consider capital gains and do not take into account reinvestment of income. Bond indices are total return indices, considering both capital gains and reinvestment income

See Chapter 1 Section 4.6 of your Study Text

80. **B** An interest rate swap is based on a notional amount and involves an exchange of the difference between the fixed rate and the floating rate of interest

See Chapter 7 Section 2.3 of your Study Text

81. **7.27**

$$\text{ROCE} = \frac{\text{Profit before interest payable and tax}}{\text{Capital employed}} = \frac{16}{220} = 0.0727 \text{ or } 7.27\%$$

The capital employed can be calculated as either

– The total finance = 60 + 130 + 30 = 220

– The net trading assets = 200 + 100 – 80 = 220

See Chapter 4 Section 7.2 of your Study Text

82. **B** Oligopoly, ie where there are only a few competing producers acting as a collective monopoly

See Chapter 2 Section 4.5 of your Study Text

83. **C**

TIME	CASH FLOW	DF	PV
	£	(6%)	£
1-4	7	$\frac{1}{0.06}\left(1-\frac{1}{1.06^4}\right)$	24.26
4	100	$\frac{1}{1.06^4}$	79.21
			103.47

The discount factor is based on the yield of a similar bond with similar risks (term and credit rating)

See Chapter 6 Section 2.3 of your Study Text

84. **C** Preference shares do not normally carry votes

See Chapter 4 Section 2.14 of your Study Text

85. **260**   Net book value = Cost – Accumulated depreciation (first two years)

or

Net book value = Residual value + Future depreciation (next six years)

ie

200 = 20 + Future depreciation (next six years)

hence

Future depreciation (next six years) = 180 = 6 × Annual depreciation

Annual depreciation = 30

Now

$$\text{Annual depreciation} = \frac{\text{Cost} - \text{Residual value}}{\text{Expected useful life}}$$

giving

$$30 = \frac{\text{Cost} - 20}{8}$$

240 = Cost – 20

Cost = £260m

See Chapter 4 Section 2.5 of your Study Text

86. **5.17**

$$(1+r) = \left(\frac{100}{\text{Purchase price}} \right)^{\frac{365}{\text{Days}}} = \left(\frac{100.00}{98.82} \right)^{\frac{365}{86}} = 1.05167$$

r = 0.05167 or 5.167%

See Chapter 6 Section 1.1 of your Study Text

87. **A**   Those offering an excess return for their level of market risk

See Chapter 11 Section 4.1 of your Study Text

88. **A**   Depreciation is a non-cash movement deducted from the project and loss account. It is therefore added back in to the cash flow statement. All the others should be deducted

See Chapter 4 Section 5.1 of your Study Text

89. **D**   Index tracking is an approach normally taken by traditional long-only fund management houses. It involves tracking a selected index and is a form of passive investment management

See Chapter 9 Section 6.2 of your Study Text

90.   **B**

Bond 1   %
Income return = £6/£100   6
Capital return = £3/£100   3
Total return   9%

Portfolio / Total return = 50% × Bond 1 total return + 50% × Bond 2 total return

8% = (50% × 9%) + 50%(x))

8 = (0.5 × 9) + 0.5(x)

8 = 4.5 + 0.5x

3.5 = 0.5x

x = 7%

Bond 2   %
Total return   7.00
Income return £5/£95   5.26
Capital return   1.74

Capital gain = £95 × 1.74% = £1.65

New price = £96.65 (95.00 + 1.65)

Therefore £97 in the closest available answer

See Chapter 6 Section 2.3 of your Study Text

91.   **C**   Other assets held are important in terms of the level of diversification amongst assets in a portfolio. The longer the term of an investment the higher the level of risk involved in that investment. The higher the level of collateral exposed to risk, the greater the risk of the investment

As such, the best answer to this is the mix of income versus capital growth since this considers returns rather than risks

See Chapter 9 Section 6.1 of your Study Text

92.   **C**   People who have turned down job offers should not be included within the unemployment statistics since they should be classified as not looking for work, and hence not unemployed

See Chapter 3 Section 3.6 of your Study Text

93.   **C**   An option is described as being in the money where it has intrinsic value, or in other words, where it would lead to a gain if exercised. Since the current market price is above the strike price it has no intrinsic value, or, is out of the money

See Chapter 7 Section 1.4 of your Study Text

94.   **C**   The current account explains the net level of imports and exports for a country

See Chapter 3 Section 4.2 of your Study Text

95.   **A**   A long futures position has a positive return when the underlying asset price increases in value, so as such an investor will only adopt this strategy, for speculative reasons, if they believe the underlying asset will increase in value

See Chapter 7 Section 1.1 of your Study Text

96. D For a defined benefit scheme, the sponsoring company bears the risk of ensuring that there are sufficient funds in the scheme to meet the obligation to pay scheme members the proportion of their final salary with the firm to be provided under the schemes rules. The amount to be contributed by the firm may from year to year

See Chapter 9 Section 6.1 of your Study Text

97. B Stock selection should not be considered when setting a client's objectives and constraints. The objectives and constraints will ultimately direct the fund manager as to which individual investments to select

See Chapter 9 Section 6.1 of your Study Text

98. C The Companies Act 2006 requires a set of financial statements to include an income statement, a balance sheet and a cash flow statement

See Chapter 4 Section 1 of your Study Text

99. B If an increase in government spending is financed through borrowing, then there will be less funds available to be borrowed by private business. As a result of this reduction of funds available to be borrowed, the interest rate will increase. An increase in interest rates will lead to lower demand for   funds (or cash balances) from companies

See Chapter 3 Section 3.1 of your Study Text

100. C The fund does not pay capital gains on gains within the fund, but when the investor sells their investment there will be CGT on any gains to the investor. So the statement 'exempt from capital tax' is incorrect

See Chapter 10 Section 1.1 of your Study Text

101. A Consumer confidence, inflation expectations and the marginal propensity to save will all have an impact on consumer spending. Exchange rates will have an impact on imports, but not on consumer spending directly

See Chapter 3 Section 2.5 of your Study Text

102. C A CFD (contract for difference) gives an investor the same return as if they owned the share, but without actually owning it. Since the share is not actually owned by the investor, they do not have voting rights

See Chapter 7 Section 2.3 of your Study Text

103. B Pension liabilities (the future pensions to be paid out to the employees) will be linked to earnings inflation, therefore will be higher when inflation is higher. Therefore they will need to have real investments, such as inflation linked bonds. Certain life assurance products also offer real returns but not all, hence the best answer is pension liabilities

See Chapter 9 Section 6.1 of your Study Text

104. C A conventional warrant gives the holder the right but not the obligation to purchase a share in an underlying company if they choose to do so. If the right is taken up by the warrant holder, the issuing company is required to create a new share to deliver to the holder of the warrant

See Chapter 7 Section 3.2 of your Study Text

105. **B** The investor currently holds an equities portfolio, and is concerned about downside risk, that is, losing money when the portfolio falls in value. To mitigate this risk, the investor requires a strategy which pays a positive return when the equities fall in value. From the available options, the strategies which best matches this description is buying a put option

See Chapter 7 Section 1.2 of your Study Text

PRACTICE EXAMINATION TWO

(105 questions in 2 hours and 20 minutes)

Questions

1.   **Which of the following is the normal life of the French government bond, known as the OAT?**

    A 20 years

    B Between seven and 30 years

    C Up to ten years

    D Life of over ten years

2.   **A company has the following items on its balance sheet.**

	£'000
Net book value of plant and machinery	42
Investments at cost	13
Inventory	35
Accounts receivables	15
Accounts payable	18
Bank overdraft	14

    What is the company's current ratio (to two decimal places)?

    Important! You should enter the answer only in numbers strictly using this format: 0.00

    Do not include spaces, letters or symbols (but decimal points and commas should be used if indicated).

3.   **A portfolio of the top UK shares has a Jensen measure of 2.0. If the return measured by the FTSE 100 over the last year is 18%, the required beta of the fund is 1.2, and the risk-free rate of return is 6%, what was the return on the portfolio (in % to 1 decimal place)?**

    Important! You should enter the answer only in numbers strictly using this format: 00.0

    Do not include spaces, letters or symbols (but decimal points and commas should be used if indicated).

4. **'Classical' unemployment refers to that part of the labour force which is**

A Involuntarily unemployed

B Unemployed because they are currently between jobs

C Unemployed as a result of a deficiency in aggregate demand

D Unemployed as a result of imperfections in the labour market causing real wages to be downwardly inflexible

5. **A six-month zero-coupon bond trades at £96.53 and a three-month zero-coupon bond is £98.41. How much additional annualised yield will be generated from holding the six-month zero-coupon bond for three months rather than holding the three-month zero-coupon bond until maturity, assuming the yield curve remains unchanged? State your answer on an annualised basis (in % to 1 decimal place).**

   Important! You should enter the answer only in numbers strictly using this format: 0.0

   Do not include spaces, letters or symbols (but decimal points and commas should be used if indicated).

6. **The performance of a UK unit trust which invests in both UK and Japanese equities should be measured by comparing its performance with that of**

A A combination of the Nikkei Index and the S&P 500 Index

B A combination of the S&P 500 Index and the FTSE Actuaries All Share Index

C A combination of the Nikkei Index and the FTSE Actuaries All Share Index

D The FTSE Actuaries All Share Index

7. **What is the premium to be paid this year on a CDS with notional value of £15m, a three year life and a spread of 15 basis points?**

A £7,500

B £22,500

C £67,500

D £75,000

8. **A Treasury Bill is issued with 91 days to maturity. The issue price is £98.20. What is the yield?**

A 7.35%

B 7.22%

C 7.17%

D 7.09%

9. **Total return bond indices**

   A   Measure the returns on all government bonds

   B   Measure the returns on all corporate bonds

   C   Measure the returns on all corporate and government bonds

   D   Take into account both capital changes and income flows

10. **Which of the following pieces of information will not be required before objectives can be set for an investment fund?**

   I   Knowledge of the client's future liquidity requirements

   II   Knowledge of the client's future liabilities

   III   Knowledge of all potential stocks which will outperform the benchmark

   A   I and II

   B   I and III

   C   I, II and III

   D   III only

11. **The following is a series of trades in stock A throughout the month of September. Using the FIFO method, what is the value of the portfolio on 28 February?**

   As at 1 February there are 12,000 shares purchased at £2.00 per share

7 February	buy 4,000 shares @ £2.20
13 February	sell 4,000 shares
22 February	buy 10,000 shares @ £2.30
27 February	sell 10,000 shares

   A   £24,000

   B   £26,400

   C   £27,400

   D   £27,600

12. **A bond pays an annual coupon of 8% and has three years to redemption. If it is priced at £97.47 with a yield of 9%, what is its duration in years (to two decimal places)?**

   Important! You should enter the answer only in numbers strictly using this format: 0.00

   Do not include spaces, letters or symbols (but decimal points and commas should be used if indicated).

13. If a bond has a price of £89.50, a coupon of 5% and a maturity of two years, which of the following is its redemption yield (internal rate of return)?

A 9%

B 10%

C 11%

D 12%

14. Compared to general insurance business, life assurance related business generally dictates that the insurance company holds more

A Longer term assets

B Treasury bills

C Commercial paper

D Certificates of deposit

15. Mortgage bonds are so called because

A They were originally issued by building societies

B They are secured upon property

C The bond holders are paid in bundles of land (no greater than one hectare) rather than coupons

D Coupon payments vary accordingly to bank and building society mortgage rates

16. A fund mainly consisting of top continental European shares is best measured against a benchmark of

A Eurotrack 100

B FTSE All Share

C DAX

D S&P 500

17. Given the following information on a fund's performance

Total return = 14.5%

Original benchmark return = 14.0%

Stock selected benchmark return = 14.2%

Timing benchmark return = 13.7%

Which of the following statements is likely to be true about the fund manager?

A Poor at security selection

B Good at market timing

C Poor at market timing

D Good at market timing and security selection

18. It is known that an asset will depreciate by £15,000 over its useful life of four years. If the expected scrap value is £2,000, what will be the net book value of the asset after one year, assuming the straight-line method is used (to the nearest £1)?

Important! You should enter the answer only in numbers strictly using this format: 00,000

Do not include spaces, letters or symbols (but decimal points and commas should be used if indicated).

19. The Dow Jones Industrial Average is based on

A The prices of all stocks traded on the New York Stock Exchange

B The prices of the largest 100 stocks traded on the New York Stock Exchange

C Only industrial companies which have been quoted on the New York Stock Exchange since 1928

D The prices of 30 blue chip stocks traded on the New York Stock Exchange

20. An investor has a choice of four bond portfolios

Portfolio	Return	Duration Relative to Market
A	12%	1.1
B	11%	1.0
C	11%	0.9
D	10%	0.8

If the risk-free rate of return is 4%, which portfolio should be chosen?

A Portfolio A

B Portfolio B

C Portfolio C

D Portfolio D

21. Which of the following pieces of information will be required before objectives can be set for an investment fund?

I Knowledge of the client's preference for risk and return

II Knowledge of the client's future liabilities

III Knowledge of the client's tax position

A I and II

B I and III

C I, II and III

D II and III

22.   A call option obliges the writer to

A   Always buy stock at the strike price

B   Always sell stock at the strike price

C   Buy stock at the strike price if the option is exercised

D   Sell stock at the strike price if the option is exercised

23.   An investor who believes the volatility in XYZ share prices is going to increase would

A   Sell a put option on XYZ shares

B   Sell a call option in XYZ shares

C   Buy a straddle on XYZ shares

D   Sell a straddle on XYZ shares

24.   The equilibrium price for a good

A   Is the price at which quantity supplied just exceeds quantity demanded

B   Is the price at which quantity demanded just exceeds quantity supplied

C   Is the fair price for the good

D   Is the price at which quantity supplied equals quantity demanded

25.   A barbell portfolio is where

A   The cash inflows match the cash outflows

B   The portfolio has bonds with durations much smaller and larger than the target duration of the portfolio

C   The portfolio has bonds with durations randomly selected around the target duration of the portfolio

D   The portfolio has bonds with individual durations similar to the desired duration of the portfolio

26.   The effective and efficient management of any portfolio requires which of the following?

    I   Clear objectives

    II   Clear performance evaluation criteria

    III   Specification of a risk-free asset

A   I and II

B   I only

C   II only

D   I, II and III

27.   A perfectly competitive market is one where

A   Each buyer and seller in the market can have a significant influence on market price

B   The many producers each have a significant influence on market price

C   Each individual buyer and seller has no significant influence on market price

D   The many customers each have a significant influence on market price

28. A fund manager who is successful at market timing will

A   Increase the beta of a portfolio prior to market rises

B   Decrease the beta of a portfolio prior to market rises

C   Increase the beta of a portfolio prior to market falls

D   Have a portfolio beta less than the beta required by the client

29. Marginal cost is

A   The addition to total cost as a result of a unit increase in profits

B   The addition to total cost when output is increased by one unit

C   The addition to average cost when output is increased by one unit

D   The addition to total profits when output is increased by one unit

30. To form a frequency table using a large sample of data requires which of the following?

    I   A decision to determine the number of groups

    II   A decision to determine the interval boundaries

    III   A clear understanding of the order of the data

A   I, II and III

B   I and II

C   I and III

D   II and III

31. What is a yield curve?

A   A plot of the gross redemption yields of bonds with various maturities at a point in time

B   A plot of the gross redemption yields of bonds with various maturities over time

C   A graph of an index of bonds of different maturities plotted over time

D   The plot of an index of bonds' accrued interest over time

32. Company X has the following assets and liabilities on its balance sheet.

	£'000
Premises	250
Computer equipment	25
Inventory	35
Accounts receivable	45
Bank loan	20
Accounts payable	40

What is the quick ratio for this company?

A   1.5×

B   1.75×

C   1.125×

D   1.0×

33. **Which of the following attributes might a warrant have?**

      I   An exercise price which may change during the life of the contract

      II   Protection against stock splits

      III   A longer time to maturity than a call option

      IV   It may be attached to a bond issue

A I, II, III and IV

B I, II and III

C I and II

D I and III

34. **A bond has three years to redemption at par and pays an 8% coupon payable at the end of each of the three years. Interest rates are 9.5% and it is currently priced at £96.24. What is the duration of this bond?**

A 2.21 years

B 3.01 years

C 2.69 years

D 2.78 years

35. **A gilt pays coupons on 7 June and 7 December each year. How many days' interest will be accrued if the bond is purchased on Friday 16 August?**

A 71

B 72

C 73

D 74

36. **For a fixed level of government spending, an increase in the tax rate will**

A Reduce the equilibrium level of national income and raise the size of the budget deficit

B Increase the equilibrium level of national income through the balanced budget multiplier, and reduce the budget deficit

C Reduce the equilibrium level of national income and the size of the budget deficit

D Leave the equilibrium level of national income unchanged and reduce the budget deficit

37. **For a normal good, the quantity demanded**

A Always has constant elasticity

B Is positively related to price

C Is price inelastic

D Is inversely related to price

38. **What is the demand curve as seen by a monopolist and firm in perfect competition respectively?**

        I   Monopolist: Downward sloping   PC: Horizontal

        II   Monopolist: Elastic   PC: Inelastic

        III Monopolist: Downward sloping   PC: Downward sloping

    A   I and II

    B   I only

    C   II only

    D   I and III

39. **An investor investing into an index tracker is wanting**

    A   Positive alpha

    B   Negative alpha

    C   Superior returns

    D   Zero alpha

40. **Three-month bills are priced at £98.30 and six-month bills are priced at £96.20. What extra holding period return will you obtain over the three-month bill by buying six-month bills and selling them in three months' time, assuming the yield curve is unchanged (in % to 2 decimal places)?**

    Important! You should enter the answer only in numbers strictly using this format: 0.00

    Do not include spaces, letters or symbols (but decimal points and commas should be used if indicated).

41. **If long-term average costs fall as output rises, the firm is**

    A   Making abnormal profits

    B   Maximising revenue profits

    C   Experiencing economies of scale

    D   Experiencing diseconomies of scale

42. **An investor buys a put option on XYZ shares, with an exercise price of 250p. The option was bought for a premium of 10p. If the price of XYZ shares on expiry of the option is 220p, what is the gain/loss made by the investor?**

    A   10p

    B   20p

    C   30p

    D   –10p

43. Market indices can be used

      I   To monitor portfolio performance measurement

      II   To form the basis of derivative securities

      III   To aid in the construction of tracker funds

A I and III

B I and II

C I, II and III

D II and III

44. The investment strategy of an investment trust compared to that of pension funds may differ because of which of the following?

      I   Investment trusts have a more predictable net cash inflow

      II   Investment trusts have a less predictable net cash inflow

      III   Investment trusts are subject to different tax treatment

A III only

B I and III

C I only

D II only

The following information relates to questions 45 to 50

You have recently met with a client who wishes you to take over the management of his equity portfolio that is currently worth £1,500,000 and is composed of 15 equities from a number of different sectors. The client believes his portfolio provides a close match to the market and has stated that the reason for asking you to take over is that he believes that under his management the portfolio has underperformed the market, returning only 8.6% when the market has returned 10% and the risk-free rate has been 5%.

An analysis of the portfolio reveals that it has a beta of 0.7 and that all of the stocks in the portfolio are positively correlated to the market, though some have quite low correlations. The riskiest share in the portfolio has a beta of +1 and has just paid a dividend of 26p, dividends have historically grown at the risk-free rate.

The FTSE index currently stands at 4500 and the FTSE 100 index future for delivery in three months stands at 4550. The client has noted a concern that the market will fall over the next three months and suggests you consider hedging the portfolio.

45. Increasing the number of stocks in the portfolio would

A Increase systematic risk

B Reduce unsystematic risk

C Move the portfolio beta towards one

D Reduce the total risk

46. **Based on the Jensen measure for the portfolio which statement is true?**

   A The portfolio has outperformed by 0.1%

   B The portfolio has underperformed by 0.1%

   C The portfolio has outperformed by 0.2%

   D The portfolio has underperformed by 0.2%

47. **The correlation between the stocks and the market means that**

   A If the market rises the portfolio will rise

   B If the market falls the portfolio will rise

   C On average the portfolio will move with the market

   D On average the portfolio will move against the market

48. **The price of the FTSE 100 futures index is 4550. If the portfolio is hedged for the next three months using the three month FTSE 100 index future value of 4500, what will be the locked-in value at the end of the period be closest to?**

   A £1,500,000

   B £1,512,000

   C £1,550,000

   D £1,665,000

49. **Calculate the price of the riskiest share in the portfolio (in £ to two decimal places)**

   Important! You should enter the answer only in numbers strictly using this format: 0.00

   Do not include spaces, letters or symbols (but decimal points and commas should be used if indicated).

50. **What is the client's portfolio Treynor measure expressed (in % to 2 decimal places)?**

   Important! You should enter the answer only in numbers strictly using this format: 0.00

   Do not include spaces, letters or symbols. (but decimal points and commas should be used if indicated).

51. **A bank that provides an interest rate cap loan for a borrower is effectively**

   A Selling an interest rate put option

   B Buying an interest rate put option

   C Selling a interest rate call option

   D Buying an interest rate call option

52. **Which of the following items are included in the UK's capital account?**

   A Expenditure of UK tourists on holiday abroad

   B The export of cars produced by Nissan in the UK

   C Insurance services provide by Lloyd's of London to overseas clients

   D The purchase by UK firms of factories and plants located abroad

53. **The original benchmark return plus selection gain plus the timing gain is equal to**

   A The return on the portfolio

   B The return on the portfolio plus the interaction gain

   C The Sharpe measure of portfolio performance

   D The return on a portfolio less the interaction gain

54. **What is the maximum maturity on issue for commercial paper in the UK market?**

   A Three months

   B Six months

   C One year

   D Five years

55. **40% of a portfolio consists of nine-year duration bonds and 60% of 11-year duration bonds. If the expected return on the portfolio is 11% and the market return and duration are 10.5% and nine years respectively, what is the risk-free rate of return closest to?**

   A 6.1%

   B 6.8%

   C 7.3%

   D 7.9%

56. **Which one of the following money market instruments is not quoted on a discount basis?**

   A Certificate of deposit

   B Commercial paper

   C Treasury bill

   D Commercial bill

57. **Which of the following statements about UK T-bills is true?**

   A They can sometimes be issued by UK corporations

   B They cannot be purchased by overseas investors

   C They cannot be resold and must be held until maturity (usually six months)

   D They are considered to be money market instruments

58. **As the average age of contributors to a pension fund decreases, trustees of the fund might require**

   A A greater proportion of the fund invested in index-linked securities

   B A greater degree of mismatching

   C A greater proportion of the fund invested in gilts

   D A greater proportion of the fund invested in all fixed income securities

59. **The best definition of an eligible bill is**

   A A forward-dated acknowledgement of a debt issued by a company which has now reached maturity

   B A bill issued by an Accepting House

   C A bill eligible to be discounted by a Discount House

   D A commercial bill which has been accepted by a bank and which the Bank of England is prepared to purchase in the money markets

60. **Gilt-edged securities transactions are usually settled how long after the trade date?**

   A On the next business day

   B Five working days

   C Ten working days

   D They are always settled on the same day

61. **In a closed economy what will be the effect on aggregate demand of a fall in government spending?**

   A A fall equal to the reduction in government spending

   B A fall greater than the reduction in spending

   C A rise equal to the reduction in spending

   D A rise greater than the reduction in spending

62. **Which of the following is the correct order in a liquidation?**

   A Preference shares, deferred shares, ordinary shares, warrants

   B Warrants, preference shares, ordinary shares, deferred shares

   C Deferred shares, preference shares, ordinary shares, warrants

   D Preference shares, ordinary shares, deferred shares, warrants

63. **An investor buys a put option with a strike of 230 pence for a premium of 25 pence. What is the investor's maximum profit?**

   A 230 pence

   B Unlimited

   C 255 pence

   D 205 pence

64. **A pension fund with an increasing average age will**

    A   Invest more in property

    B   Invest more in equities

    C   Invest more in fixed interest securities

    D   Invest in riskier assets to increase returns

---

65. **If a business has a quick ratio of 1.5, inventory of £30,000, cash of £10,000 and current liabilities of £40,000, what is the value of its receivables (to the nearest £1)?**

    Important! You should enter the answer only in numbers strictly using this format: 00,000

    Do not include spaces, letters or symbols (but decimal points and commas should be used if indicated).

---

66. **A company issues 10,000 shares with a nominal value of 50 pence for 80 pence each. What is the effect on reserves?**

    A   £5,000

    B   £8,000

    C   £3,000

    D   No effect

---

67. **Which of the following is the most likely form of investment for a UK pension fund?**

    A   Overseas equities

    B   UK Ordinary shares

    C   Corporate debt

    D   Gilts

---

68. **An investor buys an 8% bond for £105.00 just after it had paid its annual coupon. The investor holds the bond for one year and then sells it shortly after receiving the coupon, realising a total return on the bond of 4.75%. What is the price at which the bond was sold (to the nearest £1)?**

    Important! You should enter the answer only in numbers strictly using this format: 000

    Do not include spaces, letters or symbols (but decimal points and commas should be used if indicated).

69. If a company has earnings per share of 50 pence and pays a dividend of 25 pence, what is the dividend cover (to two decimal places)?

   Important! You should enter the answer only in numbers strictly using this format: 0.00

   Do not include spaces, letters or symbols (but decimal points and commas should be used if indicated).

70. The possibility that future coupons cannot be reinvested at the expected yield when holding a bond is known as

   A   Interest rate risk

   B   Reinvestment risk

   C   Coupon risk

   D   Capital risk

71. The variation margin that is payable to the clearing house in respect of exchange-traded futures is calculated with reference to

   A   The clearing house's assessment of the credit rating of the buyer

   B   The largest one day change anticipated in that particular contract

   C   The date the future was traded and its expiry date

   D   The daily change in value of the future

72. Which of the following indicates the risk of default for a bond?

   A   The coupon rate

   B   The discount to par

   C   The credit rating

   D   The sign of the credit rating

73. Which of the following is not true of an index?

   A   It shows the relative difference between values at a current date and a base date

   B   It measures the absolute difference between values at a current date and a base date

   C   The base date should not be an extreme

   D   It must be rebased historically to 100

74. In economics, the general view held is that companies in the long run will always try to

   A   Maximise output

   B   Minimise costs

   C   Maximise return

   D   Maximise profit

75. **In a perfectly competitive market, which of the following would result in a company ceasing production?**

A   Marginal revenue less than average total costs

B   Average revenue less than average variable cost

C   Marginal costs less than market price

D   Average total costs less than marginal revenue

76. **Which of the following is not true of personal pensions?**

A   It is possible to contract out of the Second State Pension into a personal pension plan

B   Employers may contribute to a personal pension plan

C   Legislation imposes a ceiling on the maximum benefits from a personal pension

D   Legislation imposes a ceiling on contributions into a personal pension

77. **An active bond fund manager considering investment over a specific period is carrying out**

A   Period analysis

B   Horizon analysis

C   Yield curve analysis

D   Fundamental analysis

78. **A convertible bond is priced at £400 and gives the right to convert into 40 shares. If the shares are currently traded at £5.40, what is the conversion value (to the nearest £1)?**

Important! You should enter the answer only in numbers strictly using this format: 000

Do not include spaces, letters or symbols (but decimal points and commas should be used if indicated).

79. **Why would a general insurance company like to invest in short term assets?**

A   To match the maturity of its liabilities

B   They offer a higher return compared with long term assets

C   Short term assets are less liquid

D   Regulators only permit the purchase of short term assets

80. **How may a property investor realise capital from their portfolio?**

I   Investing in property bonds

II   A mortgage

III   Sale and leaseback

A   I, II and III

B   II and III

C   III only

D   I and III

81. The GRY on a three-month 10% coupon gilt is 6½% and that on a six-month 10% coupon gilt is 7%. If you buy the six-month gilt and sell it after three months, what is the extra return you will generate on an annualised basic if the yield curve remains unchanged from buying the six-month rather than three-month bond?

   A   0.4%

   B   0.5%

   C   0.9%

   D   1.2%

82. Which of the following is the usual definition of total holding period return?

   A   Change in share price plus income (including reinvested income)

   B   Change in share price

   C   Change in share price plus income (including reinvested income) over the period divided by the opening share price

   D   Change in share price plus income (including reinvested income) over the period divided by the closing share price

83. Which of the following statements about investment trust companies is/are true?

      I   An investment trust company is not structured as a legal trust under trust legislation

      II   Investment trust companies are said to be closed-ended funds

      III   Investment trust companies can raise more funds by either issuing more shares or by borrowing capital

   A   I and II

   B   I only

   C   II and III

   D   I, II and III

84. A shareholder owns 4,000 shares in a company, each with a value of £3.25. The board of directors carries out a 1 for 8 rights issue at a subscription price of £2.44. What is the value of each of the rights?

   A   £0.09

   B   £1.44

   C   £0.36

   D   £0.72

85. Which of the following is not a current liability?

   A   Taxation

   B   Bank Loan

   C   Accounts payable

   D   Overdraft

86. **If the exchange rate moves from £:$ 1.64 to 1.65 the**

    A   Dollar has appreciated and US goods look expensive in the UK

    B   Dollar has appreciated and US goods look cheap in the UK

    C   Dollar has depreciated and US goods look expensive in the UK

    D   Dollar has depreciated and US goods look cheap in the UK

87. **Which of the following is the most likely outcome of the discount rate being too high?**

    A   NPV goes from positive to negative

    B   It is more likely to incorrectly reject a profitable project

    C   The NPV will be too high

    D   Interest costs will be too high

88. **Which idea requires depreciation to be included in a set of financial statements?**

    A   The accruals concept

    B   Prudence

    C   Consistency

    D   Going concern

The following information relates to questions 89 to 94

The following is an extract from the accounts of a company.

BALANCE SHEET	£'000
Non-current liabilities (3 year 6% annual coupon bond)	600
Ordinary shares with a 10p nominal value	120
Reserves	900
	1,620

The shares are currently priced at £2.40 and the bonds are currently priced at par.

The company needs to raise new funds to finance organic expansion and is considering a 1 for 4 rights issue at a price of £2.00. An alternative being considered is the issue of a convertible with the same coupon and maturity as the bonds currently in issue offering the option to convert into 200,000 shares, the conversion value is £76.80. An equivalent call option of the same term has a price of 26p.

89. **What is the debt to equity ratio for the company (in % to 1 decimal place)?**

    Important! You should enter the answer only in numbers strictly using this format: 00.0

    Do not include spaces, letters or symbols (but decimal points and commas should be used if indicated).

90. What will be the theoretical ex-rights price if the rights issue alternative is adopted (in £ to two decimal places)?

    Important! You should enter the answer only in numbers strictly using this format: 0.00

    Do not include spaces, letters or symbols (but decimal points and commas should be used if indicated).

    [   ]

91. What is the value of the proposed convertible (to the nearest £1)?

    Important! You should enter the answer only in numbers strictly using this format: 000

    Do not include spaces, letters or symbols (but decimal points and commas should be used if indicated).

    [   ]

92. What is the duration of the company's bonds (in years to 1 decimal place)?

    Important! You should enter the answer only in numbers strictly using this format: 0.0

    Do not include spaces, letters or symbols (but decimal points and commas should be used if indicated).

    [   ]

93. If the company chooses the convertible option, what will be the impact on the debt to equity ratio when the bond is first issued and when it converts, all other factors being equal

	ON ISSUE	ON CONVERSION
A	Higher	Higher
B	Higher	Lower
C	Lower	Higher
D	Lower	Lower

94. Which of the following would not fall within the reserves figure?

    A Share premium

    B Revaluation

    C Retained earnings

    D Contingencies

95.   Which of the following is a primary source of data?

A   FT article

B   Research article

C   Newswire feed

D   Survey data

---

96.   Which of the following is the correct classification of a prepayment?

A   Current asset

B   Non-current asset

C   Current liability

D   Non-current liability

---

97.   Which of the following is not a measure of dispersion?

A   Mean

B   Standard deviation

C   Range

D   Inter-quartile range

---

98.   Which of the following is a reason for setting up a revenue reserve?

A   Capitalisation issue

B   To fund future dividends

C   To fund a share buyback

D   To fund a corporation tax liability

---

99.   Free float indices were set up at the request of ?

A   Investors

B   Analysts

C   Exchanges

D   Regulator

---

100.   The asset turnover ratio is an indicator of what?

A   The level of leverage in the business

B   The efficiency of use of the firms' assets

C   The ability of the firm to generate profits

D   The ease with which the company was able to meet its interest payments

101. **The best description of the revaluation reserve is**

A   An account which shows the increase in value of tangible and intangible Non-Current Assets (not including goodwill)

B   A measure of the increase in value of inventory

C   The increase in the value of current liabilities

D   An account which shows the increase in value of all Non-Current Assets (including goodwill)

102. **What type of investment offers full or partial capital protection plus a certain type of return?**

A   Hedge fund

B   ICVC

C   Structured product

D   Wrap account

103. **What is the normal settlement period for spot FX transactions?**

A   T + 0

B   T + 1

C   T + 2

D   T + 3

104. **Which of the following is not one of the four Ps of marketing?**

A   Profit

B   Production

C   Promotion

D   Price

105. **ABC plc has the following income statement**

	£
Revenue	135
Cost of sales	85
Distribution costs	20
Administration costs	15
Other operation income	10

What is the percentage gross profit margin for ABC plc (in % to 1 decimal place)?

Important! You should enter the answer only in numbers strictly using this format: 00.0

Do not include spaces, letters or symbols (but decimal points and commas should be used if indicated).

Answers

1. **B** The French OAT has a normal life of between seven and 30 years. The JGB has 'superlongs', with lives of 20 years. The German Bund has up to ten years and the US 'T'-bond a life of over ten years

    See Chapter 9 Section 5.3 of your Study Text

2. **1.56** Current ratio is:

    $$= \frac{\text{Current assets due within 1 year}}{\text{Current liabilities falling due within 1 year}}$$

    $$= \frac{35 + 15}{18 + 14} = \frac{50}{32} = 1.5625$$

    See Chapter 4 Section 7.3 of your Study Text

3. **22.4** Actual return = CAPM expected return + alpha

    $r = r_f + \beta(r_m - r_f) + \alpha$

    $r = 6\% + 1.2(18\% - 6\%) + 2 = 22.4\%$

    See Chapter 11 Section 4.1 of your Study Text

4. **D** Thus wage demands are too high

    See Chapter 3 Section 3.6 of your Study Text

5. **1.3** Quarterly yield from yield curve ride $= \dfrac{£98.41 - £96.53}{£96.53} = 0.0195$ or 1.95%

    Annual yield from yield curve ride = 1.95% × 4 = 7.8%

    Quarterly yield from 3-month bond $= \dfrac{£100 - £98.41}{£98.41} = 0.0162$ or 1.62%

    Annual yield from 3-month bond = 1.62% × 4 = 6.48%

    Addition annual yield = 7.8% − 6.48% = 1.32%

    See Chapter 9 Section 7.6 of your Study Text

6. **C** This would be the most appropriate comparison benchmark, as the two indices closely reflect the relevant equity investment areas

    See Chapter 1 Section 4.6 and Chapter 11 Section 3.1 of your Study Text

7. **B** The CDS holder pays a spread of 15 basis points per year for the life of the CDS, or otherwise £15m × 0.0015 (i.e. 15 basis points) giving £22,500 per year

    See Chapter 7 Section 4.1 of your Study Text

8. **A** Yield $= \dfrac{100.00 - 98.20}{98.20} \times \dfrac{365}{91} = 0.0735$ or 7.35%

    See Chapter 6 Section 1.1 of your Study Text

9. **D** Indices in relation to the bond markets are total return indices. They include **both** capital gains and reinvested income

    See Chapter 1 Section 4.6 of your Study Text

10. **D** The objectives of the investment fund will depend upon the information received from the client, in terms of their objectives and/or investment constraints. These will include liquidity requirements, future liabilities, as well as areas such as tax status, time horizons and risk tolerance

See Chapter 9 Section 6.1 of your Study Text

11. **C** Follow these steps:

1.	1 Feb	12,000 shares @ £2.00 has a value of £24,000	total £24,000
2.	7 Feb	+4,000 shares @ 2.20 has a value of £8,800	total £32,800
3.	13 Feb	−4,000 shares @ 2.00 has a value of −£8,000	total £24,800
4.	22 Feb	+10,000 shares @ £2.30 has a value of £23,000	total £47,800
5.	27 Feb	−8,000 shares @ £2.00 has a value of −£16,000	total £31,800
6.	27 Feb	−2,000 shares @ £2.20 has a value of £4,400	total £27,400

The approach to apply is exactly the same as for the FIFO valuation of inventories

See Chapter 4 Section 2.8 of your Study Text

12. **2.78**

Time	Cash Flow £	DF	PV £	tPV £
1	8	$\dfrac{1}{1.09}$	7.34	7.34
2	8	$\dfrac{1}{1.09^2}$	6.73	13.46
3	108	$\dfrac{1}{1.09^3}$	83.40	250.20
			97.47	271.00

$$\text{Duration} = \frac{£271.00}{£97.47} = 2.78 \text{ years}$$

See Chapter 6 Section 2.3 of your Study Text

13. **C** Assume annual coupon and then use trial and error

$$\text{Proof: } £105 \times \frac{1}{1.11^2} + £5 \times \frac{1}{1.11} = £89.72 \approx £89.50$$

See Chapter 6 Section 4.1 of your Study Text

14. **A** A life assurance company will have longer term liabilities and therefore will not (generally) hold short-term, highly liquid assets such as T-bills, CDs or commercial paper

See Chapter 9 Section 6.1 of your Study Text

15. **B** Sometimes referred to as 'mortgage-backed bonds', these are linked to a portfolio of mortgages, i.e. the monthly mortgage payments, that are in turn linked to the underlying property itself

See Chapter 6 Section 2.6 of your Study Text

16. **A** The other indices only relate to one country's shares

See Chapter 1 Section 4.6 of your Study Text

17. **C**

Original benchmark   = 14.0%
Stock selected benchmark   = 14.2%
Timing benchmark   = 13.7%
Actual return   = 14.5%

	Actual/revised benchmark %	Original benchmark %	Gain %
Selection gain	14.2	14.0	0.2
Timing gain	13.7	14.0	(0.3)
Interaction gain (balance)			0.6
Actual return	14.5	14.0	0.5

Note: Actual, revised benchmark and original benchmark figures are given. Relevant gains are calculated from these with the interaction effect as the balancing figure

See Chapter 11 Section 4.4 of your Study Text

18. **13,250** Annual depreciation = $\dfrac{£15,000}{4}$ = £3,750

Cost = £15,000 + £2,000 = £17,000

NBV after one year = £17,000 – £3,750 = £13,250

See Chapter 4 Section 2.5 of your Study Text

19. **D** The Dow Jones Industrial Average (DJ30) consists of 30 US shares, chosen to be representative of the US economy. There is no pre-determined selection criteria based on size, instead they are chosen by the editors of the Wall Street Journal as US companies that are leaders in their field

See Chapter 1 Section 4.6 of your Study Text

20.   **C**   Return to relative duration $\dfrac{r_p - r_f}{\dfrac{D_p}{D_m}}$ for each is

$$A = \frac{12\% - 4\%}{1.1} = 7.27$$

$$B = \frac{11\% - 4\%}{1.0} = 7.00$$

$$C = \frac{11\% - 4\%}{0.9} = 7.77$$

$$D = \frac{10\% - 4\%}{0.8} = 7.50$$

See Chapter 11 Section 4.1 of your Study Text

21.   **C**   Client objectives and/or constraints include risk aversion, future liabilities and tax status, as well as time horizons, liquidity requirements and other preferences or legal constraints

See Chapter 9 Section 6.1 of your Study Text

22.   **D**   The writer of a call is obliged to sell if the holder exercises

See Chapter 7 Section 1.2 of your Study Text

23.   **C**   If volatility increases, option premium will increase for puts and calls. Thus the investor buys the straddle now hoping to sell it for more and close his position at a profit when premiums increase

See Chapter 7 Section 1.4 of your Study Text

24.   **D**   There is one price and one level of output at which supply and demand are in balance. This is known as the point of equilibrium

See Chapter 2 Section 1.1 of your Study Text

25.   **B**   A barbell portfolio is constructed with bonds that have durations distant from that of the liability

See Chapter 9 Section 7.3 of your Study Text

26.   **A**   A risk-free asset specification will not impact the actual management; it only assists in analysing performance

See Chapter 9 Section 6.1 of your Study Text

27.   **C**   Buyers and sellers are price takers in perfect competition

See Chapter 2 Section 4.1 of your Study Text

28.   **A**   An increase in beta indicates more risk than the market which is desired when the market is to rise

See Chapter 9 Section 3.1 of your Study Text

29.   **B**   Marginal cost measures the impact on total costs of one additional unit of production

See Chapter 2 Section 2.1 of your Study Text

30. **B** A frequency distribution groups the data of specific values and displays the frequency of occurrence of each bond. The order of the data is not relevant

See Chapter 1 Section 1.4 of your Study Text

31. **A** A yield curve is a 'snapshot' at one particular point in time

See Chapter 6 Section 4.2 of your Study Text

32. **C** Quick ratio $= \dfrac{\text{Current assets excluding inventory}}{\text{Current liabilities due within one year}}$

$= \dfrac{45}{40}$

$= 1.125$

See Chapter 4 Section 7.3 of your Study Text

33. **A** All attributes are possible

See Chapter 7 Section 3.2 of your Study Text

34. **D**

Time	Cash Flow £	DF(9.5%)	PV £	tPV £
1	8.00	$\dfrac{1}{1.095}$	7.31	7.31
2	8.00	$\dfrac{1}{1.095^2}$	6.67	13.34
3	108.00	$\dfrac{1}{1.095^3}$	82.26	246.78
			96.24	267.43

Duration $= \dfrac{£267.43}{£96.24} = 2.78$ years

See Chapter 6 Section 2.3 of your Study Text

35. **C** Days accrued = number of days from the last coupon payment date to the day before settlement (next business day – 19 August)

Accrued days = 7 June to 18 August (inclusive)

	7/6 – 18/8
June	24
July	31
August	18
	73

See Chapter 6 Section 2.3 of your Study Text

36. **C** An increase in tax revenue, whilst government spending remains the same, will lower the size of the budget deficit

See Chapter 3 Section 3.1 of your Study Text

37. **D** Normal goods are those which we increase our consumption of as their price falls

    See Chapter 2 Section 1.1 of your Study Text

38. **B** Monopolists face a downward sloping and inelastic demand curve. Under perfect competition the demand curve is horizontal and perfectly elastic

    See Chapter 2 Section 4.3 of your Study Text

39. **D** Index trackers want to track the index as closely as possible. Any movement away from the index represents tracking error, and it is this the fund manager is looking to eliminate

    See Chapter 9 Section 6.2 of your Study Text

40. **0.45** The holding period return is the return over the holding period of three months

    Quarterly yield from yield curve ride $= \dfrac{£98.30 - £96.30}{£96.20} = 0.0218$ or 2.18%

    Quarterly yield from 3-month bond $= \dfrac{£100 - £98.30}{£98.30} = 0.0173$ or 1.73%

    Additional holding period return = 2.18% − 1.73% = 0.45%

    See Chapter 9 Section 6.1 of your Study Text

41. **C** When the long-run average costs decline, as the size of an operation increases, the company is benefiting from economies of scale

    See Chapter 2 Section 3.1 of your Study Text

42. **B** 250p − 220p = 30p from exercise

    Less premium of 10p = 20p

    See Chapter 7 Section 1.2 of your Study Text

43. **C** Options and futures can use an index as the underlying

    See Chapter 1 Section 4.6 of your Study Text

44. **A** Pension funds are exempt from all tax, with the exception of the 10% tax credit

    See Chapter 9 Section 6.1 of your Study Text

45. **B** Increasing the number of stocks should improve diversification, i.e. reduce the unsystematic risk in the portfolio. The impact on total risk, systematic risk and beta cannot be confirmed without further information

    See Chapter 9 Section 1.2 of your Study Text

46. **A** Jensen measure $= r_p - (r_f + ß(r_m - r_f)) = 8.6 - (5 + 0.7(10 - 5)) = +0.10\%$

    A positive figure, hence the portfolio has outperformed by 0.10%

    See Chapter 11 Section 4.1 of your Study Text

47. **C** Positive correlation implies that on average the portfolio will move with the market. Only perfect positive correlation implies that the returns always move together

    See Chapter 1 Section 3.2 of your Study Text

48.   **B**

$$\text{Locked-in value} = \text{Portfolio value} \times \left(1 + \left(\frac{\text{Futures quote} - \text{Cash quote}}{\text{Cash quote}} \times \beta\right)\right)$$

$$= \pounds1,500,000 \times \left(1 + \left(\frac{4550 - 4500}{4500} \times 0.7\right)\right) = \pounds1,511,667$$

See Chapter 7 Section 1.3 of your Study Text

49.   **5.46**   The share has a beta of +1 hence the required return is the market return of 10%. With dividend growth at the risk-free rate of 5% the share price is

$$E_{xd} = \frac{d_1}{r_e - g} = \frac{d_0(1+g)}{r_e - g} = \frac{26 \times 1.05}{0.10 - 0.05} = 546p \text{ or } \pounds5.76$$

See Chapter 5 Section 3.3 of your Study Text

50.   **5.14**

$$\text{Treynor measure} = \frac{r_p - r_f}{\beta_p} = \frac{8.6 - 5.0}{0.7} = 5.14\%$$

See Chapter 11 Section 4.1 of your Study Text

51.   **A**   Interest rate options are options on futures. If interest rates rise, the short-term interest rate future will fall. If a party held a put on the future, they would, therefore, benefit if the future fell (i.e. if interest rates rose). This is effectively the same as having an interest rate cap – the party benefits if interest rates rise from the cap. The position of the bank, therefore, is equivalent to selling a put option

See Chapter 7 Section 1.1 and Chapter 7 Section 1.2 of your Study Text

52.   **D**   The capital account in the longer term aspect of the balance of payments, i.e. long-term investment flows either into or out of the UK. The current account considers the short-term flows into and out of the UK

See Chapter 3 Section 4.2 of your Study Text

53.   **D**   Original benchmark return + Selection gain + Timing gain + Interaction gain = Portfolio return

hence

Original benchmark return + Selection gain + Timing gain = Portfolio return – Interaction gain

See Chapter 11 Section 4.4 of your Study Text

54.   **C**   Commercial paper is simply a promissory note issued at discount to the face value, with maturities normally up to 12 months

See Chapter 6 Section 1.3 of your Study Text

55. **B**   Portfolio duration = $(0.4 \times 9) + (0.6 \times 11) = 10.2$ years

$$r = r_f + \frac{D_p}{D_m}(r_m - r_f)$$

$11\% = r_f + \frac{10.2}{9.0}(10.5\% - r_f) = r_f + 1.1333\ (10.5\% - rf)$

$11\% = r_f + 11.9\% - 1.1333 r_f$

$0.1333 r_f = 0.9\%$

$r_f = 6.75\%$

See Chapter 11 Section 4.1 of your Study Text

56. **A**   They are quoted on a yield basis

See Chapter 6 Section 1.3 of your Study Text

57. **D**   UK T-bills are issued by the UK government and can be freely traded in the money markets

See Chapter 6 Section 1.1 of your Study Text

58. **B**   The most suitable answer is B, as the time horizon becomes longer as the average age decreases, therefore allowing a greater degree of mismatching. The investment policy will depend upon the maturity of the fund. If the fund beneficiaries are close to retirement, it would be more appropriate to select relatively short-term safe investments. However, pension funds must also control the real rate of return and, therefore, will invest in 'real' returning assets that offer a degree of protection against the impact of inflation

See Chapter 9 Section 6.1 of your Study Text

59. **D**   Remember that a commercial bill is an IOU issued by a company. When an eligible bank has accepted it (i.e. the bank has given the IOU a guarantee), it is termed an eligible bill. This may either be kept until maturity when it will be repaid, or should the company holding this eligible bill wish to reclaim their debt earlier than the agreed time, they can simply realise their debt by selling the eligible bill on the money markets

See Chapter 6 Section 1.99 of your Study Text

60. **A**   Gilts normally settle T + 1

See Chapter 9 Section 5.3 of your Study Text

61. **B**   Due to the multiplier

See Chapter 3 Section 2.5 of your Study Text

62. **D**   Preference shareholders are always ahead of ordinary shareholders in a liquidation priority. Deferred shares will rank below these, as they have only a deferred right if certain circumstances occur. Warrant holders receive nothing on a winding-up

See Chapter 6 Section 2.6 of your Study Text

63. **D**   230p – 25p = 205p as an asset price cannot fall below zero

See Chapter 7 Section 1.2 of your Study Text

64. **C**   In order to reduce risk as the investment horizon shortens

See Chapter 9 Section 6.1 of your Study Text

65. **50,000** £40,000 × 1.5 = £60,000 = Amount of current assets less inventory

£60,000 – £10,000 cash = £50,000 receivables

See Chapter 4 Section 7.3 of your Study Text

66. **C** Issuing the shares causes an increase in share capital of £5,000 (NV only) and an increase in share premium of £3,000 (excess). Only the share premium forms part of reserves

See Chapter 4 Section 2.14 of your Study Text

67. **B** UK pension funds tend to invest the majority of their funds in the UK equity market

See Chapter 9 Section 7.8 of your Study Text

68. **102** If it generates a 4.75% return the terminal value of the investment must be

TV = 105 × 1.0475 = 109.99

Now

TV = Selling price + Coupon

Hence

Selling price + 8.00 = 109.99

Selling price = £101.99

The required format for this question is £000, hence you must round to the nearest whole pound, ie £102

See Chapter 1 Section 7.1 and Chapter 6 Section 2.3 of your Study Text

69. **2.00** $\dfrac{50p}{25p} = 2.00$

See Chapter 5 Section 3.2 of your Study Text

70. **B** Using NPV calculations, this assumes that surplus funds will be reinvested to earn a return equal to the discount rate. This may not be possible, i.e. reinvestment risk

See Chapter 6 Section 4.1 of your Study Text

71. **D** The variation margin is designed to cover daily losses made

See Chapter 7 Section 1.1 of your Study Text

72. **C** The credit rating aims to give an investor a clear perception of the quality of the bond, that is, the potential risk of default

See Chapter 6 Section 2.6 of your Study Text

73. **B** Indices are measures of relative difference

See Chapter 1 Section 4 of your Study Text

74. **D** The basic assumption is that of profit assumption and, in order for a firm to do this, the firm should produce at a point where marginal costs cut marginal revenues, i.e. MC = MR

See Chapter 2 Section 2.2 of your Study Text

75. **B** Option A would also, in the long run, lead the firm to leave the market

See Chapter 2 Section 3.1 of your Study Text

76. **C** Benefits from a personal pension depend on the performance of the fund

See Chapter 9 Section 6.1 of your Study Text

77. **B** Horizon analysis, or horizon matching, is where an active fund manager will construct a portfolio where the cash flows match the liabilities over a specific period

See Chapter 9 Section 7.4 of your Study Text

78. **216** $40 \times £5.40 = £216$

See Chapter 7 Section 3.1 of your Study Text

79. **A** General insurance companies include those offering car insurance, house insurance, and other types of generally short term insurance. Where claims are to be made, they will be within a short period of the premiums having been paid; hence the insurance company will want to keep its assets in predominantly short term and liquid investments

See Chapter 9 Section 6.1 of your Study Text

80. **B** Investing in property bonds would use capital, not realise it

See Chapter 8 Section 2.5 of your Study Text

81. **C** The final cash flow from both gilts will equal £105 (they have a 10% coupon)

MV of six-month gilt $\qquad £105 \times \dfrac{1}{1+\left(\frac{7\%}{2}\right)} = £101.45$

After three months MV of $\qquad £105 \times \dfrac{1}{1+\left(\frac{6\frac{1}{2}\%}{4}\right)} = £103.32$

$\dfrac{£103.32 - £101.45}{£101.45} = 0.0184 \text{ or } 1.84\%$

$1.84\% \times 4 = 7.36\%$

$7.36\% - 6.5\% = 0.86\%$

See Chapter 9 Section 7.6 of your Study Text

82. **C** Total holding period return includes all returns (income and capital) on the original investment

See Chapter 11 Section 1 of your Study Text

83. **D** An investment trust company (ITC) is structured as a company, not as a legal trust. An ITC is a public limited company (plc) that is listed on the London Stock Exchange. They are described as closed-ended, as there is a limit to the number of shares that they can issue, unlike unit trusts, which are described as open-ended, as they can issue as many units as possible. However, ITCs can raise more money by having a rights issue or, alternatively, through borrowing facilities

See Chapter 10 Section 1.2 of your Study Text

84. **D**

	NUMBER	PRICE £	VALUE £
Before	4,000	3.25	13,000
Rights issue	500	2.44	1,220
After	4,500		14,220

Theoretical price after = $\dfrac{14,220}{4,500}$ = £3.16

Value of the nil paid rights = £0.72 (£3.16 – £2.44)

See Chapter 5 Section 2.3 of your Study Text

85. **A** A current liability is a liability which will fall due within 12 months from the balance sheet date. A Bank Loan could fall due within 12 months, meaning the answer isn't B. Taxation is not a liability, whereas a taxation creditor would be a liability

See Chapter 4 Section 2.11 of your Study Text

86. **D** The dollar has depreciated, as it now takes $1.65 to buy £1 rather than the $1.64, i.e. it costs more dollar to buy £1, or in other words, dollars are worth less. US goods looks cheap in the UK. Consider a product that was being sold for $1.64. At the old exchange rate this would cost a UK consumer £1. When exchange rates move to $1.65, the product will remain priced at $1.64, but when this is translated into GBP the result is a lower number of GBP [$1.64/1.65 = £.994], or in other words, look cheaper to the UK consumer

See Chapter 3 Section 4.3 of your Study Text

87. **B** If the discount rate is too high, the future positive cash flows will be discounted too much, and hence will end up with a lower present value. If the future positive cash flows are too low, then there is a greater chance that they will not offset the initial cash outflow, which is unaffected by discount rates

See Chapter 1 Section 6.1 of your Study Text

88. **A** The accruals concept says that you should account for expenses when there are incurred, rather than when the cash is paid. The benefit of owning an item of non-current asset is incurred through all the years of ownership and as a result an element of expense, i.e. depreciation, should be incurred in each year of ownership. Prudence says that losses should be recognised when anticipated, and is applicable to impairments of non-current assets, rather than ongoing depreciation

See Chapter 4 Section 2.5 of your Study Text

89. **58.8**

Debt to equity = $\dfrac{\text{Interest bearing debt}}{\text{Equity shareholders funds}} = \dfrac{600}{1,020}$ = 0.588 or 58.8%

See Chapter 4 Section 7.3 of your Study Text

90. **2.32**

	NUMBER	PRICE	VALUE
Before	4	2.40	9.60
Rights issue	1	2.00	2.00
After	5		11.60

Share price = $\dfrac{11.60}{5}$ = £2.32

See Chapter 5 Section 2.3 of your Study Text

91. **107**

Value of convertible = Value of straight bond $+ \dfrac{A}{1+q} \times CR$

Value of an equivalent straight bond = par, ie £100.00

A = Value of an equivalent call option = £0.26

q = percentage change in the issued share capital if all bonds convert

$= \dfrac{200,000}{1,200,000} = 0.16667$

Conversion value = CR × Share price

76.80 = CR × £2.40

CR = 32

Value of convertible = Value of straight bond $+ \dfrac{A}{1+q} \times CR$

$= 100.00 + \dfrac{0.26}{1.16667} \times 32 = £107.13$

See Chapter 7 Section 3.1 of your Study Text

BPP
LEARNING MEDIA

92. **2.8**

Since the bond is priced at par and has a 6% coupon its GRY is 6%

Time	Cash flow	DF	PV	TPV
	£	(6%)	£	£
1	6	$\dfrac{1}{1.06}$	5.66	5.66
2	6	$\dfrac{1}{1.06^2}$	5.34	10.68
6	106	$\dfrac{1}{1.06^3}$	89.00	267.00
			100.00	283.34

$$\text{Duration} = \frac{283.34}{100.00} = 2.8334 \text{ years}$$

The required format for this question is 0.00, hence you must round to two decimal places ie 2.83

See Chapter 6 Section 2.3 of your Study Text

93. **B** When first issued the convertible will increase the level of debt with no change in shareholder's funds, therefore debt to equity is higher.

When it converts the debt level will revert to where it is at present but shareholders' funds will be higher as a result of the new shares issued, hence debt to equity will be lower

See Chapter 4 Section 7.3 of your Study Text

94. **D** Contingencies are nor reserves

See Chapter 4 Section 2.12 of your Study Text

95. **D** Primary data is information data obtained directly from the source, and can take various forms, including; scientific investigation/research, observation, discussion and market research. News articles are referred to as secondary data

See Chapter 1 Section 1.1 of your Study Text

96. **A** A prepayment is classified as a current asset

See Chapter 4 Section 2.8 of your Study Text

97. **A** Mean is not a measure of dispersion, but rather a measure of central location. Range is measured by subtracting the lowest value from the highest

See Chapter 1 Section 2.7 of your Study Text

98. **B** Retained Earnings is a revenue reserve. This can be used to fund future dividend payments. A capitalisation issue will not require a reserve to be set up since shares will be issued for free. A share buyback would be funded via the setting up of a capital redemption reserve (which is a capital reserve). A corporation tax liability would be shown as a liability on the company's balance sheet and not be shown as part of equity

See Chapter 4 Section 2.14 of your Study Text

99.　**A**　Investors are interested in knowing how many shares of a particular company are available to be traded, which is another way of describing the free float. Free float indices give a weighting passed on the available number of shares, i.e. those which investors could invest in

See Chapter 1 Section 4.6 of your Study Text

100.　**B**　The asset turnover ratio is Sales / Assets. This gives a measure of how good (or in other words, efficient) the company is at using their assets to generate sales

See Chapter 4 Section 7.2 of your Study Text

101.　**A**　The revaluation reserve captures increases in value of non-current assets, however, goodwill cannot be revalued upwards, and hence would not be included within a revaluation reserve

See Chapter 4 Section 2.14 of your Study Text

102.　**B**　A structured product provides full or partial capital protection plus a certain type of return

See Chapter 10 Section 1.2 of your Study Text

103.　**C**　Spot currency transactions normally settle on a T + 2 basis

See Chapter 3 Section 4.3 of your Study Text

104.　**A**　The four Ps are price, product, promotion, place

See Chapter 2 Section 5.5 of your Study Text

105. **37.0**

	£'000
Revenue	135
Cost of sales	85
Gross profit	50

$$\frac{50}{135} \times 100 = 0.3704 \text{ or } 37.04\%$$

See Chapter 4 Section 7.2 of your Study Text

PRACTICE EXAMINATION THREE

(105 questions in 2 hours and 20 minutes)

Questions

1. **Which of the following statements is true of Eurobonds?**

    I   They settle three business days after the trade

    II   They are bearer instruments

    III They pay coupon net of 20%. However, a bilateral agreement can reduce this to 10%

    IV   They pay coupon semi-annually

    A I and II

    B I, II and III

    C I, II and IV

    D I, II, III and IV

2. **A bond's redemption yield is 6%, with two years to maturity. The coupon is 8% and the bond is redeemable at par. What is the bond's price (in £ to two decimal places)?**

    Important! You should enter the answer only in numbers strictly using this format: 000.00

    Do not include spaces, letters or symbols (but decimal points and commas should be used if indicated).

3. **Which of the following best defines returns over a period?**

    A The change in price over the period

    B The change in price plus the income received

    C The change in price plus the income received divided by the initial price

    D The change in price plus the income received divided by the final price

4. **For a one-month holding period, which of the following is risk-free for a UK investor?**

    A One-month UK Treasury bill

    B One-month US Treasury bill

    C Three-month UK Treasury bill

    D UK Government Consol stock

5. **Given the following information for a company**

    Current ratio   = 1.8
    Quick ratio   = 1.1
    Current liabilities = £30,000

    what is the company's inventory value?

    A £18,333

    B £21,000

    C £33,000

    D £49,091

6. **If a portfolio has no specific or systematic risk, what rate of return will be obtained?**

    A Risk-free rate

    B Market return

    C Market risk premium

    D Nil

7. **A company's authorised share capital is**

    A The total share capital in the original memorandum of association

    B The total amount of share capital the company has currently in issue

    C The maximum amount of share capital the company currently has the power to issue

    D The amount of share capital the directors intend to issue

8. **£100m is invested for two years. At the end of Year 1, it has grown by 15%, after which a further £15m is injected. If the time-weighted return over the two years is 22%, what is the portfolio value at the end of the period (in £m to 1 decimal places)?**

    Important! You should enter the answer only in numbers strictly using this format: 000.0

    Do not include spaces, letters or symbols (but decimal points and commas should be used if indicated).

9. **What type of index is the CAC 40?**

    A Weighted geometric

    B Unweighted geometric

    C Weighted arithmetic

    D Unweighted arithmetic

10. **A warrant issued by the company on its own shares is essentially**

   A   A call option on the company's shares

   B   A put option on the company's shares

   C   A future on the company's shares

   D   A straddle on the company's shares

11. **If a company has after-tax cash flow of £60,000 and during the year it has depreciation of £10,000, a reduction in receivables of £7,000 and a reduction in payables of £5,000, what was its profit (to the nearest £1)?**

   Important! You should enter the answer only in numbers strictly using this format: 00,000

   Do not include spaces, letters or symbols (but decimal points and commas should be used if indicated).

12. **Which of the following will increase operating profit?**

   A   An increase in depreciation

   B   Reduction in depreciation

   C   Reduction in interest

   D   Reduction in dividends

13. **The calculation of the Jensen measure requires which of the following?**

   A   A passively managed benchmark with the same beta as that of the portfolio

   B   An actively managed benchmark with the same beta as that of the portfolio

   C   An actively managed benchmark with a different beta to that of the portfolio

   D   A passively managed benchmark with a different beta to that of the portfolio

14. **What is the internal rate of return of an 8% coupon bond with seven years to redemption trading at par?**

   A   8%

   B   8.7%

   C   9.2%

   D   9.5%

15. **An investor in an indexed equity fund is exposed to which of the following?**

      I   Specific risk

      II   Systematic risk

      III   Tracking error

A III only

B I and III

C I and II

D II and III

16. **Trading in the futures market compared to the underlying market**

      I   Requires less outlay

      II   Is less liquid

      III   Is more liquid

A II only

B I and II

C I and III

D III only

17. **What would be the present value of an annuity of £5,000 for the next six years at a discount rate of 9% (to the nearest £1)?**

Important! You should enter the answer only in numbers strictly using this format: 00,000

Do not include spaces, letters or symbols (but decimal points and commas should be used if indicated).

18. **For pre June 2005 index-linked gilts, the RPI used is how many months prior to the coupon date or redemption?**

A Eight months

B Six months

C Two months

D Four months

19. **Which of the following is the best definition of a Eurobond?**

A A bond issued by a foreign company into a domestic bond market and denominated in the currency of that country

B A bond issued by the European bank denominated in the euro into bond markets within the European Union

C A bond issued in a European currency into the US bond market via a US bank

D An international bond issue underwritten by a syndicate of banks, and sold principally in countries other than that of the currency of denomination

20. If the annual compound return on a portfolio is 8%, what would the return be over a three-month period (in % to 2 decimal places)?

Important! You should enter the answer only in numbers strictly using this format: 0.00

Do not include spaces, letters or symbols (but decimal points and commas should be used if indicated).

21. If the spot rate quote with the Euro is 1.2213 – 1.2301 € per £1 and the three month forward rate premium is 0.23 – 0.22c, how much will be received by an exporter who is hedging a €1m receipt in three months (to the nearest £1)?

Important! You should enter the answer only in numbers strictly using this format: 000,000

Do not include spaces, letters or symbols (but decimal points and commas should be used if indicated).

22. Natural unemployment could best be described as

A The level of unemployment where the only remaining unemployment is structural

B The level of unemployment where the economy is in equilibrium

C The level of unemployment where all those who wish to work are employed

D The level of unemployment where interest rates are constant

23. Where is profit maximised?

A Marginal cost = Marginal revenue

B Average cost = Marginal revenue

C Average fixed costs = Marginal revenue

D Where marginal revenue is maximised

24. The Nikkei 225 index is

A Arithmetic and weighted

B Arithmetic and unweighted

C Geometric and weighted

D Geometric and unweighted

25. In a closed economy with no government the Keynesian consumption function would be

A Steeply sloping

B Gently sloping

C A horizontal line

D A vertical line

26. **Which of the following best describes immunisation?**

    A Matching of assets and liabilities

    B Matching cash inflows and outflows

    C Matching the modified duration of assets and liabilities

    D Matching the duration of assets and liabilities

27. **Beta could be correctly described as**

    I   The correlation coefficient of the security and the market

    II   The proportion of a given fund that would have to be invested in the market portfolio to create a given risk/return profile

    III An index of a security's systematic risk relative to that of the market

    A I, II and III

    B III only

    C II and III

    D I and III

28. **In a closed economy with no government**

    A Consumption minus saving equals income

    B Desired consumption plus desired saving equals income

    C Desired saving equals desired investment

    D Consumption plus saving equals consumption plus investment

29. **Where a central bank exchanges bank notes for government bills and other securities, this is referred to as**

    A Government repurchase order

    B Open market operations

    C Credit control operations

    D Closed market operations

30. **In a situation where excess aggregate demand leads to inflation, this inflation can be described as**

    A Cost push inflation

    B Cost pull inflation

    C Demand push inflation

    D Demand pull inflation

31. **If the marginal propensity to save is 0.2, which of the following will be the marginal propensity to consume and the multiplier in a closed economy with no government?**

    A 0.8 and 1.25

    B 5 and 1.25

    C 0.5 and 5

    D 0.8 and 5

32. **In a perfectly competitive market in equilibrium**

   A   Average revenue equals price, but exceeds marginal revenue

   B   Average revenue exceeds price, which exceeds marginal revenue

   C   Average revenue equals price, but is less than marginal revenue

   D   Average revenue equals price and equals marginal revenue

33. **Which of the following is the best description of passive management of a fund?**

   A   The trustee does not appraise the performance of the fund manager

   B   The trustee does not have any involvement with the investment decisions

   C   The fund manager tries to pick stocks that will outperform the market

   D   The fund manager attempts to achieve the return on a benchmark of the appropriate risk

34. **The FTSE 250 Index is**

   A   Unweighted and arithmetic

   B   Unweighted and geometric

   C   Weighted and arithmetic

   D   Weighted and geometric

35. **A call option in Priesty plc may be purchased for £0.07. The current share price is £0.94. If the call option has an exercise price of £1.20, what will be the intrinsic value (in £ to two decimal places)?**

   Important! You should enter the answer only in numbers strictly using this format: 0.00

   Do not include spaces, letters or symbols (but decimal points and commas should be used if indicated).

36. **Treasury bills with a face value of £100 are available with three months and six months to maturity at £97.00 and £94.50 respectively. If a fund manager with a liability in three months' time decides to buy six-month bills and hold them for three months, what yield will be achieved by holding the bill over the three-month period (in % to 2 decimal places)? Do not annualise your answer**

   Important! You should enter the answer only in numbers strictly using this format: 0.00

   Do not include spaces, letters or symbols (but decimal points and commas should be used if indicated).

37. An investor has a US investment valued at $1,000 when the sterling/dollar exchange rate is £1/$1.60. If the investment increases in value to $1,150 at the end of the period and the sterling/dollar exchange rate is £1/$1.67, what is the sterling change in value (in £ to two decimal places)?

    Important! You should enter the answer only in numbers strictly using this format: 00.00

    Do not include spaces, letters or symbols (but decimal points and commas should be used if indicated).

    ┌─────────────┐
    │   │
    │   │
    └─────────────┘

38. When constructing a benchmark indexed portfolio for appraising fund manager performance, that portfolio

    I   Should be a passive portfolio
    II   Should reflect the risk that clients require
    III Should be constructed from more than one index

    A I and II
    B II and III
    C I, II and III
    D I and III

39. Which of the following would be reasons why a pension fund manager would increase their exposure to equities and reduce their exposure to gilts?

    I   The trustee becomes more willing to invest in riskier areas
    II   The average age of the contributors increases
    III The fund manager believes inflation will increase

    A I only
    B I and III
    C I, II and III
    D III only

40. The interest rate is 15%. You wish to purchase an annuity to provide £6,000 per annum for each of the next ten years. Which of the following would be the cost of the annuity?

    A £30,113
    B £28,630
    C £40,000
    D £32,317

41. **A 5% bond pays annual interest and has two years to maturity at par. If the bond is trading at £89.72, which of the following would be the yield of the bond?**

A 7%

B 9%

C 10%

D 11%

42. **At a company's year-end it had capital and reserves in the balance sheet as shown below.**

	£
Share capital	50,000
Share premium	25,000

At the following year-end, capital and reserves in the balance sheet were

	£
Share capital	75,000
Share premium	–

Which of the following has occurred during the year?

A 1 for 1 scrip issue

B 1 for 2 scrip issue

C 1 for 1 rights issue

D 1 for 2 rights issue

43. **The variance of the market returns has been calculated as 200. If a security has a beta of 0.8, which of the following will be the covariance of the security's returns and the market returns?**

A 80

B 120

C 160

D 200

44. **Which of the following is, or are, disadvantages of the mode as a statistical measure?**

I   It is distorted by extreme values

II   There may be more than one mode

III It is not appropriate for qualitative information

IV   It is difficult to calculate

A I and IV

B II and III

C II only

D I, II and IV

45. The covariance between a security and the market is 120. If the security has a beta of 0.8, which of the following must be the variance of the market?

   A 80

   B 96

   C 120

   D 150

46. Which of the following is true of gilts?

   A They pay annual coupons up to redemption at a fixed rate

   B They pay semi-annual coupons up to redemption at a fixed rate

   C They pay annual coupons up to redemption at a variable rate

   D They pay semi-annual coupons up to redemption at a variable rate

47. Which is the lowest 'investment grade' credit rating used by Moody's?

   A Baa

   B Ba

   C B

   D BBB

48. Which of the following is the correct priority on liquidation, from first to last, of the following?

   I Debenture

   II Ordinary share

   III Preference share

   IV Unsecured loan

   A I, II, III, IV

   B II, III, I, IV

   C I, IV, III, II

   D III, II, I, IV

49. A company's shares are trading at 180p. If its latest earnings were 9p per share, which of the following is the P/E ratio?

   A 0.05×

   B 5×

   C 20×

   D 2×

50. Which of the following would be the most appropriate way to assess the risk and return attitude of a client?

   A Ask what the highest return they wish to receive is

   B Ask how much they need to receive in excess of inflation

   C Ask them to pick from portfolios on their efficient frontier

   D Ask them what the highest risk they will accept is

51. **Which of the following are the usual issuers of CDs?**

    A Non-financial institutions

    B Local and municipal government bodies

    C Commercial banks and savings and loans organisations

    D Non-financial institutions which are not authorised in the country in which they issue

52. **If the spot rate for cable is $1.7770-$1.7860 and the forward rate is 0.36-0.35c pm, at what forward rate will the bank sell US dollars?**

    A $1.7895

    B $1.7825

    C $1.7736

    D $1.7734

53. **Which of the following leads to a minority interest in group or consolidated accounts of the holding company?**

    A A small number of shares held externally in one of the subsidiary companies of the holding company

    B The holding company owning a minority of shares in another company

    C Goodwill arising on a takeover

    D The holding company exercises significant influence over another company

54. **A company's shares are trading at 90p just before going ex-rights. If the rights issue is a 1 for 4 issue at 70p, what will be the value of a right (in whole pence)?**

    Important! You should enter the answer only in numbers strictly using this format: 00

    Do not include spaces, letters or symbols (but decimal points and commas should be used if indicated).

55. **Why do mature pension funds hold long term bonds?**

    A To match their liabilities

    B To comply with government requirements

    C To maximise their returns

    D To maximise their duration

56. **A fund manager wishes to invest in two securities which have betas of 0.7 and 1.3 respectively. If the fund manager wishes to construct a portfolio from these securities which has a beta of 1.0, what proportion of the fund should be invested in each security respectively?**

    A 0.7 and 0.3

    B 0.5 and 0.5

    C 0.8 and 0.2

    D 0.3 and 0.7

57. You hold £1,000 nominal value of zero-coupon bonds. If the yield is 7% and the bond has 4.5 years to maturity, what is the value of the bond (to the nearest £1)?

    Important! You should enter the answer only in numbers strictly using this format: 000

    Do not include spaces, letters or symbols (but decimal points and commas should be used if indicated).

    ```
    ┌─────────────┐
    │             │
    │             │
    └─────────────┘
    ```

58. If the dividend per share is 10.5p, dividend cover is 1.5 and net dividend yield 7%, what is the P/E ratio (to 2 decimal places)?

    Important! You should enter the answer only in numbers strictly using this format: 0.00

    Do not include spaces, letters or symbols (but decimal points and commas should be used if indicated).

    ```
    ┌─────────────┐
    │             │
    │             │
    └─────────────┘
    ```

59. What is indicated by a dividend cover figure of less than 1?

    A The company is insolvent

    B The dividend payment has been partly satisfied by accumulated profits

    C The company has exhausted its distributable reserves

    D The company has substantial distributable exceptional items

60. What is the hedge ratio if a fund manager holds £4,000,000 of UK equities and the FTSE 100 future stands at 4200?

    Important! You should enter the answer only in numbers strictly using this format: 00

    Do not include spaces, letters or symbols (but decimal points and commas should be used if indicated).

    ```
    ┌─────────────┐
    │             │
    │             │
    └─────────────┘
    ```

61. For a fund with both investments and withdrawals, which is the best measure of performance?

    A Jensen

    B Weighted Index

    C Money-weighted return

    D Simple interest

62. **Given the following fund values and capital inflows**

Time	0	6 months	1 year
Fund Value		95	133
Inflow	100	20	

what is the money-weighted rate of return?

A 10.8%

B 11.8%

C 12.5%

D 33%

The following information relates to questions 63 to 68

An analyst has made the following predictions regarding real GDP growth and inflation for the next four quarters

Scenario	Probability	Real GDP Growth	Inflation
I	0.3	+5%	+8%
II	0.5	+1%	+2%
III	0.2	–2%	–1%

The correlation coefficient between an asset the analyst is considering and real GDP growth is –0.80.

63. **What is the standard deviation of the GDP growth rate (in % to 2 decimal places)?**

Important! You should enter the answer only in numbers strictly using this format: 0.00

Do not include spaces, letters or symbols (but decimal points and commas should be used if indicated).

64. **If the economy turns out to be in the analyst's scenario III, what may be a fair description?**

A Downturn with disinflation

B Recession with disinflation

C Downturn with deflation

D Recession with deflation

65. **Which of the following assets would be most appropriate for scenario I?**

A Cash

B Commodities

C Bonds

D Interest rate swaps

66. In the event that we experience the median inflation rate, what would be the price of a share that has just paid a 20p dividend that is growing at this median inflation rate if investors require a 9% return (in £ to two decimal places)?

    Important! You should enter the answer only in numbers strictly using this format: 0.00

    Do not include spaces, letters or symbols (but decimal points and commas should be used if indicated).

67. What can we conclude regarding the asset the analyst is assessing?

    A   An increase in GDP has a positive effect on the asset price

    B   80% of the assets price movements are explained by changes in real GDP

    C   The asset returns will always fall when real GDP rises

    D   36% of the assets price movements are not explained by changes in real GDP

68. In the event that the economy moves to scenario III, which of the following economic policy actions is the government most likely to consider

    A   Raising interest rates

    B   Raise taxes

    C   Quantitative easing

    D   Reduce government expenditure

69. Goodwill is acquired under a takeover. You should

    A   Write it off immediately against reserves

    B   Treat as a fixed asset then amortise through the income statement over its useful life

    C   Treat as a fixed asset and undertake an annual impairment review

    D   Write it off against the profits for the year

70. What is the maturity of the Japanese 'superlong' bond?

    A   Five years

    B   Fifteen years

    C   Twenty years

    D   Ten years

71. A pension fund's trustees set a beta for a fund of UK equity of 0.85. The risk-free rate of return is 8% and the return of the FTSE All Share Index last year was 15%. The return on the benchmark portfolio under the Capital Asset Pricing Model would be what (in % to 2 decimal places)?

Important! You should enter the answer only in numbers strictly using this format: 00.00

Do not include spaces, letters or symbols (but decimal points and commas should be used if indicated).

72. A fund manager carrying out dedication is doing which of the following?

A Matching durations

B Matching cash flows

C Matching liabilities and assets

D Matching inflation exposure

73. If a fund has an investment horizon of five years, this means

A The investors may not remove funds within five years

B The fund manager cannot be changed within five years

C The fund's performance targets should be set with this period in view

D The fund has hedged risk for five years through derivatives

74. If a UK fund invests in UK and US mid-sized companies, a combination of which of the following two indices would be most appropriate?

A FTSE 100 and Dow Jones

B S&P 500 and FTSE All Share

C FTSE 250 and S&P 500

D FTSE 100 and S&P 100

75. A fund manager wishes to actively manage his portfolio. He is likely to engage in which of the following?

    I   Tracking

    II   Market timing

    III Stock selection

A I, II and III

B I only

C II only

D II and III

76. **CDs are**

       I   Tradable debt instruments

       II   Securities with set maturities

       III   Zero-coupon instruments

  A I only

  B I and II

  C II and III

  D I, II and III

77. **Which of the following have responsibility for banking supervision?**

       I   US Federal Reserve

       II   Bank of Japan

       III   European Central Bank

  A I only

  B II and III

  C I and III

  D III only

78. **Which of the following is not an expiry month for the NYSE Liffe future?**

  A March

  B September

  C November

  D December

79. **Which of the following is true regarding leaseholds and freeholds?**

       I   A freeholder owns the property in perpetuity

       II   A leasehold is created out of a freehold directly or indirectly

       III   A 99-year leasehold is considered to be a freehold

  A I and II

  B I and III

  C II and III

  D I, II and III

80. **Which of the following is true of the DAX Index?**

  A Weighted and geometric

  B Weighted and arithmetic

  C Unweighted and geometric

  D Unweighted and arithmetic

81. **Which of the following are responsible for managing government debt?**

        I   ECB

        II   Bundesbank

        III   Bank of France

A I only

B II only

C III only

D None of the above

82. **The JGB has a normal life of**

A Twenty years

B Between seven and thirty years

C Between two and five years

D Ten years

83. **Which of the following statements are true of preference shares?**

        I   Preference shares usually carry no voting rights

        II   All preference share dividends must be paid before any ordinary share dividends are paid

        III   Preference shares are considered to be less risky than ordinary shares

        IV   They pay a variable annual dividend

A I and II

B I, II and III

C I, II and IV

D I, II, III and IV

84. **Which of the following statements are true of the Short-Term Interest Rate Contract (STIR) on NYSE Liffe?**

        I   The size of the contract is £500,000

        II   The size of the contract is £125,000

        III   The tick size is 1 basis point, giving a tick value of £50

        IV   The tick size is 1 basis point, giving a tick value of £12.50

A I and IV

B I and III

C II and III

D II and IV

85. **Consider the following statements**

    I   Swaps are exchange traded

    II   The FTSE 100 Index future is priced at £10 per point

    III   Borrowers sell futures to hedge against an interest rate rise

Which is true?

A I and II

B I and III

C II and III

D All are true

86. **Which of the following best describes an investment trust?**

A A types of savings plan

B A type of life assurance

C A trust in which clients invest

D A company in which clients invest

The following information relates to questions 87 to 92

You are managing a fund for a wealthy private client who has a liability to meet in ten years' time but otherwise seeks to maximise returns within his specified risk tolerance. The economy is currently in a recession though the client expects it will emerge from this very rapidly in the short term.

Four bonds being considered for the portfolio are

BOND	MACAULAY DURATION (YEARS)	PRICE	GRY
W	7	96.42	5.62
X	9	103.75	5.73
Y	11	87.46	5.86
Z	13	102.46	5.94

The bond index against which the portfolio is being assessed has a duration of 10 years and the risk-free rate is currently 4.65%. Bond Z is a convertible that has a conversion ratio of 16. The shares are currently priced at £6.20 and have just paid a dividend of 47p.

87. **Three possible bond portfolios are being considered to immunise the ten year liability.**

    I   50:50 portfolio of bond X and bond Y

    II   50:50 portfolio of bond W and bond Z

    III   Equally weighted portfolio of all four bonds

Rank these alternatives in ascending order of immunisation risk

A I, II, III

B I, III, II

C II, I, III

D III, I, II

88.   If yields rise by 0.6% what will be the new price of bond X (in £ to two decimal places)?

Important! You should enter the answer only in numbers strictly using this format: 00.00

Do not include spaces, letters or symbols (but decimal points and commas should be used if indicated).

```
┌──────────────┐
│              │
│              │
└──────────────┘
```

89.   Given the client's economic outlook, which individual bond does he expect will outperform?

A   W

B   X

C   Y

D   Z

90.   What is the excess return to relative duration for bond Y (in % to 2 decimal places)?

Important! You should enter the answer only in numbers strictly using this format: 0.00

Do not include spaces, letters or symbols (but decimal points and commas should be used if indicated).

```
┌──────────────┐
│              │
│              │
└──────────────┘
```

91.   What is the conversion premium for bond Z (in % to 2 decimal places)?

Important! You should enter the answer only in numbers strictly using this format: 0.00

Do not include spaces, letters or symbols (but decimal points and commas should be used if indicated).

```
┌──────────────┐
│              │
│              │
└──────────────┘
```

92.   In relation to Bond Z's equities, what is their dividend yield (in % to 2 decimal places)?

Important! You should enter the answer only in numbers strictly using this format: 0.00

Do not include spaces, letters or symbols (but decimal points and commas should be used if indicated).

```
┌──────────────┐
│              │
│              │
└──────────────┘
```

93. **Consider the following statements**

    I   A random sample is one where every item in the population has an equal chance of being selected

    II   A random sample allows the research analyst to use his/her judgement in selecting a representative sample

    III   A random sample will always give a representative sample of the population

Which are correct?

A   I is true whereas II and III are both false

B   II and III are both true whereas I is false

C   III is true and I and II are both false

D   I, II and III are all true

---

94. **Consider the following statements**

    I   An auditor is an officer of the company

    II   An auditor is responsible for preparing the accounts to give a true and fair view

    III   If an auditor is unable to form an opinion then the auditor must issue a disclaimer of opinion

    IV   Dormant companies do not need to have their accounts audited

A   I and II are both true whereas III and IV are false

B   I and II are both false whereas III and IV are both true

C   I and III are true

D   II an IV are false

---

95. **Which of the following indices is a value-weighted, arithmetically calculated index representing approximately 900 different company shares?**

A   FT Ordinary

B   FTSE All Share

C   FTSE 350

D   S&P 500

---

96. **You will receive £750 half way through the year when the continuous interest rate was 15%. What is the present value of this sum (to the nearest £1)?**

Important! You should enter the answer only in numbers strictly using this format: 000

Do not include spaces, letters or symbols (but decimal points and commas should be used if indicated).

---

97. **Which of the following is NOT a feature of a private client fund?**

   A   Advisory dealing service

   B   Portfolio discretionary service

   C   Portfolio advisory service

   D   Discretionary dealing service

98. **An investor holds a share in a company priced at £6.20 and establishes a protective put by buying a £6.00 put at a premium of 70p. What is the breakeven price on this strategy?**

   A   £5.30

   B   £6.20

   C   £6.70

   D   £6.90

99. **What is the marginal propensity to import?**

   A   Average amount of each unit earned that is spent on imports

   B   Average amount of each unit earned that is spent on imports net of exports

   C   Amount of each additional unit earned that is spent on imports

   D   Amount of each additional unit earned that is spent on imports net of exports

100. **Which of the following is incorrect regarding credit default swaps?**

   A   They are OTC products

   B   The buyer of a CDS must also own the underlying

   C   The payout will be based upon a specified credit event

   D   The premium is based upon the issuer's spread over government bonds

101. **In a negatively skewed distribution which relationship holds true?**

   A   Mode > Median > Mean

   B   Median > Mean > Mode

   C   Mean > Mode > Median

   D   Mode > Mean > Median

102. **Capital employed is defined as**

   A   Total assets less total liabilities

   B   Current assets less current liabilities

   C   Share capital and reserves + loans + bank overdrafts

   D   Total assets less current liabilities

103. **Consider the following statements**

    I   Turnover < £6,500,000

    II   Fixed + current assets < £12,900,000

    III   Average number of employees < 50

    IV   Turnover < £25,900,000

    V   Fixed + current assets < £3,260,000

    VI   Average number of employees < 250

Meeting which combinations of conditions would allow a company to classify itself as a small company?

A   I and II

B   I and V

C   II, III and IV

D   II, IV and VI

---

104. **What is the conversion value of a bond priced at £80 offering the right to convert into 20 shares when the current share price is £3.50?**

A   £80

B   £70

C   £50

D   £30

---

105. **Company X has adopted a LIFO basis for stock valuation. You have found the following records of stock purchases and sales**

DATE	PURCHASES/(SALE)	
	UNITS	£
1/1	30	300
1/3	50	750
1/6	(45)	(950)
1/9	(10)	(200)
1/12	20	400
Year end	45	

At the year end the company's stock will be valued as

A   £525

B   £950

C   £775

D   £650

Answers

1. **A** Eurobonds pay gross annual coupon. They are bearer instruments and settle T + 3

    See Chapter 6 Section 2.6 of your Study Text

2. **103.67**

TIME	CASH	DISCOUNT FACTORS @ 6%	PV
1	£8	$\dfrac{1}{1.06}$	£7.55
2	£108	$\dfrac{1}{1.06^2}$	£96.12
			£103.67

    See Chapter 6 Section 2.3 of your Study Text

3. **C** Returns include both change in price and income

    See Chapter 11 Section 1 of your Study Text

4. **A** The one month UK T bill is free of default risk, Fx risk and reinvestment risk

    See Chapter 6 Section 1.1 of your Study Text

5. **B** Total current assets = 1.8 × £30,000 = £54,000

    Current assets less inventory = 1.1 × £30,000 = £33,000

    Therefore, inventory = £21,000

    See Chapter 4 Section 7.3 of your Study Text

6. **A** The portfolio is risk-free and will thus earn the risk-free rate

    See Chapter 9 Section 3.1 of your Study Text

7. **C** Authorised share capital is the share capital that the company is allowed to issue. Since some of it may have been retained for future issue (warrants and convertibles), it may not all be shown on the balance sheet

    See Chapter 4 Section 2.14 of your Study Text

8. **137.9** First we need to break down the two time weighted return to establish what the holding period return was for the second year. This comes to 6.09%. Then we give the initial investment by 15%, add on the 16m, and grow the total amount by 6.09%

    $$\frac{1.22}{1.15} = 1.0609 \qquad 1.0609 \times [(£100m \times 1.15) + £15m] = £137.9m$$

    See Chapter 11 Section 2.2 of your Study Text

9. **C** The CAC 40 Index is the French index which is arithmetic and weighted by market capitalisation

    See Chapter 1 Section 4.6 of your Study Text

10. **A** A warrant gives the right to buy new issue equity at a specified price on a specified future date

    See Chapter 7 Section 3.2 of your Study Text

11. **48,000**   £60,000 – £10,000 – £7,000 + £5,000 = £48,000

See Chapter 4 Section 5.1 of your Study Text

12. **B**   Interest and dividends are not part of operating profit.

See Chapter 4 Section 4.2 of your Study Text

13. **A**   The Jensen measure compares actual performance of a fund with the CAPM predicted performance for a benchmark of the same beta

See Chapter 11 Section 4.1 of your Study Text

14. **A**   For any conventional bond at par the GRY = Coupon

See Chapter 6 Section 4.1 of your Study Text

15. **D**   Equity funds are not exposed to specific risk as they are diversified

See Chapter 9 Section 1.2 of your Study Text

16. **C**   Futures are more liquid than the underlying instruments

See Chapter 7 Section 1.1 of your Study Text

17. **22,430**   Using the Annuity Discount Factor

$$£5,000 \times \frac{1}{0.09}\left(1 - \frac{1}{1.09^6}\right) = £22,429.59$$

See Chapter 1 Section 6.2 of your Study Text

18. **A**   An eight-month lag allows the next coupon (six months forward) to be calculated

See Chapter 6 Section 2.5 of your Study Text

19. **D**   A eurobond is a debt instrument issued by a borrower normally or predominantly outside of the country in whose currency it is denominated

See Chapter 6 Section 2.6 of your Study Text

20. **1.94** $\sqrt[4]{1.08} - 1 = 0.0194$ or 1.94%

See Chapter 1 Section 5.3 of your Study Text

21. **814,399**

	£1 buys €	£1 costs €
Spot rate	1.2213	1.2301
Premium	(0.0023)	(0.0022)
Forward rate	1.2190	1.2279

Sterling receipt in three months = $\dfrac{1,000,000}{1.2279}$ = £814,399

See Chapter 3 Section 4.3 of your Study Text

22. **B**   The natural rate of unemployment, known as the Non-Accelerating Rate of Unemployment (NAIRU) is where the economy is at equilibrium

See Chapter 3 Section 3.8 of your Study Text

23. **A** Profit maximisation is always where MR = MC

   See Chapter 2 Section 2.2 of your Study Text

24. **B** The Nikkei 225 and Dow Jones are both unweighted indices

   See Chapter 1 Section 4.6 of your Study Text

25. **A** As income is not absorbed by taxation on imported goods

   See Chapter 3 Section 2.5 of your Study Text

26. **D** Immunisation is the matching of durations. Dedication is the matching of cash flows

   See Chapter 9 Section 7.7 of your Study Text

27. **C** Beta is a relative measure or index number showing the level of systematic risk of an investment relative to the market portfolio. It also represents the proportion of a fund invested in the market rather than the risk-free asset. The correlation measures the relationship between two variable factors

   See Chapter 9 Section 3.1 of your Study Text

28. **D** This is demonstrated from the model of circular flow

   See Chapter 3 Section 2.1 of your Study Text

29. **B** Open market operations allow the 'soaking up' or injection of cash within an economy

   See Chapter 3 Section 3.9 of your Study Text

30. **D** Excess aggregate demand leads to consumers chasing too few goods and hence an increase in prices

   See Chapter 3 Section 3.8 of your Study Text

31. **D** MPC = 1 – MPS

   i.e. MPC = 1 – 0.2 = 0.8

   $$\text{Multiplier} = \frac{1}{1 - \text{MPC}} \text{ or } \frac{1}{\text{MPS}}$$

   i.e. Multiplier = $\frac{1}{0.2}$ = 5

   See Chapter 3 Section 2.5 of your Study Text

32. **D** Equilibrium in a perfectly competitive market is where the marginal revenue equals average revenue which equals demand, i.e. at a price (P_E). This is represented by a horizontal demand line

   See Chapter 2 Section 4.1 of your Study Text

33. **D** Passive fund management techniques would involve tracking a fund in an attempt to return the same as that fund being used as a benchmark

   See Chapter 9 Section 6.2 of your Study Text

34. **C** The FTSE indices are all weighted by market capitalisation and arithmetically calculated, except for the FT 30, which is geometric and unweighted

   See Chapter 1 Section 4.6 of your Study Text

35. **0.00**   The option is out-of-the-money, and therefore no intrinsic value

   See Chapter 7 Section 1.4 of your Study Text

36. **2.65** $\dfrac{£97 - £94.50}{£94.50} = 0.0265$ or 2.65%

   See Chapter 9 Section 7.6 of your Study Text

37. **63.62** $\dfrac{\$1,150}{\$1.67} - \dfrac{\$1,000}{\$1.6} = £63.62$

   See Chapter 3 Section 4.3 of your Study Text

38. **A**   A constructed benchmark index portfolio will always be passive

   See Chapter 11 Section 3.1 of your Study Text

39. **B**   Pension fund management would consider additional exposure to equities if there is more willingness to invest in 'risky' investments, and particularly to achieve a 'real' return to match inflation

   See Chapter 9 Section 6.1 of your Study Text

40. **A**   The cost of the annuity is the present value of the future cash flows using the Annuity Discount Factor

   $$£6,000 \times \frac{1}{0.15}\left(1 - \frac{1}{1.15^{10}}\right) = £30,113$$

   See Chapter 1 Section 6.2 of your Study Text

41. **D**   Using trial and error, the yield (GRY) is 11%

T	£	DF	PV
0	(89.72)		(89.72)
1	5.00	$\times \dfrac{1}{1.11^1}$	4.50
2	105.00	$\times \dfrac{1}{1.11^2}$	85.22
			0.00

   See Chapter 1 Section 7.1 and Chapter 6 Section 4.1 of your Study Text

42. **B**   There is no change in value on the balance sheet. Therefore we can conclude that this is a script issue that has been conducted and not a rights issue. Since the share capital has increased by 50% we have issued 50% more shares than we previously had so we must have conducted a 1 for 2 script issue

   See Chapter 9 Section 3.1 of your Study Text

43. **C**   Beta = Covariance / Variance
   0.8 = Covariance / 200
   Covariance = 0.8 x 200 = 160

   See Chapter 9 Section 3.1 of your Study Text

44. **C** The mode is the most frequently occurring item so there may be more than one mode which, by definition, suggests that it is not distorted by extreme or unusual values

See Chapter 1 Section 2.4 of your Study Text

45. **D** Beta = Covariance/Variance

0.8 = 120/Variance

Variance = 120/0.8 = 150

See Chapter 9 Section 3.1 of your Study Text

46. **B** Gilts, UK government bonds, pay semi-annual coupon throughout the life of the bond, normally at a fixed coupon rate. Currently, there are no floating rate gilts (FRGs)

See Chapter 6 Section 2.2 of your Study Text

47. **A** 'Ba' and 'B' are non-investment grade ratings. 'BBB' is the lowest S&P credit rating

See Chapter 6 Section 2.6 of your Study Text

48. **C** Ordinary shareholders are ranked below the others on liquidation

See Chapter 6 Section 2.6 of your Study Text

49. **C** $P/E = \dfrac{\text{MV of shares}}{\text{EPS}} = \dfrac{180p}{9p} = 20\times$

See Chapter 5 Section 3.6 of your Study Text

50. **C** In line with risk and return and the CAPM assumption, the efficient frontier would show the best combination of return against risk

See Chapter 9 Section 1.1 of your Study Text

51. **C** A certificate of deposit (CD) is normally issued by commercial banks or other depository institutions, essentially being tradable time deposits

See Chapter 6 Section 1.3 of your Study Text

52. **D**

Spot	$1.7770	– $1.7860
Premium	$(0.0036)	– $(0.0035)
Forward	$1.7734	– $1.7825

The bank is selling US dollars. Therefore, the customer is buying US dollars. The customer receives the worse of the two rates (the lowest number of dollars), i.e. $1.7734

See Chapter 3 Section 4.3 of your Study Text

53. **A** A minority interest holding represents the percentage of a subsidiary company that is not owned by the holding company

See Chapter 4 Section 6.1 of your Study Text

54. **16** $\dfrac{(4\times 90p)+(1\times 70p)}{5} = 86p$

86p – 70p = 16p

See Chapter 5 Section 2.3 of your Study Text

55.   A   While it is not stated explicitly, the implicit assumption is the question is referring to is a defined benefit scheme. These schemes focus on matching their future liabilities by investing into bonds where future cash flows are known

See Chapter 9 Section 6.1 of your Study Text

56.   B $(0.5 \times 0.7) + (0.5 \times 1.3) = 1$

See Chapter 9 Section 3.1 of your Study Text

57.   738 $£1,000 \times \dfrac{1}{1.07^{4.5}} = £737.52$

The required format for this question is £000, hence you must round to the nearest whole pound, ie £738

See Chapter 6 Section 2.3 of your Study Text

58.   9.52 $\dfrac{EPS}{DIV}$ = Dividend cover $\rightarrow 1.5 \times 10.5p = 15.75p = EPS$

$\dfrac{Dividend}{Market\ value}$ = Net dividend yield $\rightarrow 10.5p/0.07 = 150p = MV$

$P/E = \dfrac{Price}{EPS} = \dfrac{150p}{15.75p} = 9.52\times$

See Chapter 5 Section 3.6 of your Study Text

59.   B   If an uncovered dividend is paid, the company are drawing from previously accumulated profits

See Chapter 5 Section 3.2 of your Study Text

60.   95 $\dfrac{£4,000,000}{4200 \times £10} = 95.24$ ∴ 95 contracts, the nearest whole number as only whole contracts can be traded

See Chapter 7 Section 1.3 of your Study Text

61.   C   The money-weighted return is the IRR of a fund's opening and closing values, along with any deposits into, or withdrawals from, the fund

See Chapter 11 Section 2.1 of your Study Text

62.   B   Trial and error approach

T	£	DF	PV
0	(100)	$\times 1$	(100)
6 months	(20)	$\times \dfrac{1}{1.118^{\frac{1}{2}}}$	(18.9)
1 year	133	$\times \dfrac{1}{1.118^{1}}$	118.9
		NPV =	Nil

See Chapter 11 Section 2.1 of your Study Text

63.   **2.50**

Scenario	p	GDP	p × GDP	(GDP – $\overline{\text{GDP}}$)	p(GDP – $\overline{\text{GDP}}$)^2
		%	%	%	%
I	0.3	+5	+1.5	+3.4	3.468
II	0.5	+1	+0.5	–0.6	0.180
III	0.2	–2	$\underline{-0.4}$	–3.6	$\underline{2.592}$
			$\overline{\text{GDP}} = \underline{\underline{+1.6}}$		$\underline{\underline{6.240}}$

Standard deviation = $\sqrt{6.24}$ = 2.50%

See Chapter 1 Section 2.8 of your Study Text

64.   **D**   Two quarters of falling real GDP is the normal definition of a recession, negative inflation is deflation – disinflation is falling positive inflation

See Chapter 3 Section 3.7 of your Study Text

65.   **B**   Scenario I is characterised by high inflation. Of the assets proposed only commodities provide good coverage against inflation.

See Chapter 8 Section 1.3 of your Study Text

66.   **2.91**   Using the standard dividend valuation model:

Share price = D_1/ke – g

Where:

D_1 = next year's dividend = current dividend × (1 + growth) = 20p × 1.02

g = growth = 2% as per the info, which says to assume the share grows at the median inflation rate

ke = cost of equity = 9%, investors required rate of return

Hence, share price = (20 × 1.02)/0.09 – 0.02 = 291.4

See Chapter 5 Section 3.3 of your Study Text

67.   **D**   The asset's return and real GDP are negatively correlated, hence on average they move in opposition, though not necessarily always. To determine what proportion of the return is explained by GDP changes we need to consider the r^2 statistic, $r^2 = -0.80^2 = 0.64$, i.e. 64% of the changes in the assets return are explained by changes in the real GDP and the remaining 36% are not

See Chapter 1 Section 3.2 of your Study Text

68.   **C**   To deal with falling GDP and deflation the government will loosen fiscal and monetary policy, reducing tax rates, increasing government expenditure, reducing interest rates and quantitative easing

See Chapter 3 Section 3.1 and Chapter 3 Section 3.2 of your Study Text

69.   **C**   Goodwill should be capitalised and an impairment review undertaken over a year

See Chapter 4 Section 6.1 of your Study Text

70. **C** The 'normal' life is ten years, superlongs have a life of 20 years

See Chapter 9 Section 5.3 of your Study Text

71. **13.95** 8% + 0.85 (15% – 8%) = 13.95%

See Chapter 9 Section 3.1 of your Study Text

72. **B** Cash flow matching (dedication) is an approach which is to purchase bonds whose redemption proceeds will meet the liability of the fund as they fall due

See Chapter 9 Section 7.1 of your Study Text

73. **C** Horizon analysis is the consideration of cash flows matching liabilities over a specific time period

See Chapter 9 Section 7.4 of your Study Text

74. **C** This would be the most appropriate combination as the fund invests in mid-sized companies

See Chapter 1 Section 4.6 of your Study Text

75. **D** Tracking would indicate passive management

See Chapter 9 Section 6.2 of your Study Text

76. **B** CDs pay interest rather than being issued at a discount

See Chapter 6 Section 1.3 of your Study Text

77. **A** The best answer is the US Federal Reserve, as one of the few central banks with responsibility for banking supervision. It is worth noting, however, that the Bank of Japan does have partial responsibility for banking supervision. Please note that none of the central banks manage government debt. The Bank of England lost this responsibility to the DMO, and it is now the FSA who are responsible for banking supervision

See Chapter 3 Section 3.9 of your Study Text

78. **C** It can only be assumed that the question refers to the FTSE 100 index future traded on NYSE Liffe. The expiry months being March, June, September and December

See Chapter 7 Section 1.1 of your Study Text

79. **A** Option I is definitely correct and Option III is definitely incorrect (only a 999-year lease is considered as a freehold for valuation purposes). What is meant by Option II is unclear, but the only available option is A

See Chapter 8 Section 2.1 of your Study Text

80. **B** The DAX Index is a weighted (by market capitalisation) and arithmetically calculated index

See Chapter 1 Section 4.6 of your Study Text

81. **D** None of these are responsible for managing government debt

See Chapter 3 Section 3.9 of your Study Text

82. **D** The normal life is ten years. However, there are some 'superlongs' with a life of 20 years

See Chapter 9 Section 5.3 of your Study Text

83. **B** Preference shares pay a fixed dividend. They are also considered to be less risky than ordinary shares, as in the event of a liquidation, they are paid before ordinary shareholders

See Chapter 4 Section 2.14 of your Study Text

84. **A** The size of the contract is £500,000, with a tick size of 1 basis point (0.01%). Therefore, the '3m' STIR contract tick value is 3/12 × £500,000 × 0.0001 = £12.50

See Chapter 7 Section 1.1 of your Study Text

85. **C** I False – swaps are OTC products

See Chapter 7 Section 1.1 and Chapter 7 Section 2.3 of your Study Text

86. **D** The legal form of an investment trust is a Public Limited Company (plc)

See Chapter 10 Section 1.2 of your Study Text

87. **B** Immunisation risk is a function of the dispersion of the bonds cash flows, the lower the dispersion the lower the risk, for example a ten year zero coupon bond (zero dispersion) has no immunisation risk. Portfolio I has the lowest dispersion and portfolio II has the highest

See Chapter 9 Section 7.3 of your Study Text

88. **98.45** Modified duration $= \dfrac{\text{Duration}}{1+\text{GRY}} = \dfrac{9}{1.0573} = 8.5122$

Therefore a 1% increase in yields will give rise to an 8.5122% fall in price, ie a price fall of £8.83 (£103.75 × 8.5122%). Therefore if yields rise 0.6% prices will fall £5.30 (£8.83 × 0.6) to £98.45 (£103.75 – £5.30)

See Chapter 6 Section 2.3 of your Study Text

89. **A** If the economy emerges rapidly from a recession then we would expect interest rates to rise rapidly to control inflationary forces. If rates rise then bond prices fall and the minimum duration bond would be the least sensitive

See Chapter 3 Section 3.2 and Chapter 6 Section 2.2 of your Study Text

90. **1.10** Excess return to relative duration $= \dfrac{r_p - r_f}{D_p / D_m} = \dfrac{5.86 - 4.65}{11/10} = 1.10\%$

See Chapter 11 Section 4.1 of your Study Text

91. **3.29** Value of convertible (Conv) = 102.46

Value of shares the bond can be converted into (S) = £99.20 (£6.20 × 16)

Conversion premium $= \dfrac{\text{Conv} - S}{S} = \dfrac{102.46 - 99.20}{99.20} = 0.0329$ or 3.29%

See Chapter 7 Section 3.1 of your Study Text

92. **7.58** Dividend yield $= \dfrac{\text{Dividend per share}}{\text{Current share price}} = \dfrac{47}{620} = 0.0758$ or 7.58%

See Chapter 5 Section 3.2 of your Study Text

93. **A** A random sample is one where every item in the population has an equal chance of being selected. The analyst is *not* able to use their judgement to select a sample as this would lead to an element of bias. By its very nature a random sample will not necessarily lead to the selection of a truly representative sample

   See Chapter 1 Section 1.2 of your Study Text

94. **B** An auditor is an independent third party appointed by the shareholders to give an opinion as to whether the directors have fulfilled their obligations of producing accounts which show a true and fair view

   See Chapter 4 Section 1 and Chapter 4 Section 1.2 of your Study Text

95. **B** The FTSE All Share Index represents approximately 900 shares

   See Chapter 1 Section 4.6 of your Study Text

96. **696** $PV = 750 \times \dfrac{1}{e^{0.15 \times .5}}$

   $= 695.81$

   The required format for this question is £000, hence you must round to the nearest whole pound, ie £696

   See Chapter 1 Section 6.2 of your Study Text

97. **D** A discretionary dealing service is not a feature of a private client fund

   See Chapter 10 Section 1.2 of your Study Text

98. **D** Protective put = synthetic call

   Call breakeven = strike price + loss at strike price = £6.00 + (£0.70 + £0.20) = £6.90

   Alternatively, the cost of the put is 70p, so the share price would have to rise by 70p for the strategy to cover the cost of buying the put

   See Chapter 7 Section 1.2 of your Study Text

99. **D** The marginal propensity to import (MPM) represents the amount of each additional unit (or pound) earned that is spent on imports net of exports

   See Chapter 3 Section 2.5 of your Study Text

100 **B** The buyer of a CDS does not have to have any interest in the underlying asset.

   See Chapter 7 Section 4.1 of your Study Text

101. **A** Mode > Median > Mean

   See Chapter 1 Section 2.6 of your Study Text

102. **C** Capital employed includes all forms of finance used by the company in order to generate profits earned by the company. Any interest paid for bank loans and overdrafts is added back to the profit earned

   See Chapter 4 Section 7.2 of your Study Text

103. **B**   In order to qualify as a small company a company must satisfy two of the following three conditions:

Turnover	< £6,500,000
Fixed + current assets	< £3,260,000
Average number of employees	< 50

See Chapter 4 Section 1 of your Study Text

104. **B**   Conversion value = conversion ratio × share price = 20 × £3.50 = 70

See Chapter 7 Section 3.1 of your Study Text

105. **D**   Units sold 1/6 will be made from purchases made 1/3

Units sold on 1/9 will be made out of remaining units purchased 1/3 and 1/1

Year-end valuation of inventory is as follows.

DATE	UNITS	UNIT PRICE	TOTAL
1/1	30	10	300
1/3	50	15	750
1/6	(45)	15	(675)
1/9	(5)	15	(75)
1/9	(5)	10	(50)
1/12	20	20	400
	45		650

See Chapter 4 Section 2.8 of your Study Text

PRACTICE EXAMINATION FOUR

(105 questions in 2 hours and 20 minutes)

Questions

1. **Which of the following is the correct statement about index-linked gilts?**

   A The coupon payment only is determined by the RPI three or eight months prior to its payment date

   B The principal payment only is determined by the RPI three or eight months prior to its maturity date

   C Both the coupon payment and the principal payment are determined by the RPI three or eight months prior to the coupon date and the maturity date respectively

   D The index-linked gilt is only referred to the RPI three or eight months prior to the dates in question in an inflationary environment

2. **The Sharpe ratio is best described as which one of the following?**

   A The excess return on a portfolio divided by the portfolio beta

   B The excess return on a portfolio divided by the portfolio standard deviation

   C The degree of co-movement of a portfolio with overall market returns

   D The excess return on a portfolio over a recognised benchmark

3. **A convertible bond has a conversion ratio of 20 which is scrip protected. The company undertakes a 1 for 1 bonus issue. What will be the new conversion ratio as a result of the issue?**

   A 20

   B 40

   C 10

   D Unchanged

4. **What is the credit risk associated with purchasing a CD in the secondary market?**

   A Issuer default

   B Seller default

   C Interest rates increasing

   D Reinvestment risk upon maturity

5. **A fund manager is looking to select undervalued bonds. He/she will look to buy**

   A Bonds with a positive alpha

   B Bonds with a negative alpha

   C Bonds with a high relative duration

   D Bonds with low relative duration

6.   **Which of the following are most suitable for an unmarried 28 year-old?**

        I   Index-linked gilts

        II   Ordinary shares

        III   Unit trusts

    A   I and II

    B   I and III

    C   II and III

    D   I, II and III

7.   **An investment gives a return in Year 1 of 12%. In Year 2, it gives a return of –8%. Calculate the total compound return over the two-year period (in % to 2 decimal places).**

    Important! You should enter the answer only in numbers strictly using this format: 0.00

    Do not include spaces, letters or symbols (but decimal points and commas should be used if indicated).

8.   **In order to issue a CD in the UK, an institution must be**

    A   A bank or corporation with AAA/Aaa credit rating

    B   A bank with AAA/Aaa credit rating

    C   A bank with a UK banking licence and AAA/Aaa credit rating

    D   A bank with a UK banking licence

9.   **The following information is available from a company balance sheet.**

	£
Non-current assets	100,000
Inventory	40,000
Overdraft	30,000
Cash	40,000
Receivables	60,000
Payables	50,000
Long-term loans	80,000

    Calculate shareholders' funds (to the nearest £1).

    Important! You should enter the answer only in numbers strictly using this format: 00,000

    Do not include spaces, letters or symbols (but decimal points and commas should be used if indicated).

10. **A portfolio of £10m has given the following quarterly returns.**

    3%   5%   6%   −8%

    Calculate the final value of the portfolio (to the nearest £1).

    Important! You should enter the answer only in numbers strictly using this format: 00,000,000

    Do not include spaces, letters or symbols (but decimal points and commas should be used if indicated).

    ┌─────────────┐
    │   │
    │   │
    └─────────────┘

11. **Which of the following futures traded on NYSE Liffe have the potential to be physically delivered?**

    A   Three-month Euribor

    B   FTSE 100 Index

    C   Short-Term Sterling Interest Rate

    D   Long Gilt Notional 4%

12. **When does a spot FX transaction settle?**

    A   Same business day

    B   As agreed by the counterparties

    C   Two business days later

    D   Within five calendar days

13. **The Standard and Poor's Composite Index is an example of**

    A   Arithmetic unweighted index

    B   Geometric weighted index

    C   Arithmetic weighted index

    D   Geometric unweighted index

14. **An investor holds a portfolio of shares in Rolls Royce plc with a value of £10,000. Subsequently, Rolls Royce undertakes a 1 for 25 scrip issue. Other things remaining constant, what will be the effect on the investor's holding?**

    A   The value will fall

    B   Unchanged

    C   The value will increase

    D   It is not possible to determine the effect

15. **An investor is to receive £1,000 in three years' time with a discount factor of 9%. Calculate the present value of the investment.**

    A £730

    B £772

    C £910

    D £1,295

16. **An appropriate benchmark for a fund should always**

    A Reflect the client's preferences

    B Not have tax deducted

    C Be geographically diverse

    D Cover both equities and bonds

17. **A UK government bond is trading at a discount to its par value. Assuming interest rates remain constant over the remaining life of the bond, what would you normally expect to happen to the price as it approaches maturity?**

    A The price will rise as time to maturity falls

    B The price will fall as time to maturity falls

    C The price will remain constant over the bond life

    D It is not possible to predict the direction of price changes

18. **The £/$ spot rate is 1.6. The UK one-year interest rate is 7% and the one-year £/$ forward rate is 0.24 cent pm. What is the percentage one-year US interest rate (in % to 2 decimal places)?**

    Important! You should enter the answer only in numbers strictly using this format: 0.00

    Do not include spaces, letters or symbols (but decimal points and commas should be used if indicated).

    ```
    ┌─────────────┐
    │             │
    │             │
    └─────────────┘
    ```

19. **Why would a UK fund manager use FTSE 100 futures?**

    I   For leverage of the portfolio

    II   To lower transaction costs

    III The FTSE 100 future is usually more liquid than the underlying cash market

    A I and II

    B I and III

    C I only

    D I, II and III

20. **A portfolio is constructed as an equally weighted combination of the following.**

Bond	Yield %	Maturity Years	Duration Years
W	4	4	4
X	6	6	5
Y	5	9	8
Z	4	11	10

Assuming an immunisation policy is being adopted what is the term of the liability in years?

A   7.50

B   6.75

C   5.50

D   4.75

---

21. **Which of the following classes of assets tends to dominate UK pension funds?**

A   Fixed interest securities

B   Property

C   UK equities

D   Money market securities

---

22. **What is the highest short-term debt rating given by S&P and Moody's?**

A   A1   P1

B   A1+   P1+

C   A1+   P1

D   A1   P1+

---

23. **Which of the following central banks are responsible for managing government debt?**

I   European Central Bank

II   Bank of Japan

III   Federal Reserve

IV   Bank of England

A   None of the above

B   I, II and III

C   II only

D   I, III and IV

---

24. **Which of the following would a manager seeking undervalued bonds look for?**

A   High duration

B   Low duration

C   High positive alpha value

D   High negative alpha value

25. **If a firm is not making profit, under which of the following circumstances will they continue to produce?**

A   Marginal cost > Average fixed cost

B   They are covering fixed costs

C   Marginal costs > Average variable cost

D   They are covering total cost

26. **Predator plc purchases a company called Victim plc for £300,000. Prior to the takeover, an extract from the balance sheet of Victim plc showed the following.**

Share capital   £100,000

Share Premium account   £40,000

Reserves   £80,000

What is the amount of goodwill on acquisition (to the nearest £1)?

Important! You should enter the answer only in numbers strictly using this format: 00,000

Do not include spaces, letters or symbols (but decimal points and commas should be used if indicated).

27. **If it costs £105 to make 1,000 units of a particular good, and it costs £110 to make 1,001 units of the same good, what is the marginal cost of making the $1,001^{st}$ unit of that good?**

A   £0.11

B   £0.42

C   £3.00

D   £5.00

28. **Which of the following are not headings in the Statement of Cash Flow?**

A   Operating activities

B   Financing activities

C   Construction activities

D   Investing activities

29. **A 5% coupon gilt is currently trading at par. What is its redemption yield?**

A   0%

B   5%

C   2.5%

D   10%

30. **When considering the yield of a defined benefit pension scheme, which of the following would need to be taken into account?**

    I   Mortality rates

    II   Job transfers

    III   Inflation

    A   III only

    B   I and III

    C   I, II and III

    D   None of the above

31. **Which of the following factors would not affect the value of a call option?**

    A   Strike price

    B   The number of shares specified in the contract

    C   Share price

    D   Interest rates

32. **Which one of the following is not true for financial market indices?**

    A   They facilitate comparing the investment performance of managers with benchmarks

    B   Derivative contracts are always based on indices

    C   They can be used for monitoring the level of the market

    D   They can be used for comparing returns on asset classes

33. **The FTSE Actuaries Fixed Interest Indices comprise all of the following, except**

    A   Bond price changes

    B   Coupon payments

    C   Accrued income

    D   Weighting by size of bond issues

34. **Immunisation would be possible under all of the following circumstances, except**

    A   There is a parallel shift in the yield curve

    B   The manager plans to rebalance the portfolio duration on a regular basis

    C   The portfolio consists of zero-coupon bonds only

    D   The portfolio contains a number of callable bonds

35. **Accruals would be found in which of the following categories in a company's accounts?**

    A   Current liabilities

    B   Current assets

    C   Other income

    D   Cash

36. **All of the following are categories of non-current assets, except**

    A Investments

    B Intangible

    C Tangible

    D Inventories

The following information relates to questions 37 to 42

A young client has just won a substantial sum on the National Lottery. He has paid off his UK mortgage and debts and is looking to invest the remaining £2m to provide funds on which he can live for the rest of his life without needing to work. He is financially astute and, given the time he will now have available, he is considering

▪   A self-managed portfolio of direct investments

▪   A self-managed portfolio of collective investments

▪   A broker managed portfolio

He requires an annual income from the portfolio and, given the long-term nature of the fund, wishes both income and capital values to grow at least in line with inflation. As a small indulgence he has bought an apartment in Cannes off-plan. The apartment will be completed and must be paid for in three years at an agreed fixed price.

37. **Which of the following is not a standard service provided by a broker?**

    A Advisory execution service

    B Nominee service

    C Execution-only discretionary service

    D Portfolio discretionary service

38. **Which of the following is not a characteristic of collective investment schemes?**

    A CGT is payable by the fund on all sales of assets held

    B Funds allow a broad diversification for even a small scale investment

    C Funds are professionally managed by an experienced fund manager

    D Various funds are available with differing objectives

39. **Which of the following individual assets would be most appropriate given the clients' needs?**

    A Commodities

    B Gilts

    C Property

    D Cash

40. **Which of the following is most likely to be suitable as a benchmark for appraising the fund performance?**

    A   FTSE APCIMS Index

    B   FTSE 100 Index

    C   FTSE all-shares Index

    D   FTSE 350 Index

41. **Which of the following approaches would be the most suitable for ensuring the repayment of an interest only mortgage requiring all of the capital to be repaid in full in 20 years' time?**

    A   Riding the yield curve

    B   Indexation

    C   Tilting

    D   Immunisation

42. **The client is considering investing indirectly in property. Which of the following is not an indirect investment route**

    A   REIT

    B   Property shares

    C   Leasehold

    D   Limited liability partnership

43. **A company has inventories of £5m, receivables of £4m, cash balances of £2m, current liabilities of £7m and non-current liabilities of £2m. What is its current ratio (to two decimal places)?**

    Important! You should enter the answer only in numbers strictly using this format: 0.00

    Do not include spaces, letters or symbols (but decimal points and commas should be used if indicated).

44. **A company has operating profits of £300,000 and interest payable of £25,000. Its shareholders' funds are £1,000,000 and long-term loans are £100,000. What is its return on capital employed, where capital employed is defined as non-current assets plus working capital (in % to 1 decimal place)?**

    Important! You should enter the answer only in numbers strictly using this format: 00.0

    Do not include spaces, letters or symbols (but decimal points and commas should be used if indicated).

45. A stock has a beta of 0.8 and the risk-free return is 9%. If the market return was 15%, what would the expected return of the stock be (in % to 2 decimal places)?

Important! You should enter the answer only in numbers strictly using this format: 0.00

Do not include spaces, letters or symbols (but decimal points and commas should be used if indicated).

46. Which of the following reserves can be used to make a bonus issue?

    I   Profit and loss account reserve
    II   Share premium account reserve
    III Capital redemption reserve
    IV   Revaluation reserve

    A   I, II, III and IV
    B   I, II and III
    C   I and II
    D   I only

47. Market neutral hedge fund would be

    A   Indifferent to changes in the underlying market
    B   Take more long positions than short positions
    C   Take more short positions than long positions
    D   Sensitive to global macroeconomic events

48. Which of the following is the correct description of American and European options?

    A   American options can only be bought in America and European options can only be bought in Europe
    B   American options can only be exercised at expiry but European style options can be exercised at any time
    C   European options can only be exercised at expiry but American style options can be exercised at any time
    D   American and European options offer investors the chance to take long positions, but not short positions

49. **If a company did a 1 for 1 capitalisation, which of the following would occur?**

    I   A movement in reserves

    II   An increase in shareholders' funds

    III   A decrease in the market price of a share

    IV   A change in the nominal value of the share

    A   I and IV

    B   I and III

    C   II and IV

    D   III and IV

50. **Earnings per share is calculated from profits after deducting everything, except**

    A   Minority interest

    B   Tax

    C   Interest

    D   Dividends

51. **Which of the following methods of calculating cost, all other things being equal, is most likely to produce the highest closing inventory during a period when the price of goods are rising and inventory levels are rising?**

    A   First In First Out

    B   Last In First Out

    C   Average cost

    D   Historic cost

52. **A company has a current ratio of 1.4×, total assets of £720,000, non-current assets of £590,000 and long-term liabilities of £120,000. Which of the following is closest to the value of shareholders' funds?**

    A   £400,000

    B   £507,143

    C   £600,000

    D   £627,143

53. **A profit-seeking company is most likely to continue production in the short run if the product price at least exceeds**

    A   Total cost per unit of output

    B   Fixed cost per unit of output

    C   Average cost per unit of output

    D   Variable cost per unit of output

54. **A competitive firm will tend to expand its output, provided**

    A   Marginal revenue is positive

    B   Marginal revenue is greater than the average cost

    C   Marginal cost is less than average cost

    D   Marginal revenue is greater than marginal cost

55. **Which one of the following is most likely to contribute to the presence of monopoly in an industry?**

    A   Diseconomies of scale

    B   Legal barriers to entry into the industry

    C   An elastic market demand for the product produced by the industry

    D   Inefficiency attributable to bureaucratic decision-making procedures in the industry

56. **Which of the following accurately describes a major difference between a purely competitive firm and a monopolistic firm?**

    A   The monopolistic firm will maximise profits, and the competitive firm cannot because profits are driven down to zero in the long run

    B   The monopolistic firm maximises profit, and the competitive firm minimises costs

    C   The monopolistic firm maximises price charged, and the competitive firm maximises profit

    D   The monopolistic firm is a price maker, and the competitive firm is a price taker

57. **The interest rate risk of a bond normally is**

    A   Greater for shorter maturities

    B   Lower for longer duration

    C   Lower for higher coupons

    D   None of the above

58. **An 8%, 20-year corporate bond is priced to yield 9%. The Macaulay duration for this bond is 8.85 years. Given this information, what is the bond's modified duration (to two decimal places)?**

    Important! You should enter the answer only in numbers strictly using this format: 0.00

    Do not include spaces, letters or symbols (but decimal points and commas should be used if indicated).

59. **The gross redemption yield and flat yield on a bond are equal**

    A   When market interest rates begin to level off

    B   If the bond sells at a price in excess of its par value

    C   When the expected holding period is greater than one year

    D   If the coupon and market interest rate are equal

60. **Which bond has the longest duration?**

A Eight-year maturity, 6% coupon

B Eight-year maturity, 11% coupon

C 15-year maturity, 6% coupon

D 15-year maturity, 11% coupon

61. **As interest rates fall, which of the following statements is true of a FRN?**

A The price will rise and the yield will fall

B The price will fall and the yield will rise

C The price will remain constant and the yield will fall

D The price will remain constant and the yield will rise

62. **If the exchange rate value of sterling goes from $1.80 (US) to $1.60 (US), then the pound has**

A Appreciated and the British will find US goods cheaper

B Appreciated and the British will find US goods more expensive

C Depreciated and the British will find US goods more expensive

D Depreciated and the British will find US goods cheaper

63. **Which of the following factors is most likely to cause a nation's currency to depreciate on the foreign exchange market?**

A An increase in the nation's domestic rate of inflation

B An increase in the inflation rates of the nation's trading partners

C A decrease in the nation's domestic rate of inflation

D An increase in domestic real interest rates

64. **Which of the following will increase the value of a call option?**

A An increase in interest rates

B A decrease in time to expiration of the call

C A decrease in the volatility of the underlying stock

D An increase in the dividend rate of the underlying stock

65. **Which one of the following comparative statements about equity call options and warrants is correct?**

	CALL OPTION	WARRANT
A Issued by the company	No	Yes
B Sometimes attached to bonds	Yes	Yes
C Maturity greater than one year	Yes	No
D Convertible into the stock	Yes	No

66. A retailer originally purchased an item of inventory for £150. The item was then put on sale for £200. Subsequently, due to a change in market conditions, the retailer marked down the item's price to £140 in order to clear the obsolete inventory and it is estimated that a further £5 will be incurred in selling the item. At what value would the inventory be recognised in the balance sheet of the retailer (to the nearest £1)?

Important! You should enter the answer only in numbers strictly using this format: 000

Do not include spaces, letters or symbols (but decimal points and commas should be used if indicated).

```
┌─────────────┐
│             │
│             │
└─────────────┘
```

67. Which of the following is true of the retained earnings account shown on the balance sheet?

    I   It represents the profits generated for the financial year

    II   It is a distributable reserve and can be used to cover payment of dividends to shareholders

    III   It can be used to finance a bonus issue

    IV   It can never show a negative balance as the company would be insolvent

A I and II

B II and III

C II, III and IV

D I, II, III and IV

68. A company has an net earnings yield of 6.42%, a net dividend per share of 2.7p and a current market price per share of 140p. What is its dividend cover?

A 3.75×

B 3.00×

C 3.33×

D 4.69×

69. **A company is put into liquidation, has assets available for pay out of £975,000 and has the following creditors.**

Liquidator's expenses	£25,000
Tax authorities	£150,000
Fixed charge holders	£250,000
Trade payables	£400,000

The company has in issue £100,000 nominal of 10% preference shares in respect of which a dividend has been neither declared nor paid for the last five years. There are 200,000 ordinary £1 NV shares.

What will the ordinary shareholders receive from the liquidator upon winding-up of the company?

A   Nothing

B   25p per share

C   50p per share

D   The £1 nominal value of the share

70. **If a company does a 5 for 4 bonus issue and the cum bonus price of the shares is £8.00, what will the share price be after the bonus issue?**

A   £3.56

B   £6.40

C   £8.00

D   £10.00

71. **Gilts that are classified as longs have what minimum period to run to redemption?**

A   10 years

B   15 years

C   20 years

D   25 years

72. **In order to establish the income return on a gilt investment, which of the following yield calculations is most useful?**

A   Flat yield

B   Gross redemption yield

C   Net redemption yield

D   Yield to maturity

73. **Which of the following statements are true?**

A   The Bank of England sets the inflation rate

B   Falling retail sales would indicate inflationary pressure in the economy

C   Tourism is not part of the balance of payments

D   The RPI includes mortgage payments

74. **Which of the following are true of a gilt trading below par?**

    I   The GRY will exceed the flat yield
    II   The flat yield will exceed the GRY
    III If held to maturity, the gilt will provide a capital gain
    IV   If held to maturity, the gilt will provide a capital loss

    A   I and III
    B   II and III
    C   I and IV
    D   II and IV

75. **An investor buys 5,000 certified shares on the LSE main market for £2.18. Calculate the total price paid assuming his broker charges 0.4% commission.**

    A   10,998.10
    B   10,998.60
    C   10,999.10
    D   10,999.60

76. **What is the present value of £7,000, to be received eight years from now, if the annual interest rate is 9% (to the nearest £1)?**

    Important! You should enter the answer only in numbers strictly using this format: 0,000

    Do not include spaces, letters or symbols (but decimal points and commas should be used if indicated).

    ┌─────────────────┐
    │   │
    │   │
    └─────────────────┘

77. **Which of the following indices would be most appropriate for use as a benchmark for a portfolio of UK blue chip stocks?**

    A   FTSE 100 Index
    B   S&P 500 Index
    C   FTSE 250 Index
    D   FTSE Eurotop 300 Index

78. **The value of two stocks, A and B, in years Year 1, Year 2 and Year 3, is given below**

	YEAR 1	YEAR 2	YEAR 3
A	75p	95p	120p
B	80p	75p	87p

Taking Year 1 as the base year value of 100, what is the value of a price-relative arithmetic index for Year 3 (in index points to 1 decimal place)?

Important! You should enter the answer only in numbers strictly using this format: 000.0

Do not include spaces, letters or symbols (but decimal points and commas should be used if indicated).

79. **A fund manager achieves a return of 9% one year with a CAPM beta of 0.5. If the risk-free rate of return was 3%, what is the Treynor performance measure for this portfolio (in % to 1 decimal place)?**

Important! You should enter the answer only in numbers strictly using this format: 00.0

Do not include spaces, letters or symbols (but decimal points and commas should be used if indicated).

80. **A fixed income portfolio has achieved a return of 9% over the past year. Over the period, the average duration was 16 years. If the risk-free rate and duration of the market portfolio were 5% and ten years respectively, what is the value of an appropriate duration-adjusted performance measure?**

A   2.5

B   3.5

C   1.5

D   4.5

81. **Which of the following is not a means of representing the frequency occurrence of data?**

A   Pie chart

B   Scatter diagram

C   Bar chart

D   Histogram

82. **Which of the following is not a heading in a Cash Flow Statement of a company following International Accounting Standards?**

    A   Operating activities

    B   Investing activities

    C   Fundamental activities

    D   Financing activities

The following information relates to questions 83 to 88

An entrepreneur has just sold his business, the purchase consideration of £5m being satisfied by shares in the acquirer that the entrepreneur is obliged to hold for at least the next two years. An analyst has undertaken a regression/correlation analysis on how the price of the share (Y) relates to the passage of time, measured in months (X). Using the monthly prices of the acquirer's shares over the last ten years up to the present and has established the following regression statistics

a = £5.26

b = 2.18p

r = 0.63

The correlation of the share with the market is 0.83, its total risk is 12%, the risk of the market is 10% and the risk-free rate is 5%.

The analyst's current economic view is that the equities market is liable to fall over the next six months and may not recover over the entrepreneur's two year committed holding period.

83. **What is the current share price based on the regression model data?**

    A   £5.26

    B   £5.48

    C   £6.13

    D   £7.88

84. **What proportion of share price variations are not explained through the model by changes in time?**

    A   37.0%

    B   60.3%

    C   63.0%

    D   86.3%

85. **What is the expected return from the share under CAPM (in % to 2 decimal places)?**

    Important! You should enter the answer only in numbers strictly using this format: 0.00

    Do not include spaces, letters or symbols (but decimal points and commas should be used if indicated).

86. **What is the Sharpe measure for the share if its actual return is 9.5% (to 3 decimal places)?**

   Important! You should enter the answer only in numbers strictly using this format: 0.000

   Do not include spaces, letters or symbols (but decimal points and commas should be used if indicated).

87. **What strategy could the entrepreneur adopt to hedge himself against the anticipated share price fall?**

   A   Long future

   B   Long straddle

   C   Long put

   D   Short call

88. **An investment has systematic risk of 24% and specific risk of 18%. What is its total risk to the nearest one percent?**

   A   42%

   B   30%

   C   16%

   D   6%

89. **The minimum deposit in the sterling money market is usually**

   A   £1.0m

   B   £0.5m

   C   £10m

   D   £5m

90. **Which of the following is not true of an index-linked gilt?**

   A   There is a fixed benefit at the end

   B   They pay a low coupon

   C   They are issued with a range of maturities

   D   The coupon varies with inflation

91. **Typically, life assurance funds tend to have the greatest proportion of their assets invested in which type of securities?**

   A   Gilts

   B   Equities

   C   Property

   D   Short-term bonds

92. A fund manager has a £30m equity portfolio with a beta of 0.9 and is concerned that the index may fall. The current index level is 5400 and options available are

    5600 call priced at 120

    5200 put priced at 97

    How many options of the relevant class should be bought or sold assuming they will be held to maturity?

    A 502

    B 519

    C 536

    D 556

93. **In a semi-strong market**

    A All analysts can make superior profits

    B Technical analysts can make superior profits, fundamental analysts cannot

    C Fundamental analysts can make superior profits, technical analysts cannot

    D No analysts can make superior profits on public information

94. **An investment total risk is 25% and its specific risk is 20%. The market portfolio risk is 20% and return is 14%. The risk-free return is 6%. What is the expected return?**

    A 11%

    B 12%

    C 13%

    D 14%

95. **Which of the following will have a negative income elasticity of demand?**

    A Necessities

    B Luxuries

    C Inferior goods

    D Giffen goods

96.   **XYZ plc has the following assets and liabilities**

	£
Investments	20
Goodwill	5
Fixed assets (net book value)	15
Inventory	5
Accounts receivable	3
Cash	2
Bank loan	5
Accounts payable	2
Called up share capital	10
Revaluation reserve	15
Share premium	5
Retained earnings	13

XYZ plc has net current assets of

A   8,000

B   3,000

C   5,000

D   6,000

97.   **Your client has a high requirement for liquidity in her portfolio, and does not want to take short-term risk in her investments due to a potential need to liquidate a large element of her portfolio in the near future. Which of the following investments would be suitable?**

        I   Short-term government bonds

        II   A diversified Fund of Funds investment

        III   Long-dated high yield corporate bonds

A   II only

B   III only

C   I and II

D   I only

98.   **The Capital Asset Pricing Model gives the return necessary on an investment given the risk of the investment relative to**

A   An investments market

B   An industry

C   A global index of all securities

D   The expected national average

99.   **The return on equity ratio shows**

A   The return earned by the shareholders

B   The returned earned by the ordinary shareholders

C   The return earned by the preference shareholders

D   The return earned by the investors of the company

100. **If when prices rise 2% quantity of sales rise by 4%. What is the elasticity of supply?**

A   +2.0

B   +0.5

C   −2.0

D   −0.5

101. **You have £9,000 to invest for three years and are considering the following investments and must rank them from lowest to highest**

I   Continuous compound rate of 9.3%

II   Quarterly compound investment with a quoted rate of 2.4% per quarter

III   Monthly compound interest with a quoted rate of 0.76% per month

A   I, II, III

B   III, II, I

C   II, III, I

D   III, I, II

102. **Which of the following indices is an equally weighted, geometrically calculated index?**

A   The FTSE 100

B   The FTSE Ordinary index

C   The CAC 40

D   The S&P 500

103. **Which one of the following statements is correct?**

A   The constant in a regression equation is always positive

B   The value of a correlation coefficient is always less than or equal to or equal to 1

C   The dependent variable always explains the independent variables

D   Extrapolation and interpolation are both forms of regression analysis

104. **Consider the following statements**

I   Semi-logarithmic graphs plot the semi log of the value on the x-axis

II   Semi logarithmic graphs show constant growth as a straight line

III   Any moves away from steady percentage growth are shown by a change in the gradient

Which of the following is correct?

A   I and III are false and II is true

B   I and II are both true whereas III is false

C   II and III are true, I is false

D   I, II and III are false

105. **Which of the following is not a class of shares issued by a split level trust?**

    A Income shares

    B Capital shares

    C Zero dividend ordinary shares

    D Preference shares

Answers

1. **C** The ILG would still be referenced to the RPI in a deflationary environment. Both coupon and principal are linked to RPI, but the time lag depends upon when the bonds were issued

    See Chapter 6 Section 2.5 of your Study Text

2. **B** The Sharpe measure uses an approximation of the total risk of the portfolio to calculate the excess return to volatility. Therefore, the Sharpe measure uses the excess return over the risk-free rate of return ($r_p - r_f$) and divides this by the standard deviation of the portfolio, the standard deviation representing total risk. This would be a suitable risk-adjusted measure for an investor who is not well diversified

    See Chapter 11 Section 4.1 of your Study Text

3. **B** A 1 for 1 bonus issue, also referred to as a scrip/capitalisation issue, would double the number of shares available on conversion. Therefore, as the conversion is 'scrip protected', rather than having a conversion ratio of 20, the investor will be entitled to a conversion ratio of 40, i.e. double the original allocation

    See Chapter 7 Section 3.1 of your Study Text

4. **A** The risk is that the issuer may default on the repayment. Credit risk is the risk that the issuing corporation will not be able to repay the debt that the instrument represents. This risk of default is deemed to be less in the shorter term money markets than in the longer term bond/debt markets

    See Chapter 6 Section 2.5 of your Study Text

5. **A** The key is 'looking to select undervalued bonds'. Bonds that are undervalued will return a percentage that is higher than that expected by the Capital Asset Pricing Model (CAPM), and therefore, according to Jensen's alpha measure, will give a positive alpha

    See Chapter 11 Section 4.1 of your Study Text

6. **D** We have assumed that all would be suitable investments, as ILGs protect against inflation, ordinary shares offer long-term capital growth, both of them offer real returns, and unit trusts offer a further area of investment in order to diversify

    See Chapter 9 Section 6.1 of your Study Text

7. **3.04** Using a basic geometric (compounded) calculation

    $(1 + r) = (1 + r_1)(1 + r_2)$

    $(1 + r) = (1 + 0.12)(1 - 0.08) = 1.12 \times 0.92 = 1.0304 \therefore r = 0.0304$ or 3.04%

    See Chapter 11 Section 1 of your Study Text

8. **D** There are no specific credit rating requirements. Certificates of Deposit (CDs) are issued by depositing institutions, such as banks, being tradable instruments. Only institutions with a valid UK banking licence may issue CDs

    See Chapter 6 Section 1.3 of your Study Text

9. **80,000** From the accounting equation,

Shareholders' funds = Net assets = Total assets – Total liabilities

= (Non-current assets + Current assets – Current liabilities – Long-term liabilities)

Total assets = (Non-current assets + Inventories + Receivables + Cash)

= (£100,000 + £40,000 + £60,000 + £40,000) = £240,000

Total liabilities= (Bank overdraft + Payables + Long-term liabilities)

= (£30,000 + £50,000 + £80,000) = £160,000

Net assets = £240,000 – £160,000 = £80,000

See Chapter 4 Section 2 of your Study Text

10. **10,546,788**

£10m × 1.03 × 1.05 × 1.06 × 0.92 = £10,546,788

See Chapter 11 Section 2.2 and Chapter 1 Section 5.3 of your Study Text

11. **D** The long gilt future is based upon a notional 4% coupon bond. However, it is physically settled, with the seller of the future deciding which gilt, from a basket of 'deliverable gilts', he will actually deliver. The other contracts are cash-settled contracts, known as contracts for differences, based upon either an interest rate or an index

See Chapter 7 Section 1.1 of your Study Text

12. **C** The reference is to the institutional foreign currency market where standard settlement terms are T + 2

See Chapter 3 Section 4.3 of your Study Text

13. **C** The majority of indices around the world are arithmetically calculated, and are also weighted by market capitalisation. The S&P Composite index reflects this. The only indices that are not weighted by market capitalisation, also known as price or equally weighted indices, are the Dow Jones Industrial Average (DJIA – DJ30), the FTSE Ordinary Index (FT 30) and the Nikkei 225

See Chapter 1 Section 4.6 of your Study Text

14. **B** The ex-bonus price of each individual share will fall but not the value of total holding. The investor will have more shares but each will be worth a little less than before, meaning that the overall value of the portfolio remains unchanged. The scrip issue is another description of a bonus issue or a capitalisation issue

See Chapter 5 Section 2.4 of your Study Text

15. **B** Use the discount factor for a single cash flow to establish the present value

$$PV = \text{Cash flow} \times 1/(1 + r)^n$$

where

'r' = the discount rate at 9%

'n' = the number of years in question to be discounted, i.e. three years

Therefore, PV $= £1,000/1.09^3$

$= £772.18$

See Chapter 1 Section 6.1 of your Study Text

16. **A** The client's investment objectives will have to be considered when a fund manager decides which index to use as an appropriate benchmark. There would be little point in using an index as the benchmark if it does not reflect the client's objectives or any constraints that have been placed upon the fund manager

See Chapter 11 Section 3.1 of your Study Text

17. **A** Reflecting the reduced time to maturity. This is because the bond price must move towards par (NV), as at the date of redemption, the bond will be valued at par. Therefore, if it is currently below par, as it is trading at a discount, the price must rise

See Chapter 6 Section 2.1 and Chapter 6 Section 2.3 of your Study Text

18. **6.84** Spot rate $\times (1 + r_V) =$ Forward rate $\times (1 + r_F)$

Spot = $1.60

Fwd = $1.60 – $0.0024 = $1.5976

$r_F = 7\%$

Hence

$1.60 \times (1 + r_V) = 1.5976 \times (1.07) = 1.709432$

$(1 + r_V) = 1.0684$

$r_V = 0.0684$ or 6.84%

See Chapter 3 Section 4.3 of your Study Text

19. **D** All three are characteristics and reasons to use FTSE 100 futures contracts

See Chapter 7 Section 1.1 of your Study Text

20. **B** Immunisation is where the duration of the portfolio is matched to the term of the liability. The duration of a portfolio is the weighted average of the bond durations

Duration of portfolio = $0.25 \times 4 + 0.25 \times 5 + 0.25 \times 8 + 0.25 \times 10 = 6.75$

See Chapter 9 Section 7.7 of your Study Text

21. **C** UK equities tend to dominate UK pension funds, i.e. they have a high exposure to equities, rather than any other class of asset. This is not the case in central Europe, where most pension funds tend to have a larger proportion of their funds in bonds, particularly government bonds

See Chapter 9 Section 6.1 of your Study Text

22. **C** The full short-term ratings are

Moody's:	P1	P2	P3	
S&P:	A1+	A1	A2	A3

These are different from the traditional credit ratings of the longer term debt market, also provided by Moody's and S&P

See Chapter 6 Section 1.3 of your Study Text

23. **A** There are no central banks with responsibility for managing government debt. However, other functions that could be carried out include bank supervision, of which the Federal Reserve is responsible. The Bank of Japan also has partial responsibility for banking supervision

   See Chapter 3 Section 3.9 of your Study Text

24. **C** Duration relates to sensitivity to yield/interest rate changes. The question asks about 'undervalued bonds', therefore 'alpha values' are more appropriate, as according to the Jensen alpha measure, a bond with a positive alpha is returning more than expected, suggesting that it is undervalued

   See Chapter 11 Section 4.1 of your Study Text

25. **C** Where variable costs are covered then at least there is some contribution towards fixed costs. This, however, can only be sustained in the short term

   See Chapter 2 Section 2.1 of your Study Text

26. **80,000** Price paid – Net assets = Goodwill

   Net assets = Shareholders' funds

   £300,000 – (£100,000 + £40,000 + £80,000) = £80,000

   See Chapter 4 Section 2.9 of your Study Text

27. **D** Marginal cost is the addition to total cost of adding one additional unit of output

   See Chapter 2 Section 2.1 of your Study Text

28. **C** This would be covered by the investing activities heading

   See Chapter 4 Section 5.1 of your Study Text

29. **B** A bond trading at par will have a coupon equal to the yield

   See Chapter 6 Section 4.1 of your Study Text

30. **C** Best available answer. All are relevant to the investment process

   See Chapter 9 Section 6.1 of your Study Text

31. **B** The premium of an option is quoted per unit of the underlying asset regardless of the contract size

   Chapter 7 Section 1.2, Chapter 7 Section 1.4 and Chapter 7 Section 1.4 of your Study Text

32. **B** Whilst some derivative contracts are based on indices (FTSE 100 index future) many are based on other products (long gilt future)

   See Chapter 7 Section 1.1 of your Study Text

33. **D** Bond indices are equally weighted (unweighted) total return indices

   See Chapter 1 Section 4.6 of your Study Text

34. **D** Immunisation requires that all promised cash flows are realised and therefore is not possible if a bond can be redeemed early at the option of the issuer

   See Chapter 9 Section 7.7 of your Study Text

35.   **A**   Accruals are liabilities for costs incurred during the period

See Chapter 4 Section 2.11 of your Study Text

36.   **D**   Inventory is classified as a current asset

See Chapter 4 Section 2.8 of your Study Text

37.   **C**   There is no such thing as an execution-only discretionary service, all others are standard services

See Chapter 10 Section 1.2 of your Study Text

38.   **A**   No CGT is payable by the fund on sales of assets, however the investor must normally account for CGT when he sells his fund holdings unless they are held in a tax wrapper

See Chapter 10 Section 1.1 of your Study Text

39.   **C**   The client requires income, ruling out commodities. Neither bonds nor cash provide a long term real return. The most suitable individual investment would be property that generates income and provide a long-term real return

See Chapter 8 Section 2.2 of your Study Text

40.   **A**   The FTSE APCIMS Private Investor Index series represents a range of indices designed as benchmarks for private client use. The range exists to cover clients with differing objectives and constraints

See Chapter 1 Section 4.6 of your Study Text

41.   **D**   Since the aim is to pay a specified sum on a given future date the most appropriate strategy would be immunisation. The other approaches aim to maximise returns but provide no guaranteed future value

See Chapter 9 Section 7.7 of your Study Text

42.   **C**   Leasehold is a direct investment method, the others are indirect investment routes

See Chapter 8 Section 2.7 of your Study Text

43.   **1.57**   Current assets = Inventories + receivables + Cash = £5m + £4m + £2m = £11m

Current liabilities = £7m

Current ratio = £11m/£7m = 1.57

See Chapter 4 Section 7.3 of your Study Text

44.   **27.3**   £300,000/£1,100,000 = 0.273 or 27.3%

Remember,

Fixed assets plus working capital = Shareholders' funds + Long-term loans

See Chapter 4 Section 7.2 of your Study Text

45.   **13.8** $r = r_f + \beta(r_m - r_f) = 9\% + 0.8(15\% - 9\%) = 13.8\%$

See Chapter 9 Section 3.1 of your Study Text

46.   **A**   All reserves in shareholders' funds may be used to make a bonus issue as this is not a distribution in the form of a dividend

See Chapter 5 Section 3.5 of your Study Text

47. **A** Market neutral funds take long positions in stocks expected by the manager to outperform and short positions in stocks expected to under-perform. By having a balance of long and short positions the fund is not exposed to the general gyrations of the market (hence market-neutral); the fund generates positive returns when the long positions outperform the short positions

See Chapter 10 Section 2.1 of your Study Text

48. **C** European style options can only be exercised at expiry but American style options can be exercised at any time

See Chapter 7 Section 1.2 of your Study Text

49. **B** A capitalisation, or bonus issue, would not raise cash for the company. However, the share premium reserve (as an example) would be reduced by a corresponding increase in share capital. The market value of the share would fall, as there are now more shares than before, with no change in the net assets

See Chapter 4 Section 2.14 of your Study Text

50. **D** Earnings attributable to the ordinary shareholders are calculated as profits **after** deducting tax, minority interests, interest and preference dividends if applicable

See Chapter 5 Section 3.5 of your Study Text

51. **A** If prices are rising and inventory levels are rising, FIFO will result in the earliest, cheapest goods being sold first, and the most recently acquired, most expensive goods will be left in inventory

See Chapter 4 Section 2.8 of your Study Text

52. **B** Shareholders' funds = Total assets – Long-term liabilities – Current liabilities

Shareholders' funds = £720,000 – £120,000 – current liabilities

Current assets = Total assets – Fixed assets

$$= £720,000 - £590,000$$

$$= £130,000$$

$$\text{Current ratio} = \frac{\text{Current assets}}{\text{Current liabilities}}$$

$$1.4\times = \frac{£130,000}{\text{Current liabilities}}$$

Current liabilities = £92,857

Shareholders' funds = Total assets – Long-term liabilities – Current liabilities

$$= £720,000 - £120,000 - £92,857$$

$$= £507,143$$

See Chapter 4 Section 2 and Chapter 4 Section 7.3 of your Study Text

53. **D** This is known as a contribution to fixed costs

See Chapter 2 Section 2.1 and Chapter 2 Section 4.1 of your Study Text

54. **D** A profit maximising firm will expand output until MC = MR

See Chapter 2 Section 2.2 of your Study Text

55. **B** Monopoly is characterised by the existence of barriers to entry, allowing supernormal profit to be preserved in the long run

See Chapter 2 Section 4.2 of your Study Text

56. **D** Firms seek to maximise profits regardless of the industrial structure

See Chapter 2 Section 2.2 of your Study Text

57. **C** In general, low-coupon, long-dated bonds are the most sensitive to yield changes

See Chapter 6 Section 2.2 of your Study Text

58. **8.12** Modified Duration = $\dfrac{\text{Duration}}{1+\text{GRY}} = \dfrac{8.85}{1.09} = 8.12$

See Chapter 6 Section 2.3 of your Study Text

59. **D** Since the price of the bond will be at par and therefore there will be no capital gain or loss on redemption

See Chapter 6 Section 4.1 and Chapter 6 Section 4.1 of your Study Text

60. **C** In general, low-coupon, long-dated bonds are the most sensitive to yield changes

See Chapter 6 Section 2.3 of your Study Text

61. **C** An FRN is a floating rate note where the interest rate is regularly reset to market levels. They therefore trade near par value. If interest rates fall, the FRN coupon falls and hence, the yield falls

See Chapter 6 Section 1.3 of your Study Text

62. **C** UK investors will now get less dollars to the pound and therefore US goods will be more expensive

See Chapter 3 Section 4.3 of your Study Text

63. **A** Increases in inflation relative to other nations will erode or devalue the exchange rate over the long term

See Chapter 3 Section 4.3 of your Study Text

64. **A** A rise in interest rates will increase call premiums and decrease put premiums

See Chapter 7 Section 1.4 of your Study Text

65. **A** A warrant is a long-dated call option issued by the company where exercise results in new shares being purchased

See Chapter 7 Section 3.2 of your Study Text

66. **135**

	£
Lower of	
– Cost	150
– Net realisable value (140 – 5)	135

See Chapter 4 Section 2.8 of your Study Text

67. **B** It can be negative. A company is only insolvent if it cannot pay its debts as they fall due

See Chapter 4 Section 2.14 of your Study Text

68. **C** Dividend cover $= \dfrac{\text{Earnings yield}}{\text{Dividend yield}}$

Dividend yield $= \dfrac{\text{Net dividend}}{\text{Price}}$

$= \dfrac{2.7\text{p}}{140\text{p}} = 0.01929$ or 1.929%

$\therefore$ Dividend cover $= \dfrac{6.42\%}{1.929\%} = 3.33 \times$

See Chapter 5 Section 3.2 of your Study Text

69. **B**

	£
Assets	975,000
External creditors	(825,000)
Nominal value preference shares	(100,000)
	50,000

No. of ordinary shares = 200,000

Amount per share $= \dfrac{£50,000}{200,000} = 25\text{p}$

As the preference dividend was never declared, the preference shareholders are not entitled to their arrears of dividends

See Chapter 6 Section 2.6 of your Study Text

70. **A**

Before:	4	shares × £8 =	£32
Bonus:	5	share × nil =	£0
After:	9	shares =	£32

The new share price is therefore £32/9 = **£3.56**

See Chapter 5 Section 2.3 of your Study Text

71. **B** This is the same whether we are using the official classification (DMO's) or the FT/LSE classification. Remember, as a general rule, when you are not told which classification to use, you should use the DMO's version

See Chapter 6 Section 2.2 of your Study Text

72. **A** The question specifies income return, i.e. excluding any gain or loss on redemption. To measure the total return (before tax) we would use the GRY, which is also called the Yield to Maturity. To work out the total post-tax return, we would use the Net Redemption Yield

See Chapter 6 Section 4.1 of your Study Text

73. **D** The Bank of England sets interest rates not inflation, increasing sales indicate inflationary pressures and tourism is an invisible part of the current account

Chapter 3 Section 3.7, Chapter 3 Section 3.8 and Chapter 3 Section 3.9 of your Study Text

74. **A** If you buy a gilt below par (e.g. for £95) you will make a capital gain when you receive the £100 nominal value on redemption. This gain will be added onto the coupon to give a higher GRY than the FY

See Chapter 6 Section 4.1 of your Study Text

75. **D**

	£
Purchase cost (5,000 × £2.18)	10,900.00
Add: commission (10,900 × 0.4%)	43.60
stamp duty (10,900 × 0.5% rounded up to next £5)	55.00
PTM levy	1.00
	10,999.60

See Chapter 9 Section 5.2 of your Study Text

76. **3,513** $PV = £7,000 \times \dfrac{1}{1.09^8} = £3,513$

See Chapter 1 Section 6.1 of your Study Text

77. **A** A UK index of the largest 100 fully listed UK companies

See Chapter 1 Section 4.6 of your Study Text

78. **133.5** $\text{Year 3 Index Value} = \dfrac{120+87}{75+80} \times 100$

$$= \dfrac{207}{155} \times 100$$

$$= \mathbf{133.5}$$

See Chapter 1 Section 4.3 of your Study Text

79. **12.0** $\text{Treynor} = \dfrac{r_p - r_f}{\beta} = \dfrac{9\% - 3\%}{0.5} = 12.0\%$

See Chapter 11 Section 4.1 of your Study Text

80. **A** $\text{Return to relative duration} = \dfrac{\text{Excess return}}{\text{Relative duration}} = \dfrac{9\% - 5\%}{16/10} = 2.5$

See Chapter 11 Section 4.1 of your Study Text

81. **B** A scatter diagram shows the relationship between two variables

See Chapter 1 Section 1.6 of your Study Text

82. **C** Fundamental activities is not a heading in the cash flow statement

See Chapter 4 Section 5.1 of your Study Text

83. **D**   In the linear regression where y = a + bx,

a = intercept, ie share price £5.26 when x (time) = 0 (start of regression period)

b = slope, ie 2.18p increase in share price per period (per month)

Current period = end of ten years (120 months), hence current share price is

Share price = 526 + 2.18 × 120 = £787.6

See Chapter 1 Section 3.3 of your Study Text

84. **B**   To determine what proportion of the change in the share price is explained by time we need to consider the r^2 statistic, $r^2 = 0.63^2 = 0.397$, i.e. 39.7% of the changes in the share price are explained by changes in time and the remaining 60.3% are not

See Chapter 1 Section 3.2 of your Study Text

85. **9.98**   Under CAPM, the expected return is given by

$r = r_f + \beta(r_m - r_f)$

where

$$\beta = \frac{\sigma_s}{\sigma_m} = \frac{\sigma_i Cor_{im}}{\sigma_m} = \frac{12 \times 0.83}{10} = 0.996$$

giving

$r = 5 + 0.996(10 - 5) = 9.98\%$

See Chapter 9 Section 3.1 of your Study Text

86. **0.375**

$$\text{Sharpe ratio} = \frac{r_p - r_f}{\sigma_p} = \frac{9.5 - 5.0}{12} = 0.375$$

See Chapter 11 Section 4.1 of your Study Text

87. **C**   If the entrepreneur buys put options on the share he will establish a protective put position, protecting himself against the share price fall

See Chapter 7 Section 1.2 of your Study Text

88. **B** $\sigma_i = \sqrt{\sigma_s^2 + \sigma_u^2} = \sqrt{24^2 + 18^2} = \sqrt{900} = 30\%$

See Chapter 9 Section 1.2 of your Study Text

89. **B**   The minimum denomination for cash deposits in the money market

See Chapter 6 Section 1 of your Study Text

90. **A**   An index-linked gilt is one where the nominal value of the bond is linked to inflation. The coupon is a fixed percentage, but as it is a fixed percentage of an increasing amount, the coupon payout increases with inflation. Hence, the percentage coupon is normally quite low. The benefit that is received at the end is the nominal value of the gilt, which has increased with inflation, and is therefore not fixed

See Chapter 6 Section 2.5 of your Study Text

91. **B** Life assurance funds have a long term time horizon with relatively low liquidity needs, and as such have relatively high levels of risk tolerance. As a result, they are able to invest in equities

See Chapter 9 Section 6.1 of your Study Text

92. **A** We need to establish a protective put by buying the put option with a strike price of 5200. This will provide protection if the index falls below 5200 though, since the current index level is 5400, it leaves the first 200 points of any index loss uncovered. Below 5200 we effectively have a short hedge

To calculate the number of contracts we first need to calculate the value of the portfolio if the index falls to 5200, the value that will then need to be hedged is as follows

	£m
Current value at an index level of 5400	30.00
Loss of index falls to 5200 ($£30m \times \dfrac{200}{5400} \times 0.9$)	1.00
Portfolio value at an index level of 5200	29.00

So with the index level of 5200 and a portfolio value to hedge of £29m we have

$$\text{No contracts} = \frac{\text{Portfolio value}}{\text{Option strike} \times £10} \times \beta = \frac{£29,000,000}{5200 \times £10} \times 0.9 = 501.9, \text{ie 502 contracts}$$

See Chapter 7 Section 1.1 and Chapter 7 Section 1.2 of your Study Text

93. **D** Semi-strong efficiency implies the correct price reflects all currently available public information. No analysis will then reveal any extra information

See Chapter 9 Section 4.1 of your Study Text

94. **B** $\sigma_i^2 = \sigma_s^2 + \sigma_u^2$

$25^2 = \sigma_s^2 + 20^2$

$\sigma_s^2 = 225$

$\sigma_s = 15\%$

$\beta = \dfrac{\sigma_s}{\sigma_m} = \dfrac{15}{20} = 0.75$

$r = r_f + \beta(r_m - r_f) = 6\% + 0.75(14\% - 6\%) = 12\%$

See Chapter 9 Section 3.1 of your Study Text

95. **C** Demand for inferior goods falls as income rises

See Chapter 2 Section 1.3 of your Study Text

96. **A** Net current assets are:

	£'000
Inventory	5
Accounts receivable	3
Cash	2
Accounts payable	(2)
Net current assets	8

See Chapter 4 Section 2.2 of your Study Text

97. **D** The fund of funds investment may be diversified but it will still have a high level of risk and potential illiquidity restrictions. High yield corporate bonds will be subject to high level of interest rate and credit risk, and may be illiquid. The best answer is that the short dated government bonds are the most appropriate given the circumstances

See Chapter 9 Section 6.1 of your Study Text

98. **A** The CAPM model gives the return necessary on an investment relative to the market portfolio. Of the available answers, the best description of the market portfolio is an investments market

See Chapter 9 Section 3.1 of your Study Text

99. **B** Return on equity looks at the rate of return earned by ordinary shareholders.

See Chapter 4 Section 7.2 of your Study Text

100. **A** Elasticity of supply = $\dfrac{+4\%}{+2\%}$ = +2

See Chapter 2 Section 1.4 of your Study Text

101. **D**

TV of I = £9,000 × $e^{0.093 \times 3}$ =   11,896.27
TV of II = £9,000 × $1.024^{3 \times 4}$ =   11,963.05
TV of III = £9,000 × $1.0076^{3 \times 12}$ =   11,819.97

See Chapter 1 Section 5.3 and Chapter 1 Section 6.1 of your Study Text

102. **B** The FTSE Ordinary index is an equally weighted, geometrically calculated index. This index is also referred to as the FT 30, as it has the top 30 shares in the UK in it. The other indices that are also equally weighted are the Dow Jones Industrial Average index (DJ 30) in the US and the Nikkei 225 in Japan, although these are both arithmetically calculated

See Chapter 1 Section 4.6 of your Study Text

103. **B** The correlation coefficient measures the direction and degree of linear association between the two variables. The sign (ie + or −) indicates whether the items are positively or negatively correlated, that is whether they move in the same direction or opposite direction by the same proportion. The number indicates the strength of the correlation. Clearly it is not possible for two items to be more than perfectly correlated and hence the correlation coefficient must have a value less than or equal to 1

See Chapter 1 Section 3.2 of your Study Text

104. **C** Semi-logarithmic graphs plot the log of the value on the y-axis. On such a graph growth at a constant rate is shown as a straight line and any move away from steady growth would result in a change in the slope of the line

See Chapter 1 Section 1.6 of your Study Text

105. **C** Split level trusts may issue zero dividend preference shares but not zero dividend ordinary shares

See Chapter 10 Section 1.2 of your Study Text

PRACTICE EXAMINATION FIVE

(105 questions in 2 hours and 20 minutes)

Questions

1. What is the price of a three-year 5% annual coupon bond if the yield is 6% (in £ to two decimal places)?

    Important! You should enter the answer only in numbers strictly using this format: 00.00

    Do not include spaces, letters or symbols (but decimal points and commas should be used if indicated).

2. You have the following data in terms of return over a six-month period –8%, –5%, 5%, 8%, 9% and –9%. What is the mean?

    A   –0.3%

    B   0.0%

    C   0.3%

    D   0.6%

3. You have a single sum of £200 to invest at a rate of 2% per quarter for four years and three months. What is the terminal value?

    A   £277

    B   £278

    C   £279

    D   £280

4. A mortgage is paid monthly in arrears at a rate of 1% per calendar month. The term of the mortgage is 25 years. If the loan is for £30,000, what would the monthly repayment be (to the nearest £1)?

    Important! You should enter the answer only in numbers strictly using this format: 000

    Do not include spaces, letters or symbols (but decimal points and commas should be used if indicated).

5. **Which of the following best describes bond yields?**

    A Continuous data
    B Discrete data
    C Categorical data
    D Ordinal data

6. **If a distribution rises slowly to a peak then falls steeply back down it is**

    A Symmetrical
    B Positively skewed
    C Negatively skewed
    D Quadratically skewed

7. **Which of the following constitute secondary data?**

    I   Financial Times
    II   Surveys
    III Wall Street Journal
    IV   Investors Chronicle

    A I and IV
    B I, III and IV
    C II, III and IV
    D I, II, III and IV

8. **The rate of return of six shares last year were 12%, 10%, 3%, –5%, 1%, 9%.**

    What was the average return on the shares (in % to 2 decimal places)?

    Important! You should enter the answer only in numbers strictly using this format: 0.00

    Do not include spaces, letters or symbols (but decimal points and commas should be used if indicated).

9. **A security that lies above the Securities Market Line is**

    A Overvalued
    B Undervalued
    C Correctly valued
    D Absolutely valued

10. **A stock has a beta of 0.9, the risk-free rate is 8% and the market risk premium is 10%, what is the expected return on the stock?**

   A 9.8%

   B 16.2%

   C 17.0%

   D 17.2%

11. **The total risk on a stock is 30%, its idiosyncratic risk is 24% and the market portfolio risk is 18%. What is the stock beta?**

   A 0.33

   B 0.67

   C 1.00

   D 1.50

12. **The value per point of the NYSE Liffe FTSE 100 index future is**

   A £10

   B £5

   C £20

   D £25

13. **A put option would not contain which of the following items?**

   A The price at which you could buy

   B The quantity of shares involved

   C The price at which you could sell

   D An expiry date

14. **What is the minimum amount of a placing that must be made available to the public?**

   A 5%

   B 10%

   C 15%

   D There is no set limit

15. **Which of the following bonds would be the most responsive to a shift of 1% in yields?**

   A Low-coupon, short-dated

   B Low-coupon, long-dated

   C High-coupon, short-dated

   D High-coupon, long-dated

16. **What does the term contango describe?**

    A   When the futures price exceeds the cash market price

    B   When the futures price is equal to the cash market price

    C   When the cash market price exceeds the futures price

    D   When the option's time value exceeds its intrinsic value

17. **Which statement best describes a European option?**

    A   An option which can be exercised at any point until expiry

    B   An option traded within the European Union

    C   An option which can only be exercised on expiry

    D   An option which can be exercised only on one of several set days

18. **If the underlying is trading at 200p, strike of a call option is 190p and the call is trading at 20p, it is in-the-money by**

    A   20p

    B   10p

    C   30p

    D   −10p

19. **What is the maximum liability of the writer of a put?**

    A   Unlimited

    B   Nil

    C   Exercise price – Premium

    D   Exercise price + Premium

20. **Which of the following are true in relation to forward currency transactions?**

    I   Premiums or discounts reflect expectations of future exchange rate movements

    II   Forward transactions are only available one month, three months, six months or nine months forward

    III The rate at which the transaction will take place cannot be calculated until the currency is exchanged

    IV   Premiums or discounts reflect interest rate differentials between the two countries

    A   I and II

    B   I only

    C   III and IV

    D   IV only

21.   If a gilt is currently trading at £120 and has a flat yield of 6½%, which of the following could be the Gross Redemption Yield?

A   5½%

B   6½%

C   7½%

D   8½%

22.   A convertible trades at £130 and each £100 nominal is convertible into 50 ordinary shares. What is the premium on conversion if the shares are currently trading at £2.20?

A   18%

B   9%

C   15%

D   30%

23.   Which of the following is used to calculate the change in price of a bond, given the change in gross redemption yield?

A   Modified duration

B   Macaulay

C   Beta

D   Grossed-up net redemption yield

24.   Which of the following bonds are quoted in 32nds?

A   US T-bonds

B   German bonds

C   French OATs

D   JGBs

25.   You hold £10,000 of a 10% three-year bond (annual coupon). The yield is 8%. What is the price today?

A   £9,721.59

B   £7,938.32

C   £10,515.42

D   £11,356.65

26.   The current $/€ quote is €1.6333-€1.6428. The three-month forward is quoted at 0.92-1.03 (dis). You wish to convert €300,000 in three months. How many dollars will you receive (to the nearest $1)?

Important! You should enter the answer only in numbers strictly using this format: 000,000

Do not include spaces, letters or symbols (but decimal points and commas should be used if indicated).

27. **The current £/€ exchange rate is £1 = €2.45. If Europe experiences inflation at 2% for the next year and the UK experiences 5% inflation over the same period then**

   A   Sterling will appreciate by 3%

   B   Sterling will appreciate by 6%

   C   Sterling will depreciate by 3%

   D   Sterling will depreciate by 6%

28. **Which of the following would result in the highest duration?**

   A   Low-coupon bonds trading at low yields

   B   Low-coupon bonds trading at high yields

   C   High-coupon bonds trading at low yields

   D   High-coupon bonds trading at high yields

29. **A Treasury bill is issued with 91 days to maturity. Twenty-nine days later, it trades at £98. Which of the following is true of the bill?**

   A   Discount rate 11.8% and yield of 12%

   B   Yield of 11.8% and discount rate 12%

   C   Discount rate 8.02% and yield of 8.19%

   D   Yield of 8.02% and discount rate 8.19%

30. **A company has a 4% non-cumulative preference share in issue. In the last two years, no dividends are paid. However, in the current year, a 3p dividend is paid on each ordinary share. How much would be recorded by way of dividend by the holders of the preference shares in the current year?**

   A   7p

   B   12%

   C   4%

   D   Nil

31. **A portfolio consists of the following zero-coupon bonds.**

   Two years' maturity – market value £17m

   Three years' maturity – market value £4m

   One year's maturity – market value £7m

   What is the duration of the portfolio?

   A   1.76 years

   B   0.21 years

   C   1.89 years

   D   2.00 years

32. **If an undated gilt has a modified duration of 12.5 and duration of 13.5, what is its gross redemption yield?**

   A   12.5%

   B   7.41%

   C   8.00%

   D   8.32%

33. **If you wished to measure the performance of a fund which is 50% sterling, 50% US dollar equity, then an appropriate benchmark would be**

   A   S&P 500 / FTSE 100

   B   S&P 500 / Dow Jones

   C   FTSE 100 / FT All Share

   D   FT Actuaries / FTSE 100

34. **What is a fixed rate regime?**

   A   Where interest rates are fixed by intervention in the money markets

   B   Where interest rates and the exchange rates are fixed by the Government

   C   Where the exchange rate is fixed by the Government

   D   Where the rate of growth of the economy is stabilised

35. **An investor holds 1500 shares, with a current value of £6. The company announces a 1 for 5 scrip issue. What is the change in value of the investor's total holding?**

   A   Zero

   B   Loss of £1800

   C   Loss of £300

   D   Gain of £300

36. **Which of the following must appear in the directors' report?**

       I   Charitable and political donations over £200

       II   The ages of the directors

       III   Significant changes in fixed assets

       IV   Policy with regard to disabled employees, for companies with more than 250 employees

   A   I only

   B   II and III

   C   I, III and IV

   D   I, II, III and IV

37. **What is the profit maximising condition for a monopolist?**

   A   Marginal cost = Average total cost

   B   Average total cost = Average revenue

   C   Marginal cost = Marginal revenue

   D   Marginal cost = Average revenue

38. **An investor wishes to follow the market. Which of the following would be the most appropriate fund to invest in?**

   A   An index-linked gilt fund

   B   Emerging market debt fund

   C   Actively managed growth fund

   D   Tracker funds

39. **A share has a P/E ratio of 10, EPS of 30p and Dividend Cover of 2.4x. What is the dividend yield (in % to 1 decimal place)?**

   Important! You should enter the answer only in numbers strictly using this format: 0.0

   Do not include spaces, letters or symbols (but decimal points and commas should be used if indicated).

   ┌─────────────────┐
   │   │
   │   │
   └─────────────────┘

40. **What is the price elasticity of demand for a luxury good?**

   A   Greater than 1

   B   1

   C   Between 0 and 1

   D   0

The following information relates to questions 41 to 46

A company has experienced the following record of sales and operating profit margin over the last five years (year 5 being the most recent).

YEAR	SALES £M	MARGIN %	TAX PAID £M
1	120	5	0.84
2	132	7	2.06
3	145	9	3.28
4	160	11	4.50
5	176	13	5.72

The only non-cash expenditure is annual depreciation of £5m. The company has £60m of debt finance paying an annual coupon of 5% that matures in four years and it pays half of its earnings out as a dividend each year.

The company share price has increased rapidly in recent years but has become quite static at present and is expected to remain static in the short term.

41. **What stage is this product in its life cycle?**

   A   Introduction

   B   Growth

   C   Maturity

   D   Decline

---

42. **What was the average dividend growth rate over the period (to the nearest one %)?**

   Important! You should enter the answer only in numbers strictly using this format: 00

   Do not include spaces, letters or symbols (but decimal points and commas should be used if indicated).

   ┌──────────┐
   │   │
   │   │
   └──────────┘

---

43. **What was the free cash flow to equity for Year 4 (in £m to one decimal places)?**

   Important! You should enter the answer only in numbers strictly using this format: 00.0

   Do not include spaces, letters or symbols (but decimal points and commas should be used if indicated).

   ┌──────────┐
   │   │
   │   │
   └──────────┘

---

44. **A bond fund is considering investing in the bonds of this company, though alternatives are a 6 year FRN and a two year issue. The fund manager's expectation is that interest rates will fall, which investment would be considered optimal?**

   A   Invest in the FRN

   B   Invest in the two-year issue

   C   Invest in the bonds of this company

   D   Avoid investing and hold cash

---

45. **Which of the following would be the most suitable short-term options strategy for a fund manager who is invested in the shares of a company but considers markets to be static?**

   A   Protective put

   B   Long call

   C   Long straddle

   D   Covered call

46. **What was the interest cover on the debt in Year 3 (to 2 decimal places)?**

    Important! You should enter the answer only in numbers strictly using this format: 0.00

    Do not include spaces, letters or symbols (but decimal points and commas should be used if indicated).

    ┌──────────────┐
    │   │
    │   │
    └──────────────┘

47. **A monopolist is**

    A The only producer of goods in a market

    B The only consumer of goods in a market

    C The dominant producer in a market

    D The dominant consumer in a market

48. **IAS 2 requires that a company values inventory at**

    A FIFO cost

    B LIFO cost

    C Average cost

    D Lower of cost and net realisable value

49. **Which would be preferred by a higher rate taxpayer when interest rates are falling?**

    A Low-coupon bonds trading at low yields

    B Low-coupon bonds trading at high yields

    C High-coupon bonds trading at low yields

    D High-coupon bonds trading at high yields

50. **The Hang Seng Index is**

    A Arithmetic, unweighted

    B Arithmetic, weighted

    C Geometric, unweighted

    D Geometric, weighted

51. **Which is not one of the sub-indices of the Rogers International Commodity Index?**

    A Tropicals

    B Energy

    C Metals

    D Agriculture

52. **Which of the following are not arithmetic weighted indices?**

        I   Eurotrack 100
        II   FT Ordinary Shares Index
        III   CAC 40
        IV   Dow Jones

  A I and IV
  B I and III
  C II and III
  D II and IV

53. **A portfolio returns 15%, has a beta of 1.6 and variance of 49. The risk-free rate is 8% and market return is 12%.**

What is the Jensen measure in terms (in % to 2 decimal places)?

Important! You should enter the answer only in numbers strictly using this format: 0.00

Do not include spaces, letters or symbols (but decimal points and commas should be used if indicated).

                                        [   ]

54. **The short-term interest rate contract finishes at 94.55 in early September. What are implied interest rates for the next three months?**

  A 5.56%
  B 1.36%
  C 5.45%
  D 21.8%

55. **Which of the following is not required in a set of published company accounts for a large company?**

  A Balance sheet
  B Income statement
  C Cash flow statement
  D Company secretary report

56. **If share capital is £100m, the share premium account £70m, profit and loss reserve £125m, turnover £320m and liabilities total £130m, what is the value of all assets, both fixed and current?**

  A £425m
  B £615m
  C £190m
  D £165m

57. **If a company's working capital is £300m, with inventory of £60m and trade payables falling due within one year of £100m and after one year of £28m, what is the company's quick ratio?**

A 1.12×

B 1.4×

C 2.0×

D 3.4×

58. **What must you add back to operating profit to get cash flow?**

A Depreciation

B Increase in debtors

C Reduction in creditors

D Change in the amount held at the bank

59. **Which of the following best describes a Eurobond?**

A A corporate bond issued internationally, via a syndicate of banks

B A government bond issued in an overseas currency

C A bond issued internationally, underwritten by a syndicate of banks

D A bond issued in Europe, typically denominated in euros

60. **If r = 15%, and you require £5,000 annually over the next ten years, how much will the annuity cost?**

A £101,500

B £25,093

C £50,000

D £20,227

61. **Which of the following is not a government debt instrument?**

A OAT

B Bund

C CAC

D JGB

62. **How can an owner/occupier raise capital?**

    I   Mortgage

    II   Sale and leaseback

    III   Lease and sell back

A I and II

B I, II and III

C I and III

D II and III

63. **Which of the following is not true regarding UK unit and investment trusts?**

A They hold similar assets

B They are both subject to limitations in the amount they can invest in a single company

C They are controlled by trustees

D They are often named after the specific sector in which they invest

64. **If the interest rate is 6% and the purchaser of an annuity requires a payment of £4,000 per annum at the end of each of the next five years, what is the price of the annuity?**

A £66,670

B £22,548

C £16,850

D £18,104

65. **Which of the following statements with regard to a European and a US option is true?**

A The former can only be bought in the EU, the latter only in the US

B The US option cannot be sold before its expiry

C The US option cannot be exercised before its expiry

D The European option cannot be exercised before its expiry

66. **Where a company operates a defined benefit pension scheme, IAS19 and FRS17 require**

A Pension liabilities to be shown on the balance sheet but not pension assets

B Pension assets to be shown on the balance sheets but not pension liabilities

C Neither pension assets nor pension liabilities to be shown

D Both pension assets and liabilities to be shown

67. **Which of the following best describes variation margin for transactions on NYSE Liffe?**

A Cash deposited with the clearing house to cover daily adverse movements in futures positions

B Cash deposited with the clearing house to cover the maximum likely daily loss arising from the futures contract

C Cash deposited with NYSE Liffe to cover the maximum likely daily loss arising from the futures contract

D Cash deposited with NYSE Liffe to cover adverse movements in futures positions beyond a pre-specified point

68. **Given spot rate $/€ of 1.5226, and dollar and euro interest rates over 360-day period of 3.5% and 3.75% respectively, what is the 360-day forward premium (pm) or discount (disc)?**

A €0.0037 disc

B €0.37 disc

C €0.0037 pm

D €0.37 pm

69. **Which of the following describes an intermediaries offer?**

    A   A placing that falls below the threshold level

    B   A placing through more than one broker

    C   A subscription offer

    D   An offer for sale to the general public

70. **Which of the following are measures of market timing?**

    I   Treynor

    II   Sharpe

    III   Jensen

    A   I only

    B   II only

    C   III only

    D   I and III

71. **Which of the following statements with regard to returns are true?**

    I   Total return comprises price appreciation plus dividend yield

    II   The major stock indices are total returns indices

    III   The major bond market indices are total return indices

    A   I and II

    B   I and III

    C   II and III

    D   I, II and III

72. **A pension fund has a market value of £120m at the start of the month; just before the end of the month, it receives a deposit of a further £12m. If the fund's value at the end of the month was 16% higher than at the start, what is the return achieved by the fund manager?**

    A   16%

    B   12%

    C   6%

    D   –4%

73. **A company paid a dividend of 20p per share last year, its dividend cover was 8 and the dividend yield was 6%. What was the P/E ratio of the company?**

    A   3.33

    B   2.1

    C   1.6

    D   0.2

74. A company had a net cash flow of £140,000 over last year. During the period, inventory fell from £140,000 to £120,000, receivables increased by £12,000, and the depreciation charge was £37,000. What was the trading profit?

   A £95,000

   B £59,000

   C £104,000

   D £209,000

75. Acme plc had a trading profit last year of £3.4m. Over the period, inventory held increased by £0.2m, creditors decreased by £0.4m, while debtors rose by £0.5m. Over the period, depreciation was £0.3m. What was Acme's net cash flow (in £m to one decimal places)?

   Important! You should enter the answer only in numbers strictly using this format: 0.0

   Do not include spaces, letters or symbols (but decimal points and commas should be used if indicated).

76. Which of the following best describes the multiplier?

   A The extent to which production changes given a change in demand

   B The sum of aggregate demand and consumption

   C The ratio of the change in output brought about by a change in investment

   D The annual increase in inflation

77. Which of the following bodies would be used to help in the lending of Eurobonds?

   A The Bank for International Settlements

   B Clearstream

   C The finance ministry of the country where the bonds were located

   D EFFAs

78. All things being equal, if a proportionate tax was imposed on personal disposable income, there would be

   A An increase in aggregate demand

   B An increase in aggregate demand via the multiplier

   C An increase in the steepness of the consumption curve

   D A decrease in the steepness of the consumption curve

79. What is the primary role of Treasury Bills?

   A To control cash in the banking system

   B To raise revenue to finance long-term government borrowing

   C Influence the flow of transactions in the equity market

   D A decrease in the steepness of the consumption curve

80. **Who issues certificates of deposits?**

    A   Commercial banks and building societies

    B   Governments

    C   Companies

    D   Private customers

81. **From the following information, what is the geometric index value after one year for X and Y using Year 1 as the base?**

Year	X	Y
1	90	180
2	130	220
3	125	300

    A   113.86

    B   126.63

    C   132.87

    D   176.54

82. **An investor enters into a 3-month swap with a national principal of £10m. The investor is the payer and pays fixed at 6%. He receives LIBOR which is 7%. What is the situation for the investor at the end of three months?**

    A   The investor will receive £100,000

    B   The investor will receive £25,000

    C   The investor will pay £100,000

    D   The investor will pay £25,000

83. **Which of the following is the best description of an intermediaries offer?**

    A   An offer via more than one broker

    B   An offer direct to the general public

    C   An offer via one broker

    D   A rights issue made only to intermediate customers

84. **If the return on the market is 12%, the CAPM beta = 1.5 and the risk-free return is 4%, what is the expected return on the portfolio (in % to 1 decimal place)?**

    Important! You should enter the answer only in numbers strictly using this format: 00.0

    Do not include spaces, letters or symbols (but decimal points and commas should be used if indicated).

    [   ]

85. A fund manager has invested 80% of his portfolio in the UK and 20% in the US against a benchmark allocation of 75:25. The selected UK shares returned 16% and the selected US shares returned 14.5%.

    Comparison benchmark indices for each part of the portfolio had the following values

	UK	US
Start of year	3,000	500
End of year	3,400	580

    What interaction gain will have been experienced?

    A   −0.205%

    B   −0.125%

    C   0.125%

    D   0.205%

86. Which of the following is not an example of mental frames?

    A Self control

    B Over confidence

    C Loss aversion

    D Mental accounting

87. Which of the following is measured as a standard deviation?

    A VAR

    B Tracking error

    C Shortfall risk

    D Drawdown

88. In selecting the coefficients 'a' and 'b' in the bivariate linear regression which one of the following criteria is used?

    A Maximise the errors squared

    B Minimise the absolute value of the errors

    C Minimise the average error

    D Minimise the residual sum of squared errors

89. A bond is yielding 6.5% when interest rates are 5.7% and the gilt term spread for this maturity is 0.5%. What is the credit/default return?

    A 0.3%

    B 0.5%

    C 0.8%

    D 5.7%

90. **The liabilities of a general insurance company are best described as**

A Long-term real

B Long-term nominal

C Short-term real

D Short-term nominal

91. **Consider the following statements**

     I   Each investment opportunity will result in a single unique IRR

     II   Projects with an IRR exceeding the firm's cost of capital will always be attractive

     III   Any surplus funds can be reinvested at the IRR

A All false

B All true

C I and II true whereas III is false

D II is false whereas I and III are true

92. **A company has the following accounts receivable at the end of the year**

	£
A	15
B	20
C	30
Others	350
	415

The company experience is that 2% of the debtors default on the payment. The company has learnt that:

Debtor A has gone into liquidation

Debtor B is disputing one invoice to the value of £5,000. None of the other invoices are in dispute.

Debtor C has agreed to pay the outstanding invoices to the value of £30,000 at the end of the next month.

You are required to calculate value of the debtors for balance sheet purposes.

A £400,000

B £415,000

C £378,000

D £388,000

93. **Consider the following statements.**

    I   An equity swap exchanges the income from equities for the income from a money market deposit

    II   A currency swap exchanges both principal and interest

    III   Interest rate swaps payments are netted

Which statements are true?

A   I and II

B   I and III

C   II and III

D   All are true

94. **An analyst asked to assess the risk from investing in a company would find which of the following ratios most useful?**

A   Asset turnover

B   Return on capital employed

C   Earnings per share

D   Operational gearing

The following information relates to questions 95 to 100

A fund manager runs a portfolio on behalf of a client whose risk tolerance suggests a long-term asset allocation of 70% equities, 30% bonds. The benchmark for the equity component has returned 9% across the year, whereas the bond benchmark has returned 5%. The actual equity return achieved has been 9.1%, the bond return has been 4.3% and the actual asset allocation has been 75%:25%.

The manager has achieved this performance through a mixed management approach but is not convinced that the results have been effective and is considering switching to a core and satellite approach using ETFs as a core and a hedge fund as the active satellite.

95. **Which comment on the fund manager's performance is true?**

A   Good at stock selection, good at asset allocation

B   Good at stock selection, poor at asset allocation

C   Poor at stock selection, good at asset allocation

D   Poor at stock selection, poor at asset allocation

96. **What is the interaction gain when performance is decomposed using the Brinson Fachler method?**

A   +0.20%

B   −0.14%

C   +0.04%

D   −0.10%

97. **Which of the following characteristics is inappropriate for an equity benchmark?**

   A Specific and unambiguous

   B Relevant to the currency and preferences of the fund

   C Representative of achievable performance through a geometric weighted composition

   D Measurable and investable

98. **Which of the following is a mixed management approach?**

   A Value investing

   B Contingent immunisation

   C Portfolio tilting

   D Screening

99. **Which of the following is not a type of hedge fund?**

   A Long/short fund

   B Market neutral fund

   C Global micro fund

   D Events-driven fund

100. **Which of the following is not true of ETFs?**

   A Structured as a company

   B Priced at set valuations points throughout the day

   C Open-ended

   D Listed

101. **Potential portfolios are constructed with equal weightings of five securities with the betas noted below. Which will be least volatile?**

   A Portfolio A $+1.2 - 0.6 + 0.1 - 0.7 + 1.0$

   B Portfolio B $-0.9 + 0.7 + 0.3 - 0.8 - 1.2$

   C Portfolio C $-0.3 + 1.3 - 0.2 + 0.2 - 1.8$

   D Portfolio D $0.4 - 0.2 + 1.2 - 1.1 + 1.0$

102. **Consider the following statements.**

   I   ETCs are exchange traded

   II   NS&I investments are all tax free

   III   Investment trusts are closed-ended

   Which statements are true?

   A I and II

   B I and III

   C II and III

   D All are true

103. **A recession is defined as**

   A   A contracting economy

   B   A period of falling GDP

   C   Two consecutive quarters of falling GDP

   D   A period of high unemployment

104. **A bond is yielding 6.6% when interest rates are 5.7% and the gilt term spread for this maturity is 0.5%. What are the spread return and the credit/default return?**

	SPREAD	CREDIT/DEFAULT
A	0.4%	0.9%
B	0.5%	0.4%
C	0.4%	0.5%
D	0.9%	0.5%

105. **A convertible is in issue that has the right to convert into 20 shares. The current share price is £5.20 and call options are available on these shares maturing at the conversion date with a premium of 50p. If the convertible is converted, the issued capital of the business will rise by 4%. The value of an equivalent straight bond is £102. What is the value of the convertible?**

   A   112.0

   B   111.62

   C   110.86

   D   109.47

Answers

1. **97.33** $\dfrac{£5}{(1.06)} + \dfrac{£5}{(1.06)^2} + \dfrac{£105}{(1.06)^3} = £97.33$

   See Chapter 6 Section 2.3 of your Study Text

2. **A** $[(1 + r_1)(1 + r_2)(1 + r_3)(1 + r_4)(1 + r_5)(1 + r_6)] = (1 + R)$

   $[(1 - 0.08)(1 - 0.05)(1 + 0.05)(1 + 0.08)(1 + 0.09)(1 - 0.09)] = (1 + R)$

   $(0.92 \times 0.95 \times 1.05 \times 1.08 \times 1.09 \times 0.91) = 0.9831$

   $\sqrt[6]{0.9831} = 0.997 = (1 + R)$

   ie a loss of 0.003 or 0.3%

   See Chapter 1 Section 2.5 of your Study Text

3. **D** Using the compound factor for a single cash flow, $(1 + r)^n$

   $£200 \times (1 + 0.02)^{17} = £280$

   As the rate r is quoted for a quarter, n has to be the number of quarters

   See Chapter 1 Section 6.1 of your Study Text

4. **316** Regular repayment $= \dfrac{\text{PV of borrowing}}{\text{ADF}}$

   Now AF(1-300 @ 1%) $= \dfrac{1}{0.01}\left(1 - \dfrac{1}{1.01^{300}}\right) = 94.9466$

   Hence, Regular payment $= \dfrac{£30,000}{94.9466} = £315.97$

   The required format for this question is £000, hence you must round to the nearest whole pound ie, £316

   See Chapter 1 Section 6.2 of your Study Text

5. **A** The yield on a bond may take any value whatsoever, and so is described as continuous data

   See Chapter 1 Section 1.3 of your Study Text

6. **C** A distribution rises slowly to a peak then falls steeply back down is negatively skewed

   See Chapter 1 Section 2.6 of your Study Text

7. **B** Secondary data is information that has been collected by various companies or agencies, with the intention of then distributing or selling this data on to a third party. Primary data is information that has been obtained through observation, discussion or questionnaires

   See Chapter 1 Section 1.1 of your Study Text

8. **5.00** The arithmetic mean is the most appropriate measure, as this is looking at six different shares, rather than one share over a six-month or six-year time period

   $\dfrac{12\% + 10\% + 3\% - 5\% + 1\% + 9\%}{6} = \dfrac{30\%}{6} = 5\%$

   See Chapter 1 Section 2.2 of your Study Text

9. **B** The return from the security is higher than would be expected from the Securities Market Line (SML), suggesting that the security has performed better than expected, i.e. the security appears to be undervalued

See Chapter 9 Section 3.1 of your Study Text

10. **C** Using the Capital Asset Pricing Model (CAPM)

$$r = r_f + \beta(r_m - r_f)$$

$$r = 8\% + (0.9 \times 10\%) = 17\%$$

See Chapter 9 Section 3.1 of your Study Text

11. **C** $$\sigma_i^2 = \sigma_u^2 + \sigma_s^2$$

$$30^2 = 24^2 + \sigma_s^2$$

$$\sigma_s^2 = 324$$

$$\sigma_s = \sqrt{324} = 18$$

$$\beta = \frac{\sigma_s}{\sigma_m} = \frac{18}{18} = 1.00$$

See Chapter 9 Section 1.2 of your Study Text

12. **A** The value per index point on the FTSE 100 index future is £10 per index point. This is not to be confused with the tick value of £5.00, which is for a ½ index point move. The delivery months of this contract are March, June, September and December

See Chapter 7 Section 1.1 of your Study Text

13. **A** The price at which you could buy an item would be included within the contract specification for a call option, where the holder of the call option (long call) has the right, but not the obligation, to buy an asset at the strike (exercise) price

See Chapter 7 Section 1.2 of your Study Text

14. **D** There is no express requirement to issue a set percentage of shares. However, the issuer must ensure that the issue is said to be 'sufficiently marketable'. This may be satisfied if at least two market makers have stocks placed with them. When a number of brokers are involved, the issue can be referred to as an intermediary offer

See Chapter 5 Section 2.2 of your Study Text

15. **B** The bond that will be the most responsive in terms of its price movement will be the bond that has the highest duration. The low-coupon, long-dated bond will have the highest duration. Similarly, the low yielding bonds will have higher duration measures than higher yielding bonds

See Chapter 6 Section 2.3 of your Study Text

16. **A** A market is said to be in 'contango' when the price of the future is higher than the price in the cash market. This is the norm, as the difference between the two prices will represent the cost of carry over the time period in question

See Chapter 7 Section 1.1 of your Study Text

17. **C** A European style option is with regard to the exercise style applicable. These options may only be exercised, by the holder of the option, at the expiry of the options' life. Options that can be exercised at any time up to expiry are referred to as American in exercise style

See Chapter 7 Section 1.2 of your Study Text

18. **B** The intrinsic value of the call option is the difference between the underlying asset value and the strike/exercise price. Options that have intrinsic value are described as in-the-money (ITM). If there is no intrinsic value, they are said to be out-of-the-money (OTM). Please note that this has nothing to do with profits and losses upon exercising the option

200p – 190p = 10p

See Chapter 7 Section 1.4 of your Study Text

19. **C** It is not unlimited as the price of an asset cannot fall below zero. Thus, the worst loss is if the put is exercised such that the writer takes the stock at the strike and the stock is worthless – however, as partial compensation the writer does receive the premium

See Chapter 7 Section 1.2 of your Study Text

20. **D** The exchange rate of a forward currency transaction is agreed at the time the transaction is entered into, i.e. now. Forward transactions can be done for any maturity, and they are simply a mathematical result of the difference in interest rates in the two countries

See Chapter 3 Section 4.3 of your Study Text

21. **A** The GRY must be lower than the flat yield, as there will be a capital loss upon maturity of the bond, as the bond is currently trading above par. If the bond had been trading at par (NV) then the flat yield of 6.5% would be the same as the gross redemption yield

See Chapter 6 Section 4.1 of your Study Text

22. **A** The effective purchase price of the shares is £2.60, which is 40p higher than if the actual shares were purchased directly. This 40p premium represents the conversion premium, which equates to 18.18% of the actual trading value of the share

$$\frac{£130}{50} = £2.60 \quad \frac{£2.60 - £2.20}{£2.20} = 0.18 \text{ or } 18\%$$

See Chapter 7 Section 3.1 of your Study Text

23. **A** Modified duration measures that change in price of a bond for a 1% change in yields

See Chapter 6 Section 2.3 of your Study Text

24. **A** US T-bonds are the only overseas government bond that is quoted in 32nds. The other overseas government bonds, as well as UK gilts are quoted in decimal, ie 1/100ths

See Chapter 9 Section 5.3 of your Study Text

25. **C** Using basic discounting techniques, the present value of the bond can be established as follows

$$£10,515.42 = \frac{£1,000}{1.08} + \frac{£1,000}{1.08^2} + \frac{£11,000}{1.08^3}$$

See Chapter 1 Section 6.1 of your Study Text

26. **181,477**

The basic rules concerning discount (add) and premium (deduct) still apply whatever the quote

Spot rate	€1.6333	–	€1.6428
Add: Discount	€0.0092	–	€0.0103
Forward rate	€1.6425		€1.6531

$$\frac{€300,000}{€1.6531} = \$181,477$$

See Chapter 3 Section 4.3 of your Study Text

27. **C** Spot rate $\times (1 + r_V)$ = Forward rate $\times (1 + r_F)$

€2.45 × 1.02 = Forward rate × 1.05

Forward rate $= €2.45 \times \dfrac{1.02}{1.05}$

$= €2.38$

€ appreciation/sterling depreciation $= \dfrac{€2.45 - €2.38}{€2.45} = 0.029$ or 2.9% (3% to nearest whole number).

The best answer is sterling depreciation of 3%

See Chapter 3 Section 4.3 of your Study Text

28. **A** The bond that will be the most responsive, in terms of its price movement, to interest rate fluctuations, will be the bond that has the highest duration. The low-coupon, long-dated bond will have the highest duration. Similarly, the low yielding bonds will have higher duration measures than higher yielding bonds

See Chapter 6 Section 2.3 of your Study Text

29. **A** Discount rate is $\dfrac{£100 - £98}{£100} \times \dfrac{365}{62} = 0.118$ or 11.8%

Yield is $\dfrac{£100 - £98}{£98} \times \dfrac{365}{62} = 0.120$ or 12.0%

See Chapter 6 Section 1.1 of your Study Text

30. **C** Since the ordinary shareholders have received a dividend of 3p per share, then the preference dividend must have been paid during that year, as the dividend on a preference share is always paid first, before any ordinary dividends are paid. Please note that this is a non-cumulative preference share, so no dividends are paid in arrears for the two years of non-payment

See Chapter 4 Section 2.14 of your Study Text

31. **C** $\dfrac{(2 \times £17m) + (3 \times £4m) + (1 \times £7m)}{£17m + £4m + £7m} = 1.89$ years

See Chapter 6 Section 2.3 of your Study Text

32. C $\dfrac{13.5}{1+\text{GRY}} = 12.5$ years $\dfrac{13.5}{12.5} = 1 + \text{GRY} = 1.08 \;\therefore \text{GRY} = 8\%$

See Chapter 6 Section 2.3 of your Study Text

33. A A benchmark should be constructed so that it is described as an appropriate benchmark, used for benchmarking purposes that will be indicative of the performance that could realistically be achieved

See Chapter 1 Section 4.6 of your Study Text

34. C In order to stabilise the exchange rate, the Government will normally be unable to fix the interest rate at the same time

See Chapter 3 Section 4.2 of your Study Text

35. A He will own 300 more shares, but the price will drop to £5 after the scrip issue. Therefore his overall holding is still worth the same. This makes sense as there is no cash involved, just more shares at a lower value

See Chapter 5 Section 2.4 of your Study Text

36. C Under the Companies Acts of 1985 and 1989, the Directors' Report must contain certain key pieces of information. There is no requirement to give the age of the directors

See Chapter 4 Section 1.99 of your Study Text

37. C This is always the profit maximising condition. Where marginal costs equal marginal revenues, irrespective of the type of economic environment, firms will always maximise profits at this point

See Chapter 2 Section 2.2 of your Study Text

38. D Tracker fund use indexation where an investor will construct a portfolio that is designed to replicate the performance of a market index. This is one of the passive equity selection techniques that can be adopted by a fund manager or investor

See Chapter 9 Section 6.2 of your Study Text

39. **4.2** EPS = 30p

P/E = 10

Therefore, price =   P/E × EPS

   10 × 30p = £3

EPS = 30p

Div Cover = 2.4×

Therefore, dividend $= \dfrac{\text{EPS}}{\text{Cover}}$

   $= \dfrac{30p}{2.4} = 12.5p$

Dividend yield $= \dfrac{\text{Net dividend}}{\text{Price}} = \dfrac{12.5p}{£3} = 0.042$ or 4.2%

See Chapter 5 Section 3.2 of your Study Text

40. **A** The price elasticity of demand for a luxury good will always be negative. In fact, price elasticity of demand for any good will be negative. This is due to the fact that as the price of a good falls, the demand for that good will increase, and vice versa. Where the price fall leads to a more than proportionate increase in demand, the elasticity will be greater than 1. The fact that the actual relationship is an inverse one is not recognised when measured

See Chapter 2 Section 1.3 of your Study Text

41. **B** The product is in the growth phase that is characterised by rapid sales growth and high/expanding margins

See Chapter 2 Section 5.3 of your Study Text

42. **60**

YEAR	5	1
	£M	£M
Sales	176.00	120.00
Margin	×13%	×5%
Operating profit	22.88	6.00
Bond interest	(3.00)	(3.00)
Profit before tax	19.88	3.00
Tax	(5.72)	(0.84)
Profit after tax	14.16	2.16
Dividends (50%)	7.08	1.08

Dividend this year = Dividend n years ago $\times (1 + g)^n$

In year 5, year 1 was four years ago and hence

$7.08 = 1.08 \times (1 + g)^4$

$(1 + g)^4 = 6.56$

$(1 + g) = 1.60$

$g = 0.60$ or 60%

See Chapter 5 Section 3.3 of your Study Text

43. **15.1**

YEAR	4
	£M
Sales	160.00
Margin	×11%
Operating profit	17.60
Add depreciation	5.00
Less tax	(4.50)
FCFF	18.10
Less net interest	(3.00)
FCFE	15.10

See Chapter 5 Section 3.7 of your Study Text

44.   C   Since interest rates are expected to fall, bond prices are expected to rise. A cash holding would, therefore, be sub-optimal and an investment should be made in the bond with the highest duration. For an FRN, as the interest rate falls the coupon falls and the price remains stable, the duration of an FRN is very low irrespective of its maturity. For a normal fixed coupon bond the duration is fairly close to but slightly less than its maturity so the four year bond issued by the company is the optimal choice

See Chapter 6 Section 1.3 and Chapter 6 Section 2.3 of your Study Text

45.   D   Protective put protects against price falls. Long call benefits from price rises. Long straddle is a speculative trade that is useful when volatility is expected to rise. Covered call is useful to enhance returns in a static market, the given scenario

See Chapter 7 Section 1.2 of your Study Text

46.   **4.35**

YEAR	3
	£M
Sales	145.00
Margin	×9%
Operating profit	13.05
Interest payable	3.00

$$\text{Interest cover} = \frac{\text{Operating profit}}{\text{Interest payable}} = \frac{13.05}{3.00} = 4.35$$

See Chapter 4 Section 7.3 of your Study Text

47.   **A**   In microeconomics, the monopolist is the only producer of a good. This scenario is possible due to large barriers to entry, that make it difficult for other potential competitors entering the market, meaning that in a monopoly, profits can be made and sustained in the future

See Chapter 2 Section 4.2 of your Study Text

48.   **D**   The other options available are all methods of arriving at the cost of inventory. In accordance with IAS 2, the overall valuation of inventory in the balance sheet must be at the lower of cost or net realisable value (NRV)

See Chapter 4 Section 2.8 of your Study Text

49.   **A**   The low coupon is said to be tax efficient, from an income tax perspective. The low coupon would further suggest that the price of the bond is low, possibly below par value, giving the possibility of a tax-free capital gain (on gilts). Low-coupon and low yielding bonds will have a high duration, maximising the potential capital gain as interest rates are falling

See Chapter 6 Section 2.3 of your Study Text

50.   **B**   The Hang Seng Index is the main index of Hong Kong. It is like most world indices in that it is weighted by market capitalisation, and arithmetically calculated. The only unweighted indices are the Dow Jones Industrial Average (Dow 30), the FTSE Ordinary (30) and the Nikkei 225

See Chapter 1 Section 4.6 of your Study Text

51.　**A**　Energy, Metals and Agriculture are sub-indices but Tropicals are not. Even without knowing the exact answer, with the knowledge that Energy, Metals and Agriculture are commodities then an educated guess would lead to the answer, Tropicals

See Chapter 8 Section 1.2 of your Study Text

52.　**D**　The FTSE Ordinary (FT 30) and the Dow Jones (Dow 30) are both unweighted indices, sometimes referred to as 'equally weighted', or price relative indices. The Nikkei 225 is the other unweighted index. These indices, as they are unweighted, have the constituent elements all contributing an equal share towards the value of that index

See Chapter 1 Section 4.6 of your Study Text

53.　**0.60**　Jensen measure　　$= r_p - [r_f + \beta(r_m - r_f)]$

$= 15\% - [8\% + 1.6(12\% - 8\%)] = 0.60\%$

See Chapter 11 Section 4.1 of your Study Text

54.　**C**　Since we can assume that rates are equal to 100 – Price, in this case it will be

$100 - 94.55 = 5.45$

See Chapter 7 Section 1.1 of your Study Text

55.　**D**　No report is required by the Company Secretary

See Chapter 4 Section 2 of your Study Text

56.　**A**　Using the accounting equation

(Assets – Liabilities) = Shareholders' funds

∴ Shareholders' funds + Liabilities = Assets

(£100m + £70m + £125m) + £130m = £425m

See Chapter 4 Section 2 of your Study Text

57.　**D**　Working capital = Current assets – Current liabilities

Working capital + Current liabilities = Current assets

∴ £300m + £100m = £400m

$\dfrac{£400m - £60m}{£100m} = 3.4$

See Chapter 4 Section 2 of your Study Text

58.　**A**　Reduction in debtors and creditors as well as changes to the amounts held at the bank will result in actual money movements. Depreciation is not an actual transfer of cash

See Chapter 4 Section 5.1 of your Study Text

59.　**C**　Eurobonds are unsecured debt instruments issued by corporations or governments. The correct answer is the definition of a eurobond as described by the eurobond market regulator, the International Securities Market Association (ISMA). Eurobonds settle T + 3, and pay gross, annual coupon

See Chapter 6 Section 2.6 of your Study Text

60. **B**   Formula for the annuity

$$PV = £x \times \frac{1}{r}\left(1 - \frac{1}{(1+r)^n}\right)$$

$$= £5,000 \times \frac{1}{0.15}\left(1 - \frac{1}{(1.15)^{10}}\right)$$

$$= £5,000 \times \frac{1}{0.15}(1 - 0.2472)$$

$$= £5,000 \times \frac{1}{0.15}(0.7528)$$

$$= £5,000 \times (5.019)$$

$$= £25,093$$

See Chapter 1 Section 6.2 of your Study Text

61. **C**   The CAC 40 is an arithmetic weighted index of France. The OAT is the French government bond, the JGB is the Japanese government bond and the Bund is the German government bond

See Chapter 9 Section 5.3 and Chapter 1 Section 4.6 of your Study Text

62. **A**   The owner of property may raise further capital by borrowing through a mortgage, or selling the asset with the intention of leasing the property back from the purchaser. There is no such thing as 'lease and sell back' in the UK property market

See Chapter 8 Section 2.2 of your Study Text

63. **C**   Funds that are trusts, such as a unit trust or pension company, would have trustees, whereas funds that would be considered to be companies, such as an investment trust, would have directors who set the investment objectives of the fund

See Chapter 10 Section 1.2 of your Study Text

64. **C**

$$PV = CF \times \frac{1}{r}\left(1 - \frac{1}{(1+r)^n}\right)$$

$$PV = £4,000 \times \frac{1}{0.06}\left(1 - \frac{1}{(1.06)^5}\right)$$

$$= £4,000 \times \frac{1}{0.06}(1 - 0.74726)$$

$$= £4,000 \times \frac{1}{0.06}(0.25274)$$

$$= £4,000 \times 4.21236$$

$$= £16,849.46$$

The required format for this question is £00,000, hence you must round to the nearest whole pound, ie £16,849

See Chapter 1 Section 6.2 of your Study Text

65. **D** The terms 'American' and 'European' exercise style do not relate to the geographical regions in which these options are available for trading. An American style option offers greater flexibility in that the option can be exercised, by the holder, at any time up until expiry. A European style of exercise means that the holder may only exercise the option at the expiry date

See Chapter 7 Section 1.2 of your Study Text

66. **D** Both should be shown, although in certain circumstances a company may net one off against the other

See Chapter 4 Section 2.13 of your Study Text

67. **A** Initial margin is paid on the opening of a futures position. This is to cover the worst probable single day loss, as established by the exchange and the clearing house. Variation margin is the daily payment of losses to the clearing house, or the receipt of daily profits from the clearing house – known as 'marking-to-market'

See Chapter 7 Section 1.1 of your Study Text

68. **A** Spot rate $\times (1 + r_V)$ = Forward rate $\times (1 + r_F)$

$1.5226 \times 1.0375 = 1.5797$ = Forward rate $\times 1.035$

Forward rate = $\dfrac{1.5797}{1.0350}$ = 1.5263

Euro cheaper in terms of \$, therefore at a discount = €1.5263 – €1.5226 = 0.0037 disc

See Chapter 3 Section 4.3 of your Study Text

69. **B** A specific type of marketing operation, similar to a placing. However, the intermediary offer gives the potential for a wider shareholder base than a placing, as the distribution of share is far wider, as several 'intermediaries' are used to sell the shares. The lead intermediary will be known as the lead manager

See Chapter 5 Section 2.2 of your Study Text

70. **C** The Jensen measure, or alpha, quantifies how far above (or below) the Securities Market Line (SML) the return from a security lies at a point in time. A stock-picker would look for a security with a positive alpha, as this suggests that the share is returning more than would have been expected from CAPM, and hence when looked at on the SML, the return is greater than the SML line for that given level of risk. Sharpe and Treynor measure return as adjusted for risk

See Chapter 11 Section 4.1 of your Study Text

71. **B** In general, bond indices are total return indices, whereas equity indices Do not include income/dividend reinvestment in their calculations

See Chapter 1 Section 4.6 of your Study Text

72. **C** Value at end of month = £120m $\times$ 1.16 (being a 16% return)
= £139.2m

Cash injection = £12m

Therefore, actual growth in fund = $\dfrac{£127.2m - £120m}{£120m}$ = 0.06 or 6%

See Chapter 11 Section 1 of your Study Text

73. **B** $\dfrac{\text{Dividend}}{\text{Price}}$ = Dividend yield

    Therefore, Price $= \dfrac{\text{Dividend}}{\text{Dividend yield}}$

    $= \dfrac{0.20}{0.06} = £3.33$

    Dividend cover $= \dfrac{\text{Earnings per share}}{\text{Dividend per share}} = 8\times$

    $\Rightarrow \dfrac{\text{EPS}}{0.20} \qquad = 8\times$

    Therefore, EPS $= 0.20 \times 8 = £1.60$

    Therefore, price/earnings ratio $= \dfrac{£3.33}{£1.60} = 2.08 \approx 2.1$

    See Chapter 5 Section 3.6 of your Study Text

74. **A**

Trading profit	X
Add Decrease in inventory	20,000
Deduct increase in receivables	(12,000)
Add Depreciation	37,000
Net cash flow	140,000

Therefore, trading profit = £95,000

See Chapter 4 Section 5.1 of your Study Text

75. **2.6**

Trading profit	£3.4m
Increase in inventory	(0.2m)
Decrease in payable	(0.4m)
Increase in receivables	(0.5m)
Deprecation charge	0.3m
Net cash flow	£2.6m

See Chapter 4 Section 5.1 of your Study Text

76. **C** This is the best description of the multiplier

    See Chapter 3 Section 2.5 of your Study Text

77. **B** Since Eurobonds are mostly immobilised at Euroclear and Clearstream in Luxembourg, Clearstream is the most appropriate answer

    See Chapter 6 Section 2.6 of your Study Text

78. **D** If there was a proportionate tax imposed upon disposable income, then individuals would have less money available to spend, and if other things were to remain equal, then the steepness of the consumption diagram would decrease

    See Chapter 3 Section 2.5 of your Study Text

79. **A** The main role of T-bills in the money market is to control cash in the banking system. These are short-term (91 calendar day) instruments, that are issued by weekly tender/auction. They can be used to regulate demand for and supply of cash in the short term

    See Chapter 6 Section 1.1 of your Study Text

80. **A** Certificates of deposit are issued by commercial banks and building societies

    See Chapter 6 Section 1.3 of your Study Text

81. **C** The index after one year is $\sqrt{\left[(130\times220)/(90\times180)\right]} = 132.87$

    See Chapter 1 Section 4.4 of your Study Text

82. **B** Since the investor pays 6% and receives 7% he will actually receive money from the seller, equivalent to 1% of the nominal amount. It is calculated as (£10,000,000 × 0.01) / 4. Do not forget to divide by 4 because the rates quoted are annual but the period of the swap is only three months

    See Chapter 7 Section 2.3 of your Study Text

83. **A** An intermediaries offer is an offer via more than one broker

    See Chapter 5 Section 2.2 of your Study Text

84. **16.0** $r_e = r_f + \beta(r_m - r_f) = 4\% + 1.5\,(12\% - 4\%) = 16.0\%$

    See Chapter 9 Section 3.1 of your Study Text

85. **D** Actual portfolio performance = (0.80 × 16% + 0.20 × 14.5%) = 15.70%

    Timing portfolio performance = $\left[0.80\times\left(\dfrac{3400-3000}{3000}\right)+0.20\times\left(\dfrac{580-500}{500}\right)\right]=13.87\%$

    Stock-selected portfolio performance = (0.75 × 16% + 0.25 × 14.5%) = 15.625%

    Original benchmark performance = $\left[0.75\times\left(\dfrac{3400-3000}{3000}\right)+0.25\times\left(\dfrac{580-500}{500}\right)\right]= 14.00\%$

    Giving

	ACTUAL/REVISED BENCHMARK %	ORIGINAL BENCHMARK %	GAIN %
Selection gain	15.625	14.000	1.625
Timing gain	13.870	14.000	(0.130)
Interaction gain (balance)			0.205
Actual return	15.700	14.000	1.700

    Note: Relevant gains are calculated from the actual, revised benchmark and original benchmark figures with the interaction effect as the balancing figure.

    See Chapter 11 Section 3.1 of your Study Text

86. **B** Overconfidence is a heuristic effect

    See Chapter 9 Section 4.2 of your Study Text

87. **B** Tracking error is the standard deviation of the differences between the returns on a tracker fund and those of the index being tracked

    See Chapter 9 Section 1.1 of your Study Text

88. **D** The concept behind regression to derive the line of best fit mathematically. This requires the minimisation of the vertical distances from each value from the straight line being drawn. In performing the calculation of the sum of vertical distances, the distances are squared. This is referred to as minimising the sum of the squared errors

    See Chapter 1 Section 3.2 of your Study Text

89. **A** 6.5% − (5.7% + 0.5%) = 0.3%

    See Chapter 11 Section 3.2 of your Study Text

90. **D** General insurance liabilities are short-term nominal

    See Chapter 9 Section 6.1 of your Study Text

91. **A** All statements are false

    Investment projects can have multiple IRRs

    See Chapter 1 Section 7.2 of your Study Text

92. **D**

	£'000
Debtor A – provide in full	15
Debtor B – provide for disputed invoice	5
Debtor C – no provision required	
General provision	
350 × 2%	7
Bad debt provision	27
Debtors	415
Bad debt provision	(27)
	388

    See Chapter 4 Section 2.8 of your Study Text

93. **C** I   False – an equity swap exchanges the total return, not just income

    See Chapter 7 Section 2.3 of your Study Text

94. **D** Operational gearing is a measure of trading risk

    See Chapter 4 Section 7.2 of your Study Text

95. **C** **Actual return**   7.9%

    (0.75 × 9.1% + 0.25 × 4.3%)   } −0.1% Stock selection loss

    Timing portfolio return   8.0%

    (0.75 × 9% + 0.25 × 5%)   } +0.2% Asset allocation gain

    Original benchmark return   7.8%

    (0.70 × 9.0% + 0.30 × 5.0%)

    See Chapter 11 Section 4.4 of your Study Text

96. **C** Original benchmark return = 7.8% (0.70 × 9% + 0.30 × 5%)

		ACTUAL/REVISED BENCHMARK	ORIGINAL BENCHMARK	GAIN
		%	%	%
Selected portfolio	(0.70 × 9.1% + 0.30 × 4.3%)	7.66	7.80	(0.14)
Timing portfolio	(0.75 × 9.0% + 0.25 × 5.0%)	8.00	7.80	0.20
Interaction effect	(Balance)			0.04
Actual return	(0.75 × 9.1% + 0.25 × 4.3%)	7.90	7.80	0.10

See Chapter 11 Section 4.4 of your Study Text

Note: Relevant gains are calculated from the actual, revised benchmark and original benchmark figures with the interaction effect as the balancing figure

97. **C** A benchmark needs to be representative of achievable performance through an **arithmetic weighted** composition

See Chapter 1 Section 4.6 of your Study Text

98. **C** Portfolio tilting is a mixed management approach, ie involving both passive and active management. The approach starts with a passive benchmark portfolio then alters the weightings on a limited number of stocks, going overweight on those that are expected to outperform and underweight on those that are expected to underperform

See Chapter 9 Section 6.2 of your Study Text

99. **C** A global macro fund is a style of hedge fund, not a global micro fund

See Chapter 10 Section 2.1 of your Study Text

100. **B** ETFs are continuously priced throughout the trading period

See Chapter 10 Section 1.2 of your Study Text

101. **C** The beta of a portfolio is the weighted average of the stock betas, hence

$$\text{Portfolio A beta} = \frac{1.2 - 0.6 + 0.1 - 0.7 + 1.0}{5} = \quad +0.20$$

$$\text{Portfolio B beta} = \frac{-0.9 + 0.7 + 0.3 - 0.8 - 1.2}{5} = \quad -0.38$$

$$\text{Portfolio C beta} = \frac{-0.3 + 1.3 - 0.2 + 0.2 - 1.8}{5} = \quad -0.16$$

$$\text{Portfolio D beta} = \frac{0.4 - 0.2 + 1.2 - 1.1 + 1.0}{5} = \quad +0.26$$

The lowest value beta is portfolio C

See Chapter 9 Section 3.1 of your Study Text

102. **B** Not all NS&I products are tax free

See Chapter 10 Section 1.2 of your Study Text

103. **C** A recession is defined as two consecutive quarters of falling GDP

See Chapter 2 Section 5.1 of your Study Text

104. **B**   Credit/default risk = 6.6% − (5.7% + 0.5%) = 0.4%, spread given as 0.5%

See Chapter 11 Section 4.4 of your Study Text

105. **B**   Value of convertible = Value of straight bond + $\dfrac{A}{1+q} \times CR$

$$= £102 + \frac{£0.50}{1.04} \times 20 = £111.62$$

See Chapter 7 Section 3.1 of your Study Text